The Jewish Minority in the Soviet Union

The Jewish Minority in the Soviet Union
Thomas E. Sawyer

Dr. Sawyer investigates the status and role of Jews in
the USSR. He includes a discussion of Communist theory and
the nationality issue, particularly as it concerns the Jews,
and addresses as well the legal status of Soviet Jews as
determined by the Soviet constitutions, party directives,
legislative acts, and commitments resulting from international agreements on human and national minority rights. A central part of the study looks at the extent to which Jews have
been assimilated into the general Soviet culture and whether
they continue to play a significant role in party, governmental, and societal affairs. To provide essential background information, Dr. Sawyer presents and analyzes demographic, historical, and other relevant materials. He also
analyzes Soviet Jewish emigration, its background, and its
effects on Jews remaining in the USSR and on both internal
affairs and external relations.

Thomas E. Sawyer holds a Ph.D. in comparative government from Georgetown University. He recently retired from
the U.S. Foreign Service, where he served as a Russian language officer.

The Jewish Minority in the Soviet Union

Thomas E. Sawyer

Westview Press • Boulder, Colorado

Dawson • Folkestone, England

Published in 1979 in the United States of America by
    Westview Press, Inc.
    5500 Central Avenue
    Boulder, Colorado 80301
    Frederick A. Praeger, Publisher

Published in 1979 in Great Britain by
    Wm. Dawson and Sons, Ltd.
    Cannon House
    Folkestone
    Kent CT19 5EE

Library of Congress Number: 78-20724
ISBN (U.S.): 0-89158-480-3
ISBN (U.K.): 0-7129-0888-9

Composition for this book was provided by the author.
Printed and bound in the United States of America.

To

Professor Jan Karski of Georgetown University

scholar, mentor, and friend

Contents

Tables

Preface

In the ensuing study, an attempt is made to investigate as fully as possible what commonly has come to be known as the Soviet Jewish "question," i.e., the status and role of Jews in the Soviet Union. In that regard, an important aspect of the investigation involves the communist theoretical point of view -- as evidenced in the writings of Marx, Lenin, and Stalin -- toward the overall nationality issue and particularly, as concerns the Jews. Another important point of inquiry concerns the legal status of Soviet Jewry as determined by the Soviet constitutions, Communist Party directives, legislative acts, and other official pronouncements. In that respect, Soviet commitments resulting from the various international agreements on human and national minority rights such as the United Nations declarations and the "Helsinki Accords" are discussed and analyzed. A crucial part of the investigation focuses on the extent to which Jews have been assimilated into the general Soviet culture and whether or not they continue to play a significant role in Party, governmental, and other important societal affairs. In correlation with these investigative pursuits, appropriate demographic, historical, and other relevant materials are presented and analyzed. Also, considerable attention is given to Soviet policies and actions, both official and unofficial, aimed at the Jews as a distinct "national" group. Another highly important aspect of the investigation involves an analysis of Jewish emigration, its background, and effects on Jews remaining in the Soviet Union and on Soviet internal affairs in general (e.g., on the other "nationalities," on dissidence, on science and technology, etc.). Also discussed are the effects of Jewish emigration on Soviet external relations, particularly those with the United States. In addition, such collateral issues as the Vienna "dropout" syndrome, U.S. assistance to Soviet Jewish emigrants, the "direct" emigration channel alternative, and Soviet Jewish "departees" from Israel are discussed.

In the most fundamental of terms, one primary investigative
obligation is to render a "working definition" of what actually
constitutes a "Jew," not only in the Soviet Union, but elsewhere
as well. In that context, it is to be noted that "Judaism" and
"Jewishness" are most difficult terms to define. In fact, there
have been several recent court cases in Israel which attest to
the extreme complexity of the "Jewish" definitional problem.
In the narrower sense, "Judaism" and "Jewishness" are restricted
to the Jewish religion only. However, in the broader and more
universal application, including the Soviet example, they encompass the Jewish religion, secular culture, languages, history,
ethnicity, and even the concept of nationality itself. This broader definition, more often than not, is accompanied by a prejudice
against the Jews which not only hinders assimilation into the
general population, but, conversely, strengthens the solidarity
of the Jews as a distinct ethnic group. It is to be noted also
that the so-called Jewish "problem" is not unique to the contemporary Soviet experience -- as the turbulent history of the world's
Jews vividly illustrates. Moreover, as is well-known from the
tragedy of the Nazi era, Jewish identity, unfortunately, is not
only based on individual self-identification, but more often than
not, on what individual governments and other entities consider
a Jew to be. In many instances this prompts an inextricable
identification "mix" based on nationality, language, religion,
and, to a lesser extent, other elements contained in the Jewish
"national" heritage. This particularly has been the case in the
Soviet Union where the Jewish identification problem has been
compounded by the institutionalized internal passport procedure
where the individual's nationality, for better or worse, is "stamp-
ed" for life and largely determines individual success or failure.
　　　　Therefore, it must be recognized that the Soviet Jewish
issue is an issue of almost infinite complexity and delicacy;
an issue which not only has baffled non-Soviets, but also the
succeeding generations of Soviet officials who have been attempting to cope with it for the past sixty years. Relatedly, any discussion of the Jewish question per se, to a large extent, must
be carried out within the context of the overall nationalities
issue, which, in its own right, is a highly complex and controversial subject. Moreover, the Jewish issue, in recent years,
has attracted unprecedented attention both within and outside
the Soviet Union, and has become not only a continuing internal
irritant for the regime, but also an important factor in ongoing
Soviet-Israeli and Soviet-U.S. relations. It also has become
the subject of some contention between the Soviet and other
communist parties.

As, hopefully, will be readily apparent from the discussion carried forth in this study, the current Soviet Jewish predicament has assumed a symbolic significance far exceeding that group's actual numerical and political importance. This is due to several factors. First and foremost, the Jewish plight highlights the oppressive nature of the regime and its internal policies; not only toward the Jews and other "national" groups, but more importantly over individual freedoms. This is particularly significant with regard to a portion of the intellectual class and its apparently growing dissatisfaction with restrictions on individual lives and careers. In addition, the Soviet sanction of Jewish emigration has become a symbol of the right to reside where one wishes and also as a focal point for broader human rights. Also, the Jewish emigration "privilege" sets a dangerous precedent for other religious and ethnic groups. Moreover, Jewish strategy and tactics have been increasingly adopted by other disaffected groups. Furthermore, the Jewish issue thus far has constituted a sizable internal stumbling block to the successful implementation of the desired détente policy with the West. In addition, the Jewish emigration "prerogative" and the accompanying intensification of the Jewish problem (along with its negative ramifications) have prompted an increased awareness by many Soviet Jews of their unique heritage and have caused them to examine more closely their individual situation. This has resulted in a significant number of "assimilated" Jews taking the emigration initiative and, presumably, others at least contemplating it for future use.

Conversely, the Jewish emigration factor and the related reintensification of the Jewish problem have prompted certain negative developments; i.e., the revival of latent antisemitism in many parts of the Soviet Union. This has adversely affected higher educational and job opportunities for Jews; plus, life in general has become more difficult for those individual Jews who have attained "assimilation."

Therefore, there appears to be little doubt that the Jewish issue continues to represent a particularly thorny problem for the Soviet leadership, both in terms of domestic and foreign policy consideration. Moreover, it would seem that almost any policy initiative undertaken by the regime to resolve the Jewish impasse presents potentially undesirable consequences. A permissive policy, most certainly, would invite widespread reform demands from not only other disaffected groups, but, more importantly, from heretofore "silent" segments of the population. Whereas, an oppressive policy program would trigger external abhorrence (as is the current case) and perhaps even ostracism. There is also the distinct possibility that a continued policy of oppression

xxi

would someday ignite a catastrophic internal reaction. Consequently, the Jewish issue and its related emigration factor probably represent a long term policy dilemma for the Soviet leadership, one which may well increase in severity as the years pass.

In the preparation of this work, the author is deeply indebted to Professor Jan Karski of Georgetown University, under whose expert guidance this study was written. Professor Karski's extensive knowledge of the Soviet and Eastern European areas, as well as his unstinted patience and encouragement, provided an immeasurable assistance to the author in the preparation of this manuscript. The author also acknowledges his debt to the members of his Ph.D. dissertation committee: Professors Karl H. Cerny, Howard R. Penniman, and Stephen B. Gibert of Georgetown University, for their invaluable substantive and editorial suggestions. A special and most sincere word of gratitude the author owes to his wife, Ellen, and to his children, Tom and Kelly, for their selfless patience and enduring understanding during the author's Ph.D. study involvement. All errors of fact and judgment, of course, are the author's own.

T.E.S.

The Jewish Minority in
the Soviet Union

1
The Jewish Question as Treated in the Authoritative Communist Writings

Any discussion of communist (i.e., Marxist-Leninist-Stalinist)[1] thought on the Jewish question, to a large extent, must be housed within the context of the overall nationality issue. Moreover, the situation is complicated by the fact that there are few systematic expositions in classical Marxism, prerevolutionary Bolshevism, or in the Soviet period specifically devoted to the Jewish problem per se. Furthermore, as we shall see in the following discussion, although communist theories on nationalism (and for that matter, on Judaism) appear logical and comprehensible in principle, further investigation reveals that they, in fact, are both complex and at times, self-contradictory.

KARL MARX

In the Marxian view, the "nation" is a specific historical entity emerging from the economic necessities of rising capitalism. Relatedly, the nationality issue (and the Jewish issue per se) is an issue of a transitional nature which, in the long term, will give way to a world community with a single (socialist) culture and language. As a result, says Marx, the concept of "nation" and of "nationality," in the socialist sense, is meaningless.

Marx based this view on his well-known principle of "historical materialism" -- the philosophical concept which construes the history of mankind as a continuum of antagonistic contradictions between hostile social classes molded by dominant economic forces at given historical stages. The process is predicated upon the Marxian concept of "economic determinism," i.e., economics are the determinant factor in man's destiny and not politics.

1

In pursuing his nationality theory, Marx denied that the "proletariat," the working class catalyst to the Marxian social revolution, possessed nationality, and furthermore rejected the development of nationality as a proper goal. He admitted that national differences did exist, but found that these differences were disappearing under capitalism and predicted that they would disappear even faster after the socialist revolution.[2] He acknowledged the contradiction between "nationalism" and "internationalism," but, as noted, found its resolution in the dynamics of history. Marx believed that the nature of capitalism which the proletariat must combat was international; this was his message in the Communist Manifesto. He also believed that his theory of the international brotherhood of the working class was confirmed by the fraternization of German and French soldiers at the time of the overthrow of the Paris commune. "Class rule," he wrote then, "is no longer able to disguise itself in a national uniform; the national governments are one as against the [international] proletariat!"[3] (Italics in the original text.)

The internationalism of Marx did not cause him, however, to ignore the importance of nationality as a means to expedite the "coming proletarian revolution." He wanted to see nationalism channeled constructively, i.e., toward hastening the advent of the socialist era which he thought would first take place in large nations like France, Great Britain, and Germany -- countries sufficiently large to support a modern, industrial economy and having an historic and cultural tradition. Conversely, Marx perceived small states as "reactionary" since they had inadequate foundations for a modern, industrialized economy -- the chosen milieu for a successful, proletarian-led, socialist revolution. Therefore, he favored the absorption of small states into the larger ones.[4]

However, quite ambiguously, Marx supported claims for national independence which he judged would accelerate a subsequent socialist takeover. Thus, he did advocate Polish independence and German unification. The ambiguity of Marx's views on the nationality issue is most clearly expressed in his analysis of the Irish situation. Initially, during the 1840s, Marx opposed Irish independence on the general grounds that Ireland was too backward and that Irish nationalism was destructive of the larger British unity. The ascendancy of the English working class, Marx thought, would put an end to the Irish problem; but the absence throughout the 1850s and 1860s of any forthcoming British social revolution provoked Marx to change his mind. In December 1869, he told the Council of the

(Socialist) International that the working class of England, "the only country in which the material conditions for this social revolution had developed, would never accomplish any-thing before it got rid of Ireland."[5]

With regard to national minorities, Marx wanted the minorities to be free from each and every civil, social, and economic restriction. He vigorously opposed all manifesta-tion of national oppression as well as the hegemony of the ruling nations in the then existing multinational empires, i.e., Austro-Hungarian, Russian, and British. In that regard, Marx insisted that the English and Russian socialists support nation-al independence for both Ireland and Poland.

The right of "self-determination" and its corollary, the "right to secede," which subsequently became the corner-stone of the Leninist (Bolshevik) nationality doctrine, did not find acceptance as a socialist principle until the organization of the First (Socialist) International in 1865. Even then its elevation into a programmatic demand was largely accidental. By assuring the exercise of this right specifically to the Poles, the founders of the International appear to have been thinking of it mostly as a weapon against Russian conservatism. How-ever, they justified this position by asserting that the right of self-determination belonged to every nation and this step prepared the way for its transformation into an absolute prin-ciple of the international socialist movement.[6] Ultimately, this acceptance led to reversals of earlier attitudes of Marx on this subject.

As noted elsewhere in this study, in Marxian theory, religion is inextricably intertwined with both the nationality and Jewish questions. We see this, first and foremost, in the Marxian view of the modern state as a corollary of secular-ization, expressed by "political emancipation," i.e., the separation of politics from religious and theological considera-tions and the relegation of institutional religion to a separate and limited sphere. As Shlomo Avineri in his work The Social and Political Thought of Karl Marx notes, Marx viewed "with extreme anxiety any attempt to restore religion to the political realm." As Avineri points out, Marx goes even further, consid-ering the degree to which religion is separated from the state an index to the state's modernity. In that regard, he uses the degree of Jewish emancipation as a convenient measuring device -- "States which cannot yet politically emancipate the Jews must be rated by comparison with accomplished political states and must be considered as underdeveloped."[7]

3

The most systematic and classical communist theoretical
treatment of the Jewish question per se is a review of the writing by the Austrian Socialist Bruno Bauer, authored by the
"young" Marx in 1843.[8] In that document, Marx equates
Judaism with the power of money generally and as destructive
of the cohesion of society -- replacing the proper relationship of the human personality to other people and to things by
the mediating factor of the economic market and of money,
which, in Marx's opinion, atomizes society. In evaluating
Bauer's viewpoint, he criticizes him for taking religion at its
face value and also for not realizing the destruction of
social cohesion by the economic market. The essence of that
thesis is reflected particularly in the following excerpts from
the referred-to work:

> ...The pious and politically free inhabitant of
> New England...is a kind of Laocoon who makes not the
> slightest effort to free himself from the snakes which
> are strangling him. Mammon is the God of these people:
> they worship him not only with their lips but with all
> the powers of their bodies and souls. The earth in their
> eyes is nothing but one great stock exchange and they
> are convinced that they have no other mission here be-
> low than to become richer than their neighbors. Usury
> has taken hold of all their thoughts, excitement derives
> from some change in its object. When they travel, they
> carry their office or store, so to speak, with them on
> their backs and speak of nothing but interest and profits
> and if they turn their eyes for an instant from their own
> business it is only to turn them to the business of
> others.
> Indeed the materialistic rule of the Jew over the
> Christian world has in the United States[9] reached such
> everyday acceptability that the propagation of the
> Gospels, the teaching of Christianity itself, has be-
> come an article of commerce, and the bankrupt merchant
> deals in Gospels just as the enriched gospeler deals in
> business....
> What is the object of the Jew's worship in this
> world: Usury. What is his worldly god? Money.
> Very well then; emancipation from usury and money,
> that is, from practical, real Judaism, would constitute
> the emancipation of our time.
> ...The Jew has emancipated himself in the Jewish
> fashion not only by acquiring money power but through

4

money's having become (with him or without him) the
world power and the Jewish spirit's having become the
practical spirit of the Christian peoples. The Jews
have emancipated themselves to the extent that Christians have become Jews.

Money is the zealous one God of Israel beside
which no other God may stand. Money degrades all the
gods of mankind and turns them into commodities.
Money is the universal and self-constituted value set
upon all things. It has therefore robbed the whole
world, of both nature and man, of its original value.
Money is the essence of man's life and work, which
have become alienated from him. This alien monster
rules him and he worships it.

The God of the Jews has become secularized and
is now a worldly God. The bill of exchange is the Jew's
real God. His God is the illusory bill of exchange.

The social emancipation of Jewry is the emancipation of society from Jewry.[10]

As can be seen from these brief excerpts, Marx's views
on Judaism were decidedly harsh and negative. In fact, he
goes to great lengths to blame the Jews for the basic ills
which have befallen mankind during centuries of existence.
In one decisive swoop, he offers the Jewish people as the sole
sacrificial lamb for society's extensive shortcomings. Shades
of Hitler and antisemites everywhere!

On the whole, Marx actually contributed little original
thinking to the overall nationality question and as noted, ex-
pounded little on the Jewish question specifically.[11] However, from the presented discussion, it appears evident that
the Marxian theoretical viewpoint on both the nationality and
Jewish issues is focused on the underlying "class" concept,
i.e., that economic class membership is the distinguishing
and important factor and not the individual national and/or
religious affinity. On that theoretical basis, Marx supported
claims of national independence which led to the weakening
of the capitalistic system and opposed claims which stood in
the way of socialism. He also laid the philosophical foundation on which his disciples, Lenin and Stalin, later were to
build their nationality (Jewish) programs. Ironically, although
it cannot be said with utmost certainty that Marx was an antisemite,[12] it is interesting to note that he makes no mention
in any of his writings about the thousand years' sufferings of
the Jews -- in spite of the fact that he himself was of rabin-
nical origins.

VLADIMIR IL'ICH LENIN

There appears little doubt that Leninist theories and policies toward the nationality and Jewish questions largely were shaped by a multitude of influences generated by the world around him -- for example, the growing debate within the international socialist movement with regard to the nationality problem; the increasing national awareness of the Asian colonial areas; the experience of the Austrian national debate; the predominance of the assorted Eastern European national issues highlighted by the results of World War I; the multinational complexity of Russia vis-à-vis the immediate policy goals of Lenin, etc. Lenin, first and foremost, was a practical politician and as such, he sought to take advantage of those events which would further his immediate and short-range tactical objectives. Prior to the November Revolution, his most immediate concern was the breakup of the Russian Empire and the seizure of power by the Bolsheviks. Subsequent to the Bolshevik takeover, Leninist policies were largely governed by the more mundane necessities of diplomacy and administration.

Lenin's views on nationalism and on the Jewish issue, although colored by the expediencies of the time, basically were those of Marxian internationalism and even of cosmopolitanism. Consequently, he wrote an article in 1913 on the question of nationality which was very much in the spirit of the Communist Manifesto.

Marxism is incompatible with nationalism, even the most "just," "pure," refined and civilized nationalism. Marxism puts forward in the place of any kind of nationalism an internationalism which is growing before our eyes with every mile of railroad, with every international trust, with every workers' association.[13]

Lenin viewed national culture as a "bourgeois weapon" used to deceive the workers and disunite them. In that regard, he wrote that:

...every liberal-bourgeois nationalism carries into the proletarian ranks the greatest demoralization and causes the greatest injury to the cause of liberty and of the proletarian class struggle....It is in the name and the slogan of "national culture" -- of Great Russian, Polish, Jewish, Ukrainian culture -- that the

6

Black-Hundreds, the Clericals, and then also the bourgeois of all nationalities carry on their reactionary,
dirty business.[14] (Italics in the original text.)

For Lenin, nationality was no mere metaphysical or psychological phenomenon, but a reality rooted in the economics
of a specific historical period, more specifically in the "modes
of production." He noted that "the economic basis of these
[nationalist] movements...form the capitalist period in [a
given] national state." He also stated "that Marxists cannot
ignore the powerful economic factors...[involved] in the formation of a national state."[15] (Italics in the original text.)
        In Lenin's view, to be understood properly the problem
of nationality must be placed within its proper historical
setting.

        The categorical demand of Marxian theory in
        examining any social question is that it be placed with-
        in definite historical limits.... It is impossible to
        begin drawing up the national program of the Marxists
        of a given country without taking into account all the
        ...general historical and concrete state conditions.[16]
        (Italics in the original text.)

        At the core of the Leninist policy on the nationality ques-
tion was the principle of the "right of self-determination and
secession," a principle which Lenin steadfastly adhered to
throughout his public career. This was the principle which,
as mentioned earlier, first found acceptance in the organization of the First (Socialist) International in 1865 and which
later became the cornerstone of the Leninist (Bolshevik) nationality program. However, it should be noted that there was
growing opposition within the international socialist camp
over this principle. Rosa Luxemburg, the Polish Socialist
and contemporary of Lenin in the international socialist movement, for example, denounced the concept of the "national
state" as an "abstraction" and condemned the socialist recognition of the right of self-determination and secession as a
repetition of the "time-worn slogan of bourgeois nationalism."
Lenin took issue with Rosa Luxemburg's position and argued
that since all bourgeois revolutions tended toward the formation of national states, the principle of social democratic
support for bourgeois revolutions committed social democrats
likewise to the recognition of the right of self-determination
and secession. The denial of that right, he argued, was in

7

effect equivalent to a denial of the principle of national equality, and specifically would amount to proletarian tolerance of national oppression. "If we do not display and agitate for the slogan of the right of separation," Lenin wrote, "we play into the hands not only of the bourgeoisie but of the federalists and the absolution of the _oppressing_ nation."[17] (Italics in the original text.)

On the other hand, Lenin noted that the recognition of the right of self-determination and secession did not imply a socialist commitment to a demand for national independence in every instance. The right to secede, he stated, was uncontrollable, but the decision whether to secede or not remained in each instance with the people of the oppressed nation. The crucial question in Lenin's mind concerned the exercise of that right in each case. Acceptance of the principle of self-determination, he wrote, did not present the proletariat, whose interests generally required perpetuation of large state formations, from agitating against the secession of small states. The real solution to the dilemma created by the socialist recognition of the right of self-determination and secession resided in its corollary, the "right of amalgamation." Lenin stated that socialists who were members of oppressing nations must insist upon "freedom of amalgamation" as part of the fight against "small nation narrowmindedness, insularity, and aloofness." A little reflection by socialists, he wrote, would show that there was "no other road leading to internationalism, and the amalgamation of nations."[18]

Also contradictory to the principle of self-determination and secession, was the well-known Leninist dictum of "democratic centralism" -- the dichotomous organizational principle by which a mass participatory role in government was encouraged, however, the power of the ruling Party elite was to remain omnipotent. This concept, moreover, did not allow any federalism and regional independence initiative. Lenin recognized this contradiction and declared in 1913 that:

> The right to self-determination is an _exception_ from our general premise of centralism. This exception is absolutely necessary in view of the archreactionary Great Russian nationalism.[19] (Italics in the original text.)

It should be noted at this juncture that Lenin's self-determination and secession advocacy was concerned with capitalistic environments only, was predicated upon the class

concept, and did not apply to the envisaged socialist world.
In that regard he wrote:

> The bourgeoisie always puts its national demands
> in the foreground. It puts them unconditionally. For the
> proletariat they [the national demands] are subordinated
> to the interests of the class struggle. Theoretically, it
> is impossible to guarantee in advance whether the seces-
> sion of a given nation or its equal status with another
> nation will complete the bourgeois-democratic revolu-
> tion; for the proletariat it is important in both cases to
> ensure the development of its own class; it is important
> for the bourgeoisie to hinder this development by making
> its [proletarian] tasks secondary to the tasks of "its
> own" nation. For this reason the proletariat limits it-
> self to the so-to-speak negative demand for the recog-
> nition of the right to self-determination, without guar-
> anteeing any one nation, without entering into any
> obligation to concede anything at the expense of any
> other nation.[20] (Italics in the original text.)

A major controversy concerning the nationality issue and
relatedly the Jewish question arose from the complex nationality character of the multinational Austro-Hungarian Empire,
where the diverse nationality "mix" threatened the very life of
the Empire.

The Austrian solution to the controversy as led by the
Austrian Socialists Karl Renner and Bruno Bauer consisted of
a scheme for "national personal autonomy." By this plan, all
members of each nationality in the Empire, irrespective of
residence, were to be formed into a single public corporation
endowed with a legal personality and competent to deal with
its own national affairs. (This plan, however, necessarily
did not include the Jews since both Renner and Bauer did not
consider the Jews a "nation" and, in fact, favored their assimilation.) Among other things, these "corporations" would
organize educational and other cultural affairs of their members,
aid them in court proceedings, and levy necessary taxes to
implement these privileges. Through this plan it was hoped to
recognize national rights without destroying the political and
territorial integrity of the Empire. As a corollary to this plan,
the Austrian Social Democrats reorganized the Austrian Socialist Party into a federation of six autonomous national parties
-- Czech, German, Italian, Polish, Ruthenian, and Yugoslav.

9

The conflict between socialist interest in the formation and perpetuation of large territorial units and the state necessity of recognizing potentially destructive national claims subsequently had a profound effect on social democratic movements in other countries, particularly in Russia. Consequently, the Austrian scheme was immediately seized upon in Russia by the General Jewish Workers' Alliance (better known as the Jewish "Bund") which submitted a plan at the Second Russian Social Democratic Party Congress in 1903 for a federated Russian (Social Democratic) Party and coupled this idea with a proposal for the "national-cultural autonomy" of the Russian Jewish community. Although this plan was rejected, it gained support from the non-Jewish Social Democratic organizations in the Baltic and other regions of the Russian Empire.

Lenin was against the Austrian and more particularly the Jewish plan since he was convinced that they would undermine Party unity and encourage destructive national separatist sentiments. Moreover, he was equally convinced that the only solution to the Jewish problem lay in total assimilation and not in recognizing the Jews as a separate and distinct "national" group. However, he did advocate equal treatment for the Jews until they had attained complete assimilation.[21] His views are found in his October 1903 article in Iskra (Spark)[22] entitled, "The Bund's Position Within the Party."

> The Bund's...argument, which consists of invoking the idea of a Jewish nation, indubitably raises a question of principle. Unfortunately, however, this Zionist idea is entirely false and reactionary in its essence. The Jews cease to be a nation, for a nation is inconceivable without a territory, says one of the most outstanding Marxist theoreticians, Karl Kautsky. ... Also, more recently, in his analysis of the problem of nationalities in Austria, the same writer, attempting to furnish a scientific definition of nationality, lays down two fundamental criteria for this concept: language and territory.... The only thing perhaps remaining to the Bundists is to elaborate the idea of a separate Russian Jewish nationality, having Yiddish for its language and the Jewish Pale for its territory.
> The idea of a separate Jewish people, which is utterly untenable scientifically, is reactionary in its political implications. The incontrovertible empirical proof is furnished by the well-known facts of history and of the political reality of today. Everywhere in

10

Europe the downfall of medievalism and the development of political freedom went hand in hand with the political emancipation of the Jews, their substituting for Yiddish the language of the people among whom they lived, and in general their indubitably progressive assimilation by the surrounding population....

The Jewish question is this exactly: assimilation or separateness? And the idea of a Jewish "nationality" is manifestly reactionary, not only when put forward by its consistent partisans (the Zionists), but also when put forward by those who try to make it agree with the ideas of Social Democracy (the Bundists). The idea of a Jewish nationality is in conflict with the interests of the Jewish proletariat, for, directly or indirectly, it engenders in its ranks a mood hostile to assimilation, a "ghetto" mood.[23]

According to Lenin, only total assimilation would solve the Jewish problem and any opposition to such a solution amounted to "petty bourgeois" mentality.

The issue of assimilation...gives one an opportunity to show clearly what must be the outcome of the nationalistic vagaries of the Bundists and like-minded people....

Whoever does not espouse and defend the equal rights of nations and languages, and does not combat every kind of national oppression and discrimination, is neither a Marxist nor even a democrat. This is unquestionable. But it is equally unquestionable that the would-be Marxist who berates a Marxist of another nation on the ground of his "assimilation" is in fact nothing but a nationalistic petty bourgeois....

"Assimilation" can be cried down only by reactionary Jewish petty bourgeois who want to turn the wheel of history back and force it to run not from Russia and Galicia to Paris and New York, but the other way round.[24] (Italics in the original text.)

Lenin wrote more on the Jewish "national" issue in 1913 in his article, "Critical Remarks on the National Question."

...out of ten and a half million Jews throughout the world, about one-half live in a civilized world, under conditions favoring maximum "assimilationism,"

11

whereas only the wretched and oppressed Jews of Russia
and Galicia, deprived of legal rights and downtrodden by
(Russian and Polish) Purishkeviches,[25] live under conditions favoring minimum "assimilationism" and maximum
segregation, which includes the "Pale of Residence,"
the numerus clausus, and similar Purishkevich delights.
    In the civilized world, the Jews are not a nation;
there they have achieved the highest degree of assimilation, say Kautsky and O.Bauer. In Galicia and Russia
the Jews are not a nation; there they are unfortunately
(not through any fault of theirs, but through that of the
Purishkeviches) still a caste.[26] Such is the indisput-
able opinion of men who indisputably know the history
of the Jews.[27] (Italics in the original text.)

Thus, we can see that for Lenin the Jews constitute neither a legitimate "nation" nor a "nationality." Rather, he
prefers to depict them by the exclusionist term of "caste."
    Lenin, however, conceded that Jews were oppressed and
persecuted, more so than other elements of the Russian population. In that context, he wrote the following in his article,
"To the Jewish Workers," published in late May 1905: "...
Jewish workers suffer not only from general economic and
political oppression...but also are denied basic civil rights."[28]
    In pursuit of equal rights for Jews in Russia, Lenin
authored the so-called "Bill of National Equal Rights" in March
1914 for the Bolshevik faction of the Fourth State Duma. In
that document, he called for the "abolishment of all constitutional and other restrictions against Jews and other downtrodden nationalities (but especially Jews)." The drafted bill
proposed that:

        1. Citizens of all nationalities in Russia be
equal before the law.
        2. All constitutional laws, governmental acts,
etc., enacted against Jews pertaining to denial of residence rights, educational rights, the right to serve in
the government and in the military, the right of internal
travel and change of abode, etc., be abolished.[29]

Lenin also commented on antisemitism and its negative
effect on Russian society in an article he authored in 1919
entitled, "Concerning Jewish Pogroms":

12

Antisemitism is spreading animosity toward the
Jews....Jews are not the enemy of the workers....
Among the Jews are workers, toilers, -- they are in
the majority. They are our brothers of oppression by
capitalism, our comrades in the struggle for socialism.
...

...The shame is for them, who sow animosity toward the Jews, who sow hate toward other people.[30]

Conversely, while Lenin conceded that the Jews were
oppressed and persecuted he also maintained that:

...Jewish national culture is the slogan of the
rabbis and the bourgeoisie, the slogan of our enemies.
Whoever, directly or indirectly, puts forward the
slogan of Jewish "national culture" is...an enemy of
the proletariat, a supporter of all that is outmoded and
connected with caste among the Jewish people; he is an
accomplice of the rabbis and the bourgeoisie. On the
other hand, those Jewish Marxists who mingle with the
Russian, Lithuanian, Ukrainian and other workers in
international Marxist organizations, and make their contribution (both in Russian and in Yiddish) toward creating
the international culture of the working class movement
-- those Jews, despite the separatism of the Bund, up-
hold the best traditions of Jewry by fighting the slogan
of national culture.[31] (Italics in the original text.)

Although Lenin had no more to say of significance about
the Jewish question, he did comment further about the larger
issue of nationalism. In that regard, he argued that two principles were essential for the promotion of proletarian interests
and neither of them bore any connection to demands for "national autonomy." One of these was the demand for "political
and civil liberty and complete equality"; the other was insistence upon the right of national self-determination, a principle
which was already synonymous in Lenin's mind with the right
of separation (again, in capitalistic environments only). The
proletariat, he wrote, should not seek to propagate federalism
or like demands, but should endeavor "to unify as closely as
possible broader masses of the workers of each and every nationality for the struggle for a democratic republic and socialism in the widest possible arena." Lenin argued that self-
determination in its best sense applied to social classes, not
nations. Writing in Iskra in 1903, he wrote, "We, for our

part, will be solicitous of the self-determination, not of peoples, and nations, but of the proletariat of every nationality." (Italics added.) This is a very important statement since it represents the essence of the Leninist-Stalinist "self-determination and secession" principle -- a principle which has been widely misinterpreted by generations of non-Marxist readers. In this statement, Lenin not only adheres to traditional Marxian theory, i.e., the essence of the continuing "class struggle," but he, moreover, extends that theory to include the right of the proletariat of every nation to "determine" its own (class) identity and to "secede" from its national "bondage" in order to participate in the continuing international "class struggle" toward universal socialism.[32] Therefore, following this argument "secession" in the socialist environment should be denied!

With specific reference to the Russian situation immediately prior to the Bolshevik seizure of power, Lenin was confronted with an array of unique circumstances which demanded practical solutions if the socialist experiment in that country was to succeed. Here was a vast empire within whose boundaries resided a diverse mixture of nationalities professing different native languages, religions, and customs; many of whom desired secession from the newly established Bolshevik State as soon as possible.[33] For expediency purposes -- to gain power in the first place, and secondly to weather the early stormy days of Bolshevik rule which saw civil war and economic chaos -- Lenin as late as November 1917 continued to insist upon the "right of free separation" for the peoples of Russia (a "right," incidentally, still theoretically recognized in the prevailing All-Union constitution) and promised to recognize this right "immediately and unconditionally with regard to Finland, the Ukraine, Armenia, and any other nationality oppressed by Tsarism." However, Lenin still desired to achieve the socialist ideal of creating a great territorial state; he still wanted "as most a state, as close a tie, as great a number of nations who are neighbors of the Great Russians as possible." This continuing allegiance to the right of self-determination and secession, at least in principle if not in actual practice, was dramatized in the Bolshevik "Declaration of the Rights of the Peoples [Nations] of Russia," dated November 15, 1917, the second article of which appeared over the signatures of both Lenin and Stalin, which guaranteed "the right of self-determination of the peoples, even to the point of separation and forming independent states."[34] It is noteworthy to mention that in keeping with Lenin's view that the

14

Jews did not constitute a "nation," Jews were not specifically mentioned in the referred-to document.

The ambivalence of Lenin's policies toward the over-all nationality issue became even more evident as Lenin proceeded in his quest to consolidate his Party's rule over the entire population. As we shall see later in this study, these "revisions" in Lenin's nationality program were largely activated through his "People's Commissar for Nationality Affairs" and subsequent heir, Joseph Stalin. Conversely, we shall also see that Lenin's theoretical position vis-à-vis the "Jews" (which became that of Stalin, too) remained relatively stable, i.e., the Jews do nct constitute a nationality, total assimilation is the only means to end the Jewish problem, opposition to assimilation equates with "petty bourgeois" mentality, etc. However, Lenin's advocacy of an intervening nondiscriminative attitude toward the Jews was subsequently dropped by his successor, Stalin.

IOSIF STALIN

Comrade Koba, as the Georgian Bolshevik Iosif Vissarionovich Dyugashvili, alias Iosif (Joseph) Stalin, was known during his early revolutionary days, was the ostensible "mouthpiece," if not the actual architect of the Bolshevik Party views and policies on the nationality and Jewish questions.[35] In fact, prior to a meeting of the Central Committee of the Bolshevik faction held in Cracow, Austria, in the summer of 1913, Lenin had urged Stalin to remain in Austria and to make a study of the Austrian nationality issue. Consequently, Stalin then spent some months in Austria studying the Austrian nationality experience -- this study reportedly formed the basis for Stalin's 1913 essay on the nationality question which was entitled, "Marxism and the National Question."[36] He adheres to Lenin's views and elaborates on them.

In this essay, Stalin offered his definition of "nationhood" as follows:

> A nation is a historically evolved, stable community of language, territory, economic life and psychological make-up manifestéd in a community of culture...a nation constitutes the combination of all these characteristics taken together...the nation is not merely a historical category but a historical category belonging to a definite epoch, the epoch of rising capitalism.[37]

15

In another pre-1917 writing in which Stalin stated his opposition to the so-called "Austrian Plan" for "national personal autonomy," Stalin commented specifically on the Jewish national question, noting inter alia that the Jews are not a nationality and like Lenin, that the only solution to the Jewish problem lies in total assimilation.

> ...national autonomy is no solution for the national problem. Nay more, it only serves to aggregate and confuse the problem by creating a soil which favours the destruction of the unity of the working-class movement, fosters national division among workers and intensifies friction between them.... Bauer [the Austrian socialist] explains the impossibility of preserving the existence of the Jews as a nation by the fact that "Jews have no closed territory of settlement." This explanation, in the main a correct one, does not however express the whole truth. The fact of the matter is primarily that among the Jews there is no large and stable stratum associated with the soil, which naturally would rivet the nation, serving not only as its framework but also as a "national" market. Of the five or six million Russian Jews only three to four per cent are connected with agriculture in any way. The remaining 96 per cent are employed in trade, industry, in town institutions, and in general live in towns; moreover, they are spread all over Russia and do not constitute a majority in a single gubernia [administrative province]. Thus, interspersed as national minorities in areas inhabited by other nationalities, the Jews as a rule serve "foreign" nations as manufacturers and traders and as members of the liberal professions, naturally adapting themselves to the "foreign nations" in respect to language and so forth. All this, taken together with the increasing reshuffling of nationalities characteristic of developed forms of capitalism, leads to the assimilation of the Jews. The question of national autonomy for the Russian Jews consequently assumes a somewhat curious character: autonomy is being proposed for a nation whose future is denied and whose existence has still to be proved![38]

In refuting the (Jewish) Bundist demand for national-cultural autonomy in 1913, Stalin argued:

16

...what...national cohesion can there be...be-
tween the Georgian, Daghestanian, Russian, and American Jews?...if there is anything common to them left
it is their religion, common origin and certain relics of
national character....But how can it be seriously maintained that petrified religious rites and fading psychological relics affect the "fate" of these Jews more power-
fully than the living social, economic and cultural environment that surrounds them? And it is only on this
assumption that it is generally possible to speak of a
single nation at all.[39]

Stalin particularly thought the Bund's desire of acquiring
special Jewish rights as "socially retrogressive":

It is to be expected that the Bund will take another
"forward step" and demand the right to observe all the
ancient Hebrew holidays.... The maintenance of everything Jewish, the preservation of all the national pecu-
liarities of the Jews, even those that are patently nox-
ious to the proletariat, the isolation of the Jews from
everything non-Jewish, even of the establishment of
special hospitals -- that is the level to which the Bund
has sunk![40] (Italics in the original text.)

As all Marxists before him, Stalin adhered to the basic
communist principle of the "dialectic" of history as the foundation of his overall philosophical approach to society and its
"socialist" transformation. This included Stalin's approach
to the nationality and Jewish questions.
As Marx and Lenin, Stalin believed that the nationality
problem was rooted in the economics of the specific historical
(capitalistic) period. Also, like Marx and Lenin he believed
that the nationality problem was a phenomenon of the capitalistic epoch which would disappear once the future classless
society was attained. He initially believed that the Jewish
problem would disappear even faster.
With regard to the principle of self-determination and
secession, Stalin supported this principle and, as Lenin, re-
served its implementation exclusively for the proletarian class
in a capitalistic environment. This reservation was enunciated
by him in an article in Pravda, dated November 13, 1917, in
rebuttal to the action of the Ukrainian Rada (Council) in declaring Ukrainian independence from the newly formed proletarian-
led State.

17

They say that the conflict [subsequent Bolshevik
military attack on the Ukraine] arose over the question
of centralism and self-determination, that the Council
of People's Commissars does not permit the Ukrainian
nation to take power into its own hands and to determine
freely its own destiny....This is untrue. The Council
of People's Commissars strives precisely to put all power
in the Ukraine into the possession of the Ukrainian
nation, i.e., the Ukrainian workers, i.e., a government
of the workers and peasants, soldiers, and sailors,
without landlords and capitalists -- such precisely is
the really popular government which the Council of
People's Commissars is struggling for. The General
Secretariat [of the Rada] does not want such a government since it has no desire to do without landlords and
capitalists. In this, not centralism, lies the whole
essence [of the conflict].[41] (Italics in the original
text.)

In the same vein, Stalin, when taking note of the frequent invocation of the right of self-determination and secession by national governments hostile to the Bolsheviks,
charged that "the root of all conflicts which have arisen
between the [Soviet] borderlands and the central Soviet authority lies in the question of power." He charged that bourgeois circles were attempting to give a nationalist coloration
to these conflicts. Stalin reiterated that the principle of self-
determination and secession was a "right not for the bourgeoisie but for the working masses of a given nation. The principle of self-determination [and secession] must be a means
for the struggle for socialism and must be subordinated to the
principles of socialism."[42] This view coincides with the previously stated Leninist position that this principle in its best
sense applied to social classes only and not to nations.[43]
Therefore, Stalin, as did Lenin, conceived the right of self-
determination and secession as a "class right" whose purpose
was to further the advent of the envisaged socialist society.
    In 1920 Stalin again remarked on this subject by saying
that the "nominal" independence of (Soviet) borderland governments was an illusion, masking their real dependence on
foreign imperialism. The choice as he saw it was not between
separation from and incorporation into the Soviet Republics,
but between union with proletarian Russia and descent into
"the bondage of the international imperialists." Hence, in
this instance, since a socialist milieu was threatened, the

18

demand for separation was deemed equivalent to a "counter-revolutionary venture."[44]

Further on the question of the right of self-determination and secession, Stalin writes:

> The right of self-determination means that only the nation itself has the right to determine its destiny, that no one has the right forcibly to interfere in the life of the nation, to destroy its schools and other institutions, to violate its habits and customs, to repress its language, or curtail its rights....While combating the exercise of violence against any nation, they [the Social Democrats] will only support the right of the nation to determine its own destiny, at the same time agitating against the noxious customs and institutions of that nation in order to enable the toiling strata of the nation to emancipate themselves from them....
>
> It [the nation] has the right to enter into federal relations with other nations. It has the right to complete secession. Nations are sovereign and all nations are equal....And this gives rise to the movement, the present and future movement, the aim of which is to achieve complete democracy....[45] This complete democracy in the country is the basis and condition for the solution of the national problem....But it follows from this that Russian Marxists cannot do without the right of nations to self-determination. Thus, the right of self-determination is an essential element in the solution of the national problem [i.e., in a capitalistic environment only].[46] (Italics in the original text.)

Stalin proposed that "the only real solution [to the Soviet nationality problem] is regional autonomy, autonomy for such crystallized [geographic] units as Poland, Lithuania, the Ukraine, the Caucasus, etc." (Italics in the original text.) He noted that the advantage of regional over national autonomy is that it:

> ...does not deal with a fiction bereft [sic] of territory, but with a definite population inhabiting a definite territory...it does not divide people according to nation, it does not strengthen national partitions; on the contrary, it only serves to break down these partitions and unites the population in such a manner as to open the way for division of a different kind, division

19

according to class...it provides the opportunity for uti-
lizing the productive forces in the best possible way
without awaiting the decisions of a common centre....
Thus, regional autonomy is an essential element in the
solution of the [Soviet] national problem.[47] (Italics in
the original text.)

Further regarding the Soviet nationality issue, Stalin
advocated "...national equality in all forms (language,
schools, etc.)" as "an essential element in the solution of
the national problem." (Italics in the original text.) He
also proposed that "a new state law based on complete democracy [the socialist version] in the country is required prohibiting all national privileges without exception and all kinds
of disabilities and restrictions on the rights of national minorities."

As his final "essential element" for the universal solution of the national problem, Stalin advocated the "principle
of [the] international solidarity of workers." By this latter
"essential element," Stalin meant the organization of the
proletarian class based on international unity and not according to "demarcation" of workers by individual nationality.[48]
Hence, if class status prevailed over nationality status in the
socialist scheme of things, then the question of nationality and
national prerogatives would not matter.

As an adjunct to his nationality policy, as it specifically
relates to national culture in the Soviet Union, Stalin in his
speech before the May 1925 graduating class of the Communist
University of the Toilers of the East coined the slogan
"Proletarian in content, National in form." In essence, Stalin
explained that the "proletarian culture does not abolish national culture, but gives it content. And on the contrary, national
culture does not abolish proletarian culture, but gives it form."[49]
(Italics added.) In other words, freedom to develop nationally
combined with guidance from the center constituted the essence
of cultural autonomy. The key to the slogan lay in its proletarian content. Reduced to practice, it meant little more than
use of the national language to implement Marxist-Leninist principles. Thus, the socialist content of the national culture is
the essential ingredient; the national form is only of transitory
significance.

Stalin fully shared Lenin's internationalism, but he,
more than Lenin, was confronted with the reality of governing
a maturing "socialist" State with all the inherent administrative and diplomatic problems which go with it. Consequently,
his views and policies with regard to the arena of international

20

affairs, at least on the surface, were influenced by that real- ity. As one consequence, he attacked socialist "internation- alists" such as Karl Kautsky for advocating the creation of a single, universal language and the dying away of all other languages in the period of socialism. In his previously noted speech of May 1925 on "The Political Tasks of the University of the Peoples of the East," Stalin stated that he "had little faith in this theory of a single all-embracing language. Ex- perience, in any case, speaks against rather than for such a theory." He returned to that topic again in replying to a ques- tion from the floor during the Sixteenth Party Congress in 1930.

> I still object to this theory....I object to it be- cause the theory of the fusion of all nations of, say, the U.S.S.R., into one common _Great Russian_ nation with one common _Great Russian_ tongue is a national- jingoist, anti-Leninist theory, which is in contradiction to the basic principle of Leninism that national distinc- tions cannot disappear in the near future, and that they are bound to remain for a long time, even after the vic- tory of the proletarian revolution _all over the world_. As for the development of national cultures and national tongues taken in a more distant perspective, I have al- ways maintained, and continue to maintain, the Lenin- ist view that in the period of the victory of socialism _all over the world_, when socialism has been consolidated and become a matter of everyday life, the national lan- guages must inevitably fuse into one common language, which of course, will be neither Great Russian nor German, but something else.[50] (Italics in the original text.)

Analytical comment on specific policies and practices implemented under Stalin's rule is provided in subsequent portions of this study.

SUMMARIZATION

As mentioned earlier, Marx actually contributed little original thought to the overall nationality issue and to the Jewish question specifically. He took up the Jewish question more to refute the theories of the contemporary socialist theoretician Bruno Bauer than he did to comment on the Jewish situation per se. It is evident, however, that Marx

21

had a totally negative view of Judaism and furthermore did
not consider the Jews a "nation" -- in fact, he considered
them a "caste" or a "chimerical nation." Moreover, to Marx,
Judaism was historically obsolete and an evil in itself, "an
anti-social element" which had conquered Christianity and
which had an inherent capacity to poison other cultures. He
believed that Judaism had retained its vitality in the world
largely through a unique, historical circumstance -- one in
which the Jews had eagerly collaborated. It was Marx's contention (which, by the way, appears to be a valid historical
observation) that throughout the early stages of Christianity,
the Christians, because of their strict religious observances,
actively promoted the growth of the Jews as a predominantly
usury class. Moreover, in time, according to Marx, the
Christians themselves because tainted by what he terms the
essence of Judaism, i.e., money and the pursuit of monetary
reward. Consequently, for Marx, the question of Jewish
emancipation becomes "the question of which element in
society must be overcome in order to abolish Judaism [and its
negative effect upon society]." Thus, Jewish emancipation,
in the Marxian sense, means, ultimately, "the emancipation
of society from Judaism." Therefore, in the final analysis,
Marx paid relatively little attention to the nationality and
Jewish questions per se. His view of the world was more
concerned with the larger aspects of world history, economics,
and society -- individual national and minority problems were
only important inasmuch as they contributed to the envisaged
international socialist order.

However, he did lay the philosophical foundation
("historical materialism") upon which his disciples, Lenin
and Stalin, were to base their nationality (Jewish) programs.
In that regard, as noted previously, Lenin and Stalin as
leaders of a viable socialist State encountered daily problems
of a practical nature which were unknown to the theorist Marx.
As a consequence, Leninist-Stalinist theories and policies,
particularly when dealing with the explosive nationality and
Jewish questions, by necessity were tempered on occasion
by an awareness of the practical political expediencies of the
day. In both leaders, there appears to be on the surface at
least, an all-pervading dichotomy of thought on the nationality (Jewish) question. On the one hand, there is the negativism regarding nationality and the national state -- based
upon the Marxian conviction of the transient nature of nationalism -- and the approval of assimilation and amalgamation.
Conversely, both leaders appear to argue for the principle of

self-determination and secession. However, closer examination shows that the Leninist-Stalinist advocacy of "self-determination, secession, and amalgamation" was thought of essentially as "socially-progressive," functional requisites to individual historical stages of capitalist development, principles which would have no place or meaning in the future classless society.[51]

With specific reference to the Jewish question, Lenin, although not contrary to Marx, was, however, more liberal than Marx. He believed that total assimilation represented the ultimate solution for the Jewish problem. For Lenin, Judaism must disappear! However, both for philosophical and pragmatic reasons, Lenin was an implacable foe of anti-semitism. Ideologically, he believed that antisemitism was contrary to the fundamental socialist tenet of egalitarianism. Pragmatically, he was of the opinion that Jewish assimilation might have occurred more rapidly if not for the manifestation of antisemitism. In summation, therefore, Lenin opposed antisemitism on both theoretical and pragmatic grounds. Conversely, he advocated a policy of total destruction and assimilation in matters of religious Judaism, Zionism, and Hebrew culture. Moreover, he both distrusted and feared Jewish nationalism because of its separatism and because it was counter to his advocacy of a closely-knit, centralized revolutionary movement. For Lenin, the idea of a distinct and separate Jewish people was utterly inappropriate, unattainable in practice, and scientifically unjustifiable. He believed that the only correct solution of the Jewish problem lay in total "assimilation" and ultimate "internationalism" (the "fusion" of all nations and peoples into one society).

Stalin also rejected the Jewish claim to "nationhood" -- based on his view that the Jews did not possess either a "closed territory" or a "common language," and to a large extent were already assimilated into "foreign nations." As his Marxian predecessors, he believed that the ultimate solution to the overall nationality problem and the Jewish question in particular lay in the espoused Communist Party "internationalism" principle, whereby questions of nationalism, separatism, and other such divisive issues do not constitute a meaningful reality. However, as we shall see later in this study, Stalin's actual policies toward the Jews were to prove largely ambivalent, tempered by the expediencies of the times -- particularly during the World War II period.

Consequently, we can readily see that none of these communist thinkers -- neither Marx, Lenin, nor Stalin --

23

actually presented any definitive theoretical statement on either the Jewish question per se or on the larger question of nationality (Stalin was particularly unoriginal).[52] At best, their theoretical utterances were negative, ambiguous, and of little actual help in resolving these two issues. This ambiguity and negativism continues to this date in official Soviet policies and attitudes toward the overall nationality problem and particularly as concerns the situation of the Jewish minority in contemporary Soviet society.

However, one should note the extraordinary essence of the espoused communist view -- shared by Marx, Lenin, Stalin, and succeeding Soviet regimes -- on the Jewish question. Namely, that Jewish identity is harmful not only to socialist objectives, but to the Jewish working class and to all of mankind as well, and should be eliminated, completely and irrevocably, through total assimilation. This is classical antisemitism in its truest form. Think of it! The Jews represent the only "national" group singled out for such treatment at the hands of the communist practitioners[53] -- even though both Lenin and Stalin believed that national differences would continue to exist long after the envisaged socialist international order had been attained. Thus, it appears quite evident that at least as far as communist theory is concerned, the "Jews" are not a nation and do not deserve recognition as such.[54] However, what communist theory professes and what communist practice actually does often constitute two different realities -- as we shall see later in this study.

NOTES

1. Although Stalin's prestige in the U.S.S.R. today is rather low, his extensive contributions to communist theory and practice nonetheless must be included in any serious discussion of communist ideological concepts and attitudes.

2. Karl Marx and Frederick [sic] Engels, Manifesto of the Communist Party (New York: International Publishers, 1932), p. 28.

3. Karl Marx, The Civil War in France, with an Introduction by Frederick [sic] Engels (New York: International Publishers, 1933), p. 62.

4. Solomon F. Bloom, The World of Nations: A Study of the National Implications in the Work of Karl Marx (New York: Columbia University Press, 1941), pp. 20, 35, 40-42

[Hereafter cited as Bloom, World of Nations]; Karl Marx, Karl Marx Selected Works, ed. V. Adoratsky, 2 vols. (Moscow: Marx-Engels Institute, 1933; New York: International Publishers, 1933), 1:90-91 [Hereafter cited as Marx, Selected Works.]

5. Bloom, World of Nations, p. 38; Karl Marx and Friedrich Engels, Selected Correspondence, 1846-1895 (London: Martin Lawrence, Ltd., 1934), pp. 280-82, 290 [Hereafter cited as Marx and Engels, Selected Correspondence]; Marx, Selected Works, pp. 640-48; Vladimir I. Lenin, The Right of Nations to Self-Determination (New York: International Publishers, 1951), pp. 50-51 [Hereafter cited as Lenin, Self-Determination.]

6. Bloom, World of Nations, pp. 36-37; Rudolf Schlesinger, Federalism in Central and Eastern Europe (London: K. Paul, Trench, Trubner & Co., 1945), p. 19.

7. Karl Marx and Frederick [sic] Engels, Karl Marx and Frederick [sic] Engels: Collected Works, 45 vols., The Holy Family or Critique of Critical Criticism: Against Bruno Bauer and Company (New York: International Publishers, 1975), 4: 110.

8. Bruno Bauer, The Capacity of Today's Jews and Christians to Become Free (Zurich and Winterthur: Georg Herwegh, 1843); Karl Marx, A World without Jews, with an introduction by Dagobert D. Runes (New York: Philosophical Library, 1959) [Hereafter cited as Marx, World Without Jews].

9. For Marx, the United States represented the center of world capitalism, and as such, the epitome of the so-called "Jewish disease."

10. Marx, World Without Jews, pp. 37-45.

11. In fact, Marx in his later years never wrote or uttered an opinion on the Jewish question.

12. The noted theorist Hannah Arendt is of the opinion that Marx was not an antisemite -- rather his views were against the "evils" of the nation-state. Consequently, he attacked the "Jews" in their capacity as the "bankers" of the nation-state apparatus. See Hannah Arendt, The Origins of Totalitarianism (New York and London: Harcourt, Brace, Jovanovich, 1957), p. 34 [Hereafter cited as Arendt, Totalitarianism].

13. Vladimir I. Lenin, Sochineniya [Collected Works], 3d ed., 30 vols. Kriticheskie zametki po natsional'nomu voprosu [Critical notes on the national question] (Moscow: Gosudarstvennoe Izdatel'stvo, 1926-32), 17:129-59 [Hereafter cited as Lenin, Sochineniya, 3d ed., Vol. and page no.].

14. Ibid., 17:136.

15. Lenin, Self-Determination, pp. 10-11.

16. Ibid., pp. 14-15; Lenin, Sochineniya, 3d ed. (O prave natsii na samoopredelenie) [On the right of nations to self-determination], 17:431-32. This essay was originally published in Proveshchenie [Enlightenment], nos. 4 and 6, 1917.

17. Ibid., pp. 429-40; Vladimir I. Lenin, Natsional'nii vopros [The national question] (Moscow: Gosudarstvennoe Izdatel'stvo, 1936), pp. 45-47, 65-66 [Hereafter cited as Lenin, National Question].

18. G. Safarov, Marks o natsional'no-kolonial'nom voprose [Marx on the national-colonial question] (Moscow: Gosudarstvennoe Izdatel'stvo, 1928), p. 32; Lenin, National Question, pp. 127-30.

19. Lenin, Sochineniya, 3d ed., 17:90. (This quote is interesting in view of the Great Russian chauvinism practiced by succeeding Bolshevik/Soviet regimes.)

20. Ibid., 16:439.

21. Robert A. Kann, The Multinational Empire: Nationalism and National Reform in the Habsburg Monarchy, 2 vols. (New York: Columbia University Press, 1950), 2:158-67; Bloom, World of Nations, p. 201; Carlile Aymer Macartney, National States and National Minorities (London: Oxford University Press, 1934), pp. 148-50; Bertram D. Wolfe, Three Who Made a Revolution (New York: Dial Press, 1948), pp. 232-34, 579.

22. Iskra was the Social Democratic periodical of which Lenin had assumed sole editorship.

23. Lenin, Sochineniya, 3d ed., 6:83-85. Also see Vladimir I. Lenin, Polnoe Sobranie Sochinenii [Full Collected Works], 5th ed., 55 vols. (Moscow: Izdatel'stvo Politicheskoi Literatury, 1969), 8:72-74 [Hereafter cited as Lenin, Polnoe Sobranie].

24. Vladimir I. Lenin, Sochineniya [Collected Works], 2d ed., 45 vols. (Moscow: Gosudarstvennoe Izdatel'stvo, 1961), 17:139. Also see Lenin, Polnoe Sobranie, 24:123, 125-26.

25. Vladimir M. Purishkevich was a leading antisemitic in prerevolutionary Russia.

26. I.e., an exclusive and restrictive social group.

27. Lenin, Polnoe Sobranie, 24:125-26.

28. Ibid., 10:266-69.

29. Ibid., 25:16-18.

30. Ibid., 38:242-43.

31. Ibid., 24:122-23. Lenin was particularly against the Bundist advocacy of separate Jewish schools. See Lenin, Polnoe Sobranie, 23:375-76.

32. Lenin, National Question, pp. 9-11.

33. Peoples of all non-Russian parts of the empire opted to accept the Bolshevik invitation to self-determination and secession. In 1918 and 1919, not only did historical nations such as the Ukraine, the Baltic States, Finland, Poland, Georgia and Armenia break away; many others, even Tatars and various Cossack groups, tried to assert independence. See Robert G. Wesson, The Russian Dilemma (New Brunswick, N.J.: Rutgers University Press, 1974), pp. 84-85.

34. Lenin, Sochineniya, 3d ed., 22 (Part 2):93-94.

35. There is controversy over the actual role played by Stalin in formulating Bolshevik policies on the nationality and Jewish questions. Some scholars maintain that Lenin was the actual innovator of the Party's theories and policies on both those issues. See Boris Souvarine, Stalin, A Critical Survey of Bolshevism (New York: Longmans, Green & Co., 1939), p. 134; and Isaac Deutscher, Stalin, A Political Biography (New York: Oxford University Press, 1949), p. 117.

36. The 1913 article first appeared in the Bolshevik journal, Proveshchenie, 1913, nos. 3-5, under the title "The National Question and Social Democracy." This essay along with a number of Stalin's speeches and subsequent articles on the nationality question were compiled in Stalin's later work, Marxism and the National and Colonial Question (Moscow: Foreign Languages Publishing House, 1940).

37. Joseph Stalin, Marxism and the National and Colonial Question (Moscow: Foreign Languages Publishing House, 1940), pp. 7, 11 [Hereafter cited as Stalin, Marxism].

38. Ibid., pp. 30-31.

39. Ibid., pp. 9-10.

40. Ibid., pp. 36-37.

41. Iosif Stalin, Sochineniya [Collected Works] 13 vols. (Moscow: Gosudarstvennoe Izdatel'stvo, 1946 -), 4:7-8 [Hereafter cited as Stalin, Sochineniya].

42. Tretii vserossiiskii s'yezd sovetov rabochikh, soldatskikh i krest'yanskikh deputatov [The third all-Russian congress of the soviets of workers, soldiers, and peasants deputies] (St. Petersburg: 1918), p. 73.

43. Lenin, National Question, pp. 10-11.

44. Stalin, Sochineniya, 4:160, 352-53.

45. By "complete democracy" Stalin, of course, is referring to that "democracy" enjoyed in a strictly socialist environment.

46. Stalin, Sochineniya, 3:206-09; Stalin, Marxism, pp. 16, 49.

47. Stalin, Marxism, pp. 50-53.

48. Ibid.

49. Stalin, Sochineniya, 7:138.

50. This speech was given at the height of the koreniz-atsiya (or grass roots) program of the Party to indoctrinate the assorted Soviet nationalities in Marxist–Leninist principles through the use of the individual national languages in conducting Party and everyday business.

Joseph Stalin, Marxism and Linguistics (New York: International Publishers, 1951), pp. 50, 55-56 [Hereafter cited as Stalin, Linguistics].

51. See Joseph Stalin, Leninism, 2 vols. Eng. ed. (Moscow and Leningrad: State Publishing House, 1934), p. 363 [Hereafter cited as Stalin, Leninism].

52. However, it also appears quite evident that none of these Marxist thinkers viewed the "Jewish problem" theoretically as part of the overall "nationality issue." To them it represented a separate and distinct entity.

53. Ironically, the only such totally destructive "Jewish" policy which comes to mind is that of Nazi Germany -- although, of course, the Nazis were striving for the physical annihilation of the Jews whereas the Soviet Jewish policy has been restrained primarily to ethnocultural deprivation.

54. Unfortunately, as Hannah Arendt points out, the loss of national rights also entails the loss of political and human rights -- a circumstance which, perhaps, largely depicts the fate of not only Soviet Jews but other nationalities in the Soviet Union as well. See Arendt, Totalitarianism, pp. 299-300.

2
The Jewish Minority in the Soviet Union: Demographic and Cultural Profiles

PRINCIPAL ETHNIC GROUPS OF SOVIET JEWRY

Although Soviet Jewry is often thought of as one ethnic community, the fact is that it actually consists of several distinct communities differing in their racial origins, individual attachment to Judaism (maintaining religious laws and customs, use of Jewish dialects, etc.) and in their geographic location. These communities are of two broad categories, the "Ashkenazic" or "European" Jews, and the so-called "Oriental" or "Asiatic" Jews. As noted, these two groups are geographically and culturally distinct, though some interaction has taken place, especially as a result of World War II, when large numbers of Ashkenazic Jews fled east during the Nazi military onslaught.

The Ashkenazic group is subdivided into those Jews who have lived under the Soviet government since its establishment in 1917, the so-called "Core" Jews -- the greater portion of whom live within the pre-August 1939 European borders of the U.S.S.R. -- and those Jews known as the "Western" or "Zapadniki" Jews who were residents of regions which were annexed by the Soviets as a result of World War II, i.e., the Baltic countries, the Western Ukraine (including Bukovina and Transcarpathia), Western Byelorussia, and Moldavia. The "Core" Jews are the most highly "Russianized." The "Western" Jews are not as assimilated and as a result a greater number still speak Yiddish and observe traditional religious-cultural practices.

The Oriental or Asiatic Jewish communities consist of the Georgian, Bukharan, and Mountain or Tat Jews. The Georgian Jews, whose native language is Georgian, claim to be descended from the ten tribes of Israel exiled by Babylon in the eighth century B.C. They are among the most

29

culturally cohesive of the Jewish communities in the Soviet
Union, the family and religion being their strongest institutions. They live en masse in specific town areas, culturally
isolated, for the most part, from their Georgian national
neighbors.

The Bukharan Jews, or Oriental Jews of Central Asia,
comprise the majority of the Oriental Jewish group. Their
native language is Tadzhik, a dialect of the Persian language.
They migrated from Persia centuries ago along the "Silk Route"
and today mainly reside in the Uzbek cities of Tashkent,
Samarkand, and Bukhara, although they also live in the major
towns of other Soviet Central Asian S.S.R.s such as Ashk-
habad and Dushanbe.

The Mountain or Tat Jews, who speak an Azerbaidzhani-
Turkic language called Tat and who possess a distinct culture
of their own, reside mostly in the Soviet Autonomous Republic
of Dagestan. Many also live in Azerbaidzhan. They originally lived in mountain villages after having arrived centuries
ago from Persian Azerbaidzhan, but during the past several
decades have migrated to the cities, mostly along the Caspian
Sea coast (Derbent, Makhachkala, and Baku).[1]

According to the Soviet Census of 1970,[2] the overwhelming majority of Soviet Jews -- about 87 percent -- are
numbered in the overall Ashkenazic Jewish community group.
Of the Ashkenazic group, there are 1,633,000 "Core" Jews
living in the R.S.F.S.R., Ukraine, Byelorussia, and Kazakh
S.S.R. In addition, there are 257,000 of the other Ashkenazic
subgroup, i.e., the "Western" Jews, who live within the
territories annexed by the Soviets during the Second World
War. The three Oriental Jewish communities number 261,000
in all. It is interesting to note that the great majority of the
recent Jewish emigration from the Soviet Union is comprised
of the largely unassimilated Ashkenazic community subgroup,
i.e., the "Western" Jews, residing in the annexed Soviet
territories, and the likewise traditionally minded Oriental
Jewish communities -- the Georgian, Bukharan, and Mountain
or Tat Jews.[3]

PROBLEMS OF DEFINITION AND ANALYSIS RELATIVE TO THE
SOVIET CENSUS PROCEDURE -- ESPECIALLY AS CONCERNS
THE TOTAL NUMBER OF JEWS IN THE SOVIET UNION

There is a considerable disparity of views concerning the
total size of the Jewish population in the U.S.S.R. The lowest figure cited is the one given in the official Soviet census

of 1970 which lists a total of 2,150,707 Jews, or 0.88 percent of the total Soviet population. (Jews constitute the twelfth largest "nationality" group among 104 nationalities in the U.S.S.R.).[4]

In 1964, the Soviet publication Atlas Narodov Mira (Atlas of the Peoples of the World) conversely reported an "increasing" Jewish population of 2.5 million. In addition, an official Novosti Press Agency pamphlet in 1970 reported the total Soviet Jewish population as "about three million." (Soviet Premier Aleksei N. Kosygin used this same figure in April 1973 at a press conference in Stockholm, Sweden, as did C.P.S.U. General Secretary Leonid I. Brezhnev when speaking with a visiting U.S. Senatorial delegation in Moscow on April 3, 1973.) Western Sovietologists also use the three million figure as the most accurate approximation of the total number of Jews currently in the Soviet Union.[5]

These discrepancies are due in part to different criteria used in compiling Soviet passport and census nationality data and also, to some degree, on one's definition of the terms "nationality" and "Jew." The attributes common to most nationalities are a common descent, language, territory, political unity, customs, traditions, and religion; but no one attribute is essential either to the existence or the definition of "nationality." However, the most important of these factors are assumed to be a common territory, a common political organization, and the existence of a state, which in most cases, precedes the formation of a nationality.

According to Professor Hans Kohn:

> Nationality is formed by the [conscious] decision to form a nationality....Nationalities are created out of ethnographic and political elements when nationalism breathes life into the form built by preceding centuries. Nationalism is a state of mind, permeating a large majority of the people and claiming to permeate all its members; it recognizes the national state as the ideal form of political organization and the nationality as the source of all creative cultural energy and of economic well-being.[6]

Rupert Emerson presents the view that:

> The simplest statement that can be made about a nation [nationality] is that it is a body of people who

31

feel that they are a nation....To advance beyond it, it
is necessary to attempt to take the nation [nationality]
apart and to isolate for separate examination the forces
and elements which appear to have been the most influential in bringing about the sense of common identity
which lies at its roots, the sense of the existence of a
singularly important "we" which is distinguished from
all others who make up an alien "they." This is necessarily an overly mechanical process, for nationalism,
like other profound emotions such as love and hate, is
more than the sum of the parts which are susceptible of
cold and rational analysis.[7]

Because the importance of the componential variables
of "nationality" differs so considerably from one nationality
to the next, it is impossible to use them in a census to define
nationality. If there were a uniquely correct definition of
nationality, uniquely correct data could be gathered according to this definition. However, in the absence of such a
definition, the most practical and perhaps best way to determine "nationality" is through respondent self-identification
-- and this is precisely the nationality determining methodology used by most of the Soviet censuses, 1970 included.
    In that regard, how the nationality question is asked
or worded and the kind of instructions given to the census-
taker are most important in determining the individual respon-
ses to the nationality question.[8] In December 1926, every
resident of the Soviet Union was asked to respond to a census
questionnaire in which question number four referred to the
"nationality" (narodnost' -- tribal roots or subnationality)
of the respondent. The accompanying instructions to the
census-taker defined the term as follows:

    In this space is to be noted which nationality
    the respondent considers himself/herself a member.
    In the case that the respondent finds it difficult to
    answer the question, greater weight should be given
    to the mother's nationality. Considering that the cen-
    sus aims at determining the ethnic [ethnographic]
    composition of the population, one [the census-taker]
    should not substitute for nationality religion, citizen-
    ship, or the fact that the respondent resides in the
    territory of some [particular] republic [of the U.S.S.R.].
    The answer to the question about nationality need not

32

be the same as the answer to question number five about native language.[9] (Italics in the original text.)

The 1926 Soviet census also noted that:

Though the term narodnost' has been chosen in connection with the necessity of obtaining data on the ethnic [ethnographic] composition of the population, the determination of one's nationality has been left up to the respondent himself/herself and one [the census-taker] should not change the statements of the respondent during the interview. Persons who have lost the ties with the nationality of their ancestors may indicate the nationality which they consider themselves to be.[10] (Italics in the original text.)

Beginning with the Soviet national census of 1939, the concept of natsional'nost' was introduced which was understood to mean ethnic membership in the sense of national origin. But, in this sense, the nationality refers to nation (natsiya) and not every Soviet ethnic group has officially acquired the status of natsiya or natsional'nost', which in theory at least, denotes a common literary language, territory, economy, historical tradition, and also, a qualifying number of members (one million). To prevent confusion and possible error, a Soviet analysis of the subject had recommended that both terms (narodnost' and natsional'nost') be used in the 1970 census, but these recommendations were not heeded by the Soviet authorities. It has been suggested, moreover, that the Soviet deviation from the 1926 census narodnost' terminology was an attempt to promote the assimilation of smaller national groups with the larger Soviet nationalities, particularly with the Great Russians.[11]

As Alec Nove and J.A. Newth point out,[12] in any country the concept of Jewish "nationality" is difficult to define. Do we define a "Jew" narrowly on a strictly religious criterion or more broadly to include such characteristics as secular culture, language, history, ethnicity, and nationality? In the Soviet society, moreover, the determination of Jewish "nationality" is a particularly complicated and at times frustrating exercise. This is due in no small measure to the continuing accentuated assimilation efforts on the part of the Soviet government vis-à-vis the individual ethnic groups and also, because of the various "classifications" of Soviet Jewry which have developed over the years. For example,

33

there are the so-called "Census Jews" or those Soviet citizens who declare themselves to be Jewish or are registered as such during an official census. Since many Jewish citizens do not care to declare themselves openly as Jewish and as there is no demand for documentary proof of nationality (commencing with the 1959 census), the census procedure provides the lowest demographic accounting of the Jewish population. Another classification, the "Passport Jews," are those Jewish citizens who are registered as Jewish "nationals" on the internal passport which is obligatory for every citizen aged sixteen and older in the U.S.S.R. -- among the personal data in the passport is the bearer's nationality. The registration in the internal passport as "Yevrei" (Jewish) is mandatory for all Jewish offspring of two Jewish spouses. Upon reaching the age of sixteen, the child of a "mixed" marriage may declare himself or herself either Jewish or the nationality of the non-Jewish parent.[13] Once entered, the designation cannot be subsequently changed, regardless of future circumstances.[14] A third classification, the "Jews by descent" category includes all persons with a Jewish parent or even more distant Jewish forebear, even if the individual is registered in the internal passport system as non-Jewish. Finally, there are the so-called "Emigration Jews" among whose number are non-Jews who have familiar ties of one kind or another with Jews, e.g., spouses, and as such may emigrate together with their Jewish family.[15]

Therefore, in view of the foregoing, how does one go about defining and counting Soviet Jews? If the internal passport nationality identification is to be the vehicle, then the total number of Jews living in the Soviet Union is probably higher than the 2,150,707 figure listed in the official national census of 1970 -- perhaps close to the three million number quoted earlier in this study.[16] However, if assimilation is taken into account, either spontaneous or forced, then the 1970 census total is probably more accurate.

THE GEOGRAPHICAL DISTRIBUTION OF JEWS IN THE SOVIET UNION -- ACCORDING TO THE OFFICIAL JANUARY 1970 SOVIET CENSUS RESULTS

Approximately 1,934,000 Jews, who are 89.8 percent of the Jewish population in the U.S.S.R., live in five of the fifteen Soviet republics; concentrated in those five same republics is 83 percent of the entire population of the Soviet Union. There are 216,728 Jews, 10.1 percent, living in the ten other republics.

34

TABLE 1
The Jewish Population Concentration in Five Soviet Republics*

Republic	Number	Percentage
R S.F.S.R.	807,915	37.5
Ukraine	777,126	36.1
Byelorussia	148,011	6.9
Uzbek	102,855	4.8
Moldavia	98,072	4.6
Total	1,933,979	89.9

*Central Statistical Administration of the Council of Ministers,
U.S.S.R., Itogi vsesoyuznoi perepisi naseleniya 1970 goda
[Results of the all-union population census of 1970], 7 vols.
(Moscow: "Statistika," 1973), 4:12, 13, 14.

Jewish Population Concentration in the Russian Soviet Federated
Socialist Republic (R.S.F.S.R.)

The principal concentration of Soviet Jews is in the
R.S.F.S.R. -- 37.5 percent or 807,915 in absolute numbers.
Ten thousand or more Jews are found within only nine of the
fifty-four oblasts (regions or districts) and autonomous republics which are contained in the European part of the R.S.
F.S.R. and the Urals. There are no Jews at all in nineteen of
the R.S.F.S.R. oblasts and autonomous republics, or their
number is so small (apparently less than one thousand in each
of these administrative areas) that they do not appear in the
official 1970 census. Of the total number of Jews in the R.S.
F.S.R., 46 percent are located within the cities of Moscow
and Leningrad. Of the eighteen oblasts and autonomous republics located in the Asian or Siberian part of the R.S.F.S.R.,
Jews are found in only twelve of them; however, in two of
these, the oblast' of Novosibirsk and the "Autonomous Jewish
Oblast'" (Birobidzhan), there are 11,864 and 11,452 Jews,
respectively. Of the seven geographical regions of the European part of the R.S.F.S.R. having the most dense Jewish
population, that is, relative to the total population, the area
having the most Jews is the northwest region where Jews constitute 1.45 percent of the population -- this is because of
the relatively large concentration of Jews found in the city of
Leningrad where Jews comprise 4.11 percent of the city's
population or 162,587 in absolute figures. The area of the
most sparse Jewish concentration is the "central black soil

region" where Jews constitute only 0.13 percent of the total population. Of the three geographical regions of Siberia, which constitute the Asian part of the R.S.F.S.R., the region having the most Jews is the Far East, which includes the "Jewish Autonomous Oblast'" (Birodibzhan), where Jews constitute 0.42 percent of the population. In the other two geographical regions, i.e., Western Siberia and Eastern Siberia, Jews comprise only 0.22 and 0.23 percent of the population, respectively. The Autonomous Republic of Dagestan is the only one, except for the cities of Moscow and Leningrad, of the seventy-two regions, subregions, and autonomous republics which make up the R.S.F.S.R. in which the Jews constitute more than 1 percent of the population -- 1.55 percent to be exact. (About two-thirds of the Mountain or Tat Jewish community live in the Dagestan Autonomous Republic.) In the Autonomous Republic of Kabardino-Balkar, which is in the Caucasus and most of whose Jewish residents are of the Mountain or Tat community, the Jews constitute 0.95 percent of the population -- in the Kuybyshev Oblast' the Jews constitute 0.68 percent of the population. In all the other regions, subregions, and autonomous republics of the R.S.F.S.R., the Jews constitute less than one-half of 1 percent of the population. In the R.S.F.S.R. as a whole, Jews comprise 0.62 percent of the republic's population, as compared to 0.88 percent of the total Soviet population.[17]

Jewish Population Concentration in the Ukraine

In the Ukrainian S.S.R., according to the official census of 1970, live 36.1 percent of the total Soviet Jewish population -- or 777,126 in absolute figures. Unlike the Jewish population distribution in the R.S.F.S.R., Jews live in all the regions of the Ukraine. In the whole Ukraine the Jews constitute 1.65 percent of the population. The highest percentage of Ukrainian Jews, 9.31 percent, is found in the city of Kiev and the lowest percentage, 0.24 percent, is located in the region of Rovno. In thirteen regions Jews constitute more than 1 percent of the population. In six regions they constitute less than 0.5 percent and in the remaining seven regions between 0.5 and 1 percent of the population. Approximately 60 percent of Ukrainian Jews live in four large cities -- Kiev, Odessa, Kharkov, and Dnepropetrovsk.[18] The small number of Jews in the Western Ukraine, except for the city of L'vov, may perhaps be explained by the fact that relatively few Jews succeeded in fleeing the region in the face of the German

36

military invasion of 1941 because of the close proximity of the front and also because the Jews who survived that holocaust were permitted to emigrate to Poland following World War II.

Jewish Population Concentration in Byelorussia

In Byelorussia there are 148,000 Jews. They constitute 1.64 percent of the population -- a percentage almost identical to that of the Ukraine. A little less than one-third of them live in the capital city of Minsk. In two regions, Gomel' and Mogilev, they constitute more than 2 percent of the population. In one region, Vitebsk, they constitute 1 percent of the population, and in the three remaining regions, Minsk, Brest, and Grodno, they constitute less than 0.5 percent of the population. (The previously mentioned assumption regarding the small number of Jews in the Western Ukraine may also explain their lack of numbers in Western Byelorussia.)[19]

Jewish Population Concentrations in Lithuania, Latvia, and Estonia

According to the 1970 census, there are 65,532 Jews living in the three Baltic S.S.R.s. The largest concentration, both in absolute and relative figures, is in Latvia -- 36,680, constituting 1.55 percent of the population. The Jews of Lithuania, 23,564 in total numbers, comprise 0.75 percent of the population; and the Jews of Estonia, 5,288, comprise only 0.39 percent of the population.[20]

Jewish Population Concentrations in the Transcaucasian-Asian S.S.R.s

In the three transcaucasian S.S.R.s, i.e., Georgia, Azerbaidzhan, and Armenia, there were 97,718 Jews recorded in the 1970 census. The Jews of Georgia, 55,382 in total numbers, comprise 1.18 percent of the Georgian S.S.R. population. The Jews of Azerbaidzhan, 41,288 in total numbers, comprise 0.81 percent of that S.S.R.'s population; while in Armenia, which is the Soviet S.S.R. having the smallest number of Jews, both in relative and absolute terms, there are 1,048 Jews, constituting only 0.04 percent of the population.

In the five Central Asian S.S.R.s -- Kazakh, Uzbek, Tadzhik, Kirghiz, and Turkmen -- there were in 1970 a total of 156,333 Jews. Approximately two-thirds of them live in the Uzbek S.S.R., or 102,855 in absolute figures, constituting

0.87 percent of the population. About half of the Uzbek Jews
are concentrated in the capital city of Tashkent, with the rest
scattered throughout the republic. According to estimates
based on the number of speakers of Jewish dialects, and on
earlier official Soviet census figures, it is reasonable to assume that about one-third of the Jews of Uzbek S.S.R. are
members of the Bukharan community. In the Kazakh S.S.R.,
27,689 Jews constitute 0.21 percent of the population. About
one-third of them live in the capital city of Alma-Ata. Another
one-third live in the regions of Karaganda, Kyzl-Orda, and
Chimkent, with the remaining one-third distributed throughout
the other fourteen regions of the republic. In the Tadzhik S.S.R.,
14,615 Jews constitute 0.5 percent of the population. In the
Kirghiz S.S.R., 7,680 Jews constitute 0.26 percent of the population; and in the Turkmen S.S.R., 3,494 Jews constitute 0.16
percent of the population. In the Tadzhik S.S.R. there are
6,184 speakers of the Tadzhik tongue which is the native language of the Bukharan Jewish community -- this community
constitutes 41.6 percent of the Jewish population in that republic.[21]

Jewish Population Concentration in the Moldavian S.S.R.

Of all the Soviet S.S.R.s, the Moldavian S.S.R. (which
in 1970 had a total Jewish population of 98,072) has the largest
Jewish population relative to the population -- 2.75 percent.[22]

A COMPARISON OF JEWISH POPULATION FIGURES IN THE 1959 AND 1970 CENSUSES

According to a comparison of the results of the 1959 and
1970 censuses, there occurred a decline, both in absolute and
relative terms, in the number of Jews residing in the Soviet
Union. This trend runs counter to the general trend of population growth during the same period. In 1959, according to
official statistics, there were a total of 2,267,814 Jews living
in the Soviet Union, and by 1970 their number had declined to
2,150,707 -- a decline of 117,107 or 5.16 percent. During
that same period, the overall population growth of the U.S.S.R.
grew from 208,826,600 to 241,720,100 -- a growth of 15.8
percent.
A significant population decline occurred during the period described in the Ashkenazic Jewish group located in the
principal European S.S.R.s of the Soviet Union: in the R.S.F.S.R.

there was a decline of 67,400, and in the Ukraine there was a decline of 63,200. In six other S.S.R.s -- Byelorussia, Kirghiz, Kazakh, Turkmen, Lithuania, and Estonia -- the number of Jews decreased by a total figure of 5,300. To be noted is that there were only minor and insignificant Jewish population changes (i.e., in absolute numbers) in the Latvian and Armenian S.S.R.s. In the five remaining S.S.R.s -- Azerbaidzhan, Moldavia, Georgia, Uzbek, and Tadzhik -- the total number of Jews increased by 18,600. This growth only partially offset the significant decline of Jews registered in the Russian and Ukrainian S.S.R.s.

In view of the fact that the largest decline in the number of Jews occurred in the European S.S.R.s, while the growth in Jewish numbers occurred in the Asian S.S.R.s, it may be assumed that the decline possibly was a result of a low Jewish birth rate and the accumulated effects of intermarriage, accelerated assimilation, and the abandonment of Judaism for one reason or another. These factors in particular characterize the Jews of the R.S.F.S.R. and the Ukraine. The effect of these phenomena is relatively minor in the S.S.R.s and regions which were annexed by the Soviets following World War II, and insignificant among members of the Oriental Jewish communities which inhabit the S.S.R.s of the South Caucasus and Central Asia.[23]

In addition, low birth rates are characteristic of all urban populations which are modern and enjoy a high level of education. Even among the non-Jewish urban population, the trend is toward a declining birth rate. Among Jews this trend is relatively greater since all are city dwellers (only 2 percent of all Jews live in nonurban environments) and also because of the relatively high level of education enjoyed by the Jewish population as a whole.[24]

It is perhaps of interest to note that in the period between the 1959 and 1970 censuses the number of Jews residing in the Jewish Autonomous Oblast' (Birobidzhan) fell from 14,269, constituting 8.8 percent of the population in 1959 to 11,452, constituting 6.6 percent of the population in 1970. The number of Jews in the Jewish Region declined by 20 percent, as compared to a decline of 5.14 percent in the Jewish population in the U.S.S.R. as a whole for the same period. The decline in the region's Jewish members perhaps indicates that Jews are deserting the region -- especially since the number of rural Jews in the region has declined from a total of 2,292 in 1959 to 1,177 in 1970 -- a decline of 48.5 percent.

Among the ten "national" groups whose number decreased in the 1970 census as compared to the 1959 census, the decline of the Jews, in relative terms, was the smallest with the exception of the Moldavians. However, in terms of absolute numbers, the Jewish reduction was second only to the Poles who recorded the highest population decline.[25]

TABLE 2
Rates of Change in Jewish Population Figures Between the 1959 and 1970 Soviet Censuses*

(Growth rate = +, Reduction rate = -)

Republic	Rate of Change
Turkmen	-14.4 percent
Kirghiz	-10.2 "
R.S.F.S.R.	- 7.8 "
Ukraine	- 7.5 "
Lithuania	- 4.5 "
Estonia	- 1.8 "
Kazakh	- 1.4 "
Byelorussia	- 1.3 "
Latvia	+ 0.3 "
Armenia	+ 2.3 "
Azerbaidzhan	+ 2.7 "
Moldavia	+ 3.2 "
Georgia	+ 8.1 "
Uzbek	+ 9.0 "
Tadzhik	+17.7 "

*Central Statistical Administration of the Council of Ministers, U.S.S.R., Itogi vsesoyuznoi perepisi naseleniya 1959 goda [Results of the all-union population census for 1959], 16 vols. (Moscow: "Statistika," 1962); Soviet Census of 1970, 4:9-19,303.

THE URBAN-RURAL COMPOSITION OF THE SOVIET JEWISH POPULATION

The Jews in the Soviet Union traditionally have been urban dwellers. Of the total Jewish population of 2,150,707, some 2,105,000 or 98 percent are inhabitants of metropolitan areas -- as compared with 56 percent of the total population. While the total number of Jews has declined, the number of Jews in almost all of the primary cities of the individual S.S.R.s has increased -- 848,000 or 39 percent, live in these primary city locations. This phenomenon perhaps indicates an

40

internal migration, in recent years, of Jews from the outlying towns to the primary city areas.

The number of Jews living in rural areas declined during the period between the two censuses from 106,112, constituting 4.7 percent of the total Jewish population in 1959, to 46,056, constituting 2.1 percent of all Jews in 1970. This represents a drastic decline of 43 percent in the number of rural Jewish residents in 1970 as compared to 1959. In that regard, it should be noted that the total population of the rural areas declined during the same period from about 109 million in 1959 to about 106 million in 1970 -- a decline of less than 3 percent. Consequently, the rather significant decline in the numbers of Jewish rural dwellers should not be viewed as part of a general urbanization process in Soviet society since, as noted, the rate and proportions of the Jewish rural reductions considerably exceed that of the non-Jewish rural population.[26]

THE COMPOSITION OF THE SOVIET JEWISH POPULATION ACCORDING TO SEX

Comparable to the total non-Jewish population, the composition of the Jewish population according to sex is unbalanced -- there is a marked surplus of women. Of a total of 2,150,707 Jews in 1970, there were only 988,009 men, or 45.9 percent. For each 100 Jewish men there were 118 Jewish women, as compared with the total non-Jewish population ratio of 117 women for every 100 men. (However, in the Soviet Asian republics, there is a general numerical balance between the two sexes.) In the entire U.S.S.R. there is a total surplus of 18,921,000 women. Of this total number, 12,368,000 are Russian and 3,640,000 are Ukrainian. The number of surplus Jewish women is 175,000.

It is interesting to note that the surplus of Jewish women is not distributed uniformly throughout the Soviet Union. It is higher in the Ukraine (125.2 women to 100 men) and is non-existent in Estonia (99 women to 100 men). In terms of absolute numbers, 87,000 surplus Jewish women, or 49.8 percent, live in the Ukraine. In the R.S.F.S.R., where the total number of Jews is greater than in the Ukraine by 30,000, the surplus of Jewish women is only 50,000. This may be explained by the fact that the whole Ukrainian area was under German occupation during the Second World War, while only a small part of the European R.S.F.S.R. was so occupied. (The majority of the Jewish males either were slaughtered or sent to Germany to forced labor camps.) This assumption is strengthened by the fact that Byelorussia, which also was completely occupied by the Germans during the war, also has a relatively high surplus of Jewish women -- 119.3 women to 100 men.[27]

THE AGE STRUCTURE

The official 1970 Soviet census compilation provides statistical data on the age structure of the Jewish population of the R.S.F.S.R. only. However, it is reasonable to assume that the R.S.F.S.R. age data would be characteristic for all Ashkenazic European Jews who have lived under the Soviet government since its inception -- since their demographic characteristics are equivalent, without reference to their geographic spread. Consequently, the age data provided in the 1970 census materials probably would be characteristic for almost 90 percent of all Soviet Jews.

According to the information provided, Jewish children up to age ten constitute 7 percent of the total R.S.F.S.R. Jewish population, as compared to 18 percent among Russians. Children and youth up to age nineteen constitute 15.1 percent, as compared to 35.6 percent among Russians. In the intermediate age range of twenty to forty-nine, there is almost no difference between Jews and Russians -- 41.9 percent for Jews and 42.9 percent for Russians. The drastic difference between the two nationalities is again prominent in age groups over fifty. The fifty to fifty-nine age category among Jews constitutes 16.2 percent of the population; while among Russians it constitutes only 9.5 percent. The sixty and over age bracket accounts for 26.4 percent of the Jewish population and 12.0 percent of the Russian population. Therefore, the age group of fifty and over constitutes 42.6 percent of the Jewish population -- twice that of the Russian percentage of 21.5 in the same age bracket.

These statistical data clearly indicate that there is a decided aging process prevalent in the Jewish population -- probably principally due to the negative birth rate among Soviet Jews.[28]

THE EDUCATIONAL LEVELS

The official 1970 census report provides statistical data on Jewish educational levels in the following five Soviet S.S.R.s: the R.S.F.S.R., the Ukraine, Byelorussia, Moldavia, and

Latvia. (In these five S.S.R.s live 87 percent of all Soviet
Jews.) The census provides no data on Jewish educational
levels in Georgia or in the Central Asian S.S.R.s. Unfortunately, there is also no statistical data breakdown according to
region and other administrative units for the S.S.R.s where
census data are available.

Among the "nationalities" of the Soviet Union, the Jews
proportionally have the highest educational level, including the
Russians. In 1973, 343,000 or 16 percent of Jews were said to
have a higher education. In terms of educational level, therefore, the Jews hold first place, the Russians hold second place,
and the local majority nationalities hold third place. In absolute numbers, the Jews are third in the number of students in
higher educational institutions and third in the number of scientists (behind the Russians and the Ukrainians). They also
account for 14 percent of all Soviet physicians and writers, 23
percent of musicians, etc.[29] In addition, the gap between
first-place Jews and other "nationalities," including the second-
place Russians, is greater than that between the Russians and
the local national majorities.

It should be pointed out, however, that the relative
weight of Jews in the educated and creative manpower sectors
of the Soviet population is constantly dropping because of the
overall accelerated growth of these sectors -- in some categories even the absolute numbers of Jews are being reduced.
Whereas the relative numbers of Jewish educated manpower
are falling, most other "national" groups are gaining ground.

In 1970, 46.8 percent of the employed Jewish population
in the R.S.F.S.R. had a "higher level" of education, as compared to 6.5 percent of the employed Russian population. In
the Ukraine, 28.3 percent of the employed Jews, 9.8 percent
of the employed Russians, and 4.7 percent of the employed
Ukrainians had a "higher level" of education. In Byelorussia,
24.8 percent of the employed Jews, 14.1 percent of the employed Russians, and 4.0 percent of the employed Byelorussians
had a "higher level" of education. In Latvia, 28.5 percent of
the employed Jews, 7.7 percent of the employed Russians, and
5.9 percent of the employed Latvians had a "higher level" of
education. In Moldavia, the subject figures were Jews -- 18.4
percent, Russians -- 11.1 percent, and Moldavians -- 2.3 percent, respectively.

There are substantial differences in the educational levels
of Jews among the various S.S.R.s. It is also probable that
there are differences in educational levels of Jews on an intra-

regional basis within each S.S.R. (in addition to the differences between the two sexes and between the urban and rural populations); however, these statistical data are not provided in the 1970 census report.

The high educational level of Jews of the R.S.F.S.R., which exceeds that of Jews in the other S.S.R.s, has its origins in two factors: 1) the attraction of the R.S.F.S.R. and especially of its two major cities, Moscow and Leningrad, in which are concentrated the central institutions of government, education, science, culture, and the arts; and 2) the traditionally high degree of social mobility of the Soviet society, especially for those who are talented and who migrate from throughout the U.S.S.R. to these centers.

Jews having a "higher level" of education are the largest group among employed Jews in the four S.S.R.s: the R.S.F.S.R., 46.8 percent; the Ukraine, 28.3 percent; Byelorussia, 24.8 percent; and Latvia, 28.5 percent. In Moldavia, the largest group is composed of those Jews having a general high school education, 23.3 percent; while those having a "higher level" of education comprise the second largest group, 18.4 percent.

It is interesting to note that the educational level of the Jews of the Jewish Autonomous Oblast' (Birobidzhan) is not only lower than that of other Jews of the R.S.F.S.R., but also of the Jews of the four other S.S.R.s. Only 4.5 percent of the Jewish population in that oblast' have a "higher level" of education -- this is only a third of the comparable Moldavian percentage. Those in the Jewish oblast' having a "super-primary education of all types," including "higher," are 55 percent, 11 percent less than Moldavia.

To be noted is that the Jews of the R.S.F.S.R. lead the other nationalities of that S.S.R. both in "higher level" of educational attainment -- 46.8 percent -- and conversely in "incomplete primary" education -- 6.6 percent. The lowest percentage of employed Jews having an "incomplete primary" education, 1.8 percent however, is found in Byelorussia; while in Moldavia, the percentage for the same category is 4.4 percent.

In the R.S.F.S.R. and the Ukraine, the educational level of rural Jews is lower than that of urban Jews. In the R.S.F.S.R. urban population, those Jews who have a "higher level" of education are 34.6 percent, and those who are employed are 47.6 percent. In the rural population of the R.S.F.S.R., those Jews in the same categories are 27.4 percent and 36.2 percent, respectively. In the Ukraine, those Jews of the same categories in the urban population are 19.7 percent and 28.4 percent; while in the rural population these same categories are 12.0

and 19.0 percent. In contrast, in Byelorussia, Latvia, and
Moldavia, the educational level is higher for rural Jews than
for urban Jews.

In Byelorussia, 16.3 percent of the urban Jews have a
"higher level" of education; in Latvia the same category is
20.9 percent; and in Moldavia it is 12.6 percent. In comparison, 22.3 percent of the rural Jewish population of Byelorussia
have a "higher level" of education; in Latvia, 26.2 percent;
and in Moldavia, 13.4 percent.

The percentage of those having a "higher" educational
level among the employed urban Jews of Byelorussia is 24.7
percent; in Latvia, 28.4 percent; and in Moldavia, 18.3 percent. Whereas, the percentage of those rural employed Jews
in Byelorussia having a "higher" education is 34.0 percent;
in Latvia, 37.3 percent; and in Moldavia, 19.8 percent. From
this, it would appear that rural Jews having academic training
in Byelorussia, Latvia, and Moldavia have less difficulty in
obtaining suitable employment than in the urban areas.

The educational level of Jewish women in the Soviet
Union is almost identical to that of the Jewish men. There are
only slight differences in the representation of the two sexes
with regard to levels of education. Consequently, the number
of Jewish men possessing a "higher" education is only slightly
higher than that of Jewish women in all five of the S.S.R.s.
In that regard, 48.6 percent of all employed Jewish men in the
R.S.F.S.R. have a "higher" education, compared with 44.7
percent of the employed Jewish women. In the Ukraine, 28.6
percent of the employed Jewish men have a "higher" education,
as do 27.9 percent of the employed Jewish women. In Byelorussia, 25.6 percent of the employed Jewish men have a "higher"
education and so do 24.0 percent of the employed Jewish women.
In Latvia, the same educational equation is 29.5 percent for
employed Jewish men and 27.3 percent for employed Jewish
women. Only in Moldavia, where the general educational level
of the Jews is relatively lower than that in the other four republics, is the "higher" educational level of employed Jewish women
greater than that for employed Jewish men: 18.6 percent versus
18.1 percent.

With regard to "high school" level educational attainment,
both vocational and general, the Jewish women enjoy a greater
percentage than do the Jewish men in all five S.S.R.s -- 18.5
percent of all employed Jewish women in the R.S.F.S.R. have
a vocational "high school" education, while 15.9 percent of
them have a general "high school" education. The parallel percentages among employed Jewish men in the R.S.F.S.R. are 16.3
percent and 12.3 percent.

In the period between the 1959 and 1970 national censuses, there was a general rise in the educational level of Jews in all sectors of education in all five of the reported S.S.R.s. The rise in Jewish educational levels corresponded with the extensive expansion of the Soviet educational system during the 1960s and followed the general trend. However, there were differences in terms of levels of change, both with regard to individual sectors of education and also among the S.S.R.s. The greatest increase during the same period in question occurred in the "higher" educational category. In all five of the S.S.R.s, the increase of Jewish men with a "higher" education was greater than for Jewish women. The greatest increase in that regard, 9.1 percent, occurred among the Jewish men of the R.S.F.S.R. while the smallest increase occurred among the Jewish women of Moldavia, 3.6 percent.[30]

It should be noted, however, that the constant increase in the educational level of Jews ceased as of the 1970 census. It had been a continual advancement process up to that date. Official Soviet statistical data published subsequently indicate that there has been a decided turnabout in that process. From 1970 onward, there has been a definite decline, increasing from year to year, in the total number of Jewish students, both in institutions of higher learning and also in research. In absolute terms, the total number of Jewish students enrolled in institutions of higher learning fell from 111,900 in 1968-69 to 105,800 in 1970-71. The number fell even more drastically in 1972-73 to 88,500 and in 1974-75 to 76,200. This represents a total decline of 35,700 Jewish students since the 1968-69 academic year. In terms of percentage of the total Soviet higher educational student enrollment, the total Jewish student representation fell from 2.31 percent in 1968-69, to 1.91 percent in 1972-73, to 1.60 percent in 1974-75. Thus, the Jewish student representation declined during that total period by roughly 32 percent. In addition, between 1970 and the end of 1973, the number of Jewish fulltime postgraduate students (aspirantly) decreased by approximately 30 percent, from 4,945 to 3,456. By 1975, the number had dropped to 2,841, an overall decline of 40.24 percent from 1970. During the 1970-73 period, the total number of Soviet fulltime postgraduate students remained relatively constant -- 99,427 at the end of 1970 versus 98,860 at the end of 1973. The figures for Russian fulltime postgraduate students during 1970-73 were 59,517 and 60,647, respectively. Whereas for Ukrainians during the same period the corresponding figures were 12,248 and 12,250. (These comparative enrollment figures tend to support the claim that Jews are particularly discriminated against in their quest for higher educational opportunities.)

46

As illustration of this overall Jewish educational decline, the total number of Jewish students enrolled in Moscow higher educational institutions dropped from 19,508 at the beginning of the 1970-71 academic year to 14,985 at the start of the 1974-75 academic year. This is in decided contrast to the increased enrollment of Russian nationals in Moscow higher educational institutions from a total of 522,658 at the start of the 1970-71 school year to 540,730 students at the beginning of the 1974-75 academic year. In that regard, it is of interest that other ethnic groups, e.g., Ukrainians, Latvians, Byelorussians, Armenians, Georgians, Azerbaidzhanis, etc., also experienced a decline in total numbers attending higher educational institutions, but not as significant as that of the Jews. The decline in higher educational enrollment of Jews and other ethnic groups is due, in part, to the general leveling out of student higher educational enrollment in the U.S.S.R. -- although stricter enforcement of the nationality educational "quota system" has most certainly left its mark. (The "nationality" quota system will be discussed later in this study.)

According to the April 1974 issue of the monthly statistical publication, Vestnik Statistiki (Statistical Material), published by the Main Statistical Administration in Moscow, 4,182, or approximately 14 percent of the 29,806 persons holding doctoral degrees (said to equal postdoctoral work according to U.S. standards) in the Soviet Union at the end of 1973 were Jews. They were exceeded only by ethnic Russians, who held 16,603. Ukrainian doctoral degree holders were 2,091. There were also 23,775 Jewish "candidate of science" degree holders (purported to be the U.S. Ph.D. equivalent) of the 288,261 hol'ers of that degree at the end of 1973; there were 172,014 F ussians and 33,312 Ukrainians.[31]

JEWISH REPRESENTATION IN THE SOVIET SCIENTIFIC COMMUNITY

The term "scientific personnel" or "scientific workers" (nauchnye rabotniki) is not precisely defined. In most instances, it includes holders of advanced academic degrees and research titles, professional employees engaged in research at research institutions, and members of the V.U.Z. (higher academic institution) facilities.[32] The term is used in this study interchangeably with "scientists."

Although Jews continue to comprise a relatively large portion of Soviet "scientific workers," their importance in the

47

Soviet scientific manpower pool has declined sharply over the last twenty-five years or so and in fact appears to have been reduced to somewhat minor proportions.[33] In that regard, an analysis of the changes in the number of scientific workers is very enlightening. For example, in 1950 the proportion of Jews among scientific workers was the second largest, after the Russians, among all Soviet "nationalities." For every 3.9 Russians in that professional category, there was one Jew, and for every Ukrainian there were 1.4 Jews. Subsequent to the year 1950, there was a dynamic development of scientific research in the Soviet Union and as a result the overall number of scientific workers grew tremendously. However, while the absolute numbers of Jewish scientific workers grew from 25,125 in 1950 to 66,793 in 1971, and to 69,374 in 1975, their relative numbers declined considerably -- from 15.46 percent in 1950, to 9.47 in 1960, to 6.65 in 1971, and to 6.17 percent in 1975 -- whereas, the proportion of Russian scientific workers grew steadily. In 1950, Russians accounted for 60.9 percent of the total number; in 1960, 64.8 percent; and in 1970, 66.0 percent.[34]

In defense of the view that Jews continue to play an important, although reduced role in Soviet science, Mstislav V. Keldysh, the President of the U.S.S.R. Academy of Sciences, during an October 1972 visit to the United States remarked that 11 percent of the membership of the U.S.S.R. Academy of Sciences were Jews and also, that "many Jewish scientists are involved in highly secret and sensitive work." In addition, an article in the Soviet English-language publication, Soviet Life,[35] reported that there were "twenty Jewish members and corresponding members of the U.S.S.R. Academy of Medical Sciences."

In order to gain a better perspective of the Jewish scientific representation, the reader is encouraged to examine Tables 3 and 4 (which follow) which provide a useful, comprehensive account.

In assessing the Jewish representation and whether or not Jews continue to play a significant role in the Soviet scientific community, it is important not only to analyze the declining proportion of Jewish scientists, but also to examine their geographical distribution. In that regard, Moscow, as of January 1, 1971, contained 25.2 percent of the total number of scientific workers in the U.S.S.R. -- 233,641 out of 927,709. Of Moscow's scientific community, 10.7 percent, or 25,023 in absolute numbers, were Jewish.[36] If one divides that number, 25,023, by the total number of Jewish scientific personnel at the end of 1970, 64,392, it would appear that almost 40 percent

48

TABLE 3
National Composition of Soviet Scientific Workers 1950–73 (Main Nationalities)*

Nationality	1950	1960	1969	1970	1973
Total number of scientific workers	162,508	354,158	833,420	927,709	1,108,268
Russians	98,948(60.9%)	229,547(64.8%)	583,564(66.0%)	611,883(66.0%)	739,522
Ukrainians	14,692	35,426	95,079	100,205	120,373
Jews	25,125(15.5%)	33,529(9.47%)	63,661(7.2%)	64,392(6.94%)	67,698(6.10%)
Byelorussians	2,713	6,358	17,850	18,968	23,095
Uzbeks	845	3,748	11,254	12,140	14,330
Kazakhs	739	2,290	7,132	7,905	9,886
Georgians	4,263	8,306	17,100	18,433	21,270
Azerbaidzhanis	1,932	4,972	12,396	13,017	15,609
Lithuanians	1,213	2,959	7,482	8,168	9,794
Moldavians	126	590	2,213	2,485	2,919
Latvians	1,468	2,662	5,758	5,953	6,812
Armenians	3,864	8,001	18,708	20,194	23,873
Tatars	1,297	3,691	10,899	11,617	14,130

*Narodnoe Khozyaistvo S.S.S.R., 1922–1972, Yubileinyi Yezhegodnik [National Economy of the U.S.S.R., 1922–1972, Jubilee Yearbook] (Baku: Azerbaidzhan Gosudarstvennoe Izdatel'stvo, 1972), p. 105; Narodnoe Khozyaistvo S.S.S.R. v 1962 [The National Economy of the U.S.S.R. in 1962] (Moscow: Izdatel'stvo "Statistika," 1963), p. 584 [Hereafter cited as National Economy for (year)]; National Economy for 1964, p. 701; National Economy for 1965, p. 711; National Economy for 1968, p. 697; National Economy for 1969, p. 696; Vestnik Statistiki [Statistical Material] 3 (Moscow: Main Statistical Administration, 1968) 4:92.

49

TABLE 4
Jewish Representation in the Soviet Scientific Community*

End of Year	Total Number of Scientists	Number of Jewish Scientists	Percentage of Jewish Scientists
1950	162,508	25,125	15.46
1955	223,893	24,632	11.00
1958	284,038	28,966	10.20
1959	310,022	30,633	9.88
1960	354,158	33,529	9.47
1961	404,126	36,172	8.95
1963	565,958	49,012	8.48
1964	611,964	50,915	8.32
1965	664,584	53,170	8.00
1966	712,419	56,070	7.87
1967	770,013	58,952	7.66
1968	822,910	61,131	7.43
1969	833,420	63,661	7.21
1970	927,709	64,392	6.94
1971	1,002,930	66,793	6.65
1973	1,108,268	67,698	6.10
1975	1,123,428	69,374	6.17

*Ibid.; Narodnoe obrazovanie, nauka i Kul'tura v S.S.S.R.: statisticheskii sbornik [National education, science and culture in the U.S.S.R.: statistical material] (Moscow: "Statistika," 1977), pp. 309-10.

of the total number of Jewish scientists resided in Moscow. Also, if one would add the number of Jewish scientists living in Leningrad to that figure, the resulting percentage would be increased considerably. Consequently, it would appear that the R.S.F.S.R. and particularly, the metropolitan areas of Moscow and Leningrad contain the bulk of Jewish scientific personnel. Therefore, since the great majority of Soviet Jewish emigres, thus far, have originated from areas other than the R.S.F.S.R., it possibly can be assumed that the prevailing majority of Jewish scientific personnel still remain in the Soviet society. Consequently, it would appear that Jewish scientists continue to play a significant, although reduced role in the Soviet scientific community. However, as we shall see later in this study, for a multitude of reasons this necessarily is not the case.

NOTES

1. This section is based on the following sources:
Moshe Decter, "Jewish National Consciousness in the Soviet
Union" and "Epilogue," Perspectives on Soviet Jewry (1971),pp.
18-23 [Hereafter cited as Decter, Perspectives]; Arie L. Eliav
(Ben-Ami), Between Hammer and Sickle (New York: Signet Books,
1969), pp. 140-71.
2. The Soviet All-Union Census of January 1970 was the
most recent one to be undertaken; the next national census is
scheduled for January 1979. U.S., Foreign Broadcast Information Service (F.B.I.S.), vol. 3, no. 222, Preparations for
Census, 16 November 1976, R-8.
3. Central Statistical Administration of the Council
Ministers, U.S.S.R., Itogi vsesoyuznoi perepisi naseleniya
1970 goda [Results of the all-union population census of 1970],
7 vols. (Moscow: "Statistika," 1973), 4:9, 12, 13, 14-18,
20-151 [Hereafter cited as Council of Ministers, Soviet Census
of 1970].
4. Ibid., 4:9; Emanuel Litvinoff, ed., "Jews as a Soviet
Nationality, A Statistical Analysis," Insight 1 (Oct. 1975): 1.
5. It is interesting to note that if this estimate is correct, Soviet Jews, thus, probably constitute the second largest
(after the United States) Jewish community in the world, one
which still has an estimated half-million more Jews than Israel.
S.I. Bruk and V.S. Apenchenko, eds., Atlas Narodov Mira
[Atlas of the Peoples of the World] (Moscow: Glavnoe Upravlenie
Geodezii i Kartografii Gosudarstvennogo Geologicheskogo
Komiteta S.S.R., 1964), p. 158; Solomon Rabinovich, Jews in the
Soviet Union (Moscow: Novosti Agency Publishing House, 1967),
p. 45.
6. Hans Kohn, The Idea of Nationalism, A Study in Its
Origins and Background (New York: Macmillan Co., 1944), pp.
13-16.
7. Rupert Emerson, From Empire to Nation: The Rise of
Self-Assertion of Asian and African Peoples (Cambridge, Mass.:
Harvard University Press, 1960), p. 102.
8. For a discussion of the validity and reliability of the
census questions on nationality and language, see S.I. Bruk
and V.I. Kozlov, "Etnograficheskaya nauka i perepis' naseleniya
1970 goda" [The ethnographical science and the population census for 1970], Sovetskaya Etnografiya 6 (Moscow: 1967): 3-20.
9. Central Statistical Administration of the U.S.S.R.,
Census Division, Vsesoyuznaya perepis' naseleniya 1926 goda

51

[The all-union population census of 1926] (Moscow: Gosudarstvennoe Izdatel'stvo, 1929), p. 98 [Hereafter cited as Central Statistical Administration, Soviet Census of 1926].
 10. Ibid., p. 101.
 11. S.I. Bruk and V.I. Kozlov, "Voprosy o natsional'nosti
i yazike v predstoyashchei perepisi naseleniya" [Questions about
nationality and language in the forthcoming population census],
Vestnik Statistiki [Statistical Material] 3 (Moscow: Main Statistical Administration, 1968): 32-37 [Hereafter cited as Main
Statistical Administration, Vestnik Statistiki]; I. Sautin, "Naselenie strany i sotsializma" [The population of the country and
of socialism], Bolshevik 10 (May 1940): 17.
 12. See Alec Nove and J.A. Newth, "The Jewish Population: Demographic Trends and Occupational Patterns," in The
Jews in Soviet Russia since 1917, ed., Lionel Kochan (London,
New York, Toronto: Oxford University Press, 1970), p. 128
[Hereafter cited as Nove, "The Jewish Population"].
 13. A recent study showed that in the capital cities of
the Baltic republics, children of mixed Russian-native parents
selected the local nationality in most cases, though the frequency depended on whether the father or mother was Russian,
since children favor the father's nationality.
 14. The mass slaughter of Soviet Jews by the Nazis
during World War II was greatly facilitated by their internal
passport "nationality" identification as Yevrei (Jew). Maurice
Friedberg, "The Plight of the Soviet Jews," in Problems of
Communism (November 1970), p. 18.

   As of January 1, 1976, a "new" Soviet internal
passport system was introduced. Under this system,
all Soviet citizens, aged sixteen and older, were to be
issued internal passports, "irrespective of their place
of residence and work" (the former internal passport
system, which was first introduced in 1932, was for
urban dwellers only). According to the new passport
stipulations,"The entry [on the passport] regarding nationality is made according to the nationality of the
parents. If the parents belong to different nationalities
then the first passport to be issued records the nationality of the father or mother, depending on the wishes of
the passport recipient. Subsequently, there will be no
change in the designation of nationality." (Italics added.)
U.S., Foreign Broadcast Information Service (F.B.I.S.),
vol. 3, Soviet Decrees on Passport System, Registration;
Decrees 109 and 110 of the U.S.S.R. Government, 5

52

November 1974, R-4 [Hereafter cited as F.B.I.S., Soviet Decrees].

15. Nove, "The Jewish Population," pp. 128-29; Zev Katz, gen. ed., Attitudes of Major Soviet Nationalities, 5 vols. (Cambridge, Mass.: M.I.T. Center for International Studies, 1973), vol. 5: The Jews in the Soviet Union, by Zev Katz, "Demography," p. 1 [Hereafter cited as Katz, The Jews]; L.N. Terent'eva, "Opredelenie svoie natsional'noi prinadlezhnosti podrostkami v natsional'no-smeshannykh semyakh" [The determination of the national affiliation of children of nationally mixed families], Sovetskaya Etnografiya 3 (Moscow: 1969): 20-30 [Hereafter cited as Terent'eva, "Children's nationality"].

16. The Soviets have not published statistics on the number of "Passport Jews." Nove and Newth (see reference note 12) believe that the Soviet authorities themselves do not know the exact figure because of the lack of a system of accounting for that purpose. However, at times, as noted previously in this study, the Soviets have given Jewish population figures higher than those of the census (e.g., three million for the late 1960s and 2.5 million for 1965).

17. Council of Ministers, Soviet Census of 1970, 4:12, 16-18, 20-151.

18. Ibid., pp. 12, 152-91.

19. Ibid., pp. 13, 192-201.

20. Ibid., pp. 13-15, 273-75, 280-83, 317-20.

21. Ibid., pp. 13-15, 19-42, 202-72, 284-316.

22. Ibid., pp. 14, 276-79.

23. Central Statistical Administration of the Council of Ministers, U.S.S.R., Itogi vsesoyuznoi perepisi naseleniya 1959 goda [Results of the all-union population census for 1959], 16 vols. (Moscow: "Statistika," 1962). There is one volume for each union republic. [Hereafter cited as Council of Ministers, Soviet Census of 1959] ; Council of Ministers, Soviet Census of 1970, 4:9-19.

24. Soviet data of 1959 show that the average size of the Jewish family, "based on the nationality of the head of the family," was 3.2 compared to 3.6 for the Russians and Ukrainians, and 4.9 for the Uzbeks. The average size of a family for the U.S.S.R. was 3.7 or 13 percent higher than for Jews. Main Statistical Administration, Vestnik Statistiki, 11:95.

25. Council of Ministers, Soviet Census of 1959; Council of Ministers, Soviet Census of 1970, 4:9, 76.

26. Council of Ministers, Soviet Census of 1959; Council of Ministers, Soviet Census of 1970, 4:20, 27, 35, 43, 49, 55, 61-149.

27. Council of Ministers, <u>Soviet Census of 1970</u>, 4:20-60.

28. Ibid., pp. 365-77.

29. V.F. Samoilenko, "V.I. Lenin's Works 'Critical Notes on the Nationalities Question' and 'On the Right of Nations to Self-Determination'," <u>Voprosy Istorii K.P.S.S.</u> [Questions on the History of the C.P.S.U.] 11 (November 1976): 92-102. Educational statistics are provided in Council of Ministers, <u>Soviet Census of 1970</u>, Volume 3. By "higher educational institutions" is meant university level educational institutions.

30. Council of Ministers, <u>Soviet Census of 1959</u>; Council of Ministers, <u>Soviet Census of 1970</u>, 4:395-644; 3: <u>Uroven' obrazovaniya naseleniya S.S.S.R.</u> [The educational level of the population of the U.S.S.R.].

In the Soviet educational system the first four classes of school are defined as the "primary educational level." (Hence, the census polling procedure begins at age ten -- the age at which the first four classes are completed.) Classes five through eight are considered "incomplete high school." From class nine, high school education is divided into "general high school" and "special high school," or "vocational." There are only two classes in the "general high school" category; classes nine and ten. The "vocational high school" category is more varied. The "vocational schools" (or <u>technicums</u>) may have either a two, three, or four-year sequence; and consequently, are considered at a higher educational level than the "general high school" level. Census polling categories are: 1) "primary" (first four classes), 2) "incomplete high school" (classes five through eight), 3) "general high school" (classes nine and ten), 4) "vocational high school," 5) "incomplete high" (university level), and 6) "high" (completed university education).

31. <u>Narodnoe Khozyaistvo S.S.S.R.,1922-1972,Yubileniyi Yezhegodnik</u> [National Economy of the U.S.S.R., 1922-1972, Jubilee Yearbook] (Baku: Azerbaidzhan Gosudarstvennoe Izdatel'stvo, 1972), pp. 237-38 [Hereafter cited as <u>National Economy, 1922-1972</u>]; <u>Narodnoe Khozyaistvo S.S.S.R. v 1967</u> [The National Economy of the U.S.S.R. in 1967] (Moscow: Izdatel'stvo "Statistika," 1968), pp. 803, 811 [Hereafter cited as <u>National Economy for (year)</u>]; <u>National Economy for 1970</u>, pp. 648, 651; <u>National Economy for 1972</u>, p. 651; Statisticheskoe Upravlenie Goroda Moskvy [Statistical Directorate of the City of Moscow], <u>Moskva v Tsifrakh, 1971-1975: Kratkii Statisticheskii Sbornik</u> [Moscow in Figures, 1971-1975: A brief Statistical Account] (Moscow: Izdatel'stvo "Statistika," 1976), p.160.

[Hereafter cited as Statistical Directorate, Moscow in Figures (years)]; Main Statistical Administration, Vestnik Statistiki 4 (Moscow 1974): 92-95; Narodnoe obrazovanie, nauka i kul'tura v S.S.S.R.: statisticheskii sbornik [National education, science and culture in the U.S.S.R.: statistical material] (Moscow: "Statistika," 1977), pp. 213, 282, 313 [Hereafter cited as Education, Science and Culture].

32. Alexander G. Karol, Soviet Research and Development (Cambridge, Mass.: The M.I.T. Press, 1966), p. 78.

33. Various scholars, e.g., Mordekhai Altshuler of the Hebrew University in Tel Aviv ["Mixed Marriages Amongst Soviet Jews," Soviet Jewish Affairs 6 (December 1970)], believe that this is because many Jewish scientists are holdovers from earlier periods when access to that professional category was easier.

34. National Economy, 1922-1972, p. 105; National Economy for 1970, pp. 648, 650; Education, Science and Culture, p. 310.

35. Soviet Life, July 1972, p. 53.

36. Statistical Directorate, Moscow in Figures, 1966-1970, p. 140.

3
The Status of Jewish Ethnic Identity in Contemporary Soviet Russia

PROBLEMS OF DEFINITION -- WHAT IS "JUDAISM," AND MORE
SPECIFICALLY, WHAT CONSTITUTES JEWISH "NATIONALITY"

In any society the term "Judaism" is a most difficult term
to define. In the narrower sense it comprises religious Judaism
only. In the broader and more universal application, including
the Soviet example, it encompasses religion, secular culture,
languages (Hebrew, Yiddish, etc.), history, ethnicity, and
even the concept of nationality itself. This broader, more ambiguous, and "separatist" view of Judaism often is accompanied,
to one degree or another, by a prejudice against the Jews which
both impedes their assimilation into the general population and,
it might be argued, strengthens their solidarity as a distinct
ethnic group. It is perhaps ironic that this longstanding prejudice against the Jews, which stems originally from the traditional "Christian" view of the Jews as "nonbelievers" and as
the "killers of Christ," continues to flourish today not only in
the Soviet Union but in all communist-controlled countries of
Eastern Europe as well.
    Of interest and particular significance to the Soviet situ-
ation is the intertwining of the "national" and "religious" components which, as noted, form an integral part of the broader
essence of Judaism. In fact, religious Judaism is not only intertwined with Jewish nationality, it is to a large degree subordinated to it. Jewish "separateness" is the main adversary
and as one Soviet official remarked, "the fewer synagogues
the fewer the opportunities to congregate and to keep Jewish
separateness."[1]
    At this juncture, it may prove instructive to expound
somewhat on the conceptual notions of the term "national" or
"ethnic" identity. Brian Silver, in his article, "Social
Mobilization and the Russification of Soviet Nationalities,"

56

defines the term to mean an individual's emotional attachment to certain core symbols of his ethnic group. He adds that "national identity is a personal and subjective rather than a group characteristic" and that "it encompasses a limited set of beliefs that are defined a priori as 'national' or 'ethnic'." That same scholar defines an "ethnic group" as "those who conceive of themselves as being alike by virtue of their common ancestry, real or fictitious, and those who are so regarded by others." Furthermore, Silver notes that an individual maintains his "ethnic identity" when he remains emotionally attached to the group, even though the ethnic group may no longer preserve distinctive cultural forms. Therefore, Silver maintains, ethnic identity is not a group characteristic but an individual one.

In the same article, Silver comments that several Soviet scholars have come to recognize national or ethnic consciousness (self-identification) as a self-standing and extremely persistent indicator of nationality (or ethnicity). One leading Soviet ethnographer notes:

> Having achieved a definite stage of development, ethnic self-consciousness, like other ideological forms, can acquire a certain independent existence. It can in particular be preserved even when there is a territorial and economic break-off of separate groups of people from the basic ethnic nucleus and when there is a loss of their native language. It can grow under the influence of ideas, even when its material preconditions, such as territorial or linguistic community, are destroyed. Having achieved a definite stage of development, it is capable of reciprocal influence on the factors that gave rise to it.[2]

These conceptual approaches to "national" or "ethnic" identity are particularly pertinent and enlightening when considering the national or ethnic character of Jews in the Soviet Union. Although, as Silver points out, it may not be possible actually to determine the saliency of the individual Soviet citizen's national or ethnic identity relative to his other (emotional) attachments, we can at least assume that he is aware that he is "different" from the other national or ethnic groups -- and that as a rule it is not just the census questionnaires that stimulate such awareness. As a result of extensive population movement, mass education, and mass communications,

the Soviet citizen is widely exposed to both his own, and to
other national cultures, languages, and peoples. Furthermore,
in the Soviet society, nationality as one of the basic components
of citizenship is registered in individual work records, the personnel files of employers, in internal passports, and in other
official papers and records of crucial importance to individual
lives and careers. One important ramification of this phenomenon,
which pertains to all the Soviet "nationalities," but which is especially crucial to the Jewish ethnic status, is the continued
official cognizance of national "separateness" as a fact of life.
A consequence which has given rise to the various "Jewish" clas-
sificatory groupings discussed earlier in this study -- i.e.,
"Census," "Passport," "Jews by descent," and "Emigration"
Jews, and which also has contributed significantly to the reten-
tion of Jewish ethnic consciousness and group alienation vis-à-
vis the general Soviet society over past generations.

ASSIMILATION, ACCULTURATION, OR SEPARATION -- WHICH
BEST DEPICTS THE JEWISH EXPERIENCE IN THE SOVIET SYSTEM?

According to Vernon Aspaturian, the Soviet government,
over the years, has fostered the "Sovietization" of its varied
nationalities. He defines "Sovietization" as "the process of
modernization and industrialization within the Marxist-Leninist
norms of social, economic, and political behavior." That same
scholar notes, however, that the Soviet authorities have not
generally promoted "Russification" -- the "psychological transference of persons from a non-Russian to a Russian identity,"
although this has occurred to a certain extent as a by-product
of "Sovietization" and "Russianization." Aspaturian defines
"Russianization" as the "process of internationalizing the Russian
language and culture within the Soviet society," whereas, "Russification" is the "process whereby non-Russians are transformed
objectively and psychologically into Russians and is more an
individual process than a collective one."[3]
As evidenced in the demographic data provided earlier in
this study, it appears that the heralded "Sovietization" process
has, thus far, scarcely affected the traditional national differen-
tiations and that demographically the basic "nationality" make-
up of the Soviet Union has changed little during the more than
sixty years of Soviet rule. For example, the Russians roughly
equal the same percentage of the overall population in the 1970
All-Union Census as they did in the 1959 and 1926 censuses.[4]
Also, it is apparent that despite the tremendous absolute gains

made in the Soviet society with regard to the "social mobilization" factor, the most "backward" peoples of the pre-Revolution-
ary era remain the most "backward" today -- still led by the so-
called "former bourgeois nations," i.e., the Russians, Jews,
Ukrainians, and Georgians.

Karl W. Deutsch has observed that assimilation is likely
to be accelerated if "social mobilization," i.e., "the ["modernization"] process in which major clusters of old social, economic, and psychological commitments are eroded or broken and
people become available for new patterns of socialization and
behavior," erodes traditional attachments. The weakening of
traditional family and village solidarities, the exposure to mass
communications and modern technology, and the development of
new residential patterns, habits, and expectations, would all
seem to promote national identity change. However, Deutsch
notes that a person can assimilate without being "mobilized"
and also, that as a rule the rate of "mobilization" outruns that
of assimilation. Rapid mobilization, moreover, tends to destroy
the unity of multinational states because with increasing education and exposure to mass communications in their native tongues,
members of each nationality become more aware of their differences from other national groups and of their affinities with
persons of kindred language or heritage. Thus, according to
Deutsch, the effect of social mobilization may be to exacerbate
ethnic conflict rather than to lessen it. Furthermore, states
Deutsch, there is the possibility that both assimilation and the
strengthening of national differences or identities may occur
simultaneously among different segments of the mobilized population.[5]

However, Silver, in his article, concludes that both urbanization and exposure to Russians have been shown to have a substantial impact on the "Russification" (assimilation) of Soviet
national groups. He notes that exposure to Russians affects
urban dwellers far more than rural natives, revealing that "Russification" is a function not only of the relative proportions of
Russians in the area, but of the weakening of traditional village
ties and the exposure to modern technology, mass communications,
and an urban life-style.[6] These apparent assimilation catalysts
pertain particularly to the situation of the Jewish group inasmuch
as 98 percent of all Jews are urbanites; plus, Jews are widely
dispersed throughout the Soviet Union -- factors which no doubt
have accelerated the "Russianization" process among Jews although not necessarily "Russification."

In relation to the "modernization" process and specifically
the important role played by the Jewish group in that process,

John Armstrong has posited the notion of Soviet Jews as constituting so-called "mobilized diasporas" -- "an ethnic minority
that performs a special function in the modernization process."
He claims that such groups are more urban-oriented, higher
educated, and possess a greater degree of managerial and language skills than the local population. Because of these scarce
qualities, states Armstrong, "mobilized diasporas" obtain a
disproportionate share of the more sought-after positions in the
modernizing society. However, Armstrong also comments that
when the local nationality develops an educated class of its
own, "this apparently favored position of the minority [group]
arouses jealousy." The diaspora group then becomes "subject
to discrimination and usually ceases to perform specialized
functions"[7] -- a predicament which may very well best describe
the situation of Jews in the Soviet Union today.

In his study, "Assimilation, Acculturation, and National
Consciousness Among Soviet Jews," Zvi Y. Gitleman contends
that:

> The contradictory trends of national assertion and
> attempts to assimilate [among Soviet Jews] can be seen
> as equally "natural" or "logical" outcomes of a situation
> wherein the individual finds himself in a peculiar kind of
> unstable equilibrium, and is driven to reduce dissonance
> and stabilize his own personal situation by propelling
> himself to one of the two polar modes of behavior: assim-
> ilation or nationalism, the latter, at present, almost
> always leading to attempts to emigrate. The Soviet Jew
> finds himself in this position because the policies of the
> USSR have created an environment around him which can
> be understood as an unstable equilibrium, producing
> psychological dissonance and, of course, attempts to
> resolve it. This unstable equilibrium is created by the
> government-determined inability of Soviet Jews to
> creatively [sic] express themselves culturally as Jews,
> and hence the necessity to become acculturated into
> non-Jewish, almost always Russian, culture, and, at
> the same time, the refusal of Soviet society and the Soviet
> government to allow the Jew to assimilate completely into
> the Russian culture and assume Russian identity. Thus,
> Soviet Jews are acculturated -- they have adopted the
> culture of another social group -- but they are not assimi-
> lated -- they have not adopted that group's culture to such
> an extent that they no longer have any characteristics
> identifying them with their former culture and no longer
> have any loyalties to their former culture. Most Soviet

Jews consider themselves to be culturally Russian. However, since their internal passports designate them officially as Jews, and since the surrounding society tends to regard them as Jews rather than as Russians, they are in the curious position of being culturally Russian but legally and socially Jews. This split identity creates an internal dissonance whose resolution can be achieved by becoming wholly Jewish or wholly Russian; either they assimilate and become Russians in every sense, or they change their cultural and social identities and attempt to assimilate into another culture, the Israeli one.[8] (Italics added.)

Although the status and treatment of Jews under Tsarist and early Bolshevik rule are covered in substantive detail elsewhere in this study, it is believed pertinent to mention briefly here that under the Tsars it could be debated whether the Jews were treated as a distinct nationality or merely a religious denomination. Under the Bolshevik and later Soviet rule, there was no such ambiguity -- in spite of theoretical utterances to the contrary, the Jews were treated as a distinct ethnic group, as a nonterritorial "national" entity.

In keeping with that doctrinal approach, a Commissariat for Jewish National Affairs (Yevreiskii kommissariat or in abbreviated form, Yevkom) was established in January 1918 within the Central R.S.F.S.R. People's Commissariat for Nationality Affairs (Narkomnats) headed by Joseph Stalin.[9] In addition, so-called Jewish Sections (Yevsektsii) were organized within the overall Communist Party structure. The purpose of the Jewish Commissariat was to grapple with the cultural and economic problems associated specifically with the Jewish population by taking over and reorganizing the autonomous institutions of the Jewish community and bringing them into line with Bolshevik goals and policies. The function of the Jewish Sections was to mobilize and integrate politically those Jews who had not yet become Russian culturally, i.e., to "target" against the Yiddish-speaking majority of the Jewish population and imbue them with the ideological ideals and fervor of Bolshevism.[10] I might interject that comparable "arrangements" were made for the other "nationalities" (e.g., Poles, Letts, Byelorussians, Ukrainians, Tatars, Bashkirs, Volga Germans, Chuvash, etc.) and was part of the overall Bolshevik "indoctrinational" policy of korenizatsiya or "nativization" of the Party's ideological message. Along with this doctrinal assault, the Party attempted to substitute a secular Yiddish culture on the Jewish Community, a culture whose content was socialist. This attempt was immediately perceived and rejected

61

by members of the Jewish community as a distinctively non-Jewish importation having little, if anything, in common with Jewish culture, except possible linguistic affiliation.

The unfolding of socioeconomic and political realities in subsequent years, however, dictated an adoption of the Russian culture by the great majority of Jews, especially the Russian language, if they were to rise on the socioeconomic ladder. This Russian culture adoption ("Russianization") was particularly necessary following the advent of Stalin to power and the launching of his extensive "socialism in one country" modernization effort. This ambitious program demanded the immediate centralization of political power accompanied by the centralized direction of the nation's vast material and human resources in order to make the plan work. Multiple and possible centrifugal national allegiances could not and would not be tolerated -- the necessities of political integration were no longer compatible with the ideals of national pluralism.

At the same time, the "blossoming" of the Stalinist era temporarily brought forth a new spirit of "socialist internationalism" which attracted a large number of Jews in the hope, perhaps, of complete assimilation into the new "Soviet" culture. A hope, which we will see later, was to prove short-lived in the face of subsequent events and realities.

"Sovietization" and Linguistic Assimilation

While most Soviet scholars usually maintain that ethnic (or national) self-consciousness is distinct from and more enduring than native language,[11] these two indicators are, at the same time, acknowledged to be closely connected; plus, native language is recognized as one of the most stable of ethnic indicators. In fact, native language is usually treated by Soviet scholars as a core symbol of ethnic identity. Silver in his referred-to article, repeats the following observation made in a recent Soviet study of linguistic practices in Soviet Latvia:

> Linguistic assimilation leads not only to a change of native language but also to serious changes in national [or ethnic] self-consciousness. National language and national self-consciousness are closely related ethnic determinants. Change of the native language, although not necessarily signifying restructuring of national self-consciousness, still testifies to deep ethnic changes, to the development of assimilative processes. An incongruence of linguistic and ethnic affiliation inevitably leads to a change of national self-consciousness.[12]

62

Pursuant to this particular Soviet demographic approach
are the results of the 1970 All-Union Census which are hailed
by some Soviet scholars as factual evidence of the continuing
and accelerated assimilation of the Jewish minority into the
officially proclaimed "emerging Soviet society." At face value,
the results of the 1970 census do indeed tend to support the
espoused Soviet claim; however, as Silver cautions, "...even
without their traditional national languages, most non-Russians
might well retain a separate ethnic consciousness." Primary
exemplars of this phenomenon are the "linguistically assimilated" Jews and Volga Germans, great numbers of whom apparently
still retain their separate ethnic consciousness, although linguistically assimilated.[13]

Prevalence of Jewish native dialects among Soviet Jews.[14]
In the 1970 All-Union Census, about one-fourth of all Jews, or
25 percent, declared their attachment to Jewish dialects as the
mother tongue or as a second well-known language.[15] (Jews
who listed Yiddish as their primary language dropped from 21.5
percent of the total Jewish population in 1959 to 17.7 percent
in 1970.) Jewish women, according to the 1970 census results,
adhere to Jewish dialects to a slightly greater degree than do
Jewish men. The difference between the two sexes in the use of
Jewish dialects in the urban Jewish population is 2.6 percent,
and in the rural Jewish population, 4.2 percent. Rural Jews
adhere to Jewish dialects to a greater extent than do urban Jews.
Only 17.5 percent of urban Jews declared a Jewish dialect to be
their national tongue, while 7.8 percent declared a Jewish dialect to be a well-known second language -- this amounts to a
total of 25.3 percent of urban Jews who professed a working
knowledge of a Jewish dialect. In the rural areas, 29.6 percent
declared a Jewish dialect as a national language, and 5.8 percent declared a Jewish dialect as a well-known second language
-- or a sum total of 35.3 percent who professed a working knowledge of Jewish dialects.
    Throughout the entire U.S.S.R., according to the 1970
census results, there is not one geographical region where the
use of these Jewish dialects has ceased. However, there are
decided differences among regions in the use of Jewish dialects.
The highest number of speakers of a Jewish dialect is found in
the two autonomous S.S.R.s in the Caucasus -- Dagestan, 88
percent; and Kabardino-Balkar, 81 percent (where members of
the Georgian Jewish community speak their national language,
Georgian, which is also the language of the land in which they
reside). The percentage of speakers of a Jewish dialect, Yiddish,

63

is also high in the regions which were annexed by the Soviets during World War II: Moldavia, 52 percent; the areas of Transcarpathia and Chernovots, 54 percent; Lithuania, 63 percent; and Latvia, 49 percent. A substantial percentage of speakers of a Jewish dialect is found in the Azerbaidzhan S.S.R., 47 percent, in which a large number of Mountain or Tat Jews reside, and in the Uzbek S.S.R., 42 percent, where most of the members of the Bukharan Jews live. The lowest number of speakers of a Jewish dialect is found in the R.S.F.S.R. with less than 19 percent, followed by the Ukraine with slightly less than 18 percent -- the Ukraine, however, contains several regions in which the knowledge of Yiddish is high, e.g., Bukovina, Western Ukraine, and Transcarpathia.

Among Jews who live in large metropolitan areas, the percentage of speakers of a Jewish dialect is lower than among Jews who live in outlying settlements -- for example: Moscow City, 17 percent; Leningrad City, 15 percent; and Kiev City, 16 percent; as compared to the Moscow Oblast', 21 percent; Leningrad Oblast', 19 percent; and Kiev Oblast', 28 percent.

The highest percentage of speakers of a Jewish dialect is found in the age group over sixty, 45 percent; and the lowest frequency is in the age group of sixteen to nineteen, 2.2 percent. Therefore, linguistic assimilation, according to the 1970 census results, apparently is strongest among members of the younger generation. This would indicate that, barring an unforeseen turn of events, this linguistic assimilation trend will continue, resulting in the possible disappearance of Jewish native dialects within a generation or two. (This decline primarily reflects the lack of educational institutions in which instruction is conducted in either Hebrew or Yiddish.) In that regard, according to the 1970 All-Union Census results, 16 percent of all Jews speak Russian as a second language; 80 percent speak Russian as a native language; thus, 96 percent of all Jews are fluent Russian speakers.[16]

See tables 35 through 39 in the Appendices for additional analytical details.

Intermarriage as a Factor in the Assimilation Process

Within traditional Jewish cultures throughout the world, including those located in the Tsarist and later Soviet areas, there were severe self-imposed religious, and social sanctions against marriage outside the faith. In addition, in the past in many areas of the world, including the Russian Empire prior to 1917, marriage between Jews and non-Jews was socially frowned upon and in many instances held illegal. However, as years passed and as both Jewish and non-Jewish sanctions against intermarriage weakened, the frequency of intermarriage of Jews and non-Jews increased.

Unfortunately, there is a dearth of available representative data on Jewish intermarriage practices in the Soviet Union; however, from the information which is available it appears that the Jewish intermarriage factor depends primarily on the regional location and educational level of the particular marital partners involved. For example, it appears from the information which is available that intermarriage, in general, is far more frequent among the educated and urban dwelling strata of the Soviet population. Mordekhai Altshuler, in his study on Soviet intermarriage practices, found that in 1962 Jewish intermarriage in an old district of Tashkent inhabited mainly by traditional Oriental (Bukharan) Jews was 7.7 percent of all intermarriages; whereas, in a modern central district of the same city inhabited by the more assimilated and progressive Western (Ashkenazic) Jews, the figure stood at 33.7 percent.[17]

In 1960 a random sampling of five hundred marriages registered in Leningrad indicated that eighty-two couples, or 16.4 percent, were ethnically mixed. Of that number, sixteen marriages or 19.6 percent of all the mixed marriages sampled involved a Jewish spouse.[18]

A more comprehensive statistical picture of Soviet intermarriage practices is afforded in the 1960 study of the Ukrainian city of Kharkov -- as provided by M.V. Kurman and I.V. Lebedinskii, Naselenie bol'shogo sotsialisticheskogo goroda (The population of a large socialist city), published in Moscow in 1968 by "Statistika." The data presented (see Tables 5 and 6) indicate that Jews in that city tended to marry outside their group rather often, but less frequently than either Russians or Ukrainians.

As evidenced by the reported data, two-thirds of the Jewish women and approximately three-fourths of the Jewish men in Kharkov in 1960 married within their own ethnic group. Since Kharkov may be considered an average Soviet city as far as the size and composition of its Jewish population is concerned, Gitelman interprets these data to suggest that the rate of intermarriage of Jews in the larger Soviet cities ranges from approximately 30 to 35 percent.[19]

Alec Nove and J.A. Newth, in their extrapolations from the 1959 census, attempted to determine the proportion of "mixed" marriages in four Soviet republics -- the R.S.F.S.R., Ukraine, Byelorussia, and Moldavia. They suggest from their

65

TABLE 5
Marriages in Kharkov -- 1960

Nationality of Bride	Nationality of Bridegroom			Total Bridegrooms (Incl. Misc.)	Ethnically Exogamus (Mixed or Intergroup Marriage) Bridegrooms	
	Russian	Ukrainian	Jewish		Number	Percen
Russian	2,188	2,423	86	4,777	2,589	54.2
Ukrainian	2,241	3,643	72	6,016	2,373	39.4
Jewish	117	108	484	720	235	32.6
Total Brides (Incl. Misc.)	4,696	6,368	662	11,928	5,567	46.7

TABLE 6
Endogamy (Intragroup Marriages) Among Kharkov Ethnic Groups -- 1960

Nationality	Percentage Actually Entering Endogamous Marriage	Percentage Who Could Be Expected to Enter Endogamous Marriage by Chance	Ratio of Actual to Random (Column 1 to Column 2)
Brides			
Russian	46	39	1.2
Ukrainian	61	53	1.15
Jewish	67	5.6	11.9
Bridegrooms			
Russians	47	40	1.25
Ukrainians	57	50	1.15
Jewish	73	6.0	12.2

extrapolations that the minimum number of Jewish men with non-Jewish wives was -- (in thousands) R.S.F.S.R., 35.6; Ukraine, 7.2; Byelorussia, 0.0; and Moldavia, 0.9. They note that:

> In the R.S.F.S.R., therefore, at least one Jewish husband in seven has a non-Jewish wife (and the proportion would only be as low as this if every Jewish wife had a Jewish husband). If we were to assume a 2:1 ratio between male and female mixed marriages, then a quarter of all male Jews in the R.S.F.S.R. must have married non-Jewish wives. In the other republics considered, the extent of mixed marriages is very considerably less.[20]

A "trend" or diachronic study on Soviet intermarriage practices was conducted during the early 1960s in the city of Tashkent. This study focused on a "traditional" district in the "old city," the "October District," inhabited mainly by Asians, including Bukharan Jews, and the newer "Kuybyshev District," inhabited mainly by Europeans, including Ashkenazic Jews. In 1926 in the October District only 4.1 percent of all marriages were exogamous or "mixed"; in the Kuybyshev District, during that same year, the figure was 15.1 percent. By 1963, however, the proportion of intermarriages in the October District had reached 14.4 percent, and in the Kuybyshev District, 29.3 percent. The Soviet author of the study notes that "the proportion of inter-ethnic marriages is much higher among nationalities which constitute a relatively small percentage of the population and who live scattered among the representatives of other nations (Ukrainians, Tatars, Armenians, Jews, and others). And, by contrast, this feature is found less frequently among nations who constitute the majority or a significant proportion of the population (Uzbeks, Russians)." The data provided in this study indicate that the proportion of intermarriages involving Jews increased in the Kuybyshev District from 1926 to 1962, but that the proportion of intermarriages is much less among the presumably more traditional Jews living in the October District.[21]

Newth in his article "A Statistical Study of Intermarriage Among Jews in Part of Vilnius (Vilno-U.S.S.R.)," Bulletin on Soviet Jewish Affairs 1 (1968), discusses a Soviet study of the intermarriage phenomenon as concentrated in the Novaya Vil'nya district of Vilnius (Lithuania). This study shows that between 1945 and 1964 the rate of intermarriage for Jewish men was higher than the intermarriage rate for Jewish women and that

TABLE 7
Mixed Marriages in Tashkent, 1926-62[22]

Nationality	October District		Kuybyshev District	
	1926	1962	1926	1962
Ukrainians	–	90.0	82.0	86.0
Tatars	36.6	24.0	31.0	42.9
Armenians	–	–	28.1	36.2
Jews	–	7.7	19.2	33.7
Uzbeks	1.8	5.9	–	20.6
Russians	–	20.6	9.6	16.0

this disparity tended to increase over the years. However, as Table 8 shows, it was also noted by the same study that from about 1955 on, "there was a reduction in the proportion of both Jewish husbands taking non-Jewish wives, and (more sharply) of Jewish wives taking non-Jewish husbands."[23]

As to the consequences of Jewish intermarriage, recent Soviet analytical efforts tend to indicate that the children of mixed marriages "usually choose that nationality, the language and culture of which are most familiar."[24] Children of inter-married couples are defined according to the nationality of the mother until age sixteen whereupon they are free to choose the nationality of either parent as their own.[25] This would mean that the great majority of children from mixed marriages involving Jews choose the dominant nationality, i.e., the non-Jewish nationality. For example, in Vilnius between 1960 and 1968 only 14 percent of the children of mixed marriages chose Jewish nationality; in Tallinn, only 10 percent; and in Riga, only 6.7 percent.[26]

While there appears to be little doubt that intermarriage fosters the process of acculturation, which undoubtedly has occurred to a very large extent among Jews marrying non-Jews; evidence suggests, however, that there are certain factors which mitigate somewhat these acculturative effects of inter-marriage. For example, as noted by various scholars, it would appear evident that where the father has a decidedly Jewish family name, where the Jewish side of the family is dominant, where Jewish consciousness is high, or where the Jewish spouse is well known as being Jewish -- it would be difficult or perhaps even impossible for the children to register and be accepted as non-Jews.

TABLE 8
Proportion of Jewish and Non-Jewish Spouses*

	Percentage of Jewish Husbands with Jewish Wives	Percentage of Jewish Husbands with Non-Jewish Wives	Total Percentage
1945-49	71	29	100
1950-54	52	48	100
1955-59	77	23	100
1960-64	65	35	100

	Percentage of Jewish Wives with Jewish Husbands	Percentage of Jewish Wives with Non-Jewish Husbands	Total Percentage
1945-49	76	24	100
1950-54	68	32	100
1955-59	92	8	100
1960-64	93	7	100

*J.A.Newth, "A Statistical Study of Intermarriage Among Jews in Part of Vilnius (Vilno-U.S.S.R.)," Bulletin on Soviet Jewish Affairs 1 (1968): 68. Newth's analysis is based on data contained in O.A. Gantskaya and G.F. Debets, "O graficheskom izobrazhenii rezul'tatov statisticheskogo obsledovaniya mezh-natsional'nykh brakov" [Concerning the graphical representation of the statistical results of the investigation of intermarriages], Sovetskaya Etnografia 3 (Moscow: 1966): 109-18.

As is well known, the official Soviet position is whole-heartedly in favor of exogamous marriage which supports the immediate doctrinal policy of the "drawing together" (sblizhenie) of nations in the U.S.S.R. to foster a long-term process of national "fusion" (sliyanie) into a "Soviet people." This policy is nowhere better illustrated than in the interview comments of V.P. Ruben, Chairman of the U.S.S.R. Supreme Soviet of Nation-alities, as reported in Literaturnaya Gazeta on December 1, 1976. In this article, Ruben states that according to the 1970 census there were "7,918,502" mixed marriages in the Soviet Union; "5.5 million" of which occurred between the 1959 and 1970 censuses.[27]

This reported increase in the number of mixed marriages is reflected in a recent "trend" study conducted on mixed marriages in the Ukrainian S.S.R. from the middle 1920s to 1969. The results of this research indicate that the number of endogamous (intragroup) marriages among Ukrainians during that time diminished more than twofold from 80.3 percent to 34.3 percent; among Russians from 67.8 percent to 30.4 percent; and for Jews in the Ukraine, from 95.0 percent to 66.3 percent -- a reduction of $1\frac{1}{2}$ times.[28] Also, according to a Soviet report to the United Nations in 1963 there were in Soviet urban areas as of 1963 151 mixed families per one thousand families in the U.S.S.R. as a whole, 108 mixed families per thousand in the R.S.F.S.R., 263 mixed families per thousand in the Ukraine, and 237 per thousand in Byelorussia.[29]

Chairman Ruben in the referred-to interview consequently comments that there had been a "distinct trend in the growth of mixed marriages in recent years" in the Soviet society, a phenomenon which, according to Ruben, underscores the Brezhnev declaration that "A new historic community of people -- the Soviet people -- has taken shape among us.[30] And this means that Soviet people's traits of behavior, character, and world outlook, which are common and do not depend on social and national differences, are becoming more noticeable." This official position is also apparent in the Soviet contention that the purported reduction in overall Jewish population figures between the 1959 and 1970 national censuses is due primarily to the assimilation factor (facilitated primarily by intermarriage) and the accompanying accelerated "drawing together" of the varied Soviet nationalities.[31]

In contrast to the official Soviet viewpoint on intermarriages with regard to their importance in the projected "fusion" of the Soviet nationalities into a future consolidated "Soviet people," Armstrong makes the interesting observation that since the dispersal of Jews is much higher than that of other ethnic groups in the Soviet Union, the fact that most Jewish marriages (as evidenced by the official data) are still endogamous indicates strong ethnic cohesiveness on part of the Jewish group. This view is supported by the conclusion of Jeffrey A. Ross in his study on recent Soviet Jewish immigrants to Israel that the Soviet Jewish family, as represented by the immigrant respondents, is "a highly autonomous and self-contained unit. It functions as a strong defense mechanism against external influence. As such, it is the major carrier and transmitter of Jewish ethnic identity [among the immigrant respondents.]"[32]

71

Jewish Religion and Its Current Status

Traditionally, religion had been the nucleus of Jewish community life in pre-Communist Russia. Prior to the Bolshevik take-over in November 1917, Jews living in the territories now included in the Soviet Union had enjoyed a long history of religious semiautonomy, with their own religious institutions, customs, and modes of religious observance. Before 1917 there were religious institutions of varying size and number in every Jewish community, regardless of its geographical location or population density -- there were synagogues and prayer houses, religious schools, Talmudic academies, rabbinical courts, and so forth. Furthermore, the whole fiber of the individual Jewish "shetl" (community) was geared to the doctrinal beliefs of religious Judaism, including the economic activities, "shetl" administrative procedures, and personal attitudes of the inhabitants themselves. In essence, therefore, the synagogue and the social institutions associated with it constituted the focal point of each Jewish settlement.[33]

With the Bolshevik seizure of power in November 1917, the situation of the Jews changed drastically; and perhaps no aspect of their lives underwent a more radical change than did religion. Like all other religions in Russia, it also received the brunt of the Bolshevik doctrinal attack. In that regard, the first act of the Bolsheviks that directly affected the religious rights of the Jews was the "Declaration of the Rights of the Peoples of Russia " enacted on November 15, 1917, which rescinded all "national-religious privileges and restrictions" and promised to promote the free development of the national groups living within the confines of Russia. The wording of the declaration, itself, indicates an awareness, at the time, by Lenin and other Bolshevik leaders of the close affinity between the "national" and "religious" elements in the character of some minority groups, e.g., the Jews. Consequently, the act stressed a degree of both "national" and "religious" autonomy.

The first Bolshevik legal act directly regulating religious life in the new State was the decree of the Council of People's Commissars (signed and coauthored by Lenin) of January 23, 1918, entitled, "On Separation of Church from State and School from Church." In brief, it granted every citizen the right to profess a religion or no religion, but under certain conditions. The most important aspects of this decree, which is still in effect, are: 1) complete secularization of the State; 2) confiscation of all religious property and funds; 3) withdrawal of the status of legal entity from churches and church organizations; and 4) prohibition of religious instruction in schools. The provision of the decree which most affected the Jewish religion (as well as most other religions) was that prohibiting the teaching of religion to the young. As a result, for forty years, from 1917-57, not a single Jewish theological seminary functioned legally. In 1957 in the face of mounting criticism from abroad, the authorities did allow some concessions, including the opening of a single Yeshiva (religious seminary) in Moscow. According to Korey, this institution since its opening has ordained but two students.[34]

The next act which directly affected religious Judaism was the dissolution of the Kehilah (Jewish community center) within which the entire "national-religious" workings of the Jewish community functioned. This measure was adopted at the first conference of the "Jewish Commissariat" and the "Jewish Sections" in November 1918, and was formally adopted under the signature of the Commissar for Nationality Affairs, Joseph Stalin, in June 1919.

Soon after the Bolsheviks had installed themselves in power, they began an unrelenting, systematic attack upon all organized religions in Russia.[35] In the Jewish case, it meant the wholesale closing of synagogues, the confiscation of religious books and ritual objects, and the suppression of religious Judaism in all quarters. In most of the cases involving the closure and confiscation of synagogues, the Bolshevik authorities supplemented the legality of the action by an appeal to the public exigency: for example, many religious institutions were closed by the Yevsektsii (Jewish Sections) by turning them into emergency shelters for homeless children and the starving victims of the famine. Concurrently, a fierce campaign was initiated against clergymen of all faiths, including the ultimate penalty of arrest, prison, or deportation. The arrests and deportations of Jewish clergymen, especially rabbis, shokhtim (ritual slaughterers), and mohalim (ritual circumcisers) increased considerably in the late 1920s. In addition, throughout this campaign, antireligious propaganda of varying modes and intensity was utilized most effectively.

During these years of violent social upheaval, Hebrew, the religious Judaic language, was declared by the secular authorities to be intrinsically reactionary, irrespective of content. Consequently, Hebrew was ultimately outlawed in the late 1920s -- the only language to be so condemned in the Soviet Union. This was a particularly disastrous blow since it made it legally impossible for children to study the religious language and thus, made the study of religious subjects and Hebrew prayers extremely difficult, if not impossible.

One particularly devious, but abortive, scheme implemented by the authorities was the attempt to organize an apostatic "Living Synagogue" modeled after its Russian Orthodox counterpart, the "Living Russian Orthodox Church," which introduced drastic innovations into the religious dogmas and ritual and which was fiercely opposed to the established Church. This attempt was soon discarded, however, because of its complete rejection by all Jews regardless of their individual religious devoutness.

A second major antireligious offensive was launched in 1927-28 and was continued through most of the 1930s. During this period, many rabbis, as well as countless non-Jewish clergymen, were forced to resign from their religious posts -- a number of them being charged and imprisoned for alleged participation in various "Trotskyist plots" against the government.[36]

Contributing to the success of the Soviet government in at least temporarily reducing religious fervor among the Jewish population were the concurrent fundamental changes which were then occurring within the overall Soviet society. This was the era of the initiation of the first "Five Year Plan" (1928) with its resulting upheaval of traditional social affinities and values, and the mass movements of populations from the countryside to the urban industrial centers. Jews and other ethnic groups suddenly were absorbed into the economic, social, and cultural mainstream of the country, and were recruited into heretofore denied professional career opportunities of industry, State, and Party. As a result, for a time, a majority of Jews became alienated not only from their religion, but from their ethnic origins as well.

By the time the Stalinist constitution of 1936 was promulgated, the authorities appeared confident that the back of organized religion had been broken, thus, negating the need for further extensive repressive measures on the part of the State. Consequently, the constitution of 1936 which paid formal lip service to the freedom of religion [37] also "restored" the civil rights of those citizens, e.g., the clergy, whose rights had been deprived earlier. It was thought, at that time, that organized religion would soon die a natural death and would be of no further concern to the secular authorities.

However, the outbreak of World War II and more specifically the signing of the Soviet-Nazi "Nonaggression Pact" of

August 1939 eventually brought new territories into the Soviet
Union and with them a Jewish population of over two million.
This sudden influx of new Jewish citizens into the Soviet society
abruptly reinforced both secular and religious Judaism.

The initiation of hostilities between the Soviet Union and
Nazi Germany in June 1941 marked another era of change, a
most brutal and irrevocable one, in the situation of Jewry.
More than a million Soviet Jews, of both sexes and all ages,
were liquidated by the rapidly advancing Nazi military forces;
countless others were forced to flee. As a result, traditional
Jewish settlements and historic centers of Jewish culture were
annihilated for all time.

During the war, the Soviet authorities temporarily ceased
their antireligious campaigns and, in fact, sought to bolster
their relations with the individual religious sects, including
the Jews. In 1943 a council for the affairs of the Russian Orthodox Church and a council for all other religious cults, including
the Jewish, were established. These councils were to be "the
liaisons between the government and the leaders of the corresponding cults on questions affecting those cults and requiring
action by the government of the U.S.S.R." As a result of the
wartime emergency and the associated governmental relaxation
of former stringent religious policies, religious institutions
were quickly reestablished in many areas.[38]

Like other religious groups, the Jews enjoyed a measure
of tolerance during the immediate postwar period. However,
unlike the other religions, Jews were not included in postwar
religious bodies and conferences recognized by the Soviet
authorities. Correspondingly, the Jewish groups had no central representative body capable of establishing a focal point
of religious direction for its scattered members. This absence
of a central religious body was a significantly debilitating factor, both with regard to the conduct of internal religious affairs
and in relations with the Soviet government. As Korey points
out, this lack of a religious center was particularly harmful to
the Jews in that as a consequence formal and official contact
with coreligionists abroad was denied.[39] Consequently, the
status of Judaism, at that time, was one of internal fragmenta-
tion and almost complete isolation from the outside world.

It appears evident from the stated background description
that religious Judaism was not only the victim of the overall
Soviet frontal attack against all religion in the Soviet Union,
but was singled out for special treatment. This point is brought
out by Walter Kolarz in his study of religion in the Soviet Union:

Stalin anticipated that religious Judaism would
disappear much more quickly than other religions which
had preserved their sociological roots, and he was determined to hasten this natural process as effectively as
possible. It became clear that Stalin would not extend
to the Jews the concessions he was prepared to grant to
other religious communities.[40]

A renewed, vigorous, frontal attack against religion, and
against religious Judaism in particular, was initiated by the Soviet authorities in 1957. This assault was accompanied by a
stepped-up anti-Judaic propaganda campaign which differed
considerably from the official propaganda directed against the
other religions, and which continues to date.[41] For example,
the anti-Judaic themes noted, inter alia, that Judaism promotes
the idea that the Jewish people are a "chosen people" and a
corresponding "hatred" of other peoples, and that Judaism
advocates allegiance to another State, the State of Israel and to
the "reactionary, pro-imperialist movement of Zionism." It is
important to note in that connection that in the communist terminology "Zionism" equates with fascism and all the attributes
of a totalitarian dictatorship characterized by chauvinism and
racism. The actual essence of the Zionist movement, i.e., the
resurrection of a Jewish "national" homeland, is conveniently
misinterpreted. As a consequence, distinctions in communist
propaganda between "Jews" and "Zionists" disappear. Therefore, contemporary Soviet propaganda, under the guise of
"fighting Zionism," contains definite antisemitic overtones.
        This largely euphemistic "anti-Zionist" attack, which
apparently is designed primarily for domestic consumption,
attempts to convince the audience that the Jewish working class
has nothing in common with the capitalist Jews of Israel and
the nonsocialist world. "Zionists" and Soviet Jews who wish
to emigrate are portrayed as antisocialist malcontents who
oppose basic Marxist-Leninist teachings and values. Jews are
depicted as the "merciless enslavers of mankind" who seek to
rule the world. They also are offered as convenient scapegoats
not only for failures within the Soviet system, but on the international scene as well. In brief, the traditional Marxian vir-
ulence of blaming the Jews for the world's ills is brought into
play.
        Unfortunately, there are decided pragmatic ramifications
resulting from the described media attack. Jews not only are
discriminated against with regard to jobs and higher educational
opportunities, they, moreover, are thought of collectively as

76

"traitors" to the Soviet homeland. Relatedly, a feeling of "distrust" has pervaded the Party hierarchy and the general public -- not only against those Jews who seek emigration, but also against any Jewish citizen regardless of his emigration intent.

In commenting on the status of religious Judaism in the Soviet Union, it is interesting to note that the Oriental Jewish communities (Bukharan, Mountain, and Georgian Jews) traditionally have enjoyed a greater latitude of religious freedom under communist rule than the Western (Ashkenazic) Jews. According to Rothenberg, this disparity of treatment is due primarily to the greater extent of religious devotion on the part of the Oriental Jews and to the correspondingly greater measure of defiance which could be expected from them in the face of any denial of their basic religious rights.[42]

The synagogue remains the only officially recognized Jewish institution in the Soviet Union today. In that regard, there are conflicting reports as to the total number of currently active synagogues and officiating rabbis. In a reported interview in 1976, Vasilii Grigor'evich Furov, Deputy Chairman of the Council on Religious Affairs, U.S.S.R. Council of Ministers, states that there now remain two hundred synagogues, out of a prerevolutionary figure of some five thousand, of which ninety-two (the figure usually quoted by the Soviet Press) are registered.[43] Similarly, another Soviet official, Iosif Shapiro, also a member of the Council on Religious Affairs, notes that "there are now about two hundred Judaic religious societies (synagogues) in the Soviet Union. Ninety-two of them are operating synagogues."[44] Deputy Chairman Furov also remarks that there currently are fifty rabbis in the Soviet Union who remain professionally active.[45]

In an interview conducted early in 1976, Vladimir Aleksey-evich Kuroedov, Chairman, Council for Religious Affairs, U.S.S.R. Council of Ministers, also remarked that there are two hundred remaining synagogues in the Soviet Union, ninety-two of them registered. He, however, differed from his colleague, Furov, with regard to the total number of active rabbis in the country -- according to Chairman Kuroedov, there are only thirty. Kuroedov also commented that since there are only thirty rabbis, many synagogues only function on an "occasional basis." He noted also that there are only fifteen theological schools for all religious denominations. (According to Rabbi Yakov Fishman, Chief Rabbi for the City of Moscow, and also the previously mentioned Soviet official Iosif Shapiro, there were ten rabbinical students studying at the Moscow Yeshiva in 1976.)

Although a number of other official Soviet sources repeat the same synagogue statistics, still other Soviet officials state

that there remain no more than "several dozen" operating synagogues plus "more than three hundred Jewish meeting houses"
[sic] in the Soviet Union today. In addition, Chief Rabbi Fishman, in a personal interview conducted on May 17, 1976, with
the Israeli Russian language newspaper, Nasha strana, stated
that he is the "sole remaining rabbi for sixty operating synagogues." This latter figure corresponds with the figure of sixty-
two operating synagogues most frequently identified by Jewish
organizations located outside the U.S.S.R.[46]

According to official Soviet sources, religious Jews comprise only 3 to 6 percent of all Jews in the R.S.F.S.R. and the
Ukraine; 5 to 9 percent in the Baltic Republics; and 7 to 12 percent among Georgian, Bukharan, and Mountain Jews. Conversely,
non-Soviet sources and also Chief Rabbi Fishman maintain that
there is a noticeable increase in religious awareness among Jewish young people in contemporary Soviet society.[47] It has been
noted, on occasion, that this latter circumstance, if indeed actual,
probably stems from the fact that religion reinforces both the separate identity and national aspirations of the particular ethnic
group and provides an ideological and organizational link
(through communal worship, study groups, etc.) between such
disparate elements of the population as the liberal intellectuals,
the technical and managerial class, and workers and peasants
who have a traditional religious upbringing. In some cases,
religious expression may be even a convenient cover for nationalist or ethnic sentiment. This is particularly true, it is believed,
among Jews, even for those who are professed atheists, as a
means of expressing national or ethnic identity and self-initiated
alienation from the general Soviet culture.

The Current Status of Native Jewish Educational Institutions

During the intensified Korenizatsiya or "nativization" period during the 1920s, Jewish Yiddish language schools were encouraged and indeed vigorously supported by the Bolshevik authorities.[48] As a result, there were 336 Yiddish language schools
established in 1923-24; 775 Yiddish language schools established
in 1927; and by 1930 their number grew to 1100. School enrollment in those schools during 1923-24 totaled 54,173 students.
In 1927-28, about 50 percent of all Jewish elementary school-
children in the Ukraine attended Yiddish language schools, as
did about 56 percent in Byelorussia; but only approximately 8
percent did so in the R.S.F.S.R. It must be emphasized, however, that at no time during the entire Soviet era has more than a
bare majority of Jewish children attended native Jewish schools.[49]

The Soviet constitution of 1936 reaffirmed in Article 121 the right of "instruction in schools...in the native language." Similar provisions were made in the constitutions of all the union and autonomous republics. In addition, in August 1962, the U.S.S.R. ratified the United Nations Educational, Scientific, and Cultural Organization (UNESCO) Convention Against Discrimination in Education, which obliged it, according to Article 5 (1c), "to recognize the rights of members of national minorities to carry on their own educational activities, including the maintenance of schools and...the use or the teaching of their own language." However, even before the U.S.S.R. ratified the UNESCO Convention, a Soviet law was adopted on April 16, 1959, entitled "Concerning the Strengthening of the Connection of the Schools with Life and Furthest Development of the System of Peoples' Education in the R.S.F.S.R." Article 15 of that law declared: "...the education in schools will be conducted in the native language of the students. The right is given to parents to decide with what language in schools to register their children."[50] There is also the statement made by the Soviet government to UNESCO: "The Union of Soviet Socialist Republics reports that every Soviet citizen may have his children taught in any language he wishes."[51]

In 1961, the Twenty-second Party Congress adopted a Party program in which the Soviet commitment to the teaching of native language was reemphasized. It assured "the complete freedom of each citizen in the U.S.S.R. to speak and to rear and educate his children in any language, ruling out all privileges, restrictions, and compulsion in the use of this or that language."[52]

However, in spite of these legal "guarantees," there is not a single native Jewish educational institution in existence in the contemporary Soviet Union.[53] World War II, for all practical purposes, marked the end to Jewish schools in the U.S.S.R. Several attempts after the war to reestablish such schools proved unsuccessful. Even the few Jewish schools which had remained open in the Jewish Autonomous Region of Birobidzhan until the late 1940s were closed.[54]

The reasons for the current lack of native Jewish schools are due to a number of factors. For example, there is the argument most advanced by the Soviet authorities that Jewish assimilation into the Russian culture, over the years, has alleviated the need for a separate Jewish school system. On the surface of things, this would appear to be a logical circumstance resulting from the long-term "Russianization" process which has largely characterized the Jewish population. However, in going beyond that superficial reasoning and considering the early banning by the authorities of the culturally essential Hebrew language and its replacement by an inferior Yiddish substitute, plus, the tragic and extensive misfortunes which befell the Jews as a result of World War II and the totality of the Soviet effort to build a "Russianized" Soviet peoples' conglomerate, one can readily see that "natural" assimilation represents neither the chief nor only reason. It would appear, based on the findings presented here and elsewhere in this study, that the demise of native Jewish educational institutions is due largely to the deliberate long-term Soviet policy objective of "fusing" the varied nationalities into one distinct "Soviet people." In pursuit of that ultimate goal, it would appear expedient to curtail, whenever possible, the continued "cultural socialization" of succeeding generations of disparate ethnic groups, particularly in view of the probable threat that they represent to the continued well-being of the monolithic Soviet Party State. The Jews, in particular, because of their widespread dispersal and, for all practical purposes, lack of a distinct territorial base, represent a prime target for the espoused Soviet policy program. The available, ample evidence underscores the intensity of that effort.

The Contemporary Jewish Literature, Press, and Theatre

A distinctive Jewish press and book publishing first appeared in Russia during the second half of the nineteenth century. Under subsequent communist rule, there was a decided expansion of both Yiddish language and of Soviet Jewish, i.e., communist, literature in the 1920s and the early 1930s, followed by a drastic decline and total cessation by the late 1940s. In the first three decades after the Bolshevik Revolution, there were scores of State-supported Jewish (Yiddish) newspapers, periodicals, magazines, and almanacs; publishing houses produced hundreds of thousands of Jewish books. For example, in 1932, titles of 653 Yiddish language books were printed, with a circulation of more than 2.5 million. However, by 1948 the Jewish publishing structure, for all practical purposes, was totally dismantled, including the shutting down in November 1948 of the prestigious Moscow Yiddish publishing enterprise, Der Emes. The Yiddish language newspaper by the same name, which was published by this enterprise, was closed down in 1939; its World War II successor, Ainikeit, ceased operation in 1948.

80

In 1959, Yiddish language publications were slowly and hesitantly reintroduced with the release of two Yiddish language volumes, by classic Yiddish writers long dead, in limited editions of thirty thousand. In 1961, three more classics were published. (These Yiddish classics are identified in the following paragraph.) Since 1959 there has been a total of only approximately two dozen Yiddish language books published in the Soviet Union, four in 1970.[55]

Other and more recent official Soviet sources claim that between 1955 and 1970 there were 466 books by Jewish authors published in fifteen Soviet languages in a total edition of more than forty-six million copies. According to these same sources, beginning in 1956 more than 120 books by Jewish authors and fifty in the Yiddish language have been published. Also reportedly published in the Yiddish language were one-volume editions of the Jewish literary classics of Sholom Aleichem, Mendel Moicher Sforim, E.L. Perets, and D. Bergelson -- in thirty thousand copies each. The selected works of the "father of Soviet

TABLE 9
Publication of Jewish Books and Brochures in the U.S.S.R., 1968-70*

Year	1968-70 Total Titles in all languages (foreign & Soviet)	Total Titles in languages of the U.S.S.R.	Jewish Publications	
			No. of Titles	No. of Copies (000's)
1968	75,699	72,651	2	10
1969	74,587	72,137	8	40
1970	78,875	75,731	4	10

*Pechat' S.S.S.R. v 1968 godu [Publications of the U.S.S.R. in the year 1968] (Moscow: Izdatel'stvo "Kniga," 1969, p. 10; Pechat' S.S.S.R. v 1969 godu [Publications. of the U.S.S.R. in the year 1969] (Moscow: Izdatel'stvo "Kniga," 1970), p. 10; Pechat' S.S.S.R. v 1970 godu [Publications of the U.S.S.R. in the year 1970] (Moscow: Izdatel'stvo "Kniga," 1971), p. 10.

Jewish literature, " Osher Shvartsman, reportedly came out in
ten thousand copies. There also were said to be published
two editions of six-volume works by Sholom Aleichem -- in
225,000 and 150,000 copies each. These same Soviet sources
also claim that there are some seventy Yiddish language writers
in the Soviet Union today -- prose writers, poets, and play-
wrights.[56]

Immediately prior to World War I, there were thirteen
Yiddish and two Hebrew language newspapers published in
Russia, with a total circulation of several hundred thousand.
Although suppressed during the war, the Jewish press flourished
after the March Revolution and in the period 1917-18 there
were some 170 different Jewish periodicals published. Of
course, immediately after the Bolsheviks gained power, communist publications multiplied and noncommunist publications
ceased altogether. In addition to the Yiddish language newspaper published directly by the Yevsektsii (Jewish Sections of
the Communist Party), originally known by its German name, Di
Varnheit (truth), and later in August 1918 changed to the corresponding Yiddish name, Der Emes, there were twenty-one
Yiddish language newspapers in 1923-25, twenty-six in 1926,
and forty in 1927 -- all subsidized by the government. By
1935 there were Jewish dailies in Moscow, Kharkov, Minsk,
and Birobidzhan.

By the late 1930s the number of available Jewish periodicals declined considerably. Consequently, by 1939 in the
entire R.S.F.S.R. the only Jewish newspaper which remained
was that of Birobidzhan. Also, in that same year only seven
Jewish periodicals remained in the entire country, with a
total circulation of 38,700. Although a brief and limited revival of Jewish cultural activity occurred during World War II,
it was abruptly curtailed in 1948. Between 1949 and 1953,
hundreds of Jewish literary figures were imprisoned, executed,
or deported for alleged crimes against the State, and almost
without exception, the remaining Jewish cultural institutions
were closed.[57]

There are only two Yiddish language periodicals in the
Soviet Union today. One is the monthly Sovetish Heimland
(Soviet Fatherland), published in Moscow since 1961, at
first (prior to 1965) as a bimonthly with a professed circulation of 25,000 copies per issue, at a reported sales price of
50 kopecks per copy. It is edited by a "Jew," Aron Vergelis;
is an organ of the U.S.S.R. Writers Union, deals mostly with
Soviet themes, contains a sheet for Yiddish language self-study;

has news on Jewish concerts, Yiddish writers' activities, plus reports some Jewish cultural news from abroad. It frequently prints material of genuine literary quality, reportedly contributed by more than one hundred Soviet Jewish writers. According to a December 1976 Vechernaya Moskva article, Sovetish Heimland is exported to more than thirty countries.

In addition, there is the Birobidzhaner Shtern (Birobidzhan Star) which is mostly a two-page translation into Yiddish of the Russian language Birobidzhanskaya Zvezda province newspaper, and which reportedly is published five times per week. According to official Soviet statistics published in 1970, the circulation of the Birobidzhaner Shtern is 12,000. It is reportedly possible to subscribe to it "anywhere in the Soviet Union."[58]

TABLE 10
Publication of Newspapers in the U.S.S.R., 1968-70*

Year	Total Number of Newspapers	Total Number of Jewish Newspapers
1968	7,289	1
1969	(n.a.)	(n.a.)
1970	7,231	1

*Pechat' S.S.S.R. v 1968 godu, p. 68; Pechat' S.S.S.R. v 1969 godu, p. 68; Pechat' S.S.S.R. v 1970 godu, p. 68.

TABLE 11
Publications of Journals and Periodicals in the U.S.S.R. in 1968 and 1970*

Year	Total Number of Journals & Periodicals	Total Number of Jewish Journals & Periodicals
1968	1,078	1
1970	1,131	1

*Pechat' S.S.S.R. v 1968 godu, pp. 59-60; Pechat' S.S.S.R. v 1970 godu, pp. 59-60.

Under Bolshevik rule, a permanent Jewish State Theatre was established in Moscow in 1919. Jewish theatrical life, in which the new communist government initially took special interest, prospered in many areas of the country. For example, there were the Jewish Theatrical College and the Jewish State Theatre in Minsk, Jewish departments at the Kiev Institute for Drama, and by the mid-1930s there were eighteen permanent Jewish theatres located throughout the Soviet Union. However, by the end of the 1930s, their number had diminished considerably, and finally, in 1948, the last vestige of Jewish theatrical life, including the dominant Jewish State Theatre in Moscow was closed by the Soviet authorities.

There is no permanent Jewish theatrical establishment in the Soviet Union today. However, a still-functioning touring Yiddish repertory company was formed in Moscow in 1962 by the former Moscow Jewish State Theatre actor and "Honored Artist of the R.S.F.S.R.," Veniamin Wolf Shvartser. Yiddish amateur theatre groups also now perform in Vilnius, Riga, and Birobidzhan.[59]

The Jewish Resettlement Initiative

In keeping with the Marxian "tillers of the soil" philosophy and also to alleviate the dire economic difficulties which engulfed Soviet Jewry in the immediate post-Civil War period (and as an alternative to the avowed Zionist territorial objective), the Soviet authorities, during the 1920s and 1930s, made extended attempts to resettle the Jews on land in so-called Jewish "national" districts -- Kalinindorf in the Kherson province, Novo-Zlatopol'ye and Stalindorf in the Ukraine, and also in the Crimea.[60] An early advocate of such territorial resettlements was Lenin, who in an article "Critical Remarks on the National Question " supported the necessity of providing future territorial areas for "nations" deprived of them. He wrote:

It is beyond doubt that in order to abolish all national oppression it is extremely important to create autonomous areas even of the smallest dimensions, each with an integral uniform national composition of population, towards which the members of the given nationality, scattered in different parts of the country, or even of the world, could "gravitate" and with which they could enter into relations and free associations of every kind.[61]

For that purpose, a special governmental body, Gesel-
schaft far ainordenung af erd Arbetndike Yidn in F.S.S.R.
(Society to settle working Jews on the land in the U.S.S.R.),
known as "Geserd," or in the Russian language abbreviation,
"Komzet" (Komitet po Zemel'nomu Trudyashchikhsya Yevreiev
-- The Committee for the Rural Placement of Toiling Jews), was
established in January 1925.[62] It was composed of leading
members of the Yevsektsii as well as such foremost Soviet
State officials as the Soviet President, Mikhail Kalinin; the
Commissar for Foreign Affairs, Georgi Chicherin; the Commissar
for Foreign Trade, Leonid Krassin; the Vice-Chairman of the
Supreme Soviet, Peter Smidovich; and also the well-known
diplomat and later Commissar for Foreign Affairs, Maxim Litvinov.
The original proposal of this body called for the resettlement of
approximately 500,000 Jews by the end of 1926 on allocated
land in the Ukraine and in the Crimea.[63] However, in the face
of acute competition for land in those areas and the considerable hostility shown by the native Ukrainian and Tatar populations toward the Jews, relatively few Jews, in fact, were resettled, as called for by the plan.

In March 1928 the Soviet government announced that the
province of Birobidzhan in the Soviet Far East would become a
Jewish autonomous oblast' (region)[64] and available for resettlement. This was an area of over 36,000 square kilometers
situated close to the Chinese border, along the shores of the
Amur River. The idea for the Birobidzhan Jewish settlement
originated in the People's Commissariat of Agriculture and
was strongly supported, for obvious strategic purposes, by the
Commissariat for Defense.

In support of the Birobidzhan settlement project, the
Soviet authorities launched an extensive propaganda campaign,
both among Soviet Jews and among Jews abroad. Although
Jews offered oral support to the project, relatively few of them
actually migrated. In 1928 a total of 654 Jews migrated to the
Birobidzhan area; there were 555 new Jewish settlers in 1929;
860 in 1930; 3,231 in 1931; 14,000 in 1932; and 3,005 in 1933.[65]

On May 7, 1934, a decree of the Presidium of the Central
Executive Committee of the U.S.S.R. officially proclaimed the
Birobidzhan area the Jewish Autonomous Oblast'. On that occas-
sion, the President of the Soviet Union, Mikhail Kalinin, en-
larging on his earlier view that the Birobidzhan settlement was
necessary to preserve the Jewish "nationality," observed the
following:

85

The creation of such a region is the only means of
a normal development for this nationality. The Jews in
Moscow will have to assimilate....In ten years' time
Biro-Bidzhan will become the most important guardian of
the Jewish-national culture and those who cherish a
national Jewish culture must link up with Biro-Bidzhan.
... We already consider Biro-Bidzhan a Jewish national
state.[66]

In spite of these grandiose plans and efforts, the Jewish
colonization of the Birobidzhan territory never reached full frui-
tion. This failed partly because of the inclement climate and
soil and of insufficient financial resources. Moreover, by the
mid-1930s, Soviet industrialization and its accompanying
"social mobilization" of the Soviet masses became dominant
on the Soviet scene, providing heretofore unequalled job opportunities.
Also detrimental to the Birobidzhan resettlement movement
were the vast collectivization programs, the extensive Stalinist
purges, and the outright denial of further settlement in the area
during World War II. According to the official results of the
1970 All-Union Census (which is the most recent Soviet national
census), there remain only 11,452 Jews in the Birobidzhan area.
(For comparison purposes, out of a total Birobidzhan area population of 172,449, there are 144,286 Russians and 10,558 Ukrainians.) Of the region's five representatives in the Soviet of
Nationalities of the Supreme Soviet, only one, Lev B. Shapiro,
is a "Jew."[67]
Consequently, in view of the decidedly unsuccessful
history of the Birobidzhan resettlement attempt, and the pro-
nounced apathy shown to it over the years by the Jews, it appears evident that this long-enduring experiment represents
neither a "national" homeland nor a symbolic cultural rallying
point for Soviet Jews. Conversely, the Birobidzhan model continues to be the most important official showplace for exhibit-
ing the alleged resolution of the Jewish problem, and moreover
at the outset could have been considered as a sincere attempt
to give "nationhood" status to the Jews.
In spite of the fact that the Birobidzhan experiment ultimately emerged as an unfulfilled chapter in the ongoing saga of
Soviet Jewry, it, nonetheless, represents an intriguing and
highly imaginative conception on the part of the Soviet authorities.
At the same time, it epitomizes the characteristic ambiguity prevalent in Soviet policies and practices vis-à-vis the Jewish group.

There appears to be little doubt, for example, that the Birobidzhan resettlement initiative was partially prompted by the drastic economic condition of Jews in the aftermath of the First
World War and Civil War hostilities. Something had to be done
to alleviate the misery of so large an ethnic group, not only for
the group's own salvation, but more importantly, for the salvation of the large cities to which the Jews had flocked in large
numbers following the wartime emergencies.

Also, one could argue that the projected transference of
large numbers of Jews from scattered urban areas to the rural
Birobidzhan territory represented a sincere desire on the part
of some Soviet officials, e.g., the Soviet President, Mikhail
Kalinin, to bestow "nationhood" status on the Jews. After all,
the Birobidzhan resettlement would conform with the ideological
"nationhood" prerequisites of "territorial integrity" and "association with the soil." In that connection, the then President
of the Soviet Union, Mikhail Kalinin, expressed the hope in
1934 that "when 100,000 Jews had settled" in Birobidzhan, the
Soviet government would consider declaring it a "Soviet Jewish
Republic."[68] Also, a 1936 decree stated that "for the first
time in the history of the Jewish people its ardent desire to
create a homeland of its own, to achieve national statehood,
is being realized" (in Birobidzhan).[69] However, this optimism
proved to be ephemeral, for Stalin, in his November 25, 1936,
speech, "On the Draft Constitution of the USSR," without
specifically mentioning either the Jews or Birobidzhan, declared
that three conditions must be fulfilled for autonomous regions
to become constituent Soviet republics. "First, the republic
must be a border republic, not surrounded on all sides by
Soviet U.S.S.R. territory." "Second, the nationality which
gives its name to a given Soviet republic must constitute a
more or less compact majority within that republic." "Third,
that republic must not have too small a population; it should
have a population of, say, not less, but more than a million."[70]

As mentioned briefly previously, official motivation for
resettling Jews in the Birobidzhan territory also stemmed from
strategic considerations, i.e., to safeguard the far eastern
frontier; most notably from Japan with whom a disastrous war
had been fought in 1904-05 and with whom renewed hostilities
were considered a distinct possibility. This motivation perhaps
is attested to by the official statement published in 1932 declaring that "the masses of the Jewish toilers, who are perme-
ated with loyalty and devotion to the Soviet regime, are going
to Biro-Bidzhan...they are not only fighting for their country,

not for a new fatherland, as the U.S.S.R. is already for them, but for strengthening the Soviet Union in the Far East."[71]

Also as noted previously, it is probable that some Soviet officials hoped that by creating an autonomous Jewish territorial unit, which perhaps would be later transformed into a State unit, that both Soviet and foreign Jews would abandon Zionism and religious Judaism. In that regard, Aleksandr Chemerisky, secretary of the Yevsektsii (Jewish Sections of of the C.P.S.U.) boasted in 1928 that "the autonomous Jewish territory will be the heaviest blow to the Zionist and religious ideology."[72]

Thus, we can see the apparent contradictions inherent in the espoused official views and policies toward the Birobidzhan resettlement issue. Some officials, most notably Kalinin, saw the experiment as a primary means to solidify Jewish national aspirations and attain statehood status. Others saw it as a means to strengthen the physical security of the new Soviet State (i.e., in the far eastern regions), while still others viewed it as a means to negate the world-wide appeal of international Zionism and religious Judaism. The most important Soviet actor, Joseph Stalin, as we saw earlier, apparently was against the Birobidzhan project from the outset, at least as far as the ultimate attainment of Jewish statehood status was concerned. Furthermore, as we shall see later in this study, Jewish migration to Birobidzhan during World War II was completely stopped, and immediate postwar Jewish attempts to revive immigration to Birobidzhan were refused by Stalin. (Ironically, following Stalin's death, Jewish immigration to Birobidzhan was revived by the Soviet leadership as "State policy" and continues to this date in that capacity.) He also rejected postwar Jewish immigration proposals for the Crimea as constituting a possible security threat to the Soviet State.

A more sinister aspect of the Jewish resettlement issue reportedly occurred during the early 1950s when Stalin allegedly planned forced mass Jewish relocations to Eastern Siberia. However, unlike the intent of the original Birobidzhan resettlement initiative, this latter resettlement attempt was designed primarily to rid the metropolitan areas of unwanted Jewish population concentration and influence. Only the death of Stalin in March 1953 reportedly prevented the actual carrying out of this relocation effort.[73]

The Birobidzhan project is important also in that in spite of its inherent policy contradictions and haphazard execution, it illustrates the growing solidification of Stalin's ascendancy to supreme power in the Soviet leadership hierarchy and, relatedly, demarcates the stiffening of official policy toward the Jews. Conversely, it also indicates the power dichotomy within the leadership hierarchy up to that time, a situation which was to change drastically beginning in 1936. One might even say that Stalin's indirect rejection of statehood for the Jews in 1936 -- relative to the Birobidzhan resettlement issue -- represented a foreboding to the Jewish group of things to come.

The Revival of Ethnic ("National") Consciousness Among Soviet Jews

There exists today among many Soviet Jews a decided reawakening of their ethnic or "national" consciousness. This phenomenon is evident not only in the large numbers who have already emigrated, but also in many who have remained behind in the Soviet Union.

Gitelman, in his referred-to work "Assimilation, Acculturation, and National Consciousness " attributes this reawakening to several factors. First of all, World War II was a great shock for many Soviet Jews who were well on their way to assimilation in the 1930s. The Jewish tragedy experienced in the war and government attempts to minimize or ignore it stirred many Jews into a Jewish consciousness which they did not previously have.

Another and most important catalyst to the Jewish consciousness was the Soviet acquisition, during the war, of the Baltic Republics, Eastern Poland, and Bessarabia-Bukovina, which brought into the U.S.S.R. over two million new Jewish citizens, a large portion of whom still retained allegiance to religious traditions, Hebraic culture, and Zionist ideas. The entry of this Jewish population into the U.S.S.R. did much to revive the ethnic consciousness among many Jews; and in fact, these "Zapadniki" or "Western" Jews were later to play an all-important role in inspiring and guiding the Jewish "national" revival of the 1960s and 1970s. It is also pertinent to note the prominent role played by these "new" Jews in the recent Jewish emigration exodus from the Soviet Union.

A third and perhaps the most important stimulus to the revival of Jewish ethnic consciousness was the establishment of the State of Israel in 1948. This fact is attested to by the tremendous spontaneous reception which Soviet Jews gave to Golda Meir, Israel's first ambassador to the Soviet Union, upon her arrival in Moscow in 1948. The establishment of a

89

recognized Jewish homeland, for many Soviet Jews, sparked
the first real awakening of their Jewish identity and opened
for them a possible, albeit as yet distant, means to leave the
country.[74]

While Soviet antisemitism can be considered a constant
factor in the arousal and maintenance of Jewish ethnic consciousness, its greatest impact occurred during the so-called
"black years," 1948-52, when the last vestiges of Jewish culture were apparently eradicated and when an intense, extensive
antisemitic campaign, climaxed by the "doctors' plot," threatened every Jew. It was at this time that many Jews decided
that it was time to leave.[75]

Another important factor supportive of the revival of Jewish
ethnic consciousness was the Israeli victory in the Arab-Israeli
War of 1967, particularly in light of the definite anti-Israeli posture of the Soviet government and its concurrent pro-Arab stance.
Relatedly, the Soviet media undertook an immediate vituperative
campaign against Israel, Zionism, and Judaism, with direct and
indirect antisemitic inclusions. This campaign was intensified
at the beginning of the 1970s with the appearance of the Jewish
emigration factor. Concurrently, there emerged a decided consensus among the Soviet leadership and other segments of the
population that the Jews who emigrate are "traitors." This
feeling of "distrust" was enlarged to include those Jews who
did not emigrate and for all practical purposes remained loyal
Soviet citizens. These actions on the part of the government
did much not only to strengthen the Jewish consciousness in
those Jews who had already maintained some vestiges of it,
but more importantly sparked a Jewish awareness in many Jews
who heretofore considered themselves "assimilated."

Of course, the ongoing Soviet propaganda effort which
largely refuses to distinguish between "Jews," "Israelis," and
"Zionists" adds fuel to the Jewish ethnic consciousness revival
in the Soviet Union. As noted, this largely euphemistic "anti-
Zionist" (i.e. antisemitic) campaign has been intensified to
heretofore unheard of dimensions in recent years, primarily to
combat the continuing Jewish exodus to Israel. At the same
time, the effort attempts to attack the notion of the existence
of an international Jewish culture and denies that the Jews are
indeed a "nationality," but merely an ethnic group.

An additional factor contributing to the resurging Jewish
awareness of ethnic "separateness" from the general Soviet
culture, in recent years, is the continuing governmental antagonism directed against the Jewish dissident activists and the
ongoing drama of related "show trials." By all accounts, the

Jewish activist movement has been all but decimated by the imprisonments, exiles, and deportations of its most capable
leaders. More recently, the official campaign to disrupt the
Jewish activism has been enlarged to include accusations of
such nefarious activities as direct espionage involvement on
behalf of the Western governments, theft, arson, illegal currency transactions, etc. As a consequence, all Jews in the
Soviet Union have been made amply aware of their "distinctive-
ness" and of the apparent reality that their future in Soviet
society is tenuous, to say the least.

NOTES

1. Joseph B. Schechtman, Star in Eclipse: Russian Jewry
Revisited (New York: Thomas Yoseloff Publishers, 1961), p. 146.
2. V.I. Kozlov, Dinamika chislennosti narodov: metologiya issledovannia i osnovnye faktory [The dynamics of population statistics: research methodology and basic facts] (Moscow:
"Nauka," 1969), p. 48; Brian Silver, "Social Mobilization and
the Russification of Soviet Nationalities," American Political
Science Review, 68 (March 1974): 46-48 [Hereafter cited as
Silver, "Social Mobilization"].
3. Ibid., p. 49; Vernon V. Aspaturian, "The Non-Russian Nationalities," in Prospects for Soviet Society, ed. Allen
Kassof (New York: Praeger Publishers, 1968), pp. 159-60.
4. However, recent demographic trends indicate that
the Russians and other European Slavs are losing ground to the
non-Slavic elements in Soviet society with regard to population
increase. The 1970 All-Union Census confirms that the birth
rate of non-Europeans is decidedly higher than that of Europeans.
The peoples of Central Asia and the Caucasus far outdistance
the Russians and other Slavs, as well as the Baltic peoples, in
their overall population growth rate. (The Russians, according
to the 1970 Census, constitute 53.4 percent of the total population as compared to 54.8 percent in 1959). If the current demographic trend continues, it is quite probable that the Russians
will no longer constitute a majority within several decades. This
reality, of course, could present profound difficulties for the
continued Russian leadership role and perhaps also accounts
for the current accelerated "merging together" nationalities policy
of the Soviet government. Council of Ministers, Soviet Census
of 1970, 4:9, 12, 16-18, 20-151.
5. Karl W. Deutsch, Nationalism and Social Communication: An Inquiry in the Foundations of Nationality, 2d ed. (Cambridge, Mass.: M.I.T. Press, 1966), pp. 162-63; Karl W.

Deutsch, "Social Mobilization and Political Development,"
American Political Science Review 60 (September 1961): 494,
514.

6. Silver, "Social Mobilization," p. 64.

7. John A. Armstrong, Ideology, Politics, and Government in the Soviet Union, rev. ed. (New York: Praeger Publishers, 1967), pp. 131-35.

8. Zvi Y. Gitelman, "Assimilation, Acculturation, and
National Consciousness Among Soviet Jews" (Prepared for delivery at the annual meeting of the American Historical Association, New Orleans, December 1972), pp. 2-3 [Hereafter cited
as Gitelman, "Assimilation and Acculturation"].

9. The Narkomnats, established on November 8, 1917,
was originally intended to serve as an intermediary between the
central Soviet organs and the minorities and to assist the government in dealing with problems of a purely national character.

10. Zvi Y. Gitelman, Jewish Nationality and Soviet Politics, The Jewish Sections of the CPSU, 1917-1930 (Princeton:
N.J.: Princeton University Press, 1972), pp. 122, 123, 137,
260-61 [Hereafter cited as Gitelman, Jewish Sections].

11. For example, the Soviet sociologist, I.Kon writes:

> First of all, not every linguistic assimilation is
> voluntary. It happens that minorities are simply deprived
> of an opportunity to cultivate their languages, since they
> are not taught in schools and are not used in cultural life.
> ... But even a complete linguistic assimilation [as in
> the case of the Jews and the Volga Germans], the loss of
> one's native language and its transformation into a dialect,
> is not tantamount to a disappearance of other ethnic dif-
> ferences. A person may speak the language of the majority
> and yet consider himself a member of a national minority.
> It is not accidental that our censuses separate the question
> about one's native language from that about one's ethnic
> affiliation.

I. Kon, "Dialektika razvitiya natsii" [Dialectic of the
development of nations], Novyi mir 3 (Moscow: 1970): 145.

12. Silver, "Social Mobilization," p. 48.

13. Ibid., p. 65.

14. The term Jewish dialect means: among Ashkenazic
Jews, Yiddish; among Georgian Jews, Georgian; among Bukharan
Jews, Tadzhik; among Mountain or Tat Jews, Tadzhik; and among
Crimean Jews, Tatar (the Crimean Jews were almost completely

annihilated during the Second World War and there remain only a few hundred survivors today). Hebrew, not being recognized by the Soviet authorities as a national language, is not included in the census.

15. This query regarding use as a "native or second language" was not asked during the 1959 All-Union Census.

16. Council of Ministers, Soviet Census of 1970, 4:9, 20-321, 331-83.

17. Nove, "The Jewish Population," p. 144; Mordekhai Altshuler, "Mixed Marriages Amongst Soviet Jews," Soviet Jewish Affairs 6 (December 1970): 30-32 [Hereafter cited as Altshuler, "Mixed Marriages"].

18. A.G. Kharchev, Brak i sem'ya v SSSR [Marriage and Family in the U.S.S.R.] (Moscow: "Statistika," 1964), p. 193, cited by Gitelman, "Assimilation and Acculturation," p. 21.

19. M.V. Kurman and I.V. Lebedinsky, Nasilenie bol'-shogo sotsialisticheskogo goroda [The population of a large socialist city] (Moscow: Izdatel'stvo "Statistika," 1968), cited by John A. Armstrong, "Soviet Foreign Policy and Anti-Semitism," Perspectives on Soviet Jewry (1971), pp. 62-64 [Hereafter cited as Armstrong, "Soviet Foreign Policy and Anti-Semitism]; Gitelman, "Assimilation and Acculturation," p. 22.

20. Nove, "The Jewish Population," p. 143.

21. K. Kh. Khanazarov, "Mezhnatsional'nye braki -- odna iz progressivnykh sblizheniya sotsialisticheskikh natsii," Obshchestvennye nauki v Uzbekistane ["Intermarriage -- one of the progressive drawing togethers of socialist nations," The Social Sciences in Uzbekistan] 10 (1964): 29-30, cited in Gitelman, "Assimilation and Acculturation," pp. 25-26; Altshuler, "Mixed Marriages," pp. 30-32.

22. Ibid.

23. J.A. Newth, "A Statistical Study of Intermarriage Among Jews in Part of Vilnius (Vilno -- U.S.S.R.)," Bulletin on Soviet Jewish Affairs 1 (1968): 68. Newth's analysis is based on data contained in O.A. Gantskaya and G.F. Debets, "O graficheskom izobrazhenii rezul'tatov statisticheskogo obsledovaniya mezhnatsional'nykh brakov" ["Concerning the graphical representation of the statistical results of the investigation of intermarriages"], Sovetskaya Etnografia 3 (Moscow: 1966): 109-18.

24. Literaturnaya Gazeta [Literary Gazette], 24 January 1973, p. 13.

25. It is ironic that this Soviet maternal nationality criterion, at least up to age sixteen, corresponds to Judaic law (Halakha) which bases the "Jewishness" of an individual

on the mother's national origins, differing, however, in that
the Judiac identification is for life. Encyclopedia Judaica, vol.
10 (Jorusalem, Israel: Keter Publishing House Ltd., 1971), pp.
24, 59.
    26. L.N. Terent'eva, "Opredelenie svoiei natsional'noi
prinadlezhnosti podrostkami v natsional'no-smeshannykh sem'-
yakh" [Identifications of individual national affiliations among
juveniles in nationally mixed families], Sovetskaya Etnografiya
[Soviet Etnography] 3 (1969): 20-30; Nove, "The Jewish Population," p. 129; Council of Ministers, Soviet Census of 1926, pp.
98, 101; F.B.I.S., Soviet Decrees.
    27. "A Union of Equals," Literaturnaya Gazeta (Moscow)
1 December 1976, p. 10 [Hereafter cited as Literary Gazette,
"Union of Equals"].
    According to comments made in a lecture on "The Commu-
nist Party and Future Development of Nationality Relations,"
given by an unidentified lecturer on March 13,1975 , at the
Conference Hall of the Moscow Znaniye [Knowledge] Society --

    Virtually all geographically dispersed nationalities
    were reduced numerically during the last decade. The
    primary reason for this reduction was the increase of
    mixed marriages in the U.S.S.R., particularly involving
    members of geographically dispersed nationalities [for
    example, the Jews]. Even in 1959, more than one out of
    every ten marriages included spouses of different nation-
    alities.

    28. V.T. Zinich and V.I. Naulko, "Kul'turno-bytovoe
sblizhenie narodov Ukrainskogo S.S.R." ["The cultural-social
drawing together of the peoples of the Ukrainian S.S.R."] ,
Sovetskaya Etnografiya 6 (November-December 1972): 28-37.
    29. United Nations, General Assembly, 25 September
1963, Manifestations of Racial Prejudice and Religious Intolerance (A/5472), Add. 1, p. 48.
    30. This "Soviet nation" or community is defined in the
Soviet publication, Leninizm i natsional'nyi vopros v sovremennykh usloviyakh [Leninism and the national question under contemporary conditions] (See Reference note 31) as:

    The Soviet nation is a new historic, social, and
    international community of people having a homeland, ter-
    ritory, economy, culture which is socialist in its content,
    a federal all-national state and a common goal to build
    socialism which has resulted from a socialist transforma-

tion and a drawing nearer of workers classes and strata, nations and nationalities.

In 1959, 10.2 percent of all families in the U.S.S.R. were the product of mixed marriages; in 1970, this figure was almost 14 percent. Yurii V. Bromlei, "Ethnic Aspects of Contemporary National Processes," Istoriya S.S.S.R., 3 (May-June 1977): 19-28, as cited in American Association for the Advancement of Slavic Studies, The Current Digest of the Soviet Press, vol. 29, no. 28 (Columbus, Ohio: American Association for the Advancement of Slavic Studies, August 10, 1977), "Soviet Ethnic Integration: What Is It?," p. 3. [Hereafter cited as American Association for Slavic Studies, Current Digest (vol., no., and article title)].

31. Literary Gazette, "Union of Equals"; see also P.N. Fedoseyev, et. al., Leninizm i natsional'nyi vopros v sovremennykh usloviyakh [Leninism and the national question under contemporary conditions] 2d ed. (Moscow: Politizdat, 1974).

32. Armstrong, "Soviet Foreign Policy and Anti-Semitism," pp. 62-67; Jeffrey A. Ross, "Alienation and Self Image: The Development of Emigration-Nationalism Among Soviet Jews" (Prepared for delivery at the annual meeting of the International Studies Association, New York, March 14-17, 1973), p. 10 [Hereafter cited as Ross, "Alienation and Self-Image"].

33. Joshua Rothenberg, "Jewish Religion in the Soviet Union," in The Jews in Soviet Russia since 1917, ed. Lionel Kochan (London, New York, Toronto: Oxford University Press, 1970), pp. 159-60 [Hereafter cited as Rothenberg, "Jewish Religion"].

34. S.S. Studenikina, gen. ed., Istoriya sovetskoi konstitutsii v dokumentakh 1917-1956 [The history of the soviet constitution in documents 1917-1956] (Moscow: Gosudarstvennoe Izdatel'stvo, 1957), pp. 57-58, 109-110 [Hereafter cited as Studenikina, History in Documents]; Rothenberg, "Jewish Religion," pp. 161-62; William Korey, The Soviet Cage, Antisemitism in Russia (New York: Viking Press, 1973), p. 43 [Hereafter cited as Korey, Soviet Cage].

35. Although Lenin's prerevolutionary writings emphasized the need to distinguish between Party and State attitudes toward private religious conviction, he personally believed that pervasive antireligious propaganda and broader education of the masses would eliminate the vestiges of "religious prejudices" over time. Therefore, while he formally called for guarantees of freedom of conscience and separation of church and state, his measures

95

were designed to cope with what was viewed as a temporary phenomenon. Vladimir I. Lenin, Polnoe sobranie sochinenii [Full Collection of works], 5th ed., vol. 12: "Sotsializm i religiya" ["Socialism and religion"], pp. 143-45; vol. 17: "Ob otnoshenii rabochii partii k religii" ["Concerning the Attitude of the workers' party toward religion"] (Moscow: Gosudarstvennoe Izdatel'stvo, 1960), p. 431; Rothenberg, "Jewish Religion," p. 162.

36. Rothenberg, "Jewish Religion," pp. 161-69; Idem., The Jewish Religion in the Soviet Union (New York: KTAV Publishing House, Inc., 1971), pp. 6, 39-66, 101, 164-67.

37. Article 124 of which reads: "In order to ensure freedom of conscience, the church of the U.S.S.R. is separated from the State, and the school from the church. Freedom of religious worship and freedom of anti-religious propaganda is recognized for citizens." However, in digesting Soviet constitutional rights "guarantees" it is prudent to keep in mind the essentially propagandistic nature of these constitutional utterances and that, in most instances, they do not reflect the reality of the internal Soviet situation.

38. Rothenberg, "Jewish Religion," pp. 171-72.

39. Ibid., p. 173; Korey, Soviet Cage, p. 42. According to a New York Times article of November 27, 1976, a World Jewish Congress initiative (as yet unanswered) to establish a relationship with the Soviet government controlled Moscow Jewish religious leadership was made during November 1976. "Official Jewish Leaders in Soviet Union Seek Link to International Groups," New York Times, 27 November 1976. Conversely, a Soviet Mennonite delegation of six was allowed to attend a Mennonite conclave in the United States in July 1978. "Soviet Delegation Warmly Greeted By Mennonites," Washington Post, 28 July 1978. Additionally, Soviet Russian Orthodox clergymen, over the years, have been allowed to attend external religious meetings on a regular basis.

40. Walter Kolarz, Religion in the Soviet Union (New York: Frederick A. Praeger, 1961), p. 388.

41. During the same period, a substantial number of the remaining synagogues, including the large synagogues of L'vov and Chernovtsy were closed.

42. See Rothenberg, "Jewish Religion," pp. 176-79.

43. Every functioning Soviet religious body is required by law to register with the authorities.

44. Soviet law recognizes two types of religious organizations, which are referred to collectively as "religious associations." The first designation is that of the religious "societies"

which are administered by "groups of twenty" (dvatsaka), and
the second consists of groups of believers, "not numerous
enough to organize a religious society." Rothenberg, "Jewish
Religion," p. 179. (The Law on Religious Associations of
April 8, 1929, was published in Sobranie uzakonenii i rasporyazhenii rabochekrest'yanskovo pravitel'stva R.S.F.S.R., no. 35,
1929, text no. 353; amendments: Sobranie uzakonenii, etc.,
no. 8, 1932, text no. 41, 116. "Instructions," on following the
law were issued October 1, 1929, and were published in the
Byuleten N.K.V.D., R.S.F.S.R., no. 37, 1929. English translations of both texts can be found in Church and State Under
Communism, a special study prepared by the Law Library of
Congress, Washington, D.C., 1964, pp. 12-17, 18-24).

45. Khronika Tekushchikh Sobytii [Chronicle of Current
Events], no. 41 (August 3, 1976), cited in Radio Liberty Research Bulletin, no. 16, April 22, 1977, pp. 1-2, Novoe
Vremya [New Time], 16 (April 16, 1976): 30 [Hereafter cited
as Novoe Vremya]. The average age of Jewish clergymen is
above seventy. Rothenberg, "Jewish Religion," p. 182.

46. Kuroedov's remarks were presented in a lecture to
the staff of the Great Soviet Encyclopedia, reported in the
previously mentioned Chronicle of Current Events publication
and also in Izvestiya (Moscow) 31 January 1976; Nasha strana
[Our Country], 17 May 1976 [Hereafter cited as Nasha strana];
Novoe Vremya, p. 30; American Association for Slavic Studies,
Current Digest, vol. 28, no. 51 (January 19, 1977), "Jewish
Culture Seen Thriving in the U.S.S.R.," p. 7 [Hereafter cited
as American Association for Slavic Studies, "Jewish Culture"].

47. Ibid.; "Facts Refute Slander of Zionists," Tribuna
(Prague) 17 October 1973 [Hereafter cited as Tribuna, "Slander
of Zionists"]; U.S., Foreign Broadcast Information Service,
(F.B.I.S.), vol. 3, Concerning an Anti-Soviet Campaign, 13
December 1976, R-3 [Hereafter cited as F.B.I.S., Anti-Soviet
Campaign]; Nasha strana; Rothenberg, "Jewish Religion," pp.
185-86; Idem., "The Fate of Judaism in the Communist World,"
in Religion and Atheism in the U.S.S.R. and Eastern Europe,
ed. Bohdan R. Bociurkiw and John W. Strong (Toronto: University of Toronto Press, 1973), p. 231.

48. Hebrew was outlawed in the 1920s an an instrument
of Zionism.

49. Gitelman, Jewish Sections, pp. 333, 337, 351-52,
365-66, 371; Solomon M. Schwarz, The Jews in the Soviet Union
(Syracuse, N.Y.: Syracuse University Press, 1951), p. 18
[Hereafter cited as Schwarz, Jews in the Soviet Union];

Kommunisticheskaya akademiya komissiya po izucheniyu natsio-
nal'nogo voprosa, Natsional'naya politika VKP (b) v tsifrakh
[The Communist academy commission for the study of the nation-
ality question, The national policy of the VKP (b) (Communist
Party), in figures] (Moscow: Izdatel'stvo Kommunisticheskoi
Academii, 1930), p. 278.

50. United Nations, Commission on Human Rights, Study
of Discrimination in Education (Doc. E/CN.4/Sub.2/210), 5 January 1961, p. 6; Konstitutsiya (osnovnoi zakon) Soyuza Sovetskikh Sotsialisticheskikh Respublik [The Constitution (the basic
law) of the Union of Soviet Socialist Republics] (Moscow:
Izdatel'stvo "Izvestiya Sovetov Deputatov Trudyashchikhsya
S.S.S.R.," 1960) [Hereafter cited as U.S.S.R.,Constitution].

51. United Nations, Commission on Human Rights, Periodic Reports on Human Rights Covering the Period 1960-1962
(Doc. E/CN.4/861/Add.2), 20 December 1963, p. 42.

52. Pravda [Truth] (Moscow), 2 November 1961.

53. According to a recent Czech report, a "faculty of the
Yiddish language" was recently activated in the Pedagogical
Institute in Leningrad. Tribuna, "Slander of Zionists."

54. Elias Schulman, A History of Jewish Education in the
Soviet Union (New York: KTAV and Brandeis University Press,
1971), pp. 146-65.

55. Schwarz, Jews in the Soviet Union, pp. 139-41; C.
Abramsky, "The Biro-Bidzhan Project, 1927-1959," in The Jews
in Soviet Russia since 1917, ed. Lionel Kochan (London, New
York, Toronto: Oxford University Press, 1970), pp. 62-75
[Hereafter cited as Abramsky, "The Biro-Bidzhan Project"];
Pechat' S.S.S.R. v 1970 godu [Publications of the U.S.S.R.
in the year 1970] (Moscow: Izdatel'stvo "Kniga," 1971), p.10.

56. F.B.I.S., Anti-Soviet Campaign, R-4; American
Association for Slavic Studies, "Jewish Culture," p. 7; U.S.,
Foreign Broadcast Information Service (F.B.I.S.), vol. 3, 14
January 1977, Izvestiya Denies Existence of 'Jewish Question,'
R-11 [Hereafter cited as F.B.I.S., Izvestiya Denies].

57. Abramsky, "The Biro-Bidzhan Project," pp. 62-75;
Joseph Brumberg and Abraham Brumberg, "Sovyetish Heymland,"
in The Unredeemed, Anti-Semitism in the Soviet Union, ed. R.I.
Rubin (Chicago: Quadrangle, 1968), pp. 83-96; Gitelman, Jewish
Sections, pp. 127-28, 333, 351-52, 365-66, 371.

58. F.B.I.S., Izvestiya Denies; Vechernaya Moskva
[Evening Moscow], 7 December 1976; Soviet Life, October 1972,
p. 48.

59. Schwarz, Jews in the Soviet Union, pp. 140-42;
Soviet Life, May 1972, p. 17.

60. Schwarz, Jews in the Soviet Union, pp. 151-54.

61. Vladimir Il'ich Lenin, Sochineniya [Collected Works], 2d ed., 45 vols. (Moscow: Gosudarstvennoe Izdatel'stvo, 1961), vol. 27, p. 158.

62. "Ozet" -- a semiprivate auxilliary to "Komzet" was formed to enlist public support, both at home and abroad, for land colonization efforts. Some authors give the date of the creation of "Komzet" as August 24, 1924. See Guid G. Goldman, Zionism Under Soviet Rule (1917-1928) (New York: Herzl Press, 1960), p. 111.

63. It is interesting to note that in response to the Soviet government's appeal to world Jewry for needed funds for this project, an assistance agreement was signed with the American Jewish "Joint Distribution Committee." A similar Soviet monetary appeal was made to support the later Birobidzhan settlement project.

64. This is an important acknowledgement to the Jewish "national" status since in the Soviet system of government, the term oblast' denotes a smaller, yet distinct, "national" entity. See Samuel N. Harper and Ronald Thompson, The Government of the Soviet Union, 2d ed. (Toronto, New York, London: D. Van Nostrand Co., Inc., 1949), p. 52.

65. Abramsky, "The Biro-Bidzhan Project," pp. 66, 68, 70-71.

66. S. Dimanshtein, ed., Yidn in F.S.S.R. [Jews in the U.S.S.R.] (Moscow: Zamlbuch, Der Emes, 1935), pp. 31-38, as cited in Abramsky, "The Biro-Bidzhan Project," pp. 72-73 [Hereafter cited as Dimanshtein, Yidn in F.S.S.R.].

67. Shapiro is also Party First Secretary of Birobidzhan. Council of Ministers, Soviet Census of 1970, 4:76.

68. Dimanshtein, Yidn in F.S.S.R., pp. 31-38.

69. Pravda (Moscow), 26 November 1936,as cited in Katz, The Jews, "Basic Views on Jews and on their National Attitudes," p. 1.

70. Stalin, Leninism, p. 584.

71. Published in the Geserd periodical, Tribuna, Issue no. 9, 1932, as cited in Abramsky, "The Biro-Bidzhan Project," p. 69.

72. Aleksandr Chemerisky, "Biro-Bidzhan -- der grosser onzog," in Oktiabr, 30 March 1928, as cited by Abramsky, "The Biro-Bidzhan Project," p. 69.

73. Aleksandr I. Solzhenitsyn in his book, The Gulag Archipelago, 1918-1956 (New York: Harper & Row, 1973) -- see author's Footnote no. 48, bottom of p. 92 -- repeats the often-heard speculation that Stalin in 1953 planned a forced relocation

of Soviet Jews to Eastern Siberia where barracks reportedly had
already been prepared for them alongside the railroad tracks of
the Trans-Siberian Railroad. This alleged plan, which was to
follow the hanging of the "doctors' plot intriguers" on Red Square,
was shelved following Stalin's death. This alleged plan was
said by Western press sources at the time to have been included
in Khrushchev's famous denunciation of Stalin before the Twentieth Party Congress in February 1956.

Roy Medvedev, in his brief May 1970 samizdat [self-
published] article wrote the following about the same subject:

> ...the organs of the N.K.V.D. hastily prepared for
> a massive expulsion of the Jews from all the main cities
> of the U.S.S.R....In several districts of Kazakhstan,
> barracks for Jews were urgently erected. A text of an
> appeal to the Jewish people, which several distinguished
> scientists and cultural leaders of Jewish nationality had
> to sign "requesting" resettlement, was prepared; several
> large factories passed resolutions for the eviction of
> Jews, [and] in several regions of the country pogroms
> and slaughters of Jews were carried out.

Roy A. Medvedev, Blishnevostochnii konflikt i yevreiskii
vopros v S.S.S.R. [The near-eastern conflict and the Jewish
question in the U.S.S.R.] (Moscow: A samizdat [self-publish-
ed] document authored in May 1970) [Hereafter cited as Medvedev, Near-Eastern Conflict].

74. In fact, many Soviet Jews openly started to declare
themselves citizens of the new Jewish State and professed
loyalty to it.

75. Soviet emigre Aleksandr Voronel, however, opines
that the reawakening of ethnic consciousness among Soviet
Jewry is less connected with intensified antisemitism than
with the "growth of Jewish culture in their midst" -- a resent-
ment that Soviet society had deprived the Jews of their literature, their religion, and rooted traditions. He also credits the
pursuit of education as a "supreme value in itself" and its subsequent denial by the Soviet authorities as chiefly responsible
for the "radicalization" of Soviet Jews in recent years. See
Aleksandr Voronel, "The Social Pre-Conditions of the National
Awakening of the Jews in the U.S.S.R.," in Aleksandr Voronel
and Viktor Yakhot, eds., Jewishness Rediscovered: Jewish
Identity in the Soviet Union (New York: Academic Committee
on Soviet Jewry and the Anti-Defamation League of B'nai B'rith,
1974), pp. 25-37 [Hereafter cited as Voronel and Yakhot,

Jewish Identity]; Emanuel Litvinoff, ed., "Captive Scientists: Their Central Role in the Struggle for Freedom," Insight 1 (May 1975): 2 [Hereafter cited as Litvinoff, "Captive Scientists"].

4
The Legal Status of Jews in the Soviet Union

THE JEWS IN PRE-SOVIET RUSSIA -- A BRIEF ACCOUNT

The Tsarist Period

As noted elsewhere in this study, antisemitism as practiced in the Soviet Union today is not a phenomenon initiated
by the current Soviet leadership; it prevailed in Russia long before the communists came to power. In fact, the pre-1917
history of Jews not only in Russia, but in most of Eastern Europe
as well, was one of anti-Jewish prejudices, discrimination,
hostility, and often outright hatred and persecution. For successive Tsarist regimes, the essence of policy toward the
Jewish minority was one of either oppression or total assimilation. Tsar Ivan IV (1533-84) perhaps expressed it best: "Bap-
tize the Jews who consent to baptism and drown the rest."[1]
Consequently, there was no official identification of Jewish
nationality per se, only of Jewish religion. Any Jew who became Russian Orthodox or Catholic ceased to be categorized as
a Jew. Relatedly, Jews who adopted Christianity immediately
became free of all legal restrictions and limitations.[2]
The Jews have constituted an important segment of Russian
society since the days of antiquity. They first settled in Eastern
Europe in the days of the "Second Temple," several centuries
before the birth of Christ. Long before the Christian era, they
had already settled in the Caucasus; by the second century
A.D. they appeared in Georgia, and by the eighth century they
were in the Crimea (where they comprised the largest single
ethnic group) and in Lithuania. By the time of the Tatar invasion
in the thirteenth century, Jews had already settled along the
banks of the Don, Dnieper, and Volga Rivers. However, as we
shall see in this chapter, the ensuing "Jewish problem" in
Russia was not inherently Russian. It was inherited by the

Russians as a result of their piecemeal absorption of the Polish-Lithuanian territories commencing in the mid-seventeenth century. By then, great numbers of Jews had already settled in Poland where they had been invited in the Middle Ages as a result of circumstances favorable both to the various Polish governments which were eager to stimulate commercial life, and to the Jews, heretofore persecuted in Western Europe, who were granted a considerable degree of cultural autonomy and economic opportunity.[3]

With regard to the Jewish settlements, it is interesting to note that the early Jewish settlers vied with the powerful Byzantine church in seeking converts for their own faith among the pagan peoples in whose midst they lived. This contest centered particularly among the Khazars, a heterogeneous people of Finnish-Turkish origin who, between the seventh and tenth centuries, dominated the region between the Sea of Azov and the Volga River. Although some of them converted to Christianity and later to Islam, the most important elements, including the Khazar king and nobility, embraced Judaism.

During the reign of the Jewish "kagans," the Khazar Kingdom rose to great power and prosperity. It also sought to protect Jewish rights whenever possible. As a consequence, many Jews fleeing Byzantine persecution sought asylum in the Khazarian Jewish kingdom. Ironically, in decided contrast to today, the non-Jewish subjects under Khazar rule held the Jews in high esteem -- as clever merchants, carriers of culture, as well as for their physical prowess and bravery.

Khazar rule witnessed the blossoming of Jewish life and the emergence during the tenth and eleventh centuries of Jewish communities in the principality of Kiev. Relatedly, in 1016, after fifty years of fighting, the Khazar kingdom was completely vanquished by Kievan Russia, and a large portion of the Jewish-Khazarian population was removed to the Kiev principality.

Although Christianity eventually became the state religion of Kievan Russia and subsequent intolerance toward the Jews grew, their position until about the sixteenth century was much better than that of Jews in Western Europe. The Russian Jews were free men and as members of the city merchant class enjoyed freedom of worship. Throughout the Middle Ages, there was no physical segregation of Jews in Russia and most Jews lived in the cities. More importantly, there does not appear to be any indication of general antisemitic feelings. In fact, many Jews fleeing persecution in Western Europe found refuge in post-Kievan Russia.

103

The latter part of the fifteenth century, however, saw the rise of a movement known as the "Judaizing heresy," which had serious consequences for the Jews. This movement was so-called because it resulted in many apostasies from the Christian church, among them some prominent Russian ecclesiastics and a number of high-ranking government officials as well. For a time, practically the entire government of the Moscovite Russia was composed of either Judaizers or sympathizers.

As a direct result of Christian backlash to the Judaizing heresy and the concurrent fear of rising Jewish influence, anti-semitism grew. This antisemitic trend is also reflected in Tsar-ist policies which began to discriminate against the Jew at this time. From the sixteenth century, when the Moscovy Tsardom set about consolidating independent principalities into a unified empire, it became the government policy not to admit Jews into its territories, even for temporary purposes. Thus, in 1727, a decree was issued that "all Jews found to be residing in the Ukraine and in other Russian towns shall be forthwith expelled beyond the frontier and not permitted under any circumstances to reenter Russia." In 1742 another governmental edict reaf-firmed the decree of banishment and nonadmission, an excep-tion being made for those who would embrace the Greek-Ortho-dox faith.[4]

Catherine II ascended the throne of Imperial Russia in 1762 and continued the anti-Jewish policies of her predecessors. In her first year of reign, she issued a manifesto permitting the immigration of all foreigners except Jews. As before, the basic concern was that of not wanting to arouse the religious sensitivities of the population.

Such was the Tsarist "Jewish" policy until the year 1772, when, as a result of the first partition of Poland, Russia inher-ited a Jewish population of two hundred thousand. Through the subsequent Polish partitions of 1793 and 1795, which added other Polish-Lithuanian provinces, the number of "new" Jews grew to nine hundred thousand. Consequently, since it was no longer possible to resort to banishment as a means of solv-ing the Jewish problem, the government sought to limit Jewish rights through special legislation. As a result, the first govern-mental decree concerning the partitioned territories, issued by Catherine II on August 16, 1772, distinguished between the new Jewish and non-Jewish subjects. The non-Jews were promised that they could exercise the same rights throughout the Russian Empire as they enjoyed under their former government. The Jews, however, were told that they would be restricted in the exercise of their rights to the specific territories in which they were

104

living at the time of the partition. Hence, the so-called "Jewish Pale of Settlement" was officially established in Russia. Moreover, even within the Pale, Jews were singled out from among the Christian populace for discriminatory legislation through the imposition of a double tax burden.

An attempt to solve the Jewish problem was made during the early years of the reign of Aleksandr I -- influenced, no doubt, by the wave of liberalism which was then sweeping Western Europe. In November 1802, the Tsar ordered the creation of a "Committee for the Amelioration of the Jews," for whom the committee subsequently recommended "a minimum of restrictions, and a maximum of liberties." The committee also decided to invite representatives from the individual Jewish communities to come to the capital to advise the government on the needs of their people.

A "Statute Concerning the Organization of the Jews " was issued on December 9, 1804. Prefacing this new charter was a preamble stating that it was prompted by a "solicitude for the welfare of the Jews as well as for the native population of those provinces in which these people are allowed to live." Although the proclamation reaffirmed the existence of the Pale of Settlement, it also permitted Jews to send their children to all schools of the empire and offered inducements to those Jews who would engage in agriculture (similar to the Bolshevik/Soviet Jewish agrarian objective). The statute stated that "when the Jews shall evince diligence and application in agriculture, manufacture, industry, and commerce, the government will adopt the necessary measures for equalizing the taxes imposed on them with those levied on the other subjects of the empire."

With the general conservative political reaction in Europe following the Congress of Vienna, the emerging liberal tendencies in Russia suffered a decided setback and during the reign of Nicholas I (1825-55) the position of the Jews became exceedingly difficult. For the first time in Russia, Jews were conscripted into military service, often accompanied by enforced conversion to Christianity. The "Statute of Conscription and Military Service" promulgated on August 26, 1827, provided that in addition to supplying recruits to serve a term of twenty-five years, Jews also had to produce cantonists (juvenile conscripts) from the ages of twelve to twenty-five. In addition, in 1844 Nicholas I formally abolished the kahal, the Jewish community administration, in response to the "rebellious" spirit exhibited by some Jewish communities to his policies.

In April 1835, a new code of regulations was issued which confirmed the anti-Jewish legislation of the law of 1804 and

105

appended the restrictive bylaws promulgated since that time.
In addition, the Pale of Settlement was now clearly defined.
It consisted of Lithuania (provinces of Kovno, Vilno, Grodno,
and Minsk); the southwestern provinces (Vohlyn and Podol
without any territorial restrictions); Byelorussia (Vitebsk and
Mogilev minus the villages); Little Russia (Chernigov and
Poltava minus the crown hamlets); New Russia (Kherson, Ekat-
erinoslav, Taurida, and Bessarabia minus Nikolaev and Sevas-
topol); the province of Kiev minus the capital; and the Baltic
provinces (for old settlers only). In addition, rural settlements
located within the immediate proximity of the western frontier
were to be closed to Jews.

After the disastrous Crimean War, it became clear to the
Tsarist government that if Russia were to regain her prestige
as a great power, changes would have to be made in her system
of government. This realization was responsible for the period
of "Great Reforms" during the reign of Aleksandr II (1855-81)
which resulted in the abolition of serfdom, the granting of local
self-government, and the institution of court and military service reforms. The Jews also benefited. The military conscription cantonist system was abolished; laws favoring special
classes of Jewry were enacted; some Jews were accorded the
right of unrestricted residence and the opportunity for government service. It was during this period also that educational
opportunities for Jews increased and many Jewish parents took
advantage of the occasion to place their children in the Russian
school system.

Soon after, the movement for Jewish emancipation suffered
another setback as a result of the Polish uprising in 1863, which
adversely affected all national minorities in Russia. The heretofore extensive "Russification" efforts on the part of the government were largely curtailed. Discriminatory statutes against
Jews reappeared during the later years of Aleksandr II's reign.
For example, in the matter of military conscription, a law of
May 9, 1878, obligated Jews as a group to military service.
Thus, in the event of failure to fill the assigned quota of recruits,
Jews who for family reasons were entitled to exemptions would
be drafted to make up the deficiency. Similar discriminatory
policies were sought against Jews in the field of education. In
fact, there was a widespread clamor for a numerus clausus for
Jewish students in the educational system.[5]

Following the assassination of Aleksandr II in 1881, a
new era of officially sanctioned discrimination and downright
persecution of the Jews began, lasting until 1917. Jews were
expelled from Moscow, they were denied jobs in the civil

service, and they were strictly confined to the Pale of Settlement. In addition, opportunities for Jews to study in the higher educational institutions and to work in the professions became greatly limited. In fact, in 1887, restrictive quotas for Jews seeking secondary and higher education were enacted -- 10 percent for schools within the Pale of Settlement, 5 percent for outside the Pale of Settlement, and 3 percent for St. Petersburg and Moscow. These quotas were subsequently reduced even further to 7, 3, and 2 percent, respectively. Also, on November 8, 1889, during the reign of Aleksandr III, a governmental decree was enacted which restricted the admission of "non-Christian," i.e., Jewish, Muslim, and Karaite lawyers seeking entrance to the bar. Although the decree was not specifically directed at the Jews, only they actually were affected. Soon thereafter, the government reportedly allowed and sometimes even encouraged mass pogroms in which great numbers of Jews were either killed or forcibly displaced.[6]

As Solomon M. Schwarz points out, throughout most of the history of the Jews under Tsarist rule, legislative and administrative restrictions against the Jews greatly impeded, if not made impossible, the assimilation of the Jewish masses into the mainstream of Russian life. Even under the enlightened rule of Aleksandr II, the avowed governmental policies of assimilation were not complete. This is evidenced in the March 1856 decree which ordered all officials "to revise all existing legislation regarding the Jews, so as to bring them into harmony with the general policy of merging this people with the native population, so far as the moral status of the Jews will allow it." (Italics added.) Consequently, for the bulk of Russian Jewry, life under the Tsars was one of continuing harsh oppression and often of dire economic difficulty.[7]

Pertinent Jewish demographic realities. From the annexation of the Polish territories to the national census of 1897, the number of Jews in the Russian Empire increased, through natural growth, to approximately five million, the overwhelming majority of whom continued to reside in the Pale of Settlement. Within the Pale, which had an overall population of 42.2 million in 1897, Jews accounted for 11.6 percent of the population. In other parts of the Empire, with 85.1 million inhabitants, Jews represented less than one-half of 1 percent of the total population. More than four-fifths of the Jews within the Pale lived in urban communities and accounted for nearly 40 percent of the urban population. Of the total 4.9 million Jews concentrated in the Pale of Settlement, one-third lived in so-called "market towns,"

107

otherwise known as the <u>shetl</u>, of which Jews often were the only inhabitants. Their cultural identity remained "Jewish," and the mother tongue of nearly 97 percent was Yiddish.[8]

Before the 1917 revolutions, most of the Jews in the Pale of Settlement were engaged in commercial trade and crafts. As of 1897, about 50 percent of the Jews in Russia were craftsmen, hired hands, and workers in small factories. About 40 percent were shopkeepers and commercial agents of one kind or another. In addition, another 5 percent were engaged in professional careers; only 2.5 percent were farmers. It is also said that between 30 and 35 percent of the total Jewish population at the time was dependent, to one degree or another, on relief provided by the international Jewish welfare organizations. This was due to the fact that the socioeconomic pattern of the Jewish minority still bore the imprint of the economic catastrophe which had befallen feudal Poland's Jewish community at the time of the Polish collapse and in the early stages of Russian rule. Many so-called Jewish "businessmen" lacked capital and business equipment, frequently had no place of business, and in most instances, had to rely on short-term credit at high interest rates. The condition of Jewish artisans was likewise. Similarly, the factory working conditions for the Jews were abominable and wages were pathetically low.

The miserable socioeconomic conditions of the Jews were compounded by the hostilities of World War I which brought the military front to the very doorstep of many regions of the Pale of Settlement. As a result, not only were great numbers of Jews killed or forcibly displaced, but many more faced starvation and economic ruin. This plight became even more desperate in the ensuing Civil War catastrophe since many more Jews were killed as a result of war-related pogroms. Individual Jews, however, did find heretofore denied economic and professional opportunities. Disruption of normal supply channels and shortages created loopholes through which individual enterpreneurs and middlemen made economic profit. Also, the Civil War disruption allowed a number of Jews to enter the government organizations of the newly established and hard-pressed Bolshevik regime, which eagerly sought their services.[9]

<u>Jewish emigration -- 1880-1914.</u> Between 1880 and 1914 one-third of the Jewish population emigrated; some 70 percent went to the United States. According to available data, between 1880 and 1890, 135,003 Jews arrived in the United States from Russia. Similar to today's situation, worldwide public opinion was soon organized on behalf of the Jews and diplomatic protests

were made on the subject by individual foreign powers. It is also ironic that in mirror-like reflection of current history, the only path then opened to the Jews for complete emancipation lay in the emigration route. Also, as a result of their taking the emigration initiative, all Jews were accused of disloyalty and government-sponsored antisemitic policies and practices increased. Also comparable to today's situation, fear was expressed by some Jewish leaders at the time that emigration would undermine the struggle for complete emancipation of the Jewish masses in Russia.[10]

Jewish political expression. As mentioned earlier, a large element in Russian antisemitism, both official and popular, arose from the fact that religious Judaism was a faith alien to the national Russian Orthodox Christianity and that the Tsar was both the spiritual and secular head of the Russian Empire. Consequently, Jews were never accepted on an equal status and were continually discriminated against in all aspects of life. In answer, significant numbers of Jews in the nineteenth century eagerly joined the ranks of the revolutionary activists and indeed, did participate in every phase of revolutionary activities.
There were two leading anti-Tsarist movements in the 1800s -- the Narodniki (Populists) and the Zemlya i Volya (Land and Freedom). In both these organizations, Jews played a leading role. Aaron Zundelevich and H. Magat were leaders in the Narodniki movement, and Nicholas Utin, sometimes referred to as the "first Russian Marxist", was a leader in Zemlya i Volya. Paul Axelrod and Lev Deich were also Jewish revolutionary activists in this era. All were assimilationists and their attitude toward religion, history, and even the traditional past of their own people was a negative one.[11] In that regard, Zundelevich wrote:

> For us, Jewry as a national organism did not present a phenomenon worthy of support. Jewish nationalism, it seemed to us, had no raison d'etre. As for religion, that cement which combines the Jews into one unit, it represented to us complete retrogression.[12]

The Jewish revolutionaries, including the Marxists, maintained that emancipation of the Jews depended on emancipation of the Russian people, with whom, they believed, the Jews should completely assimilate. They were confident that the Jewish problem would be solved with the liberation of the masses. According to Louis Greenberg, although the Jewish revolutionaries did not admit it, and perhaps even were not fully conscious of it, probably the disabilities from which their own people suffered did much to contribute toward their own interest in the revolutionary movement.[13]

According to Harry G. Shaffer, by 1897, Jews accounted for one-fourth of all political prisoners in Russia. In 1903, Count Witte claimed that 50 percent of all revolutionaries were Jews and attributed this to the unjust way Jews had been treated under Tsarist rule, e.g., denial of civil rights, lack of career and economic opportunity, physical abuse, residential restrictions, etc. Witte's estimate of the numbers of Jewish revolutionaries perhaps is lent credence by the existence of the then only mass workers' party in Russia, the Jewish "Bund."

Since for a Jew joining a Marxian revolutionary party represented a conscious and deliberate break with Jewish tradition, religion, and culture, Jews much more readily joined the Menshevik rather than the Bolshevik faction of the Russian Socialist Democratic Party. This is because for the "internationalist" Jew, the Mensheviks represented the more Western, more internationalist, and more universal wing of the socialist movement. For the Jewish social democratic "revolutionary," the advent of socialism meant a better life for all peoples, and not merely a better life for one particular nationality such as the Jews. On the other hand, the Bolshevik faction, at this time, appeared to have significant nationalist characteristics, i.e., it was totally immersed in the Russian situation and gained its primary support from the Great Russian nationality group.[14]

An important catalyst to the Jewish political consciousness was the debacle of the First Russo-Japanese War (1904-05) which had triggered widespread public outrage against the Tsar and his government. (In fact, the noted historian, George Vernadsky, claims that this war was the "outward cause of the first Russian revolution [of 1905].")[15] As a direct consequence of that war and its related public demonstrations, strikes, and general disorder, Nicholas II was forced to yield to the general demands for constitutional government. As a result, on August 6, 1905, an "advisory" body known as the duma (which later evolved into a legislative body) was established; and on October 17th of that same year, the Tsar granted a constitutional government. It, thus, was in this immediate time period and liberal milieu that a number of Jewish political parties were formed and Jewish "revolutionary" zeal reached new heights.[16]

Consequently, prior to the 1917 revolutions, there emerged a multitude of Jewish political parties, espousing either Zionist, socialist, or religious doctrines. One of them, and perhaps the most important in terms of its influence upon the subsequent course of historical events, was the "General League of Jewish Workingmen in Lithuania, Poland, and Russia"; more commonly known as the Jewish "Bund." The Bund was a Marxist party founded in 1897, which for a time was an integral part of the Russian Socialist Democratic movement. It was the first Jewish political party to attempt a "synthesis" of general political goals whose attainment would assure both the modernization of the Russian Jewish "nationality" and the preservation of its Jewish identity. As is well-known, the withdrawal of the Bundists from the Russian Social Democratic Party Convention in London in 1903 in support of Jewish nationalist causes afforded Lenin and his followers the majority vote and hence, control of the central Russian Social Democratic Party apparatus. This action on the part of the Bundists also precipitated the split in the Russian Socialist Democratic ranks which gave birth to Bolshevism as a distinct political movement.[17]

The Zionist Party, founded in 1905, espoused Jewish resettlement in Palestine and the use of the Hebrew and Yiddish languages in Russian Jewish public life. The Zionist Workers' Party, founded in 1906, wanted Jewish resettlement in one specific territory, not necessarily Palestine, to construct a Jewish socialist order. The Jewish Socialist Workers' Party, also founded in 1906, desired extraterritorial nationality parliaments or sejms which would have jurisdiction in political, cultural, and economic matters.[18] The Poalai Tsion (Labor Zionist) Party, founded in 1906, a Zionist and also Marxian party, advocated a Jewish socialist resettlement in Palestine. There were also the Russian Constitutional Democratic Party and the nationalistic Folkspartei (People's party) led by the historian Simon Dubnow. In 1917, various Jewish religious political parties emerged, e.g., the Masores V'Kherus or Tradition and Freedom Party; the Shomrai Yisroel or Guardians of Israel Party; the Kneses Yisroel or Assembly of Israel Party; the Akhdus Yisroel or Unity of Israel Party; and the Adas Yisroel or Community of Israel Party.

By 1917, the most prominent Jewish political parties in Russia were the Zionist Party with 300,000 members and the Bund, with 33,700 members. There were also the United Jewish Socialist Workers' Party (also known as the Farainigte)[,19] the Poalai Tsion Party, and the Folkspartei. In addition, individual Jews belonged to the various non-Jewish socialist political parties, including the Bolshevik and Menshevik factions of the Russian Socialist Democratic Party.[20]

The general Jewish apathy toward the Bolshevik faction is demonstrated by the fact that only 958 Jews joined the Bolsheviks

111

prior to 1917, while the total Party membership in January 1917 was 23,600. Moreover, less than 5 percent of Jewish C.P.S.U. members in 1922 had been Bolsheviks prior to 1917. Reportedly, only 1,175 Jews joined the Bolsheviks in 1917.[21]

Most of the socialist-oriented Jews supported either the Bund or the Menshevik faction of the Russian socialist movement. Of the approximately one hundred Jewish delegates to the Russian Socialist Democratic Party Congress in 1907, fifty-seven were Bundists. One-fifth of the Menshevik delegates were Jews.

By 1917, however, some prominent Bolshevik leaders were "Jews." In fact, of the twenty-one Central Committee members in August 1917, six were "Jews": Trotsky, Kamenev, Sokolnikov, Sverdlov, Uritskii, and Zinoviev. Trotsky, who was second only to Lenin in the overall Bolshevik leadership, held the highly sensitive posts of the People's Commissar for Foreign Affairs and head of the Military-Revolutionary Committee. Other prominent "Jews" during the Bolshevik rise to power included Joffe (later chief delegate to the Brest-Litovsk peace talks), Radek, Axelrod, Rozovskii, and Chudnovskii (who directed the arrest of the Provisional government). In addition, 20 percent of the delegates to the All-Russian Conference of the Bolshevik Party held in Petrograd on April 20, 1917, were "Jews."[22]

Further regarding the presence of "Jews" in the Marxian movement, it is perhaps ironic that there was apparently, at the time, a widespread view, both domestic and foreign, that the Marxian-socialist movement was predominantly Jewish. For example, there was the intellectual view that the Marxian-socialist movement was a basically Jewish movement, but not a movement of the Jewish race as a whole. That is, the direction of the proletarian revolt had been directed mainly by the Jew -- "his energy, his international quality, his devotion to social revolution" -- and was not peculiar to Russia, but was present throughout the industrialized areas of the western world.[23] Another illustration is presented in the so-called "Balfour Declaration," i.e., the British decision to allow Palestine as a national home for the world's Jews, a partial British motive for which reportedly being a desire to keep the new Marxian (i.e., "Jewish") leadership in Russia in the war against Germany. On the domestic scene, this viewpoint was promoted not only because of the high visibility of the "Jewish" leaders in the Russian Marxist-socialist movement, but perhaps more importantly by the relatively large numbers of Jews, who in 1917, suddenly rushed to fill the governmental posts vacated by the fleeing Tsarist officials.

112

Apart from their high visibility among the top leadership of the Bolshevik Party, the presence of "Jews" in the Marxian movement was also dramatized by the relatively large numbers of "Jews" in the Bolshevik secret police apparatus, the dreaded "Cheka" (Vecheka). The Bolshevik motivation for largely employing "Jews" as well as other national minorities as Cheka agents is not entirely clear; however, one could assume that these people could hardly be suspected of harboring Tsarist loyalties in view of their past oppression by successive Tsarist governments. "Jews" and the other national minorities as well apparently were attracted to the Cheka by the lure of physical power and the opportunity to "get even" with the Russian population for past crimes inflicted against them. However, since the Cheka was the most hated and feared organ of Bolshevik power, anti-Jewish feelings among the Russian populace increased in direct proportion to Cheka terror.[24]

The Transitory Period (1917)

The overwhelming majority of Russia's Jews hailed the first and democratically oriented revolution of March 1917 and the accompanying overthrow of Tsarist rule. The newly established Provisional government, as one of its first legal acts (the Act of April 2, 1917), enacted the full emancipation of the Jews together with all other national minorities. Its key provision read: "All the limitations on rights of Russian citizens imposed by hitherto existing laws on the basis of religion, creed, or nationality are hereby revoked."[25] As a result, Jewish community life bourgeoned almost overnight -- cultural activity among Jews increased at a feverish pace; schools, relief work, publishing in both Hebrew and Yiddish, opening of new synagogues, and expansion of trade union activity. Political activity also reached heretofore unknown intensity. As previously mentioned, new Jewish political parties emerged, older parties redrafted their party programs to reflect the newly won freedoms, and a host of new political initiatives were embarked upon. As mentioned earlier, Jews, in record numbers, assumed administrative posts in local and central governmental bodies and in general exerted an energetic political presence throughout the country.

Concurrent with this Jewish political reawakening, Jewish national consciousness also soared to new heights. This is best illustrated in the endorsement by all the Jewish political parties of the principle of "extraterritorial, national-cultural autonomy." One might add that all the principal non-Jewish

political parties, except the Bolsheviks, also fully endorsed
the principle. The Socialist Revolutionary Party endorsed it in
May 1917; the Menshevik Socialist Democratic Party favored the
proposal in August 1917; and the Constitutional Democrats back-
ed the principle in July of that same year.

It should be interjected at this point, however, that the
referred-to "extraterritorial national-cultural autonomy" idea
did not originate in the glow of the March 1917 utopia. As noted
in Chapter 1 of this study, the Austrian Marxists espoused the
same principle decades earlier. In fact, the Jewish Bund leaders,
at the same time, had eagerly adopted the principle from the
Austrians and in turn, had engaged in lengthy polemics on the
subject with Lenin who was vehemently opposed to it.

The Jewish political scene in March 1917 was characterized by the following three dominant tendencies: 1) the several
middle-class groups, of a Zionist, non-Zionist, or orthodox
character, more or less closely aligned with the Russian Constitutional Democrats; 2) the social Democratic elements which
supported either Mensheviks or Bundists; and 3) a number of
socialist-Zionist, socialist-territorialist, and kindred groups,
in which general politics espoused a moderate Russian or Ukrainian socialism.

It is important to note that the Bolshevik Party, called the
Communist Party after March 1918, as such did not figure at all
in Jewish politics, nor did it have among its leaders any individuals familiar with or active in Jewish community life -- those
individual "Jewish" Bolsheviks, as pointed out earlier, having
been completely assimilated into the Russian culture. In fact,
the individual "Jewish" Bolsheviks were rabid anti-"Judaists"
who sought the complete destruction of all aspects of Judaic
culture and tradition. As such they were prominent in the ranks
of the "Jewish Sections" which led the Party's subsequent campaign to eradicate Judaism. Furthermore, the Bolsheviks had
conducted practically no agitation or propaganda among the Jews
prior to 1917; and as noted previously, Jewish rank-and-file
membership in the Party was relatively of minor proportions.[26]

With regard to the Jewish community's attitude toward the
Bolshevik Party, it was ambivalent but it is believed that the
majority of Jews, conscious of their Jewishness and determined
to preserve it, were against the Bolshevik movement at its inception. It could not be otherwise. Several Bundist leaders,
at the time, maintained that the Bolsheviks constituted a distinct
threat to all the gains made since the collapse of Tsarism and
possibly could even provoke a counter-revolution. In addition,

Jews commonly feared the Bolshevik cultural, economic, and political policies. They had much to lose from the Bolshevik prohibition of free commerce since many were traders and artisans. In addition, many Jews were well aware of Lenin's negative view toward Zionism and Jewish tradition. However, some Jews reportedly also took pride in that individual "Jews," e.g., Trotsky, Sokolnikov, and others, had gained prominence in the Bolshevik ranks.[27] How wrong they were since, as noted, these Bolshevik "Jews" had already deserted their Jewishness and had eagerly embraced the anti-"Judaic" doctrine of the Bolshevik Party.

As a consequence of their newly won freedom and political awareness, the Jewish political parties in March 1917 decided to hold an All-Russian democratically elected Jewish Congress for the purpose of coordinating Jewish community activities in the new democratic state. The elections were held in the autumn of 1917 (before the Bolshevik coup), but because of the subsequent unsettled political conditions, the Congress never met. The results of the election are important, however, in that they demonstrate the relative strength of the individual Jewish political parties at the time. The reports of the 193 kehillas (local Jewish administrative units) in nine provinces in the Ukraine showed that the Zionists had 36 percent of the delegates, the Bundists had 14.4 percent, the Akhdus Party had 10 percent, the United Jewish Socialist Workers' Party had 8.2 percent, the Poalai Tsion Party had 6.3 percent, and the Folkspartei had 3 percent. Similar electoral trends were evident in the Jewish Congressional elections held in January 1918. In that election the Zionists received more votes than all the other parties together (some 60 percent) while the socialist-oriented parties amassed no more than 25 percent. The orthodox parties received 12 percent. These results show that the Zionists were clearly the majority party and that Jewish ethnic consciousness was prevalent throughout the Jewish community. They also represent what the Bolsheviks must have considered a decided threat to the ideological and programmatic objectives of the Bolshevik Party. Primarily because of this potential opposition, the Zionist movement was marked for early liquidation by the Bolsheviks upon assuming power.[28]

THE JEWISH ROLE IN CONTEMPORARY SOVIET POLITICS

The history of Russia's Jews in Tsarist times was one characterized by a high degree of volatility, civil denial, and personal tragedy. But following the Tsarist downfall in March

1917, the Jewish minority, almost overnight, became both
politically aware and more than ever before, conscious of
its Jewish heritage. It rushed into the mainstream of public
life but at the same time sought to retain its Jewish identity.

This newly won status was to be ephemeral, however,
for later Soviet rule resumed, in most respects, traditional
discriminatory policies and practices. Like the Tsars the succeeding Soviet rulers sought to solve the Jewish question through
assimilation while enacting restrictive policy measures designed
to curb unwanted Jewish influence. The basic contradiction between assimilation and exclusion was not only to remain, but
was to be extended.

This declining Jewish societal role is perhaps best reflected in the actual Jewish participation in the Soviet political
process. According to Roy Medvedev in his brief samizdat (self-
publication) article of May 1970, at the beginning of the 1920s
no less than one-fourth of the Party's Central Committee membership were Jews. That same source notes that at the Fourteenth
Party Conference in November 1927, more than 10 percent of all
the delegates were Jewish.[29] In 1939, out of 139 members (including alternates) of the Party's Central Committee, fifteen, or
10.8 percent, were Jews. The Jewish Central Committee repre-
sentational percentage dropped to 3 percent in 1952, to 2 percent
in 1956, and to a mere 0.3 percent in 1961.[30]

Today, there appears to be only one admittedly "Jewish"
member, Veniamin Emmanuilovich Dymshits (Deputy Chairman,
Council of Ministers, and former Chairman, State Committee
for Material and Technical Supply) among the full membership
of the Central Committee. Aleksandr Chakovsky, the editor of
the Moscow Literary Gazette, who also is admittedly "Jewish,"
was made a candidate member of the Party's Central Committee
apparatus in 1971. There are no Jews today, whatsoever, in the
top Party organ, the Politburo -- the last "Jew," Lazar M. Kaganovich, having been removed in 1957. There also do not appear
to be any identifiable "Jews" among the key Party figures either
in the central Party apparatus or among the first secretaries of
provincial and district Party organizations. The lone exception
is the July 1970 appointment of Lev B. Shapiro as the First Secretary of the Party organization in the Jewish Autonomous Oblast'
of Birobidzhan.[31]

Official Soviet figures purport Jewish membership in the
Party in 1922 at 5.2 percent of the total Party membership.
Since then, the percentage has declined. Jews made up 2.8
percent of the Party membership in 1960 and about 1.6 percent
in 1965. According to one Western observer, Jews had the

highest Party membership relative to their total population among all nationalities in the U.S.S.R. during the mid-1960s. It has been estimated that 210,000 Jews, or about 16 percent of the adult Jewish population (one in every six) were Party members in 1969 -- about 1.5 percent of the total Party membership at the time.[32]

According to official Party membership figures as of January 1, 1976, there are 294,774 Jewish Party members constituting 1.9 percent of the total Party membership of 15,638,891. Also nine out of every ten young Jews between the ages of fourteen and twenty-eight are Young Communist League members. These figures are most interesting in that Jews apparently remain by far the most "Party saturated" ethnic group, with approximately three times the U.S.S.R. average -- and almost twice the Russian membership percentage. Thirteen percent of the total Jewish population, based on the 1970 census figures, are Party members.[33] However, this phenomenon should hardly be surprising since the Party traditionally has been an urban-oriented political organization and Jews are overwhelmingly (98 percent) an urban community. In addition, the Jews as a highly educated and presumably career-minded group would naturally seek Party membership to further their individual careers and status. Party leadership, of course, is another matter and as highlighted above, the Jewish members of the Party, for some time now, have been relegated to relatively subordinate Party positions. For a detailed analysis of the nationality composition of the C.P.S.U. as of January 1, 1976, see Table 12 which follows.

A critical indicator of the political role of Jews in Soviet society occurs in the membership in the All-Union Supreme Soviet and in the individual republic supreme soviets -- since the election of delegates to these governmental bodies is a Party-dictated choice with only one name appearing on the ballot. In 1937, forty-seven Jews were elected (of 1,143 members) to the All-Union Supreme Soviet, thirty-two to the Soviet of the Union (569 members), and fifteen to the Soviet of the Nationalities (574 members). In the first election of the All-Union Supreme Soviet following the war, in January 1946, only five Jews were elected to the Soviet of the Union (601 members).[34] (No figures are available for the Soviet of Nationalities membership.) In 1950, there were only two Jews elected to the 678-member Soviet of the Union and but three to the 638-member Soviet of Nationalities. In 1958, only three Jews were to be found among the 1,364 members of both houses of the All-Union Supreme Soviet. This in spite of the fact that the official 1959 All-Union Census lists a total Jewish population of 2,267,814. The total 1962 Jewish

117

TABLE 12
The Nationality Composition of the Communist Party of the U.S.S.R. (C.P.S.U.) as of January 1, 1976*

	Absolute Figures	Percentage of Total Party Membership	Percentage of Respective National Populations (Based on 1970 National Census)
Total Members and Candidates	15,638,891	100.0	100.0
Main Nationalities			
Russians	9,481,536	60.6	7.4
Ukrainians	2,505,378	16.0	6.2
Byelorussians	563,408	3.6	0.6
Uzbeks	321,458	2.1	3.5
Kazakhs	282,471	1.8	5.3
Georgians	259,520	1.7	8.1
Azerbaidzhanians	232,223	1.5	5.2
Lithuanians	106,967	0.7	4.0
Moldavians	67,707	0.4	2.5
Latvians	65,116	0.4	4.6
Kirghiz	49,542	0.3	3.3
Tadzhiks	63,611	0.4	3.4
Armenians	234,253	1.5	6.5
Turkmenians	48,021	0.3	3.2
Estonians	49,739	0.3	5.0
Bashkirs	55,122	0.4	4.6
Jews	294,774	1.9	13.3
Mordvinians	73,464	0.5	5.8
Tatars	300,714	1.9	5.1
Chuvash	83,109	0.5	4.8

*Partiinaya Zhizn' [Party Life] 10 (Moscow: Izdatel'stvo "Pravda," May 1976):13-22; Central Statistical Administration, U.S.S.R., Itogi vsesoyuznoi perepisi naseleniya 1970 goda [Results of the all-union population census of 1970] 7 vols. (Moscow: "Statistika," 1973), 4:9-11.

118

representation among 1,443 All-Union Supreme Soviet deputies consisted of but five Jews -- in 1966, there were five Jewish deputies out of 1,517.[35] Six Jews were elected to the All-Union Supreme Soviet on July 14, 1974,to represent a total Jewish citizenry of 2,150,707. Veniamin E. Dymshits (who is also Deputy Chairman, Council of Ministers) and academician Yuriy Khariton were elected to the 767-member Soviet of the Union. Four others, including Lev B. Shapiro, Party First Secretary in Birobidzhan, and Aleksandr Chakovsky, Editor of the Moscow Literary Gazette, were elected to the 750-member Soviet of Nationalities.[36]

With regard to Jewish representation in the individual republic supreme soviets, of the total number of 5,312 deputies elected to these governmental bodies in 1959, only fourteen were Jews. There was only one Jewish deputy among the 835 R.S.F.S.R. Supreme Soviet deputies, one Jew among the 457 corresponding deputies in the Ukraine, and but two Jews among the 407 deputies in Byelorussia. Of the 281 deputies in Moldavia, where Jews numbered 3.3 percent of the population, there was not a single Jew; and of the 200 deputies in Latvia, where Jews constituted 1.7 percent of the population, no Jew was chosen. However, in Lithuania in 1959, Jewish representation in the supreme soviet there corresponded with the percentage of Jews in the republic's population, with three Jewish deputies out of the total 209 Lithuanian Supreme Soviet membership.[37] In 1971, there was a total of 6,058 Jews in all Soviet organs in the U.S.S.R., only nineteen in the republics' supreme soviets.[38]

Official Soviet spokesmen have recently pointed out, however, that among the deputies to elective bodies of Soviet power, from the U.S.S.R. Supreme Soviet to the local soviets, eight thousand deputies (out of a total of approximately 2,200,000) are Jews.[39] Although this number, at first glance, appears proportionally significant, it is evident from the previously provided data that these "elective" positions are of little or no actual political significance.

It would appear that the provided data support the view that the sociopolitical position of the Jews in Soviet society has deteriorated, to a significant degree, both in the country as a whole and in the individual union republics. Although the Jews are allowed to join the Party and respond to a greater degree (per population) than any other nationality group (Russians included), apparently, they are barred from Party/State leadership roles. This in spite of the fact that, according to official Soviet sources, some 340,000 Jews, over the years, have been awarded orders and medals for heroism and courage in "defense of the fatherland," and for "valiant labor and successes in

119

political, economic, scientific, and cultural activity." These
awards included, inter alia, 117 "Hero of the Soviet Union,"
80 "Hero of Socialist Labor," 123 "Lenin Prizes" (about 11 per
cent of all winners), and 1,478 Jews, or 12 percent of all winners,
received the "U.S.S.R. State Prize."

This situation is compounded by the apparent reality that
the great bulk of the Soviet Jewish population has not yet emigrated, and perhaps never will. In cognizance of that possible
circumstance, Soviet Jewish activist leaders now reportedly desire to focus their attention not only on emigration rights, but
also on religious and political rights and for a better life in
general for Jews in the contemporary Soviet Union.[40]

Thus, we can see from the discussion carried forth in the
chapter that the envisaged promise of full emancipation for
Russia's Jews following the fall of Tsardom in 1917 was short-
lived; and in fact, the Jews, as a group, are decidedly worse
off today than they were in the transitory period of 1917.

THE LEGAL STATUS OF JEWS ACCORDING TO THE SOVIET CON-
STITUTIONS, LEGISLATIVE ACTS, AND PARTY RESOLUTIONS

The Marxist-Leninist Concept of Law and Legality

Prior to delving into the complicated question of what
constitutes the legal status of Jews in the Soviet Union, it might
be expedient to discuss somewhat the concepts of "law" and
"legality" as formulated in Marxist-Leninist ideology.

The basic principle is that the law operating in a given
society is determined by that society's socioeconomic system,
and that its origin and development over a long period is connected with "class contradictions, socioeconomic inequality,
and the resultant political relations of domination and subjuga-
tion."[41] "The individuals who rule in these conditions," Marx
and Engels wrote, "besides having to constitute their power in
the form of the state, have to give their will, which is determined by these definite conditions, a universal expression as
the will of the state, as law."[42] (Italics in the original text.)
Ergo, law in a given society represents essentially the will of
the particular ruling class at a given time in that society's history. Consequently, law in a contemporary socialist environment such as the Soviet Union represents essentially the will
of the ruling proletarian class -- or in more factual terms, its
surrogate, the Party/State apparatus. Thus, individual and
other minority interests, by definition, are of inconsequential

legal and moral importance. It is ordained that what is good for
the well-being of the working class ultimately will prove beneficial for all, regardless of lingering "bourgeois" pretentions.

Marxism also emphasizes the "intimate interconnection"
between the state and law. "Each historical type of state (e.g.,
slave-holding, feudal, bourgeois, socialist) has its own type of
law." Marxism does not recognize either the primacy of law over
the state or the state over law. It regards them as a "dialectical
unity since in each concrete society, state and law are a product
of the same socioeconomic system and political conditions."
Marxists also take the thesis that since law is indissolubly bound
up with the state, it is to wither away, along with the state, in
the future classless and stateless communist society.[43]

Sources of Soviet Law

The principal and dominant source of the Soviet system of
law reportedly is the statute, that is, a normative act adopted by
the higher organs of state power and carrying the highest juridical
force. Ostensibly, for the U.S.S.R. as a whole, statutes are
issued by the Supreme Soviet of the U.S.S.R. and for the union
and autonomous republics by their respective legislative bodies.
According to the Soviet interpretation, statutes are indefeasible,
which means that they "must be fulfilled unconditionally and that
no other organ, with the exception of the Supreme Soviet of the
U.S.S.R. can rescind or suspend their operation."[44]

Types of Soviet Law

The Soviet constitution is the "most important" source of
Soviet law and the "highest type" of law. As is known, each
union and autonomous republic has its own constitution. However, those of the union republics must conform with the supreme
all-union instrument and relatedly, those of the autonomous republics must conform with the constitutions of both the all-union
and of the individual union republic of which it is a part.[45]
Specific types of Soviet law, which in some instances are unique
to the Soviet system, are as follows:

State or constitutional law. Constitutional law allegedly
is regarded by Soviet juridicial writers as the central branch of
the legal system since it deals not only with the political system and the organization of state power, but lays down the basis
of the entire social system, notably the economic system.

121

Administrative law. Administrative law is closely connected with constitutional law and "embraces social relations in the sphere of state administration (and not power); that is, it deals with the legal forms of concrete executive and administrative activity by government ministries and other organs exercising the day-to-day administration of various spheres of social life."

Financial law. Financial law is an aggregation of legal rules regulating the "activity of state organs and legal relations connected with it in the sphere of the budget, taxation, state credit, and other spheres of state financial activity." Financial law is closely allied with constitutional and administrative law.

Labor law. Labor law deals with "the regulation of the labor relations of industrial and office workers."

Civil law. Civil law reportedly is mainly connected with the "economic sphere of social life, with relations involving property, distribution, and exchange." In the civil law sphere there are three basic groups of regulation -- 1) relations between "socialist" organizations, e.g., state, cooperative, and mass organizations; 2) relations between citizens and social organizations; and 3) relations between citizens.

International private law. International private law deals with property relations involving the participation of "Soviet citizens and clerical persons and foreign elements."

Land law. Land law is designed to "ensure the rational use of land, minerals, waters, and forests."

Collective-farm law. As a separate branch of law, collective-farm law regulates relations in the organization and activity of collective farms and also, relations between the collective farms and their members.

Family law. Family law lays down the "conditions and procedures governing the contract and dissolution of marriage, the rights and duties of the spouses, regulates the relations between parents and children, guardianship and patronage, measures for the protection of the family, and the interests of mothers and children."

122

Criminal law. Criminal law is designed to provide "protection for the social and state system, socialist property, and the person and rights of citizens against criminal encroachments."

Corrective-labor law. Corrective-labor law applies to persons sentenced to penalties entailing "deprivation of liberty." Such sentences usually are served in so-called "corrective-labor colonies," involving exile to a specified locality.

International public law. International public law regulates relations in the international sphere involving "states maintaining diverse political, economic, and cultural relations."[46]

Concept of "Socialist Legality"

Soviet legal science allegedly regards "socialist legality" as the "precise observance and execution of the Soviet constitution and the laws and subordinate enactments based on it by all state organs, mass organizations, persons in office, and citizens. Socialist legality is a most important guarantee of the social, economic, political, and other rights and freedom of citizens. The protection of the rights and freedoms of citizens is a key element of socialist legality, and one of the principal immediate tasks of the regime of socialist legality" (i.e., within the Marxian class context). Moreover, in the socialist concept of legality "everyone is equal before the law, and the laws are equal for all."[47]

Historical Factors Pertinent to the Jewish Legal Position

As Jacob Miller notes, "among those features of the Soviet mental world which have influenced thought on the Jews, perhaps the most decisive is the traditional Russian sense of cultural identity."[48] In both pre-Soviet and Soviet Russia, an individual's cultural affinity was and remains an all-important distinguishing identification. This is particularly true of the legal situation of the Jews since Soviet theories and practices vis-à-vis them proceed from both a national and religious perspective. Consequently, the Jews (as well as other "national" groups) are victimized by a "double jeopardy" situation, one which is both complex and at times self-contradictory.

The basis of the Bolshevik approach to the overall nationality issue lay in the fundamental communist theoretical principles of the "dialectic," the "dynamism of history," and the exposition of "class" versus "bourgeois nationalist" prerogatives. With regard to the Jews, as evidenced in the theoretical writings, the Bolshevik theoreticians specifically denied that the Jewish community had those specific characteristics

123

considered essential for nationhood, i.e., a "closed territory of settlement" and a "large and stable stratum associated with the soil." On the other hand and in spite of this theoretical denial, the Bolshevik leaders ostensibly did recognize the Jews as a distinct "nationality." An early recognition occurred in March 1914 in the so-called "Bill of National Equal Rights," which Lenin authored for the Bolshevik faction in the Duma in which the envisaged legal status of Jews was clearly defined. As noted previously, the proposed bill provided for "the abolishment of all constitutional and other restrictions against Jews and other downtrodden nationalities (but especially Jews)." It also stipulated that citizens of "all nationalities" would be equal before the law and specifically urged the removal of legal barriers against Jews, including educational and residential restrictions, and barriers to careers in the government, military, and liberal professions.[49]

Upon seizing power in 1917, the Bolsheviks again specifically identified the Jews as a distinct "nationality" in projecting on the programmatic objectives of the Russian Communist Party:

> On the part of the workers of those nations, who in the capitalist era, were oppressors, special consideration is called for in attitudes toward the national spirit of oppressed nations [natsii] (for example, on the part of Byelorussians, Ukrainians, Poles toward Jews, on the part of Tatars -- toward Bashkirs, etc.)[50] (Italics added.)

Also a Party resolution, "Theses on the Immediate Tasks of the Party in Connection with the National Program," adopted at the Tenth Party Congress in March 1921, specifically mentioned Jews among examples of nationalities and national minorities:

> 4. In addition to the...nations and peoples which possess a definite class structure and occupy definite territory, there exist within the R.S.F.S.R. various casual national groups, national minorities, interspersed among compact majorities of other nations, who in most cases neither possess a definite class structure nor occupy a definite territory (Letts, Esthonians [sic], Poles, Jews, and others). The policy of Tsarism was to exterminate these minorities by every possible means, including massacre (Jewish pogroms).

124

Now that national privileges have been abolished and the equality of nationalities established, and the right of national minorities to free national development is guaranteed by the very nature of the Soviet system, the duty of the Party towards the toiling masses of these national groups is to help them to make the fullest possible use of the right to free development which they have secured.[51] (Italics added.)

Further recognition of the Jews as a distinct, albeit non-territorial, "national" group was formally extended in January 1918, when a Commissariat for Jewish Affairs (Yevkom) was established within the R.S.F.S.R. Central People's Commissariat for Nationality Affairs (Narkomnats) headed by Joseph Stalin. In addition, so-called "Jewish Sections" (Yevsektsii) were organized within the Party structure to deal with the cultural and economic problems associated specifically with the Jewish population. The function of these "Jewish Sections" was to mobilize and integrate politically those Jews who had not become Russian culturally, i.e., the Yiddish-speaking Jewish majority.[52] Although these specific initiatives were designed to bring about the ultimate and total assimilation of the Jews and were consistent with the intervening Leninist nondiscriminative policy toward the Jews, they, nonetheless, did represent a tacit recognition of the Jewish group as a distinct "national" entity within the Soviet society.

Another indication of the tacit recognition of Jewish "nationality" was the acceptance of Yiddish as the "native" tongue of the Jewish community. (According to the 1926 census, 70.4 percent of Jews considered Yiddish as their native tongue).[53] Thus, the Byelorussian Republic decreed in law that Yiddish was among the four official languages of the government.[54] Furthermore, Article 13 of the R.S.F.S.R. constitution of 1925 stipulated that citizens of that republic "have the right to use their native language [presumably including Yiddish] freely in meetings, in the courts, in administrative bodies, and in public affairs... [and] have the right to receive education in their native tongue."[55] Also, the Bolshevik ideological message to the "Jewish street," as carried out by the referred-to "Jewish Sections" of the Party, was to be conducted primarily in the Yiddish language.

In view of these recognitions, one may infer that additional recognition of Jewish "nationality" occurred in the November 15, 1917, governmental decree, the "Declaration of Rights of the Peoples of Russia," which proclaimed the "free development of national minorities and ethnic groups inhabiting Russian territory."

125

It also formally abolished "all national and national-religious privileges and restrictions."[56] Another implied recognition was the first Soviet constitution of July 10, 1918,[57] which stated in Article 22   that:

> The Russian Soviet Federated Socialist Republic recognizing the equality of rights of all citizens, irrespective of their race or nationality, declares the establishment or toleration on this basis of any privileges or advantages, or any oppression of national minorities or restriction of their equality, to be contraventions of the fundamental laws of the Republic.[58]

This assertion of the principle of equal "national" rights is echoed in the constitutions of the individual republics. For example, the referred-to 1925 constitution of the R.S.F.S.R., in Article 13, declared that "oppression of national minorities in whatsoever form, [and] any restriction of their rights... are wholly incompatible with the fundamental laws of the Republic."[59]

A particularly important legal recognition of individual Jewish "national" identification is represented in the establishment by governmental decree in December 1932 of the so-called "internal passport system" -- by which all urban residents aged sixteen and older were obliged to acquire internal passports.[60] Among the identifying personal data contained in these internal passports was a reference, "Point 5," to the bearer's "nationality" -- in the case of Jews, the "nationality" was to be listed as Yevrei (Jewish). The registration in the internal passport as "Jewish" was and remains mandatory for all Jewish offspring of two Jewish spouses, regardless of the wishes of the offspring in question -- although through bureaucratic mix-up, downright bribery or through forgery, individual registrations, on occasion, have been recorded to reflect a non-Jewish identity. The child of a "mixed" marriage, at age sixteen, may declare the "nationality" of either parent. Once entered, the "nationality" designation cannot be subsequently changed, regardless of future desires or circumstances.[61] Unfortunately, the internal passport vehicle has outgrown its original limited purpose of coping with a severe housing shortage in the major urban areas. It now serves a host of both official and unofficial uses which, more often than not, are detrimental to the general well-being of the individual Jewish bearer. (As previously noted, a tragic example of this was the ready-made identification and subsequent extermination of count-

126

less Jews in the wake of the advancing Nazi forces during the Second World War.)

Further credence to the official recognition of the Jews as a distinct "national" group is illustrated in the various Jewish resettlement initiatives sponsored by the Soviet authorities during the 1920s and 1930s -- the most notable being the establishment of the "Jewish Autonomous Oblast'" of Birobidzhan by decree of the Presidium of the Central Executive Committee of the U.S.S.R. on May 7, 1934.[62] This recognition is particularly emphasized in the Jewish "national" aspirations proclaimed by no less an authority than the then President of the Soviet Union, Mikhail Kalinin. (See Chapter 3, "The Jewish Resettlement Initiative," for details.) The Birobidzhan resettlement attempt although evidently failing in its intended mission as the national "homeland" for the Jewish population, nevertheless, continues to represent a clear indication of the ostensible acceptance of the Jews as a distinct "national" group.

In view of the foregoing "acknowledgements," a further juxtaposition of the Jews and "nationality" perhaps is reflected in the various Soviet criminal codes. For example, Article 8 of the law on the Fundamentals of Criminal Jurisprudence of the U.S.S.R. and the Union Republics stipulates that all citizens (presumably irrespective of race or national origin) are "equal before the law and the courts." Moreover, the R.S.F.S.R. Criminal Code of 1922, as previously mentioned, provides a minimum of one year's imprisonment for "agitation and propaganda arousing national enmities and dissensions." (Here, the Jews should represent a prime "national" group for protection.) Also, the R.S.F.S.R. Criminal Code of 1927 calls for imprisonment of "no less that two years [for] propaganda and agitation aimed at arousing national and religious enmities, and dissensions." (Here again, the Jews come to mind as a prime group for protection.) More recently, Article 74 of the Criminal Code of the R.S.F.S.R., dated January 1, 1961, entitled "Infringement of National and Racial Equal Rights," specifies that "any direct or indirect limitation of rights or the establishment of direct or indirect privileges" on grounds of race or nationality will be punished by either "deprivation of freedom" for a period of from six months to three years or by exile from two to five years.[63] (Most certainly, the wording of this article is broad enough to cover all "national" groups -- including the Jews.)

The Constitutional "Guarantees" and Their Significance

As previously mentioned, the All-Union constitution represents both the "ultimate source" and the "highest type" of Soviet law. In addition, "socialist legality" is said to be recognized as the "precise observance and execution of the Soviet [All-Union] constitution and the laws and subordinate enactments based on it by all state organs, mass organizations, persons in office, and citizens." Therefore, the All-Union constitution must be looked to (in theory if not in actual practice) as the fundamental legal instrument for defining duties, rights, and privileges of Soviet citizens.

In that context, the All-Union constitutions of 1936 and 1977 provide a number of constitutional "guarantees" pertinent to both the national and Jewish issues.[64] "Guarantees," however, coined in the essence of the socialist reality which perpetuates the subordination of "minority" rights and privileges to those of the ruling working class -- which, in the Soviet example, is represented by the Party/State apparatus.[65] Consequently, most of the "rights" and "privileges" accorded to the individual, as well as to the various national interests, are restricted by such caveats as "conformity with the interests of the working class, [or with] the aims of building communism, [or] for the purpose of strengthening socialism, and the power and prestige of the Soviet State."

Of particular significance to the Jewish legal position are the following constitutional prerogatives spelled out in both the 1936 and 1977 All-Union constitutions. Article 124 of the 1936 constitution (repeated in Article 52 of the 1977 constitutional document) provides for "freedom of religious worship for all citizens." (Italics added.) Article 34 of the 1977 constitution states that "citizens of the U.S.S.R. shall be equal before the law, irrespective of origin, social and property status, nationality or race...language, [or] attitude toward religion." That same article notes that the "equality of citizens...shall be insured in all fields of economic, political, social, and cultural life." An article of particular pertinence to the Jewish "national" issue is contained in Article 86 of the 1977 constitution which lists the Jewish Autonomous Oblast' (Region) among the designated "autonomous oblasts" of the R.S.F.S.R. As noted previously, this is an important official recognition since in the Soviet system of government, the term oblast' denotes a smaller, yet distinct, "national" entity.

It is interesting to note also that although the 1977 constitutional instrument contains similar, and in most cases,

128

identical civil and national rights as its 1936 predecessor, it limits these rights and privileges with subtle caveats.[66] For example, Chapter 6 of the 1977 constitution, "Citizenship of the U.S.S.R.: Equality of Citizens," stresses the unity of Soviet citizenship for the whole of the Soviet Union, the equality of all citizens before the law, and the provision of equal rights for citizens in all spheres of economic, political, social, and cultural life. However, Chapter 7, "The Basic Rights, Freedoms,and Duties of Citizens of the U.S.S.R.," begins with a rather ominous introductory Article -- Article 39, which states: "Exercise by citizens of rights and freedoms must not harm the interests of society, the state, and the rights of other citizens."

In addition, religious freedom apparently has been curtailed in the new constitution by the prohibition of "incitement of hostility and hate on religious grounds," a stipulation which would seem to lend itself to fairly broad interpretations (Article 52). A rather broad religious restriction is contained in Article 66 which makes it obligatory for parents to "educate their children to be worthy members of the socialist society."

The most ominous Article of all is Article 59 which stipulates that the "exercise of rights and freedoms shall be inseparable from the performance by citizens of their duties." This nexus could be interpreted to mean that citizens may enjoy their constitutional rights and privileges only to the extent that they carry out their duties under the provisions of the new constitution. Most noteworthy of these extensive citizenry obligations is Article 62 which obliges the citizens "to safeguard the interests of the Soviet state, [and] to strengthen its power and prestige." These duties, moreover, are stated in the broadest possible of terms in an apparent effort to encompass any activity not sanctioned by the Soviet authorities.[67] With specific reference to the nationalities question, the 1977 constitution omits any demand for the ultimate "fusion" (sliyanie) of Soviet nationalities; however, at the same time, the centralistic tendencies appear to have been strengthened, with a resulting diminution of union republic powers.

Leonid I. Brezhnev, Party General Secretary and Chairman of the Presidium of the Supreme Soviet, remarks on this phenomenon in his speech to the plenum of the C.P.S.U. Central Committee on May 24, 1977. He notes the multinational character of the Soviet State, says it works well, that there is no need to change it, and that the new constitution provides for greater initiative to be taken at the union republic levels. He also comments that:

...[the 1977 constitution] like the Constitution
of 1936, says that the sovereign rights of the Union Republics are protected by the Union of the S.S.R. The
safeguards of these rights are also retained. Moreover,
new ones are being added....On the other hand, the progressive rapproachement [sblizhenie] of the nations and
nationalities of the U.S.S.R. prompts the need to strength-
en the Union elements of the state. This is reflected in
the very definition of the U.S.S.R. as a single Union
multinational state. The strengthening of the all-Union
principles is reflected also in some other provisions [of
the 1977 constitution].[68]

Comment

From the foregoing passages, it would appear, on the
surface at least, that Jewish rights and privileges are well-
protected by the appreciable array of "guarantees" spelled out
in the various constitutional instruments, legislative acts,
and Party resolutions. In addition, individual Soviet governmental "Jewish" policies and practices, as noted, over the
years, tend to substantiate the legal position of the Jews as a
distinct "national" group.

However, as the discussion in this and other chapters
points out, constitutional and other fundamental rights and privileges are couched within the Marxian class concept and as
such, individual and minority prerogatives are of little actual
consequence. They have to "conform with the interests of the
working class and [with those of] the Soviet state."[69] This is
particularly detrimental to Judaic religious and cultural practices which, to a large degree, are built on traditional observances -- observances considered "socially retrogressive" by the
Soviets.

Furthermore, throughout Soviet history, communist doctrine
toward the Jews has remained relatively the same, i.e., the Jews
do not constitute a "nation" and, therefore, do not deserve "nationhood" treatment. In fact, they have been singled out by the
Soviet authorities for especially expeditious assimilative action.

In addition, the prevailing Party doctrine on the nationality
issue depicts Soviet society as a "society of mature socialist
social relations, in which a new historical community of people,
the Soviet people, has emerged."[70] (Italics added.) In practical
terms, this communist jargon means that the centralist and largely oligarchial rule of the Party is to be strengthened and disparate

130

"petty bourgeois" nationalistic pretensions are no longer to be tolerated. One could assume from the prevailing Party definition that Jewish nationalist aspirations would fall under the "petty bourgeois" nationalistic category.

SOVIET "COMMITMENTS" RESULTING FROM PARTICIPATION IN INTERNATIONAL AGREEMENTS ON HUMAN AND NATIONAL MINORITY RIGHTS

This subchapter focuses on Soviet "commitments" arising from the participation in the various United Nations covenants and conventions[71] on the human and national minority rights issue, as well as on comparable Soviet "commitments" resulting from the "Helsinki Accords" -- i.e., the Conference on Security and Cooperation in Europe, Final Act. It is to be noted that these agreements contain similar and in some instances, identical human and national minority rights provisions. This repetition is due apparently to a coincidence of two major factors: 1) the protracted polemical effort conducted by the "free world" to combat Soviet intransigence on the human and national minority rights issue, and 2) a continuing attempt by the "newly emerging" areas to seize this issue as a means to further their own egalitarian objectives vis-à-vis the developed nations of the world. Also, the agreed-upon provisions in certain instances reflect a common international viewpoint, particularly concerning prerogatives of national (i.e., "statist") sovereignty over human and national minority rights. (Relevant provisions of these agreements as well as those of the basic United Nations Charter are provided as Appendices to this study.)

Pertinent United Nations Agreements on the Human and National Minority Rights Issue

The "Universal Declaration of Human Rights." On December 10, 1948, the General Assembly of the United Nations in its Resolution 217 (III) A adopted a "Universal Declaration of Human Rights" (see U.N. Doc. A/811). The voting was forty-eight for and none against. The following eight states abstained: Byelorussia, S.S.R.; Czechoslovakia; Poland; Saudi Arabia; Ukraine, S.S.R.; the U.S.S.R.; The Union of South Africa; and Yugoslavia. Most readers will find this abstention consensus particularly incongruous. "Racist" Saudi Arabia and South Africa in the company of such avowed "classless" societies as the Soviet Union, Czechoslovakia, Poland, and Yugoslavia. (What strange bedfellows politics makes! Evidently these diverse

131

societies share a mutual sensitivity to the human rights issue.)
The declaration, as such, is not a legally binding instrument
(particularly, of course, on the nations which abstained); however, its provisions either do constitute general principles of
international law or represent basic concerns of humanity.
More important, is its status as an authoritative guide to the
interpretation of the United Nations' Charter. In that capacity,
the declaration has decided indirect legal effect, and it is regarded by many as a part of the "law of the United Nations."

The declaration calls for inter alia the equality of all human beings regardless of race, color, sex, religion, national
or social origin, and political persuasion (Articles 1 and 2).
It also advocates equal rights before the law and equal protection from the law (Articles 6 and 7); freedom of movement (including the right to leave any country, including one's own) and
residence (Article 13); freedom to the right of nationality (Article
15); freedom of expression (Article 19); freedom of employment
and education (Articles 23 and 26); and freedom of thought, conscience, and religion (Article 18).[72]

It should be pointed out that automatic observance of the
provisions of the 1948 declaration is required by the ratification
of the two subsequent 1966 United Nations agreements; the
"International Covenant on Economic, Social, and Cultural
Rights," and the "International Covenant on Civil and Political
Rights."[73]

Illustrative of the Soviet Union's position and perhaps
also its ambiguity on the international human and national minority rights issue are the contributions of the Soviet representative during the General Assembly debates on the draft of the 1948
declaration. The Soviet representative considered that the draft
declaration did not satisfy the three conditions which were, in
the opinion of the Soviets, indispensable to the completion of
the declaration, namely: a guarantee of "basic freedoms for all,
with due regard to the national sovereignty of states [a recurring
Soviet theme]; a guarantee that human rights could be exercised
with due regard to the particular economic, social, and national
circumstances prevailing in each country [again a recurring Soviet
insistence in international debates on the human and national
minority rights issue]; and a definition of the duties of citizens
to their country, their people, and their state [which, more or
less, puts the issue in a "proper" Marxian context]."

The Soviet representative also considered that the article
dealing with the freedom to disseminate ideas did not solve the
problem of freedom of expression, and moreover, made no provision for the free dissemination of "just and lofty ideas [i.e.,

of the socialist persuasion]." He argued that if freedom of expression was to be effective "the workers must have the means of voicing their opinions, and for that they must have at their disposal printing presses and newspapers" -- a "guarantee" provided in the 1936 Soviet All-Union constitution, but ironically absent from the 1977 Soviet All-Union constitutional instrument. In addition, the Soviet representative advocated that the right to street demonstrations should be guaranteed and drew the Assembly's attention to a defect in the declaration which he considered to be fundamental: the "absence of provisions guaranteeing the rights of national minorities."[74] (Of course, the Soviet delegate's remarks pertained to the nonsocialist world only and not to the "complete democracy" allegedly enjoyed in the Soviet society.)

These particular Soviet amendment proposals are pertinent in that they not only depict the Soviet position but, moreover, exemplify the decided terminological gulf between the socialist and nonsocialist worlds. The Soviet conception of the human and national minority rights prerogative is focused only on the external capitalistic world -- it has no pertinent reality in the internal socialist environment, whereas the nonsocialist spokesmen perceive the issue as both international in character and as largely descriptive of the internal socialist milieu.

The dichotomous Soviet position is particularly reflected in the following specific amendments proposed by the Soviet representative during the 1948 deliberations:

Article 15 (Right to a Nationality)
The cases and the procedure of depriving a person of his nationality must be determined by national legislation. (Italics added.)

Article 18 (Individual Freedom of Thought)
Every person shall have the right to freedom of thought and freedom to practice religious observances in accordance with the laws of the country and the dictates of public [i.e., socialist] morality. (Italics added.)

Article 19 (Freedom of Opinion and Expression)
1. In accordance with the principles of [socialist] democracy and in the interests of strengthening international co-operation and world peace, every person shall be guaranteed by law the right to the free expression of his opinions and, in particular, to freedom of speech and

133

of the Press, freedom of assembly, and freedom of artistic
representation. The use of freedom of speech and the Press
for the purposes of propagating fascism and aggression or
of inciting to war between nations shall not be tolerated.
    2. In order to ensure the right of the free expression
of opinion for large sections of the peoples and for their
organizations, State assistance and co-operation shall be
given in providing the material resources (premises, printing presses, paper, and the like) necessary for the publication of democratic [i.e., socialist] organs of the Press.[75]

The 1948 deliberations also brought out what was to prove
to be continued Soviet intransigence over the external travel (emigration) right. According to a United Nations study entitled
Study of Discrimination in Respect of the Right of Everyone to
Leave Any Country, Including His Own, and to Return to His
Country (United Nations, 1963), when the pertinent article (13-2)
was discussed by the Third Committee of the General Assembly
in the autumn of 1948, the Soviet delegate expressed no opposition to the right "to leave any country, including his own," but
did propose an amendment which would add the words "in accordance with the procedure laid down in the laws of that country."
He commented that the proposed amendment "in no way modified
the basic text of the article" and that: "In the Soviet Union...
no law prevented persons from leaving the country, but anyone
desiring to do so had, of course, to go through the legally prescribed formalities." The proposed amendment was subsequently rejected as "unnecessarily restrictive," by a vote of seven
in favor, twenty-four against, and thirteen abstentions. Ironically, "racist" Saudi Arabia was among those few nations supporting the Soviet proposal.[76]

The "International Convention on the Elimination of All
Forms of Racial Discrimination." This convention was unanimously adopted by the United Nations General Assembly on
December 21, 1965.[77] It was subsequently opened for signatures on March 7, 1966, and signed by seventy-one states.[78]
This convention essentially reflects, although with more specificity, the same rights and privileges accorded in the 1948 declaration (in fact, the post-1948 agreements are intended to com-
plement and in some cases supersede the 1948 pact). As an
example of its specificity, Article 1 of the 1965 convention
stipulates that:

In this convention, the term "racial discrimination" shall mean any distinction, exclusion, restriction or preference based on race, colour, descent, or national or ethnic origin which has the purpose or effect of nullifying or impairing the recognition, enjoyment or exercise, on an equal footing, of human rights and fundamental freedoms in the political, economic, social, cultural or any field of public life.[79]

Other passages reflect comparable emphasis.

Although the Soviet Union abstained from the December 21, 1965, voting, it subsequently ratified the convention on January 22, 1969.[80]

The "International Covenant on Economic, Social, and Cultural Rights." This covenant was unanimously adopted by the United Nations General Assembly on December 16, 1966.[81] It was signed by thirty-nine states and stipulates human and national minority rights, more or less, comparable to those advocated in the 1948 and 1965 agreements, including the right to national cultural development and higher educational opportunity. The Soviet Union again abstained in the voting; however, subsequent Soviet ratification was given on September 26, 1973.[82]

The "International Covenant on Civil and Political Rights." This covenant was also unanimously adopted by the United Nations General Assembly on December 16, 1966, and again, the Soviets abstained.[83] It was signed by thirty-eight states (the Soviet Union subsequently signed on March 18, 1968) and for the most part, reiterates and in some cases enlarges upon those human and national minority rights guarantees advocated in the previous agreements. On the other hand, Article 18-3 offers the restriction that:

Freedom to manifest one's religion or beliefs may be subject to such limitations as are prescribed by law and are necessary to protect the public safety, order, health, or morals or the fundamental rights and freedoms of others.[84]

Although at first glance this limitation appears similar to the caveat expressed in Article 39 of the 1977 Soviet All-Union constitution which states that: "Exercise by citizens of rights

135

and freedoms must not harm the interest of society, the state,
and the rights of other citizens,"[85] reflection, on the contrary,
indicates a positive awareness of the need to safeguard majority
rights while advocating minority freedoms. Whereas, the stated
Soviet stipulations could be construed as an all-pervasive means
to restrict individual or minority rights and privileges.

The "International Covenant on Civil and Political Rights"
was ratified by the U.S.S.R. Supreme Soviet on September 26,
1973.[86]

The "Optional Protocol to the International Covenant on
Civil and Political Rights." This protocol, which also was
passed by the General Assembly on December 16, 1966, adds
to the machinery for implementing the "Civil and Political Rights"
covenant. It was signed by fourteen states, only one of which
by 1971 had ratified it. The Soviet Union abstained.[87]

Article 1 of the protocol is particularly pertinent to our
study. It states that:

> A State Party to the Covenant that becomes a party
> to the present Protocol recognizes the competence of the
> Committee [the so-called "Human Rights Committee" set
> up in Part IV of the Covenant on Civil and Political Rights]
> to receive and consider communications from individuals
> subject to its jurisdiction who claim to be victims of a
> violation by that State Party of any of the rights set forth
> in the Covenant. No communication shall be received by
> the Committee if it concerns a State Party to the Covenant
> which is not a party to the present Protocol.[88]   (Italics
> added.)

Although, as noted, the Soviet Union did ratify the "International Covenant on Civil and Political Rights," it has not yet
ratified the related protocol. This omission is particularly significant in that without ratification, Article 1 of the protocol
specifically forbids the referred-to United Nations "Human Rights
Committee" from receiving appeals from individuals or organizations alleging violations of rights. Instead, the two 1966 covenants provide that governments themselves will report on their
own human rights performances.

This concession, of course, supports the espoused Soviet
contention of ultimate national sovereignty jurisdiction over the

136

human and national minority rights issue. It also supports
Soviet efforts to control its internal dissident and minority
problems. A fact readily recognized by Soviet dissidents and
minority groups who have long complained of their inability to
appeal directly to an international body that could check into
the internal situation and bring remedial pressure to bear on
the Soviet government.

The "Helsinki Accords" and the Human and National Minority Rights Issue

The Conference on Security and Cooperation in Europe
(the "Helsinki Accords"), which opened at Helsinki on July 3,
1973, and continued at Geneva from September 18, 1973, to
July 21, 1975, was concluded at Helsinki on August 1, 1975,
with the signing of the "Final Act" by thirty-five nations, including the Soviet Union and all the Eastern European countries.
Follow-up meetings are called for by terms of the agreement,
the first of which was to be held in Belgrade, Yugoslavia in
1977.[89]

Included among the priority issues dealt with by the Conference members was the issue of human and national minority
rights. The resulting human and national minority rights provisions agreed upon in the Final Act reaffirm the rights and privileges enunciated in the previous international agreements. In
that essence, the Final Act states that:

> In the field of human rights and fundamental free-
> doms, the participating States will act in conformity with
> the purposes and principles of the Charter of the United
> Nations and with the Universal Declaration of Human
> Rights. They will also fulfill their obligations as set
> forth in the international declarations and agreements in
> this field, including inter alia, the International Coven-
> ants on Human Rights, by which they may be bound.[90]

Special emphasis in the Final Act provisions is given to
freedom of emigration, primarily motivated by Western concerns
over the Soviet Jewish emigration question:

> The participating States will deal in a positive and
> humanitarian spirit with the applications of persons who
> wish to be reunited with members of their family,[91] with
> special attention being given to requests of an urgent

137

character such as requests submitted by persons who
are ill or old.

They will deal with applications in this field as
expeditiously as possible.

They will lower when necessary the fees charged
in connexion [sic] with these applications to ensure that
they are at a moderate level.

Applications for the purpose of family reunification
which are not granted may be renewed at the appropriate
level and will be reconsidered at reasonably short intervals
by the authorities of the country of residence or destination,
whichever is concerned; under such circumstances fees will
be charged only when applications are granted....

They confirm that the presentation of an application concerning family reunification will not modify the
rights and obligations of the applicant or of members
of his family. [92]

As noted, the other human and national minority rights
provisions of the Helsinki Agreement largely reiterate comparable rights and privileges contained in the previous international agreements on this subject.

The significance of Helsinki. The Helsinki Agreement is
neither legally binding nor a treaty in the proper sense. However, as a political statement of intent signed at the highest
governmental levels, it does carry considerable moral and political persuasion. Consequently, the human and national minority
rights provisions contained in its Final Act are of distinct importance, not only in their own right, but more importantly when
linked with the earlier United Nations agreements on the human
and national minority rights issue.

As noted, in most instances, the provisions of the Final
Act compare substantially with similar provisions in the previous United Nations agreements. However, provisions in the
Final Act which relate to a person's right to travel (emigrate)
are considerably more restrictive in scope. Whereas, the 1948
Universal Declaration of Human Rights provides that "everyone
has the right to leave any country, including his own, and to
return to his country" (Article 13-2), and the International Covenant on Civil and Political Rights states that "everyone shall
be free to leave any country, including his own" (Article 12-2),
no such broad statement of principle is made in the Final Act.
Instead, "Basket III" ("Cooperation in Humanitarian and Other

138

Fields") focuses on the more limited aspects of the right of external travel based on the "reunification of families" and for
"marriages between citizens of different states." In that connection, it should be remembered that all emigration from the
U.S.S.R. prior to the Helsinki Conference had been based only
on the grounds of family reunification; and as noted previously,
it remains predominant today as the chief vehicle for leaving
the country. However, it must also be taken into consideration
that, as previously pointed out, the Final Act specifically binds
the participating members to "conformity with the purposes and
principles of the Charter of the United Nations and with the
Universal Declaration of Human Rights," as well as with "the
obligations set forth in the international declarations and agreements in this field," including the "International Covenants on
Human Rights" (in which the provisions on travel and emigration
are considerably more extensive).

Since the signing of the Final Act, the Soviet Union has
indeed relaxed certain emigration procedures based on the family reunification principle. For example, early in 1976, the
Soviets lowered the existing fee for an exit visa from four hundred to three hundred rubles;[93] the requirement for a "character
reference" (the so-called kharakteristika) from the emigration
applicant's local Party leader was replaced by the lesser requirement for a certificate of employment from his or her job
supervisor; children under the age of sixteen were to be included in family passports without charge; the payment of a
forty ruble application fee for travel documents was made mandatory only if the request was granted; and the waiting period
between appeals against rejected applications was reduced
from one year to six months.

There is the viewpoint that the Soviets made significant
and at the time, miscalculated concessions at Helsinki with
regard to the human and national minority rights guarantees
spelled out in Basket III and in Principle VII of the Final Act.
While it is true that the dissident elements in the Soviet Union,
and in Eastern Europe as well, have indeed seized upon these
"pledges," it is also true that these "concessions" achieved
what appear to be primary Soviet objectives for calling the
Helsinki meeting; i.e., the recognition of post-War II European
borders, the acceptance of Soviet diplomatic presence in
Western European Councils, and continuing Soviet access to
Western technology. The Soviets also were successful at
Helsinki in getting the "family reunification" principle accepted
as the chief grounds for emigration.

139

In addition, in assessing the tangible results of Helsinki, it is important also to remember that essentially the same human and national minority rights "commitments" contained in the Final Act provisions are espoused in earlier international agreements to which the Soviets either were a direct signatory or endorsed indirectly. Also, many of these same rights "guarantees" are already well covered in the various Soviet constitutional instruments. Consequently, it would appear that the Final Act "commitments," in themselves, do not represent a distinctive unilateral leverage for Soviet compliance. Their main importance, if any, rests in their linkage with previously enacted international agreements and in what moral persuasion they can exert on Soviet attitudes.

The Soviet Position on the Human and National Minority Rights Issue

Authoritative Soviet sources maintain that the U.S.S.R. has remained the "consistent champion" of the human and national minority rights cause and that, in fact, most of the international guarantees are already contained in the Soviet All-Union and regional constitutions (which, in fact, they are). These same sources argue that the West, on the other hand, has used the human and national minority rights issue as a pretext for "interference in the internal affairs of socialist countries" and for "violations of a country's sovereignty,"[94] a position steadfastly adhered to by the Soviets over the years -- as evidenced in repeated Soviet "abstension" in international voting on the human and nationality minority rights issue.

In defense of its own record in the human and national minority rights field, the Soviets argue that the West also has problems with fulfillment of the Basket III provisions; however, they maintain that they, themselves, are adhering to these provisions -- particularly with regard to emigration on grounds of family reunification. In addition, the Soviets continually define the human and national minority rights issue largely as pertaining to the fulfillment of "social" rights -- such as the right to education, employment, medical care, social security, etc. Also, the Soviets now point to their new constitution as the ultimate example of human and civil rights perfection.

The continuing intransigence of the Soviet position is perhaps best illustrated in the fact that in spite of the relative insignificance of the current internal Soviet dissident threat, Soviet preoccupation with maintaining effective internal control apparently overrides any concerns about Western views of internal repressive measures. It would appear, judging from past performance, that the Soviet leadership fears that any relaxation of control over internal dissidence and the question of minority rights could trigger a burgeoning explosive atmosphere, both within the U.S.S.R. and throughout the general Eastern European area. The Soviets apparently believe that any points of contention with the West over its internal human and minority rights policies are a manageable item. Consequently, Soviet "concessions" to the West with regard to internal Soviet policies and practices have been both few in number and consonant with the Soviet viewpoint.

Consideration of the Soviet Position

In the interest of maintaining proper intellectual objectivity, it is expedient to point out that contentions of national sovereignty over domestic situations is not peculiar to the Soviet Union. Practically all nations, including the United States, support that particular prerogative of statehood. This is reflected in the fact that all nations require that international agreements prior to implementation first must be ratified by the appropriate domestic organ or organs. In the United States, our constitutional system decrees the "ratification" responsibility to the Congress. In the Soviet Union, that responsibility is given to the Supreme Soviet of the U.S.S.R. Other governments have comparable constitutional arrangements.

Relatedly, it should be noted that the United States, in spite of its continuing advocation of the principle of international human and national minority rights, has only signed two of the described international agreements and this was done in belated fashion. It was not until October 5, 1977, that President Carter finally signed the covenants on "Economic, Social, and Cultural Rights," and on "Civil and Political Rights." Even in doing so, congressional ratification was not expected anytime in the near future.[95]

In that same context, it is of interest that relatively few nations, thus far, have ratified any of the referred-to international agreements. In fact, as of September 1973, reportedly only three western nations -- Sweden, Denmark, and Norway -- had, so far, ratified the two 1966 covenants.[96]

Another consideration is that like the United States, the Union of Soviet Socialist Republics essentially represents an extensive "federation." Therefore, it is important to distinguish

141

that in both societies, the American and the Soviet, the term "national minority" has neither legal meaning nor legal application. This is an especially important point when assessing Soviet "commitments" to international agreements on the national minority rights issue.

Another point of consideration lies in the very nature of the United Nations' organizational structure. As is well-known, resolutions passed by the General Assembly membership have little, if any, binding application. Only decisions reached by the United Nations' Secretariat have any real political significance. Therefore, it probably can be safely assumed that individual agreements attained through General Assembly resolution, at most, represent only a moral incentive for international compliance. A postscript to this apparent contemporary reality is the fact that, more often than not, the really crucial international issues (e.g., S.A.L.T., M.B.F.R., etc) are denied to the international quorum and restricted to "superpower" deliberation only. Thus, the essence of the Soviet "commitment" to the various General Assembly agreements on the human and national minority rights issue rests solely on moral grounds; the legality of such a "commitment" is highly questionable.

On the other hand, the veracity of the Soviet human and national minority rights "commitment" perhaps is best attested to by the observation that one of the very rights and privileges acknowledged by the Soviets in several of the referred-to international agreements[97] is basically "legally" denied in the Soviet Union, i.e., the right to conduct religious instruction. While several "token" religious training facilities are currently functioning in the Soviet Union, religious instruction to children is still, for all practical purposes, prohibited, as called for by the still-effective January 23, 1918, decree entitled "On Separation of Church from State and School from Church," and most recently reiterated in the 1977 All-Union constitution (Article 52).[98] This fact, coupled with the longtime official outlawing of Hebrew, the religious Judiac language, prompts one to question both the motives and integrity of the Soviet international "commitment" on this subject.

Finally, as Hannah Arendt succinctly points out:

> ...contrary to the best-intentioned humanitarian attempts to obtain new declarations of human rights from international organizations, it should be understood that this idea transcends the present sphere of international law which still operates in terms of reciprocal agreements and treaties between sovereign states; and, for the time being, a sphere that is above the nations does not exist.[99]

142

NOTES

1. As quoted in Harry G. Shaffer, The Soviet Treatment of Jews (New York, London, Washington: Praeger Publishers, 1974), pp. 3-4 [Hereafter cited as Shaffer, Soviet Treatment].

2. It is interesting to note the similarity in Tsarist and Soviet policies toward the Jews, i.e., the assimilationist objective.

Nove, "The Jewish Population," p. 127; Salo W. Baron, The Russian Jew Under Tsars and Soviets (New York and London: The Macmillan Co., and Collier Macmillan Publishers, 1964), pp. 6-7 [Hereafter cited as Baron, The Russian Jew].

3. Shaffer, Soviet Treatment, p. 3; Schwarz, Jews in the Soviet Union, pp. 6-7; Gitelman, Jewish Sections, p. 17; Simon M. Dubnow, History of the Jews in Russia and Poland: From the Earliest Times Until the Present Day, 3 vols., trans. I. Friedlander (Philadelphia: The Jewish Publication Society of America, 1916-20) 1: 52 [Hereafter cited as Dubnow, History of the Jews]; S. Ettinger, "The Jews in Russia at the Outbreak of the Revolution," in The Jews in Soviet Russia since 1917, ed. Lionel Kochan (London, New York, Toronto: Oxford University Press, 1970), p. 16 [Hereafter cited as Ettinger, "Outbreak of the Revolution"]; Louis Greenberg, The Jews in Russia: The Struggle for Emancipation, 2 vols. (New York: Schocken Books, 1976) I:1 [Hereafter cited as Greenberg, Jews in Russia].

4. Greenberg, Jews in Russia I:1-7.

5. Ibid., I: 8-11, 92, 96-97; Ettinger, "Outbreak of the Revolution," pp. 15-24.

6. Baron, The Russian Jew, pp. 29-30, 48; Abram Leon Sachar, A History of the Jews (New York: Alfred A. Knopf, Publishers, 1972), pp. 310, 313-15; Ettinger, "Outbreak of the Revolution," pp. 16-18; Greenberg, Jews in Russia, II: 19-47.

7. Schwarz, Jews in the Soviet Union, p. 9; Greenberg, Jews in Russia, I:91; Leonard Schapiro, Introduction to The Jews in Soviet Russia since 1917, ed. Lionel Kochan (London, New York, Toronto: Oxford University Press, 1970), p. 1 [Hereafter cited as Schapiro, "Introduction"].

8. Schwarz, Jews in the Soviet Union, pp. 10-13; Gitelman, Jewish Sections, p. 17.

9. Schwarz, Jews in the Soviet Union, pp. 14, 18-21; Gitelman, Jewish Sections, pp. 19-23; Baron, The Russian Jew, pp. 54, 75-98.

10. Gitelman, Jewish Sections, pp. 17-25; Ettinger, "Outbreak of the Revolution," p. 22; Greenberg, Jews in Russia, II:59-62, 73.

11. Schapiro, "Introduction," pp. 1, 3-4; Shaffer, Soviet Treatment, p. 5; Greenberg, Jews in Russia I:146-48; Joel Cang, Tho Silont Millions - A History of the Jews in the Soviet Union (London: Rapp and Whiting, Ltd., 1969), pp. 25-27 [Hereafter cited as Cang, Silent Millions].

Hannah Arendt states that the schism between rich Jews ("bankers of the State") and intellectual Jews (the "poor" Jews) prompted both Jewish intellectual anti-Jewish denunciation and hatred against the state and society -- and promoted the revolutionary zeal of individual Jewish intellectuals. Arendt, Totalitarianism, p. 64.

12. Greenberg, Jews in Russia, I:148.

13. Ibid.

14. Shaffer, Soviet Treatment, p. 5; Schapiro, "Introduction," pp. 3-4.

15. George Vernadsky, A History of Russia, 6th rev. ed. (New Haven: Yale University Press, 1961), p. 261 [Hereafter cited as Vernadsky, History of Russia].

16. Greenberg, Jews in Russia, II:10-13; Vernadsky, History of Russia, pp. 264-67.

17. Schwarz, Jews in the Soviet Union, pp. 47-49; Gitelman, Jewish Sections, pp. 25-46.

18. Similar to the Austrian nationality scheme promoted by the Austrian Socialists Bruno Bauer and Karl Renner.

19. The United Jewish Socialist Workers' Party was formed in May 1917 by the merger of the Zionist Workers' Party with the Jewish Socialist Workers' Party.

20. Gitelman, Jewish Sections, pp. 46-51, 64, 71-74, 105.

21. Ibid., pp. 97-98, 100-101, 105.

22. Ibid., pp. 105-06; Baron, The Russian Jew, pp. 202-03, 205; Cang, Silent Millions, p. 19.

23. Hillaire Belloc, The Jews (Boston, New York: Houghton Mifflin Co., 1922), pp. 55-56.

24. Gitelman, Jewish Sections, pp. 113-14, 117. The correct terminology for the Bolshevik secret police organ is the "Vecheka" (The All-Russian Extraordinary Commission for Combating Counter-Revolution, Sabotage, and Speculation). Local subcommissions of the organization were known as the "Cheka." The Vecheka was established on December 6 or 7, 1917. See Leonard Schapiro, The Communist Party of the Soviet Union, rev. & enl. ed. (New York: Vintage Books, 1971), pp. 165-66.

25. Ettinger, "Outbreak of the Revolution," p. 14.

26. Ibid., pp. 14-15; Schwarz, Jews in the Soviet Union, pp. 90-92; Gitelman, Jewish Sections, p. 105.

27. Gitelman, Jewish Sections, pp. 117-18.
28. Ibid., pp. 77-79. The Zionist movement in Russia was aided by the Balfour Declaration, published in November 1917, granting British approval of Palestine as a Jewish national homeland. Ettinger, "Outbreak of the Revolution," p. 27.
29. Medvedev, Near-Eastern Conflict.
30. Cited in Korey, Soviet Cage, p. 56.
31. Soviet Life, May 1972, p. 17; U.S., Foreign Broadcast Information Service (F.B.I.S.), vol. 2, USSR Domestic Affairs -- "Briefs," 24 July 1970, B-5.
32. T.H. Rigby, Communist Party Membership in the U.S.S.R., 1917-67 (Princeton, N.J.: Princeton University Press, 1968), pp. 383-88; J.A. Newth and Zev Katz, "Proportions of Jews in the Communist Party of the Soviet Union," Bulletin on Soviet and East European Affairs 4 (1969): 38.
33. Partiinaya Zhizn' [Party Life] 10 (Moscow: Izdatel'stvo "Pravda," May 1976): 16 [Hereafter cited as Party Life]; "Addendum to Dr. Rigby's Article on C.P.S.U. Membership," Soviet Studies 28 (October 1976): 615; American Association of Slavic Studies, Current Digest, vol. 23, no. 51 (January 18, 1972), "Zionists Called Imperialist Agents," pp. 11-12.
34. Schwarz, Jews in the Soviet Union, pp. 354-55.
35. Nove, "The Jewish Population," p. 152; Council of Ministers, Soviet Census of 1959.
36. "How Many Jews Are There in the Soviet Union?" Soviet Life, July 1972, p. 53 [Hereafter cited as Soviet Life, "How Many Jews?"]; The American Jewish Committee, American Jewish Yearbook 1976 (New York: The American Jewish Committee, 1976), p. 397; Council of Ministers, Soviet Census of 1970, 4:9.
37. Nove, "The Jewish Population," pp. 152-53.
38. Yakov Kapeliush, "Yidn in Sovetnfarband" [Jews in the Soviet Union], Sovetish Heimland 9 (1974): 177.
39. "The Truth About Jews in the U.S.S.R.," Moscow News, 21 February 1976 [Hereafter cited as Moscow News, "Truth About Jews"]; Soviet Life, "How Many Jews?" p. 53; American Association for Slavic Studies, "Jewish Culture," p. 7; American Association for Slavic Studies, Current Digest, vol. 28, no. 7 (March 17, 1976), "Soviet Freedoms Defined and Defended," p. 3 [Hereafter cited as American Association for Slavic Studies, "Soviet Freedoms"].
40. Moscow News, "Truth About Jews"; "We'll stay, but not quietly," The Economist, 6 August 1977 [Hereafter cited as Economist, "We'll Stay"].
41. V.M. Chkhikvadze, ed., The Soviet State and Law (Moscow: Progress Publishers, 1969), p. 192 [Hereafter cited as Chkhikvadze, Soviet State].

145

42. Karl Marx and Friedrich Engels, The German Ideology (Moscow: Marx-Engels-Lenin Institute, 1964), p. 357.

43. Chkhikvadze, Soviet State, pp. 194-95, 219.

44. Ibid., pp. 221-22.

45. Ibid., p. 227.

46. Ibid., pp. 240-62.

47. Ibid., pp. 266-71.

48. Jacob Miller, "Soviet Theory on the Jews," in The Jews in Soviet Russia since 1917, ed. Lionel Kochan (London, New York, Toronto: Oxford University Press, 1970), p. 44 [Hereafter cited as Miller, "Soviet Theory"].

49. Lenin, Sochineniya, 3d ed., 17:292.

50. Ibid., 24:96.

51. Stalin, Marxism, p. 84.

52. Gitelman, Jewish Sections, pp. 122, 133, 137, 260-61. A modern, more sinister version of the Yevkom/Yevsektsii concept occurred in the late 1960s with the establishment of a "Jewish Department" and "Jewish Sections" within the newly created Fifth Chief Directorate of the K.G.B. -- again, to deal specifically with the so-called Jewish problem. See Chapter 5, "Reorganization of the K.G.B. to Meet the New Jewish Challenge," for details.

53. See Central Statistical Administration, Soviet Census of 1926.

54. Prakticheskoe reshenie natsional'novo voprosa v Belorusskoi S.S.R. [The practical resolution of the national question in Byelorussia, S.S.R.], Part I (Minsk: 1927), p.120.

55. Studenikina, History in Documents, p. 532.

56. Ibid., pp. 56-58. An English language version is provided in Yuri Akhapkin, First Decrees of Soviet Power (London: Lawrence & Wishart, 1970), pp. 31-32.

57. Actually, this was the R.S.F.S.R. constitution of 1918 since the U.S.S.R. formally did not exist at that time.

58. Studenikina, History in Documents, p. 147.

59. Ibid., p. 531. Similar equal "national" rights provisions are included in the constitutions of other republics -- Article 15 of the Byelorussian constitution (1919), Article 32 of the Ukrainian constitution (1919), Article 7 of the Georgian constitution (1922), etc. Ibid., pp. 189, 197,340.

60. As previously mentioned, a new, and all-inclusive internal passport ruling implemented in January 1976, made it compulsory for all Soviet citizens, aged sixteen and older, to acquire internal passports, regardless of their domicile or place of work. F.B.I.S., "Soviet Decrees."

61. Pravda (Moscow), 28 December 1932; F.B.I.S., "Soviet Decrees."

62. Abramsky, "The Biro-Bidzhan Project," pp. 72-73; see also Schwarz, Jews in the Soviet Union, pp. 151-54. The official designation of Birobidzhan as an "autonomous oblast'" as mentioned elsewhere in this study is particularly pertinent since this particular identification signifies a distinct "national" administrative region.

63. Ugolovnyi Kodeks R.S.F.S.R. [Criminal Codes of the R.S.F.S.R.] (Moscow: Gosudarstvennoe Izdatel'stvo Yuridicheskoi Literatury, 1922), p. 18; Ugolovnyi Kodeks R.S.F.S.R. (Moscow: Gosudarstvennoe Izdatel'stvo Yuridicheskoi Literatury, 1953), p. 23; Ugolovnyi Kodeks R.S.F.S.R. (Moscow: Gosudarstvennoe Izdatel'stvo Yuridicheskoi Literatury, 1964), p. 39.

64. Verbatim constitutional texts are given in U.S.S.R., Constitution, pp. 23-29; and in U.S., Foreign Broadcast Information Service (F.B.I.S.), vol. 3, Special Report, Text of the U.S.S.R. Constitution, 7 June 1977, pp. 1-28 [Hereafter cited as F.B.I.S., Constitution Text]. (Pertinent verbatim English language texts are also provided as Appendices.)

65. Although, the 1961 C.P.S.U. program declared that the Soviet Union was now a "state of the whole people" and no longer a "dictatorship of the proletariat" -- ostensibly, as a result of the achievement of socialism and the transition to the "full-scale construction of communism."

66. As an illustration of the apparent conservative mentality of the authors of the 1977 constitution, Roy Medvedev contends that "in one of the working groups on the new constitution, it was decided to cross out from the draft on citizens' rights [chapter 7] a statute on the right of free exit and entry to the U.S.S.R. 'They will shout that we adopted that point under pressure,' allegedly said one of the Central Committee secretaries supervising work on the constitution." "Drive on Dissidents Creates Ominous Atmosphere," Washington Post, 5 June 1977 [Hereafter cited as Washington Post, "Ominous Atmosphere"].

67. F.B.I.S., Constitution Text.

68. TASS (Moscow), 5 June 1977.

69. See U.S.S.R., Constitution; F.B.I.S., Constitution Text.

70. F.B.I.S., Constitution Text.

71. According to The American Heritage Dictionary of The English Language, New College ed. (Boston, New York, Atlanta, Dallas, Palo Alto: American Heritage Publishing Co., Inc. and

Houghton Mifflin Co., 1975), a "convention" signifies "an international agreement dealing with a specific subject...a general agreement or acceptance." Whereas, the same source defines a "covenant" as a "binding agreement or contract between two or more parties." (Italics added.)

72. See United Nations, Official Records of the Third Session of the General Assembly, Part I (Lake Success, N.Y.: United Nations, 1948), p. 71 [Hereafter cited as United Nations, Official Records]; United Nations, Yearbook on Human Rights for 1948, Part 3 (Lake Success, N.Y.: United Nations, 1948), pp. 457-68 [Hereafter cited as United Nations, Yearbook on Human Rights for (year)].

73. United Nations, Yearbook on Human Rights for 1966, pp. 437-50.

74. United Nations, Yearbook on Human Rights for 1948-1949, pp. 532, 534.

75. United Nations, Yearbook on Human Rights for 1947, p. 459.

76. Jose D. Ingles, Study of Discrimination in Respect of the Right of Everyone to Leave Any Country, Including His Own, and to Return to His Country (Lake Success, N.Y.: United Nations, 1963), pp. 85-87.

77. The convention is annexed to Resolution 2016 (XX) of the General Assembly. See also Ian Brownlie, Basic Documents on Human Rights (Oxford, Clarendon Press, 1971), pp. 237-42 [Hereafter cited as Brownlie, Basic Documents].

78. The act of signing a convention or covenant is indicative of a state's general agreement and the support of the provisions of the treaty as well as intent to consider submitting it to the appropriate domestic body (or bodies) for ratification.

79. Brownlie, Basic Documents, p. 239.

80. Sovetskaya Rossiya [Soviet Russia] (Moscow) 27 September 1973 [Hereafter cited as Soviet Russia]; "Moscow ratifies 2 U.N. Covenants on Human Rights," New York Times, 28 September 1973 [Hereafter cited as New York Times, "Moscow Ratifies Covenants"].

81. The covenant is annexed to Resolution 2200 (XXI) of the General Assembly. See United Nations, Yearbook on Human Rights for 1966, pp. 537-41; and Brownlie, Basic Documents, pp. 199-210.

82. Soviet Russia; New York Times, "Moscow Ratifies Covenants."

83. This covenant is also annexed to Resolution 2200 (XXI) of the General Assembly. See United Nations, Yearbook on Human Rights for 1966, pp. 442-50; Brownlie, Basic Documents, pp. 211-31.

84. United Nations, Yearbook on Human Rights for 1966, pp. 449-50; also see Brownlie, Basic Documents, p. 219.

85. F.B.I.S., Constitution Text.

86. Soviet Russia; New York Times, "Moscow Ratifies Covenants."

87. "The "Optional Protocol" is also annexed to Resolution 2200 (XXI) of the General Assembly. See United Nations, Yearbook on Human Rights for 1966, pp. 450-54; and Brownlie, Basic Documents, pp. 232-36.

88. United Nations, Yearbook on Human Rights for 1966, pp. 450-51; Brownlie, Basic Documents, p. 232.

89. U.S., Department of State, Bureau of Public Affairs, Office of Media Services, Conference on Security and Cooperation in Europe, Final Act (Washington, D.C.: U.S. Government Printing Office, 1975), p. 75 [Hereafter cited as U.S.,Conference on Security].

90. Ibid., p. 81.

91. Family reunification has been, and remains, the only valid emigration "reason" accepted by the Soviet government.

92. U.S., Conference on Security, p. 114.

93. However, emigrants to Israel and other such "fascist" countries are still required to pay the additional five hundred ruble fee for renunciation of Soviet citizenship.

94. "December 10 Is Human Rights Day: In the Struggle for Genuine Humanism," Izvestiya (Moscow), 10 December 1976; U.S., Foreign Broadcast Information Service (F.B.I.S.), vol. 3, Soviet Newspapers Report Ratification of Rights Pacts, 28 December 1973, A-1.

95. "U.S. Fulfilling Promise, Signs 11-Year-Old Rights Pacts at U.N.," New York Times, 6 October 1977.

96. Soviet Russia.

97. I.e., the "Universal Declaration of Human Rights" (Article 18), the "International Covenant on Economic, Social, and Cultural Rights" (Article 13-3), and the "International Covenant on Civil and Political Rights" (Article 18-1).

98. See Studenikina, History in Documents, pp. 109-10; and F.B.I.S., Constitution Text.

99. Arendt, Totalitarianism, p. 298.

5
Soviet Policies and Actions, Official and Unofficial, Aimed at the Jews as a Distinct "National" Group

THE OFFICIAL NATIONALITIES POLICY

In spite of continued Soviet official statements to the contrary, any discussion of Soviet policies and actions directed specifically toward the Jewish minority inevitably must be housed within the context of the overall nationalities policy. That policy, as reflected in Communist Party resolutions, the Soviet constitutions, and public law, is based on the ideological acceptance of the concept of national self-determination and on the legal recognition of the right of all nationalities within the Soviet system either to sovereignty or various degrees of autonomy.

As mentioned previously, the overall nationalities issue and its related problems of national "separateness" and dissension have represented a particular area of concern for the communist leaders since the inception of the regime in 1917. As early as July 27, 1918, the Council of People's Commissars was obliged to issue a decree aimed at destroying the "anti-Semitic movement at its roots."[1] In addition, the R.S.F.S.R. Criminal Code of 1922 provided a minimum of one year's imprisonment for "agitation and propaganda arousing national enmities and dissensions." Also, the R.S.F.S.R. Criminal Code of 1927 provided for imprisonment of "no less than two years [for] propaganda and agitation aimed at arousing national and religious enmities and dissensions."[2] Furthermore, it is quite apparent that the current Soviet leadership is aware of and concerned about national relations in the Soviet Union. Politburo theoretician Mikhail A. Suslov has identified ethnic antagonism as one of the three major conflicts confronting Soviet society today; and a 1972 C.P.S.U. Central Committee resolution recognized the nationality problem as "one of the critical sectors in the [ongoing] struggle between socialism and capitalism."[3]

From the Soviet perspective, "bourgeois nationalism" represents a distinct threat to the very existence of the Soviet State because of the State's intrinsic multinational character. The Soviet leadership, however, using a variety of methods, has, thus far, managed to control the inherent explosiveness and centrifugal potential of the nationality issue. The leadership has accomplished this by tolerating and, on occasion, even encouraging, i.e., within acceptable ideological limits, the cultural diversity as represented by most ethnic groups. Representatives of leading national groups have been coopted and allowed significant opportunities for personal advancement in the Party, government, and other important societal sectors, although these opportunities largely are limited to their individual national areas.

Nevertheless, ethnic pressures have continued to build, resulting in the amendment of the Party theory of national relations. In the new Party Program, adopted in 1961 at the Twenty-Second Party Congress, it was stated that in the new period of communist construction, "...the nations [of the U.S.S.R.] will draw closer together, and their [ultimate] complete unity will be achieved."[4] This new formula was cast in dialectical terms. It affirmed that separate national cultures were to flourish by a "drawing together" (sblizhenie) stressing cultural phenomena common to all Soviet groups until the final dialectical leap to the achievement of "complete [socialist] unity" (sliyanie). This "drawing together" concept has continued in vogue and subsequently emerged as the leading nationalities theme of the Party in the deliberations of the Twenty-Fourth Party Congress held in the spring of 1971.[5] It since has received even greater emphasis as the Party's fundamental nationalities doctrine.

Relatedly, the C.P.S.U. leadership currently is seeking to spur the integration of the nationalities by linking the economies of the various republics more closely together. Proliferating economic linkages are being fostered by the development of the republican economies on the basis of a "scientific division of labor," i.e., economic development in each republic is to proceed on a specialized rather than on a universal basis (similar to the Khrushchev "specialization" proposal to the Council for Mutual Economic Assistance membership). The Party also plans to create large industrial or energy-producing centers of regional magnitude in the various republics. The Nurek hydroelectric facility in Tadzhikistan, for example, will eventually supply power to all the Central Asian republics and will, therefore, serve as an economic link between these republics. It is hoped that because of these regional industrial and energy-producing centers, interrepublic migration will increase, and the assorted nationalities will become

151

increasingly integrated. Ironically, this plan is reminiscent of
the Stalinist advocacy of "regional autonomy" as the "only real
solution" to the nationality problem:

[Regional autonomy] does not divide people according to nation, it does not strengthen national partitions; on
the contrary, it only serves to break down these partitions
and unites the population in such a manner as to open the
way for division of a different kind, division according to
class...it provides the opportunity for utilising the productive forces in the best possible way.[6]

In apparent recognition of the persisting nationalities schism,
C.P.S.U. spokesmen caution that it would be a "mistake to declare at this time that a 'Soviet nation' has been formed. A merger
of nationalities will take place only under full communism." Interestingly, the added caution is given that "premature declaration
of the existence of a monolithic [Soviet] nation would arouse the
ire of nationalistically oriented elements within the various republics."[7] (An official acknowledgment perhaps of the underlying volatility of the Soviet nationalities problem.)

The Continuing Ambivalence of Soviet Policy

A very real danger facing the Soviet system with regard to
the continuing nationalities problem appears to be the apparent
politicization of nationalism within the Party and especially within the Party leadership. This danger is emphasized by current
Soviet demographic trends which indicate accelerated and superior growth rates for the non-Slavic elements of the population.
Also, during the early 1970s there were definite indications that
individual high-ranking C.P.S.U. leaders such as Ukrainian Party
chief Shelest, Georgian Party chief Mzhavanadze, and Estonian
Party chief Kebin were becoming more and more influenced by
their respective local national affiliations. This inclination is
particularly reflected in the individual attempts by such leaders
to gain even more local autonomy than was permitted during the
"liberal" early 1970s period.
In that context, it should be noted that stemming from the
amorphous state of early post-Stalinist politics, national and
local particularism has become increasingly entrenched in Soviet
political life. The apparent diffusion of authority in the central
collective leadership prompted compromise and delay in central
decision making which allowed local Party leaders heretofore
unheard-of autonomy within their local spheres of authority.

152

The fact that several of the more important regional leaders were also Politburo members ensured that the nationality issue would not be merely a matter between Moscow and the provinces, but also a political issue in the Kremlin. There is evidence that following the aggregation of ethnic tensions caused by the intensified "Russification" program of the Stalinist period, national or ethnic pressures resurfaced in the struggle for power immediately following Stalin's death and played an important role in the efforts of contending leaders to obtain support. For example, L.P. Beria, in his abortive bid for power in 1953, allegedly championed local national rights. It reportedly was his view that the predominance of Russians in the leadership of the non-Russian republics had to be reversed. Concurrent with Beria's brief rise in the Central Committee Presidium, a Central Committee Plenum decision was passed on June 12, 1953, stating that the post of First Secretary in every republic had to be held by a local "national" and not by a Russian sent from Moscow. This policy ploy on Beria's part apparently was an attempt to use the divisive nationalities issue as a prime means to wrestle supreme power in the immediate post-Stalinist Party hierarchical struggle. However, Beria's initiative on behalf of local nationalism was ephemeral, since it was viewed by Khrushchev and the rest of the Kremlin collective leadership as an "anti-Party" attempt to "aggravate nationalist tensions between Russians and non-Russians as well as tensions between the central leadership in Moscow and the local leadership in the republics."[8] Consequently, Beria's quest for power was "derailed" and he was summarily deposed.

In the post-Khrushchev era, the nationalities issue once again came to the forefront in the continuing power struggle going on behind closed Kremlin doors. In the end, Party General Secretary Leonid I. Brezhnev was able to take advantage of conflicting local interests, play one local leader against another, and broaden his power base. In his quest for power, Brezhnev initially openly identified himself with the policy of giving preference to the less-developed Soviet areas with regard to economic development programs. That strategy, however, ultimately contributed to the mounting concern of several influential members of the Politburo, particularly Party theoretician Mikhail A. Suslov, that emphasis on local versus regional economic development would exacerbate local national "separateness" and dissension. As a consequence, Brezhnev, once his power base was solidified, abruptly reversed his position in his report to the Twenty-Fourth Party Congress in which he vigorously supported the espoused "Soviet people" concept as the fundamental nationalities doctrine of the C.P.S.U.[9] This inclusion apparently signalled Brezhnev's personal identifi-

cation with a tougher policy toward local nationalism and evidently also was intended to elicit expressions of loyalty to Moscow
where Brezhnev was "first-among-equals" in the collective Party
leadership.

As illustrated, the continuing official attitude toward the
nationalities issue largely has been an ambivalent one. This is
reflected particularly in, what appears to be, the considerable
behind-the-scenes ideological dispute on the important, though
largely hidden issue of Russian nationalism. Although Russian
nationalism is publicly discouraged, Soviet leaders have long
recognized its importance in the continuing competition for supreme power in the leadership hierarchy; plus, they have recognized the fact that the Russian language and the Russian people
provide the cement that holds the Soviet multinational conglomerate together. In that connection, individual Party leaders such
as Brezhnev, former First Deputy Premier Dmitri Polyansky, and
others are said, on occasion, to espouse strong Russian nationalist sentiments.[10] Further ambivalence in the official attitude
is shown in policies and practices directed specifically toward
the Jews -- which will be the subject of the following discussion.

THE JEWISH PREDICAMENT

Western Viewpoints

The Western Sovietologist, Leonard Schapiro, opines that
the fate of Soviet Jewry is intricately interwoven with the fate of
the political system of the U.S.S.R.: "The Jew suffers more than
the other Soviet citizen from the circumstance that he lives in a
totalitarian state, in which the principles of tolerance and equality
before an independent law are not observed." That same scholar
observes that much of what the Soviet Jews suffer is not directed
against the Jew alone, but rather any "nationality" and against
any religion in the Soviet Union. But, he notes that:

> ...the national consciousness of the Jew, where it
> exists, revolves around...religion and Zionism....Propa-
> ganda against priests does not...arouse hostile feelings
> against Armenians or Georgians, let alone against Russians.
> In contrast...lurid stories about the alleged immorality and
> dishonesty of a particular rabbi...suitably caricatured with
> a hooked nose and other distinctive Jewish features...stim-
> ulate hostility against the Jew as such....[This creates]
> a sense among non-Jews that the Soviet authorities treat

154

the Jews as second-class citizens, and that the Jews are, therefore, "fair game." The same line of reasoning applies to anti-Zionism.[11]

Another eminent scholar, Hans Morgenthau, observes that:

...there exists a residue of popular anti-Semitism in Eastern Europe which makes anti-Semitic arguments plausible because they meet the prejudices, the emotional preferences, of the population at large. However, the first objective reason why one might argue that anti-Semitism is inevitable not only in the Soviet Union but in any strictly totalitarian country seems to me to be the basic pretense of totalitarianism, and that it is the only source of truth and virtue available to a particular society. For this reason, it must be hostile to any religion not subservient to it.[12]

Still another Western Sovietologist, Alex Inkeles, perceives Soviet attitudes as a function of stress which develops when there is a "shift from class interest to ethnic interest: a class-based party becomes a ruler of an ethnic nation-state and comes to identify the class interest with [certain] racial or ethnic interests."[13] Vivid illustration of this in the Soviet example rests in the apparent leadership preference of the Russian national group over all other national entities -- as typified in the famous Stalin Red Army banquet toast of May 25, 1945:

I should like to drink to the health of our Soviet people ...and first of all to the health of the Russian people. I drink first of all to the health of the Russian people because it is the most outstanding of all the nations forming the Soviet Union....It has won in this war universal recognition as the leading force in the Soviet Union among all the peoples of our country....The confidence of the Russian people in the Soviet government was the decisive force which ensured the historical victory over the enemy of mankind -- fascism.[14]

More recently, this same Russian national preference was reiterated by Party General Secretary Brezhnev in his praise of Russian "revolutionary energy, selflessness, diligence, and profound internationalism" in his report to the Twenty-Fourth Party Congress.[15]

Inkeles and others note that in the Soviet Union there has been a very high rate of social mobility into the elite; as a consequence, many of the new "elites" bring with them many folk prejudices, including antisemitic sentiments.[16] (Former Soviet Party boss Nikita S. Khrushchev perhaps represents a prime example.) In addition, there still exist in the Soviet system what many western observers believe to be socioeconomic reasons for national dissension and prejudice, e.g., competition for job and higher educational opportunities (particularly in view of the reported higher educational "national quota" system).

Also, it is postulated that antisemitism often serves as a useful vehicle for relieving tensions both within the Soviet Union and between the Soviet Union and the individual countries of Eastern Europe; particularly in times of crisis -- a notable case in point is the 1968 Czech crisis. In that crisis, the Soviets blamed the Czech "troubles" solely on so-called "Zionist agents" who, according to the Soviets, were attempting to hand Czechoslovakia over to "international Zionism." Regarded by the Soviets as chief "Zionist culprits" were such Czech dignitaries as Eduard Goldstuecker, former Chairman of the Czechoslovak Writers' Union; Frantisek Kriegel, Czech Politburo member and Chairman of the National Front; Ota Sik, Deputy Premier; and Bohumil Lomsky, Minister of Defense. According to the Soviets, the "treacherous" activities of these individuals prompted the Soviet military intervention. [17]

Background to the Current Situation

During the early period of communist rule when the ideological fervor of "internationalism" and the "classless society" prospered, antisemitism was vigorously combatted by the communist leadership and Party. Even during the early years of Stalin's rule, no official antisemitism reportedly was practiced. In fact, Stalin himself told a Jewish Telegraphic Agency representative in January 1931 that antisemitism was "a phenomenon profoundly hostile to the Soviet regime and is sternly repressed in the U.S.S.R." He, in fact, referred to antisemitism as "a survival of the barbarous practices of the cannibalistic period." [18] Indeed, under Stalin's early rule, "Jews" (i.e., individual assimilated "Jews") continued to occupy high official positions. For example, Lazar M. Kaganovich remained as one of the Party's chief lieutenants, Maxim Litvinov was Foreign Minister, and Lev Mekhlis was a high security official. (Although it possibly could be argued with some validity that the continued presence of individual "Jews" in prominent positions was due primarily because Stalin's power position within the Party had not yet solidified, and he, therefore, was compelled to share his leadership role with other Party leaders, some who, incidentally , were "Jews.") [19]

156

A new era in the history of Soviet Jewry was ushered in at the time of the signing of the U.S.S.R.-Nazi Germany Nonaggression Pact in August 1939, when anti-Jewish discrimination reportedly became an integral part of official Soviet policy. According to the prominent Soviet dissident, Andrei Sakharov, antisemitism entered into the policy of the "highest [Soviet] bureaucratic elite" at that time.[20] As one direct consequence, the "Jew," Maxim Litvinov, was abruptly removed from his Foreign Minister's post, although this dismissal could also be seen as a diplomatic necessity in view of the new Soviet-Nazi alliance. This was the time also of the sudden influx of about two million "new" Jews into the Soviet Union from the incorporated territories of Poland, the Baltic states, and Moldavia. Substantial numbers of them were either handed over directly to the Nazi "allies" for immediate extermination, herded back to the German interior for subsequent extermination or forced labor, or exiled to forced labor camps in remote regions of the Soviet Union.

Following the Nazi invasion of the U.S.S.R. in June 1941, a wartime dualistic Jewish "situation" developed in the Soviet Union. One result was the creation of the Jewish "Antifascist Committee" in Moscow on April 7, 1942 (reportedly at the suggestion of the Soviet Foreign Minister) whose membership included the most prominent Soviet "Jewish" personalities, including the then Soviet Foreign Minister's Jewish wife, Madame Molotov (Zhemchuzhina), Central Committee member S.A. Lozovsky, General Aaron Katz, and cultural figures Shlomo Mikhoels, Itzik Fefer, and Ilya Ehrenburg. It was the first solely "Jewish" representative body since 1917 and the first "Jewish" central public body since the C.P.S.U. "Jewish Sections" were disbanded in 1930. A prime Soviet motivation for the formation of the committee was to win Western Jewish sympathy and material support for the Soviet wartime cause.[21]

The essence of such a committee is particularly pertinent to this study -- prominent Soviet personalities were allowed, and moreover, "encouraged" to come forward and be recognized, with the Government's blessing, as "Jews." Nothing could be more counter to the basic tenets of both Leninist and Stalinist theory on the "Jews," which denied Jewish "national" status and preached total and immediate assimilation. Although this deviation represented only a wartime expediency, it, nonetheless, illustrates what appears to be the continuing Soviet ambivalence on the Jewish issue.

Also, of a "positive" nature, Jews fought well in the war and reportedly had one of the highest ratios of "Hero of the Soviet Union" (the highest military honor) among all nationality groups.[22]

157

On the "negative" side of the coin, antisemitism was extensive not only throughout the Nazi-occupied Soviet territories and at the front, but in the inner parts of the country as well. Jewish survivors, returning after liberation to their former areas of residence, usually encountered both popular antisemitism and official discrimination. In that connection, it is reported that in 1942 the Soviet authorities disseminated a "secret" order establishing quotas for Jews in particular prominent positions.[23] In addition, Soviet defector Igor Gouzenko states that a "confidential" decree of the Party Central Committee was sent in 1939 to all directors of higher educational institutions establishing quotas of admission for Jewish students. He also comments that in the summer of 1945 he was told by the then chief of the "secret division of Soviet Intelligence" that the Central Committee had sent "confidential" instructions to directors of all factories to remove Jews from responsible positions.[24] Concurrently, there developed during the war a deepening Russian nationalism, almost bordering on xenophobia, with the result that those ethnic groups linked with "internationalism" e.g., the Jews, soon became a convenient target for prejudice and other discriminatory practices.

Three years after the end of the war, which more or less marked the beginning of the Cold War era, a particularly dark period for Soviet Jewry emerged. It was during those years that Jewish cultural institutions, including Yiddish language newspapers, publishing houses, schools, and theatres were once again closed by the Soviet authorities. Jewish authors and other intellectuals were arrested en masse and either deported or imprisoned; some were even executed. The wartime Jewish Antifascist Committee was abruptly disbanded in November 1948 and many of its members were either imprisoned or, as in the case of the Committee's chairman, Shlomo Mikhoels, more drastically discarded (Mikhoels was killed in an alleged "traffic accident"). It was during those years also (in January 1953 to be exact) that the so-called "doctors' plot" was hatched by Stalin in which seven of the alleged defendants, charged with the assassinations of several highly placed officials and the planned assassination of several others, were Jewish. The "plot" was subsequently exposed as a fabrication following the death of Stalin in March 1953.[25]

At the same time as these "black years" of Soviet Jewry were ripening, Stalin, according to his daughter, Svetlana Alliluyeva, was becoming more and more a Russian chauvinist and also, increasingly antisemitic. She writes that Stalin's antisemitic feelings were gradually transformed, over the years, "from political hatred to a racial aversion for all Jews bar none."

In that respect, both she and Khrushchev comment that Stalin's growing antisemitism was responsible for Alliluyeva's divorce from her first husband, Grigory Morozov, who happened to be a Jew. (Stalin had Morozov deported.) In fact, Khrushchev claims that Stalin "ordered" his daughter to divorce Morozov solely "because he was a Jew." Relatedly, according to Khrushchev, Stalin's heir apparent, G.M. Malenkov, soon thereafter followed Stalin's example and forced his daughter also to divorce her Jewish spouse. Both Alliluyeva and Khrushchev agree that Stalin eventually regarded all Jews as "treacherous and dishonest." In that essence, according to Khrushchev, Stalin viewed members of the Jewish Antifascist Committee as "agents of American Zionism " and considered their post-War II proposal to establish a Jewish State in the Crimea as an attempt by "American imperialism" to wrest the Crimea away from the Soviet Union. (Interestingly, Khrushchev subsequently "concurred" in Stalin's rejection of the Crimea resettlement proposal because he too feared "that in case of another war the Crimea might become a landing place and the enemies' bridgehead against the Soviet Union"; perhaps indicative of Khrushchev's personal antisemitism also.)[26]

Perhaps reflective of Stalin's personal antipathy toward the Jews is the comment of the late U.S. Ambassador to the Soviet Union, Charles "Chip" Bohlen, who is quoted as saying that Stalin had once remarked to him that "he did not know what to do" with the Jews: "I can't swallow them, I can't spit them out; they are the only group that is completely unassimilable."[27] In addition, Milovan Djilas, the dissident Yugoslav communist, reports a boast allegedly made to him by Stalin in 1946 that there were no Jews, whatsoever, in the Central Committee apparatus of the C.P.S.U.[28]

During these latter years of Stalin's reign, discrimination reportedly heightened against the Jews not only within the Party and State bureaucracy, but also in other sectors of the Soviet system, including admissions to the higher educational institutions. Roy Medvedev, in his brief May 1970 samizdat article, reports that during Stalin's "anticosmopolitan" campaign in the late 1940s and early 1950s, Jews were "cleansed" from the central Party governmental hierarchy (Central Committee, Council of Ministers, etc.), from the provincial and regional branches of the Party, from the military, from the diplomatic service, and the organs of the K.G.B. and the M.V.D. (Ministry of Internal Affairs), from the procuratorship (similar to our Attorney-General Office), from the courts, and from many other organizations.[29]

According to Medvedev, even after Stalin died in March 1953, Jews were continued to be denied "...access to positions in the higher Party apparatus, in the provincial and regional branches of the Party, in various kinds of central ideological institutions, in the higher organs of the military leadership, in the diplomatic service, in the organs of the K.G.B., and in the procuratorship." He also reports that Khrushchev continued to maintain the restrictive admissions quotas for Jews for many of the higher educational institutions, and that especially low quotas were set for Jews seeking entrance to military academies, military schools, and certain "special" civilian higher educational facilities. Also continued to be restricted was the size of the Jewish "leadership" in the scientific and cultural sectors, a situation which will be discussed in detail later in this study.[30]

Evidence of the continuation of officially sanctioned anti-semitic policies and practices following Stalin's death is also illustrated in the comments attributed to Khrushchev and to other leading Party dignitaries at the time. Khrushchev in a 1956 interview with a visiting French Socialist delegation acknowledged that popular prejudice against the Jews did play a role in affecting the Party's policies. He declared that:

> Should the Jews want to occupy foremost positions in our republics, now it would naturally be taken amiss by the indigenous inhabitants. The latter would ill-receive these pretensions, especially as they do not consider themselves less intelligent nor less capable than the Jews. Or, for instance, when a Jew in the Ukraine is appointed to an important post and he surrounds himself with Jewish collaborators, it is understandable that this should create jealousy and hostility toward Jews.[31]

Khrushchev subsequently claimed, in a speech to a Party-organized meeting of artists and intellectuals in December 1962, that were Jews to continue to occupy top posts, it would tend to create antisemitism.[32]

On that same subject, Yekaterina Furtseva, the late Soviet Minister of Culture, told a correspondent of the National al Guardian in 1956 that:

> The Government has found in some of its departments a heavy concentration of Jewish people, upwards of 50 percent of the staff. Steps were taken to transfer them to other enterprises, giving them equally good positions and without jeopardizing their rights.[33]

With regard to his own personal antisemitism, Khrushchev is reported to have commented angrily during the 1956 riots in Poland that there were too many Abramovitzes and Rabinovitzes, their names changed to end in "ski," in the Polish Party and government.[34] Conversely, Khrushchev continually denied the existence of any kind of antisemitism in the Soviet Union. He told former President Eisenhower in 1959 that "the Jewish people in the Soviet Union are treated like everyone else" and remarked to Bertrand Russell, the British philosopher, in 1963, that "there never has been...any policy of anti-Semitism in the Soviet Union since the very nature of our multinational socialist State precludes the possibility of such a policy." He reiterated that theme in a speech in March 1963 in which he stated that "no Jewish problem exists here [in the Soviet Union] and those who invent it are singing a foreign tune."[35]

While it is true that following the death of Stalin, the era of mass arrests and imprisonments came to an end -- Khrushchev subsequently released hundreds of thousands of political prisoners, including many Jews -- it is also true that Khrushchev, beginning in 1957, launched a renewed offensive against organized religion, particularly against religious Judaism. Many of the remaining synagogues, including the largest synagogues in L'vov and Chernovtsy were forced to close; and the ongoing propaganda campaign against religious Judaism increased in intensity and in vituperation.[36]

During the early 1960s (1961-64), the Khrushchev government also initiated an intensive campaign against so-called "economic crimes," which included such law violations as pilferage, bribery, and currency speculation. In May 1961, the Presidium of the Supreme Soviet adopted a decree extending earlier laws covering misappropriation of State property and illicit trading to embrace a host of newly designated "economic offenses." At the same time (May 1961), the Presidium reintroduced the death penalty for such offenses -- a punishment that had been dropped in 1947. The campaign, which was vigorously carried out on both the judicial level and on the propaganda level, soon appeared to take on a decidedly anti-Jewish character. Those individual cases involving Jewish defendants were extensively reported in the Soviet news media, often in inflammatory articles, usually disproportionate to the overall ratio of Jewish and non-Jewish citizens involved in such crimes. Furthermore, jail sentences imposed on Jews appear to have been particularly severe -- of the nearly 250 persons known to have been executed for economic crimes between 1961 and 1964, more than half reportedly were Jews.

A study of the economic crimes trials conducted by the
International Commission of Jurists concluded:

> ...there has been an insidious and sometimes
> subtle propaganda campaign directed against the Jewish
> people of the Soviet Union, specifically against those
> charged with economic crimes and also against the sup-
> posed general characteristics of Jews that have been
> reiterated for centuries...the number of Jews receiving
> death sentences and severe terms of imprisonment is
> greatly disproportionate to their number as a minority
> group.
>
> The charge has been raised of Jewish persecution
> linking their difficulties over synagogues or Passover
> bread with the unwelcome attention which Jewish defend-
> ants have received in the [Soviet] press in connection
> with economic crimes.[37]

As we shall see in subsequent portions of this chapter,
the largely discriminatory "Jewish" policies carried forth under
the Khrushchev government continue, in even more intensity,
today.

Spreading Antisemitism and its Effects Upon the Jewish Situation

The emergence of antisemitic, Russophile organizations
and sentiments. Largely in response to a number of determinant
factors, e.g., the high profile of the internal Jewish dissident
activism, the large number of Jewish citizens seeking emigration, the Soviet pro-Arab stance in the Middle East and its accompanying vitriolic anti-Zionist (i.e., antisemitic) propaganda
campaign, and the vehemence of international public opinion in
support of Soviet Jews, a growing wave of antisemitism reportedly has resurfaced in the Soviet Union in recent years.

Concurrent with this antisemitic revival has been the reported emergence of strong Russophile sentiments among influential elements of the population, including among high-ranking
members of the Party, military, and the intelligentsia.[38] This
Russian "xenophobia" has expressed itself, in one instance,
in the reported formation of the so-called Za Rodinu (For the
Motherland) movement and Rodina (Motherland) clubs throughout the country. These clubs allegedly periodically meet to
assess the strength of Russian "patriotism" and also to discuss
ways of combatting unwanted Jewish influence in the country
for which most members reportedly favor total emigration as the

most effective remedial action. The membership in these clubs now reportedly numbers in the several millions. Other ramifications of this Russophile resurgence have been the growth of circles of "Russite" writers and artists, and renewed intellectual interest in Russian Orthodox Christianity and the preservation of Russian historical monuments and churches. Ironically, one of the causes attributed to this resurgence of the Russian national consciousness is the "tacit, if grudging, recognition in recent official policy of the 'right' of Soviet Jews to reclaim their homeland in Israel [permitting by analogy a similar 'right' for Russians to repossess traditional Russia]."[39]

Discrimination in employment. There appears to be considerable evidence available to support the contention that Jews are indeed subject to continuing discriminatory policies and practices in employment. According to Soviet emigre Mikhail Zand, in approximately January 1970 there was a meeting in the Science and Higher Education Section of the Central Committee of the C.P.S.U. attended by the leading Soviet academicians, military personnel, and chaired by U.S.S.R. Academy of Sciences Chairman Mstislav Keldysh. The topic of discussion was the removal of Jews from prominent positions in which they could affect national security. The participants in the meeting were asked how long it would take to rid their organizations of Jews. The scientific representatives estimated seven years; but the military representatives at the meeting allegedly refused to answer, expressing concern that precipitous action might adversely affect military capabilities. As a result of the meeting, a circular, apparently issued by the U.S.S.R. Council of Ministers, was distributed concerning the "undesirability of employment at responsible levels in institutions connected with defense, rocket, atomic, and other secret work of persons belonging to a nationality the state organization of which [Israel] pursues an unfriendly policy in relation to the U.S.S.R." Consequently, Jews ostensibly were to be denied employment in such governmental bodies as the U.S.S.R. Ministry of Foreign Affairs, the Ministry of Defense, the Intelligence Services, the Academy of Sciences, and the Ministry of Foreign Trade.[40]

Medvedev, in his previously mentioned samizdat article, apparently refers to the same U.S.S.R. Council of Ministers' circular for he notes: "And thus, we see, as the replacement of the previous formulas about the 'non-indigenous population,' which served as a basis for discrimination against Jews... there are new formulas regarding 'persons belonging to a nationality the state organization of which pursues an unfriendly policy in relation to the U.S.S.R.'"[41] Medvedev also makes the interesting observation that apparently even those "Jews" who are not identified as such in their internal passports also are not exempt from discriminatory practices since "personnel departments and special departments [in institutes, factories, etc.] continue to consider these people as Jews....In recent years, in many closed institutions [i.e., closed to Jews], in the hiring for responsible jobs, and even in several universities, a questionnaire is filled out in which there are two columns: 'father's nationality' and 'mother's nationality'."[42] (If either parent is "Jewish" the application is to be denied.)

Pursuant to the Zand and Medvedev observations, it apparently was indeed intended by the Soviet authorities to replace Jews who held responsible positions, although the original estimate of within "seven years" appears somewhat accelerated. That possibility is attested to by the January 15, 1975, Radio Australia report that Soviet Premier Aleksei N. Kosygin had told former Australian Prime Minister Whitlam in Moscow that "many Jewish scientists and technologists had applied for exit but the Soviet Union could not let them all go at one time." He reportedly added that "within four or five years, when other people were trained to take their place, their emigration vouchers would be looked at sympathetically."

Jews, for all ostensible purposes, reportedly have been virtually eliminated from the diplomatic service of the U.S.S.R. in which they once were prominently represented. There reportedly are very few, if any, Jewish ambassadors today and no Jews are being admitted to diplomatic training schools. Even the foreign service in the commercial field, is reportedly closed to Jews.[43]

Jews also have been virtually eliminated from leading positions in the Soviet military. From the end of World War II up to 1953 over three hundred high-ranking Jewish officers in the Soviet Army were pensioned off, among them sixty-three generals. Today there are very few Jews, if any, left in such positions and no Jews are being admitted to military academies.[44]

In recent years, there also has been reported a host of ongoing discriminatory practices levied specifically against Jewish scientists, professors, writers, and other intellectuals, involving, inter alia the right to publish, obtain or change employment, travel outside the country, carry on research considered related to national security, maintain professional contact with foreign colleagues, etc. -- in effect, discriminatory practices tantamount to complete exclusion from all professional activity.[45]

Perhaps typical of such discrimination is the case of a
world-renowned Jewish scientist and Corresponding Member of
the U.S.S.R. Academy of Sciences, Veniamin Levich. Levich,
once his emigration plans became known, was summarily dismissed from his position as head of the research institute he had
founded and also, was relieved of his teaching responsibilities
at the prestigious Moscow State University. He was no longer
allowed to publish and in addition, his name was immediately
expunged from scientific journals and books. Other Jewish intellectuals, such as physicist Veniamin Fain and sinologist Vitaly
Rubin, suffered comparable denigrations.

A discriminatory practice which has aroused considerable
protest in the West is the denial to Jewish scientists of the right
to attend international conferences, even those held in the Soviet
Union. For example, physicists and magnetism specialists Aleksandr Voronel, Mark Azbel, and Mosei Gitterman were excluded
from the International Conference on Magnetism which took place
in Moscow in August 1973, and Professor Levich was excluded
from the Fourth International Biophysics Conference held in Moscow
in August 1972.

In addition, Jewish intellectuals, once dismissed from their
professional positions, find it extremely difficult, if not impossible,
to find suitable employment in their fields. This is an extremely
difficult and even dangerous predicament since unemployed persons
in the Soviet Union are subject to legal prosecution under the so-
called "parasite" law. In fact, both Levich and Rubin, after losing
their jobs, were formally accused of "parasitism" although not pro-
secuted in a court of law.[46]

Discrimination in higher education. Perhaps a most crucial
aspect of alleged discrimination against the Jewish minority concerns
the "quota system" in the admission practices of universities and
institutes, which represent the key to individual career fulfillment.[47]
The quota system was first officially justified in a major work entitled
Social progress, published in Gorky in 1970 by the leading Kremlin
ideologue, V. Mishin. In that work, Mishin advocates a sharp reduction in the number of specialists with higher education and endorses
the numerus clausus as the prime means to accomplish that end. (It
should be noted that since the early 1950s there has been a glut of
secondary school graduates seeking admission to Soviet higher educational institutions. To alleviate the situation and also, to channel
more Soviet youths into the hard-pressed active labor ranks, the Soviet authorities had earlier sought a solution by enacting the controversial Educational Reform Act of 1958.) The essence of the quota system operates on the principle of "equivalent-balance," i.e., the representation of any national or ethnic grouping in overall higher

165

educational enrollment should be as the relation of the numerical size of that group to the total U.S.S.R. population. This existence of a numerus clausus and in some instances even numerus nullus spells disaster for the great majority of Jews seeking higher educational opportunities, since Jews represent approximately only 1 percent of the total population.[48] As one consequence, according to Aleksandr Voronel, this increasing lack of higher educational and professional career opportunity prompts more and more Jewish intellectual families to emigrate.[49]

There are varying figures available regarding the numbers of Jews allowed into these higher educational institutions -- Zand quotes the figure of 3 percent as the most universal admissions quota for Jews.[50] Medvedev notes that the quota system "varies from city to city and from university to university." For example, he asserts that the quota on Jews is less in Kiev than it is in Moscow, less at Moscow State University than at Moscow State Polytechnical Institute.[51] As noted earlier, in military academies, diplomatic and intelligence training schools, Jews are excluded altogether. It is even claimed that Jews are now excluded altogether from admission to Moscow State University, Leningrad State University, as well as "other first class universities."[52]

In that connection, it is reported by several Soviet sources that Jews are now being compelled as a result of the described restrictive quotas to seek higher educational opportunities in Siberia and in the Asian republics where university admission practices are considerably freer.[53] This possibly accounts for the relatively high proportion of Jewish students in these republics where the overall Jewish population is not all that significant.

Although authoritative Soviet sources maintain that the described quota system applies to all national and ethnic groups and does not single out the Jews for special treatment, the fact remains that the Jewish minority has been the group most adversely affected by the policy's implementation. This is borne out by the rather drastic reduction in recent years in the total Jewish representation in both the student higher educational and scientific manpower sectors. (Relevant and detailed statistical data are provided in Chapter 2.)

The Soviets also present what on the surface appears to be the valid contention that as a multinational and formally federalized system, it must adhere to stipulated national higher educational quotas to ensure equal higher educational rights for its citizens, i.e., according to the prescribed national "equivalent-balance" concept. In that context, the Soviet authorities maintain that the Jewish minority, over the years, had achieved a superior higher educational imbalance at the expense of the other ethnic groups. (A point perhaps supported by the decidedly disproportionate Jewish higher educational percentages

up to 1970.)[54] In all objectivity, this contention appears to have
some logical and legal merit, particularly, when considering the
fact that higher educational quotas, albeit of a different kind,
are also a fact of life in the United States and in most other countries. However, in most noncommunist countries, higher educational quotas are neither centrally dictated nor designed to limit
minority higher educational participation. On the contrary, most
are spawned on a local basis and as in the case of the United
States, designed to protect specific individual and minority higher educational interests, according to some determinative criterion
such as intellect, sex, race, or religion, even to the possible
detriment of majority higher educational prerogatives. (The Supreme Court Bakke litigation is a case in point.) Even the restrictive "out-of-state" admissions quota system which is practiced
in most American state universities is designed to protect the
higher educational rights of a distinct minority (the citizenry of
the particular state) from infringement by the "outside" majority
group, even though the individual state institution, in most instances, receives considerable "outside" (federal) financial
support.

Therefore, in spite of the Soviet contentions, their possible
legal merit, and the existence of prevailing "restrictive" higher
educational admissions quotas in other countries, the fact remains
that the Soviet quota system is not only singularly catastrophic to
Jewish higher educational hopes (as evidenced in the referred-to
statistical data), but, moreover, is morally unjustified. It is
morally unjustified because the Soviet quota system basically
treats the Jews (and certain other ethnic groups as well) as a
distinct "national" group, which is to their decided disadvantage;
yet, official Soviet utterances refuse to concede Jewish "nationality." (The age-old dichotomy persists!) In addition, the espoused "equivalent-balance" quota system perpetuates the Great
Russian national dominance at the expense of minority interests
and aspirations. This is evidenced in the increasing numbers of
Russian nationals in the higher educational and scientific manpower sectors. Another refutation of the expressed Soviet contentions is evidenced in both the timing of the increased higher
educational restrictions (they concur with accelerating Jewish
emigration) and their coincidence with other restrictive measures
apparently designed to thwart the Jewish emigration initiative --
e.g., the "educational reimbursement" tax, more stringent and
increased "parasite" law enforcement, etc.[55]

Escalation of repressive measures against the Jewish minority. A growing campaign has been initiated by the Soviet

167

authorities not only to harass Jewish and other activists, including imposing individual jail sentences, exiles, and psychiatric detentions, but to discredit and eliminate them by attempting to link them with "treasonable" activities allegedly carried out on behalf of foreign intelligence. Medvedev concludes in a paper privately circulated in Moscow that: "These are not routine actions of the K.G.B. but were [actions] sanctioned at the highest Party level."[56] Medvedev believes that a basic decision was taken by the Politburo in the fall of 1976 to heighten dramatically the pressure on the activists and to cut off their contacts with the West, from which they draw moral support.[57] A prime example of this renewed Soviet "vigilance" concerns prominent Jewish human rights activist Anatoly Shcharansky, who was arrested on March 15, 1977, and formally charged on June 1, 1977, with "treason and espionage" against the Soviet State under Article 64-A of the R.S.F.S.R. Criminal Code. Conviction under this Article could result in a prison term of ten to fifteen years, or even death.[58] (Shcharansky is a charter member of the Moscow-based "Orlov Group" which sought to monitor Soviet compliance with the Helsinki Agreement on Human Rights.)

As part of the Shcharansky scenario, several U.S. Embassy Moscow, officials who had maintained personal contact with members of the Moscow Jewish community, were accused by the Soviets of involvement with Shcharansky in alleged intelligence-gathering activities on behalf of American Intelligence.[59] In addition, Los Angeles Times correspondent Robert C. Toth was similarly charged because of his personal contacts with Shcharansky and with another Jewish citizen from whom he was accused of receiving "State secrets." It should be noted that all the Americans involved had been subjected previously to constant Soviet harassment tactics designed to curtail their individual contacts among the Jewish activist community, including constant surveillance, late-night telephone calls, denial of internal travel permission, etc.[60]

Reorganization of the K.G.B. to meet the new "Jewish Challenge." In the 1960s, pursuant to the awareness of the Soviet leadership that dissent in the Soviet Union was becoming a serious problem, the Committee for State Security (K.G.B.) apparatus was reorganized with a view to coping more effectively with it. As a consequence, a new K.G.B. directorate known as the "Fifth Chief Directorate" was established in late 1966 or early 1967 to deal with this increasingly "dangerous" phenomenon; it was charged with the "political security" function and concerned with specified segments of the Soviet

168

population -- "religious groups, the intelligentsia, nationalist groups, and former political prisoners."[61]

Correspondingly, in 1970-71, the age-old Party concept of the Yevkom (Jewish Commission) was resurrected with the establishment of a so-called K.G.B. "Jewish Department" probably located within the newly established Fifth Chief Directorate organization. "Jewish Sections" (Yevsektsii), or on occasion, a single K.G.B. officer tasked with the responsibility for Jewish matters, reportedly were then located in individual localities where Jews constituted a significant portion of the population.[62]

In its assigned role as the regime's arm for monitoring the "Jewish Street," the K.G.B. undertook a host of activities aimed at disrupting and ultimately negating the distinctive threat to the Soviet system which Jewish activism was thought to represent. By all accounts, this assigned K.G.B. role has accelerated in recent years to the point where it now encompasses every known coercive tactic, ranging from routine surveillance and harassment to the ultimate accusation of espionage and betrayal.

The most common K.G.B. procedures used against Jewish activists involve such widespread tactics as mail and telephone monitoring, censorship activities, unannounced detention and interrogation, employment blacklisting, house arrest, conscription for military service, and character assassination. The more serious aspects of the K.G.B. offensive which are becoming more prevalent are depicted in the following individual examples. In 1973, two young Jews, Mark Nashpits and Boris Tsilionok, were sentenced to five years' exile for their part in a peaceful demonstration in Moscow; another Jew, Luzar Lubarsky, was sentenced to four years in a corrective labor camp for "anti-Soviet slander" under Article 190-1 of the Criminal Code; and several other Jews were threatened with similar prosecution. In addition, in 1975 Dr. Mikhail Shtern was sentenced to eight years' imprisonment on charges of "accepting bribes"; and in 1976 Jewish activists Boris Chernobyisky and Iosif Ass were charged under Article 206 of the Criminal Code with "malicious hooliganism," a charge which could bring five years' imprisonment. Of course, the culmination of the K.G.B. offensive, thus far, is reflected in the 1977 treason charges levied against Jewish activist Anatoly Shcharansky, a charge which, as noted, carries a minimum penalty of ten years' imprisonment and a maximum penalty of death.

In addition to these "Jewish responsibilities," the individual K.G.B. units reportedly routinely receive all Jewish emigration applications from the Visa and Registration Department (O.V.I.R.) of the Ministry of the Interior and in actuality, "process" these

169

applications. That is, the local K.G.B. units initiate contact with the applicant's employer, review the applicant's personal history statement, call in selected applicants for "interviews," and make recommendations regarding approval or disapproval of the individual application.[63]

Intensification of the antisemitic propaganda campaign. As a result of the Six-Day War in June 1967, and the Soviet Union's involved support of the Arab cause in that war, the Soviet media launched a vituperative campaign against Israel, Zionism, and Judaism, with direct and indirect antisemitic inclusions. Since the early 1970s the antisemitic overtones of that campaign have been intensified under the guise of "fighting Zionism" to heretofore unheard of dimensions.

Of course, the regime's campaign against Zionism dates further back than the June 1967 war. As pointed out earlier, Soviet fears and concerns about the so-called "Zionist threat" go back to the inception of the communist government in November 1917, when Russian Zionism and the Hebrew language were marked for early extinction by the regime. But, never has the Soviet effort been so vociferous as it is today.

Illustrative of the particularly virulent nature of most of the literature connected with this Soviet campaign is the book, Polzuchaya kontrrevolyutsiya (Creeping Counterrevolution), written by Soviet author, Vladimir Begun, and published in 1974. Pertinent excerpts from this book include the following:

> ...the specific interest of Jewish chauvinists is the encitement of antisemitism....imaginary antisemitism is the tried and tested weapon of Zionists....Antisemitism can occur as the spontaneous reaction of the oppressed strata of the toiling population to their barbarous exploitation by Jewish bourgeoisie....We do not grieve today if our fathers, grandfathers, and great-grandfathers desperate in their distress and want, treated their oppressors disrespectfully, regardless of whether they were native or alien by blood.... [The Jewish religion is] an extremely reactionary monotheistic religion... [and the] synagogue remains a potential basis for subversive activity.[64]

The author also holds the "Zionists" responsible for the 1968 upheavals in both Poland and Czechoslovakia. Most interesting is the author's use of nonexistent religious Judaic writings (which were later exposed as forgeries) to depict the "hostile nature" of religious Judaism and the alleged Zionist threat of

170

"world domination." Ironically, these quotations reportedly
were taken word-for-word from a 1906 Russian pamphlet circulated
by the antisemitic "Black Hundred" in collaboration with the Tsarist secret police in order to provoke pogroms as reprisal for the
1905 revolution.[65]

A comparable work, Against Zionism and Israeli Agression,
written by Soviet writer Dmitri Zhukov includes the following
passages:

> The foundation of Zionism has always been and remains
> religion....The Zionists proceed from the idea that God pro-
> claimed the Jews as "His chosen people."...It was precise-
> ly this that gave birth in antiquity to the savage provision
> of the Talmud which taught the Jews to hate people of a
> different faith, the "Goyim," to fool them in every way
> and, when opportunity arose, to destroy them. It is pre-
> cisely this that inspires the present Zionist thugs to com-
> mit those "heroic deeds" the documents of this collection
> mention: to destroy entire villages, not sparing women
> and children, to rape little girls.[66]

In illustration of the extensive nature of this current campaign, similar works, all apparently officially sanctioned, include:[67]

> Vozniak, N.V., Their True Face (Kiev: Noyve Knigi
> Ukrainy, 1974).
> Sitnikov, G.O. and Verest, G.V., Together They Do
> Black Business (Kiev: Novye Knigi Ukrainy, 1974).
> Mitin, N., ed., The Ideology of International Zionism
> (Moscow: The Political Literature Publishing House, 1974).
> Brodsky, R., The Truth About Zionism (Moscow: Novosti,
> 1974).
> Savtsov, V.Y. and Rozenblum, N.Y., The Black Webs
> of Zionism (Kiev: Literature of the Ukraine, 1974).
> Belenki, M.S., Judaism (Moscow: The Political Liter-
> ature Publishing House, 1974).

In addition, there were the earlier "classics" by the Ukrainian
author Trofim Kichko entitled, Judaism Without Embellishment
(1963), and Judaism and Zionism (1968), which more or less set
the stage for the current works.

This largely euphemistic "anti-Zionist" (i.e., antisemitic)
offensive is triggered by the spontaneous desire on the part of a
considerable number of Jews to emigrate. In response, articles

and editorials in the press, commentaries on television and widely-circulated books attempt to dissuade Jews from emigrating. Life in Israel is depicted in the most deplorable of terms, noting, _inter alia_, the "unfriendly"reception accorded Soviet immigrants, the housing shortage and spiraling inflation, Israel's continuing "militarization" posture, and the "probability of perpetual war," etc. Concurrently, the Soviet campaign expounds on the equal rights and opportunities afforded to Jews as members of the working class in the Soviet "socialist" society, as "guaranteed" by the constitution and other laws.[68]

This campaign,which apparently is intended primarily for domestic consumption, attempts to convince Jews (and probably other ethnic groups as well) that regardless of supposed external cultural ties, the Jewish working class has nothing in common with the "reactionary" capitalist Jews of Israel and the nonsocialist world. The campaign attempts to portray "Zionists" as anti-socialist, anti-Soviet, and as holding values which are contradictory to those of the Soviet people (including Jews). In addition, the ongoing campaign stresses the "unity of Soviet culture" and the "integral" role which Jews and Jewish culture play in it. It also denies the existence of an international Jewish culture and attempts to link Zionism to imperialism. At the same time, Soviet spokesmen, ironically, have found it necessary to rebuke the Soviet press and literary circles for continuing to use "absolutely incorrect terms" such as the "Jewish people" and even the "Jewish nation." These spokesmen have also admonished the press and even the authors of the Great Soviet Encyclopedia publication to refer to Jews as an "ethnic group" and not as a "nationality."[69]

Reflection on the Antisemitism problem. Discussion of whether or not officially sanctioned antisemitism flourishes today in the Soviet Union would not be complete without consideration of the following. Is Soviet policy toward the Jewish minority specifically "antisemitic" in nature or would comparable policy initiatives be enacted against any "deviant" group, regardless of its ethnic affiliation? There is reason to believe that indeed comparable policies would be implemented against any group whose members continue to proclaim their "national" uniqueness in direct opposition to both basic Leninist-Stalinist principles and sixty years of continuous State efforts to the contrary. This peculiarly "nonsocialist" attitude is compounded by the insistence of many of the group members to seek "abandonment" of the Soviet society altogether by emigrating -- a "sin" regarded as unforgivable by most of the Party elite and general public. Ipso facto,

172

such individuals, according to the prevailing Soviet mentality, must be considered "traitors to the Soviet Motherland" and as "enemies of the working class."[70]

In pursuing this question, it is believed pertinent to point out that in contradistinction to the Western moralistic principle of protection of the rights of the innocent, no such ethical concern apparently is prevalent in the Soviet Union, at least as far as Jewish rights are concerned. As we have seen in the preceding portions of this chapter, the innocent are punished right along with the guilty, if nothing more than by the prevailing wave of antisemitism which is sweeping the Soviet Union. It is also evident that the generality of the recent policy measures directed specifically against the Jews (e.g., the restrictive employment policies) precludes any fine delineation between guilty and innocent; all are to suffer. In addition, even in those measures of alleged more general application, e.g., the higher educational quota system, the Jews are victimized the most.

Significant to this question of whether or not antisemitism is indeed embedded in the referred-to policy initiatives is the corresponding question of whether or not popular antisemitism is extensive in contemporary Soviet society. The investigation carried forth in this study strongly indicates that it is. Perhaps also supportive of this contention are the data accumulated by the "Harvard Project on the Soviet Social System," conducted in 1950-51. In its interviews of 329 Soviet refugees, approximately 60 percent held negative stereotypes of Jews. In spite of its relative age, the Harvard study is still thought pertinent to the current Soviet situation.[71] Consequently, the view must be taken that the Soviet policy in question is indeed inherently antisemitic, regardless of its possible hypothetical applicability to other groups.

If indeed Soviet policy with regard to the Jewish minority is to be judged basically antisemitic, then the additional question could be asked -- what is to be the extent of the Soviet liability for this infraction? As enunciated previously in this study, Jews in the Soviet Union today apparently are denied basic rights and privileges "guaranteed" not only through the various Soviet constitutions, Party resolutions, and other official enactments, but also through Soviet "commitments" resulting from international agreements concluded with other sovereign nations on the human and national minority rights issue. However, in spite of what may be considered the questionable legality of the Soviet policy actions, the fact remains that the reality of the international system promotes, at most, only a final judgment of moral wrongdoing on the part of the Soviet government. There is no available legal indictment alternative.

173

Furthermore, it should be noted that the intensity of the current Soviet antisemitic propaganda campaign, the severity of the official crackdown on Jewish activism, and the apparent limitations placed on Jewish educational and career opportunities tend to support the view that a widescale anti-Jewish purge is currently going on in the Soviet Union. As we shall see in the following chapter in our discussion of the Jewish emigration issue, this view is complemented by the apparent Soviet decision to "let the Jews go."[72]

NOTES

1. Izvestiya (Moscow), 27 July 1918.
2. Ugolovnyi Kodeks R.S.F.S.R. [Criminal Codes of the R.S.F.S.R.] (Moscow: Gosudarstvennoe Izdatel'stvo Yuridicheskoi Literatury, 1922), p. 18; Ugolovnyi Kodeks R.S. F.S.R. (Moscow: Gosudarstvennoe Izdatel'stvo Yuridicheskoi Literatury, 1953), p. 23.
3. "Preparations for the 50th Anniversary of the Formation of the Union of Soviet Socialist Republics," Partiinaya Zhizn' [Party Life] 5 (March 1972): 12.
4. U.S., Foreign Broadcast Information Service (F.B.I.S.), vol. 7, Special Report, Text of Khrushchev Draft Program at the 22nd C.P.S.U. Congress, October 1961, p. 69.
5. Joint Publications Research Service (J.P.R.S.), General Secretary Brezhnev's Report at the 24th C.P.S.U. Congress (Arlington, Va.: Joint Publications Research Service, December 20, 1971), Special Report No. 54742-1, pp. 89-94 [Hereafter cited as J.P.R.S., Brezhnev Report].
6. Stalin, Marxism, pp. 50-53.
7. Unidentified public (Znanie) lecturer, Moscow, March 21, 1973.
8. Soviet Analyst, March 2, 1972; S. Talbot, ed., Khrushchev Remembers, with an Introduction by E. Crankshaw (Boston: Little, Brown & Co., 1970), pp. 329-30 [Hereafter cited as Talbot, Khrushchev Remembers].
9. See J.P.R.S., Brezhnev Report, pp. 89-94.
10. Radio Liberty, Target Area Listener Report No. 200-70, June 22, 1970, Soviet Leadership Divided on Anti-Semitism?; Carl A. Linden, Soviet Politics and the Revival of Russian Patriotism (Washington, D.C.: The Institute for Sino-Soviet Studies, the George Washington University, n.d.), pp. 1-76 [Hereafter cited as Linden, Revival of Russian Patriotism].
11. Schapiro, "Introduction," pp. 6-8. For pertinent

174

examples of the continuing Soviet antisemitic effort see the
subsequent subchapter, "Intensification of the Antisemitic
Propaganda Campaign."

12. Hans J. Morgenthau, "The Jews and Soviet Foreign
Policy," Perspectives on Soviet Jewry (1971), p. 86.

13. Alex Inkeles, "Anti-Semitism as an Instrument of
Soviet Policy," Perspectives on Soviet Jewry (1971), pp. 76-
83 [Hereafter cited as Inkeles, "Anti-Semitism"].

14. Quoted in Hans Kohn, "Soviet Communism and Nationalism: Three Stages of a Historical Development," in Soviet Nationality Problems, ed., Edward Allworth (New York and London:
Columbia University Press, 1971), p. 59; Izvestiya (Moscow),
25 May 1945.

15. J.P.R.S., Brezhnev Report, pp. 89-94.

16. Inkeles, "Anti-Semitism," pp. 76-83. A study of the
top Party leadership on both national and regional levels in 1958
and 1962 shows that almost one-half of them have peasant fathers.
Furthermore, only 6 percent have whitecollar origins, while a little
more than a quarter have proletarian origins. Almost 40 percent
of the leadership either acquired no education beyond the secondary school level or attended only Party institutions. Of those who
completed college, 40 percent studied engineering and 30 percent
agronomy -- "narrowly specialized and highly applied skills."
George Fischer, The Soviet System and Modern Society (New York:
Atherton Press, 1969), pp. 65-117

17. As illustration of the Soviet propaganda offensive
see Vladimir Begun, "An Unarmed Invasion," Neman, no. 1
(1972).

18. New York Times, 15 January 1931; Pravda (Moscow),
30 November 1936.

19. There are those observers who even argue that as
late as the early 1950s, Stalin was still concerned about "Jewish" opposition within the Party hierarchy. In that context they
opine that "Stalin's last anti-Jewish campaign, the 'doctors'
plot', [was] a means to an end: the last great purge...of the
old members of the Soviet Politburo." This position is supported
by the former Soviet leader, Nikita S. Khrushchev, who also
described the "doctors' plot" as a prelude "aimed at the removal
of the old Politburo members and the bringing in of less experienced persons so that these could extol him [Stalin] in all
sorts of ways." See Paul Lendvai, "Jews Under Communism,"
Commentary, December 1971, p. 70 [Hereafter cited as Lendvai,
"Jews Under Communism"]. The Khrushchev quote reportedly
was contained in his secret speech to the Twentieth Party Congress in February 1956 as cited in Basil Dmytryshyn, U.S.S.R.:

A Concise History (New York: Charles Scribner's Sons, 1965), p. 263.

20. Andrei Sakharov, Progress, Coexistence, and Intellectual Freedom (New York: W.W. Norton, 1970), pp. 65-66.

21. Eynikayt (Ainikeit) was the official news organ of the Committee. In addition to serving Soviet propaganda purposes, it also was a source of information about Jewish life in the U.S. S.R. See Shimon Redlich, "The Jewish Antifascist Committee in the Soviet Union," Jewish Social Studies 31 (January 1969): 25-36; and Talbot, Khrushchev Remembers, p. 259.

22. Solomon M. Schwarz, Yevrei v Sovetskom Soyuze (1939-1965) [Jews in the Soviet Union: 1939-1965] (New York: The American Jewish Committee, 1966), pp. 43-177 [Hereafter cited as Schwarz, Yevrei]; R. Ainsztein, "Soviet Jewry in the Second World War," in The Jews in Soviet Russia since 1917, ed., Lionel Kochan (London, New York, Toronto: Oxford University Press, 1970), pp. 269-87.

23. Armstrong, "Soviet Foreign Policy and Anti-Semitism," p. 67.

24. Igor Gouzenko, The Iron Curtain (New York: Dutton Publishers, 1948), pp. 157-58.

25. Schwarz, Jews in the Soviet Union, pp. 198-231; Also see Svetlana Alliluyeva, Twenty Letters to a Friend (New York: Harper & Row, 1967) [Hereafter cited as Alliluyeva, Twenty Letters]; and B.D. Weinryb, "Antisemitism in Soviet Russia," in The Jews in Soviet Russia since 1917, ed., Lionel Kochan (London, New York, Toronto: Oxford University Press, 1970), pp. 307-11 [Hereafter cited as Weinryb, "Antisemitism in Soviet Russia"]; Talbot, Khrushchev Remembers, pp. 261-62.

26. Alliluyeva, Twenty Letters, pp. 162, 197-98, 206, 217; see Talbot, Khrushchev Remembers, pp. 260, 262-64, 269, 292-93; Arieh Tartakower, "The Jewish Problem in the Soviet Union," Jewish Social Studies 31 (January 1969): 290-91 [Hereafter cited as Tartakower, "Jewish Problem"]; J.B. Salsberg (Saltzberg), "Anti-Semitism in the U.S.S.R.?" Jewish Life (February 1957), p. 38, as cited in Korey, Soviet Cage, p. 53 [Hereafter cited as Salsberg, "Anti-Semitism"]; Cang, Silent Millions, pp. 135-36.

27. See Charles Eustis Bohlen, Witness to History, 1929-1969 (New York: W.W.Norton, 1973).

28. Milovan Djilas, Conversations with Stalin (New York: Harcourt, Brace & World, 1962), p. 154.

29. Medvedev, Near-Eastern Conflict.

30. Ibid.

176

31. Quoted in Korey, Soviet Cage, p. 53; also see Realites (Paris), May 1957, p. 104; Decter, Perspectives, p. 14.

32. Khrushchev's comments were quoted from the London Observer, 13 January 1963.

33. National Guardian, 25 June 1956.

34. See Alexander Werth, Russia: Hopes and Fears (New York: Simon and Schuster, 1969), p. 25.

35. Richard Cohen, ed., Let My People Go (New York: Popular Library, 1971), p. 10; Pravda (Moscow), 28 February 1963; Ibid., 30 March 1963; Ibid., 8 March 1963.

36. See Rothenberg,"Jewish Religion," pp. 176-79.

37. Cang, Silent Millions, pp. 156-67; "Economic Crimes in the Soviet Union," Journal of the International Commission of Jurists (Summer issue, 1964), pp. 3-47.

38. Such political "opposites" as former First Deputy Premier Dmitri Polyansky and novelist/historian Aleksandr Solzhenitsyn are purported to harbor strong Russophile beliefs.

39. Linden, Russian Patriotism, pp. i, 1-2, 27; also see Associated Press (Moscow), 29 November 1976; and Reuters (Moscow), 25 September 1975.

40. Mikhail Zand, Yevreiskii vopros v S.S.S.R. (Tezisy) [The Jewish Question in the U.S.S.R.: Theses] (Moscow: A samizdat [self-published] document authored in May 1970) [Hereafter cited as Zand, Jewish Question]; see also Medvedev, Near-Eastern Conflict.

41, Medvedev, Near-Eastern Conflict.

42. Ibid.

43. Ibid.; Tartakower, "Jewish Problem," p. 293; Zand, Jewish Question.

44. Tartakower, "Jewish Problem," p. 293. According to Medvedev (see Near-Eastern Conflict), no Jews have been allowed to enter Soviet military academies since 1967.

45. In response to their total professional exclusion, Jewish scientists in Moscow conceived the idea of holding informal seminars in their homes, a practice which culminated in their launching of an international seminar on "Collective Phenomena and the Applications of Physics to other Fields of Science" which was to be held in Moscow from July 1-5, 1974. Although the proposed "home seminar" initiative received widespread international support, it was subsequently squelched by the Soviet authorities.

46. "The Fate of a Russian Pariah," Washington Post, 3 April 1976 [Hereafter cited as Washington Post, Russian Pariah"]; Litvinoff, "Captive Scientists," pp. 3-7; Reuters (Tel Aviv), 27 November 1974.

47. Revised and more discriminatory Jewish higher educational quotas reportedly were levied in 1968. Voronel and Yakhot, Jewish Identity, pp. 25-37.

48. N. Dewitt, Education and Professional Employment in the U.S.S.R. (Prepared for the National Science Foundation by the Office of Scientific Personnel, National Academy of Sciences, National Research Council, Washington, D.C.: U.S. Government Printing Office, 1961), p. 3 [Hereafter cited as Dewitt, Soviet Education]. Other "national" groups such as the Ukrainians, Latvians, Byelorussians, Armenians, Georgians, Azerbaidzhanis, etc., also experienced a decline in total numbers attending higher educational institutions, but not as significant as the Jews. See National Economy for 1970, pp. 648, 651; National Economy for 1972, p. 651; Statistical Directorate, Moscow in Figures, 1971-1975, p. 160.

49. Voronel and Yakhot, Jewish Identity, pp. 25-37.

50. Zand, Jewish Question.

51. Medvedev, Near-Eastern Conflict.

52. Washington Post, "Russian Pariah."

53. Radio Liberty, Listener Report, no. 13-73, March 6, 1973, Pyatigorsk Student Listener to RL Speaks of Jewish Communities Springing Up in Siberia; Radio Liberty, Background Information, Report no. AR-8-73, June 8, 1973.

54. See Dewitt, Soviet Education.

55. In the Soviet Union, so-called "parasites" (persons without steady employment) are subject to legal prosecution and imprisonment "for up to two years" under the provisions of Article 209 of the R.S.F.S.R. Criminal Code. See Vedomosti R.S.F.S.R., 33 (869) [Herald of the R.S.F.S.R.], August 14, 1975.

56. The Medvedev paper is discussed in Washington Post, "Ominous Atmosphere."

57. Ibid.

58. Shcharansky subsequently was sentenced by a Moscow court to thirteen years' "imprisonment and hard labor" for alleged espionage activities on behalf of the U.S. government. The Supreme Court of the R.S.F.S.R. also levied a concurrent seven-year sentence on Shcharansky for "anti-Soviet agitation and propaganda." See "Scharansky [sic] Verdict: 13 Years Prison, Labor," Washington Post, 15 July 1978. In 1971, the Soviet authorities were forced by adverse international opinion publicly to eschew treason charges which had been levied under Article 64 (which specifies "flight abroad" as a treasonable act) of the R.S.F.S.R. Criminal Code against the so-called "Leningrad hijackers."

59. In recent years, the U.S. Department of State has made it a practice to assign at least one Jewish officer to the Political Section of the Embassy in Moscow for reportorial purposes.

60. "Soviet Charges [sic] a Key Jewish Human-Rights Activist With Treason," New York Times, 2 June 1977 [Hereafter cited as New York Times, "Soviet Charges a Key Jewish Activist"]; New York Times, 16 June 1977; Los Angeles Times, 12 June 1977.

61. See John Baron, "The Control Mechanism," in Understanding the Solzhenitsyn Affair: Dissent and Its Control in the U.S.S.R., ed. Ray S. Cline (Washington, D.C.: The Center for Strategic and International Studies, Georgetown University, 1974), pp. 8-13 [Hereafter cited as Baron, "Control Mechanism"].

62. Ibid.

63. See Emanuel Litvinoff, ed., "Open Assault on Jews and Judaism," Insight 1 (July 1975): 1 [Hereafter cited as Litvinoff, "Open Assault on Jews"]; Idem, "Captive Scientists," p. 4; "Two Moscow Jews Face Charge of 'Hooliganism' After Protest," Christian Science Monitor, 3 November 1976; New York Times, "Soviet Charges a Key Jewish Activist" ; "A Picnic with the K.G.B.", Washington Post, 24 November 1974; Baron, "Control Mechanism."

64. Vladimir Begun, Polzuchaya kontrrevolyutsiya [Creeping counterrevolution] (Minsk: Izdatel'stvo "Belarus," 1974), pp. 16-17, 46, 51, 57, 60, 71, 78-79, 83-84, 90.

65. The prime example is the turn-of-the-century forgery and classic antisemitic writing, the Protocols of the Elders of Zionism. See Lendvai, "Jews Under Communism," p. 67.

66. Dmitri Zhukov, Against Zionism and Israeli Aggression (Moscow: Nauka Publishing House, 1974), as cited in Litvinoff, "Open Assault on Jews," p. 6.

67. These publications, of course, are in addition to the extensive array of central and regional press, television, and public lecture coverage of the subject.

68. See U.S.,Foreign Broadcast Information Service (F.B.I.S.), vol. 3, Izvestiya Rebuts Zionist Claims about Soviet Jews, 12 January 1977, R-2.

69. Radio Liberty, Research Report, no. RL-235/73, July 26, 1973, An Intensification of the Antisemitic Campaign in the Soviet Press; "Moscow vs. Zionism," Washington Post, 11 November 1976; U.S., Foreign Broadcast Information Service (F.B.I.S.) "Pravda Official Rebukes Soviet Press for Softness on Zionism," Trends in Communist Propaganda, 31 October 1973, pp. 30-31 [Hereafter cited as F.B.I.S., "Pravda Offical Rebukes"].

70. This Soviet inclination, unfortunately, has been assisted on occasion by premature declarations of allegiance to the State of Israel by individual Soviet Jews.

71. See Raymond A. Bauer, Alex Inkeles, and Clyde Kluckhohn, How the Soviet System Works (Cambridge, Mass.: Harvard University Press, 1956).

72. Although there apparently has been a Soviet leadership decision to allow a sizeable number of Jews to leave the Soviet Union, certain "necessary" or nutzliche Juden have been retained in the Soviet system in relatively important positions, albeit in definitely consultative roles rather than in policy making capacities. For example, there is G.A. Arbatov, director of the prestigious U.S.A. and Canada Institute in Moscow (who is thought to be at least part Jewish) and also, Bentsion Milner, currently deputy director of the Institute of Systems Research, Moscow, and formerly a departmental chief in the U.S.A. and Canada Institute.

6
The Jewish Emigration Issue

PERTINENT BACKGROUND

The current Jewish emigration reality does not represent a
new phenomenon in mass Jewish migrations from Russia to Israel
(and before its formation, Palestine). In actuality, there were
several previous Russian Jewish "waves" or aliyah (a Hebrew
word which literally means "ascents") prior to the recent exodus.
Both the first wave, which lasted from 1882 to 1903, and the
second wave, which lasted from 1904 to 1913, consisted of predominantly Jews from Russia. They established the first Jewish
agricultural colonies, created the first kibbutz settlements, and
founded both the Histadrut (the Jewish Federation of Labor) and
the main political parties which remain the dominant political
forces in Israel today. The third wave of immigrants, which occurred between 1919 and 1922, was also composed predominantly
of Jews from Russia. In the subsequent waves of immigration
(1923-26, 1932-39, and the immediate post-1948 Israeli period),
Soviet Jews did not play a prominent role, although considerable
numbers of Jews from the "annexed territories" did proceed to
Israel following their repatriation to Poland as a result of the
Soviet-Polish Repatriation Agreement of March 25, 1957.[1]
In commenting on background thought pertinent to the current emigration situation, reiteration should be made of the tremendous impact which the founding of the State of Israel on May
14, 1948, had on Soviet Jewry (and on world Jewry as well). The
realization that a "national Jewish homeland" now existed, coupled with the actual presence of Israeli diplomatic representatives
in Moscow (following the 1948 Soviet recognition), ignited a spontaneous "national" reawakening for many Soviet Jews. Of equal
importance, from that reawakening there developed what would
prove to be an ever-growing Jewish disavowal of allegiance to
the Soviet Union and a concurrent demand for the "right to emigrate."

181

It is with some irony to note that in 1948 the then senior Soviet representative to the United Nations, Andrei Gromyko, who is the current Foreign Minister, actually spoke in favor of the creation of the Jewish State -- to diminish British control in the area and also to promote budding Soviet diplomatic initiatives for the Middle East. Relatedly, the U.S.S.R. was one of the first countries to recognize Israel, granting de jure recognition within two days. The Soviets also provided the young Israeli State with desperately needed military weapons (mostly from Czechoslovakia) during Israel's initial military encounters with the Arab nations.[2]

JEWISH EMIGRATION IS NOT UNIQUE

Contrary to the popular belief, the exodus of Jews from the Soviet Union in recent years does not represent a unique national experience in the affairs of the Soviet State. In fact, there have been a number of comparable ethnic emigrations, albeit less extensive in size, in recent Soviet history. For example, under the terms of the Soviet-Polish Repatriation Agreement which was concluded on March 25, 1957 (it was subsequently extended until September 30, 1957, and then again until March 31, 1959), some two hundred thousand Polish citizens were repatriated to Poland.[3] Interestingly, it has been estimated that probably 7 or 8 percent of these repatriates were Jews.

Another pertinent example involves the repatriation of Spanish nationals, commencing in the fall of 1956. These individuals, for the most part, had been youngsters who had been sent to the Soviet Union in the late 1930s by the Spanish Republican Government. According to "official" Spanish governmental data, as cited by Korey in The Soviet Cage, between 1956 and 1959 a total of 1,899 adults had been repatriated under this program.[4]

Other examples are the continuing repatriation of substantial numbers of Greek nationals to Greece, and Koreans to Korea. Included among the Greek repatriates are those who fled during the Greek Civil War and those whose ancestors settled in Russia centuries ago.[5] The Korean repatriates come from the estimated seven thousand Koreans remaining in Sakhalin, where they were sent by the Japanese in 1942-43.

More recent and possibly more noteworthy examples of non-Jewish ethnic migrations from the Soviet Union, of course, involve the ongoing departures of ethnic Germans and Armenians. Since 1971 (up to June 1, 1977), approximately thirty-eight thousand ethnic Germans have left the Soviet Union; after the Jews, they

182

form the largest group of current Soviet emigrants. In 1976 alone, 9,704 ethnic Germans departed the U.S.S.R. and resettled in the Federal Republic of Germany.[6] In the more distant past, between 1950 and 1969, 21,988 ethnic Germans emigrated from the U.S.S.R. -- this number includes the approximately 14,000 who were former prisoners-of-war or were from Memel (German Lithuania). Also in recent years, the outward flow of Armenian nationals from the Soviet Union has substantially increased -- up to June 1, 1977, eleven thousand Armenians had emigrated.[7] This increase is illustrated especially in the so-called "direct" emigration channel to the United States, i.e., not involving intervening "third-country" transit, where Jews and Armenians, for the period 1973-76, together constituted 90 percent of the U.S.-bound Soviets receiving exit permits. Whereas Jews constituted 66 percent and Armenians 24 percent of this group at the beginning of the period, the ratio was reversed at the end of 1976, with Jews accounting for 30 percent and Armenians 60 percent.[8]

Reflection on the Armenian exodus brings to mind the ironic circumstance that the Soviet Union had fostered its own version of "Zionism" -- or "return to the homeland" movement -- which prospered in the immediate post-War II period. Through this "movement," an attempt was made, which was largely successful, to lure back former citizens, who, during the war and before, had migrated to the far-flung corners of the earth. This large-scale "repatriation" effort was directed toward most, if not all, of the individual nationalities, e.g., Russian, Ukrainian, Byelorussian, Georgian, etc.; but particular attention was given to urging Armenians to return. Although many did return under this program, the success of the Armenian repatriation effort subsequently was clouded by the fact that many of the "returnees" became disaffected and consequently, proved "unassimilative." Furthermore, like the Jews, the Armenians have maintained extensive family ties outside the U.S.S.R. which have contributed to their national "separateness" and emigration propensity. Consequently, similar to the Jewish case, the Soviet authorities apparently made a reluctant decision to allow the Armenian "nonconformists" to leave.

In addition to these emigrations, the Soviet authorities have the extreme Jewish emigration example set by Poland commencing in the late 1950s (and gaining particular momentum during the "Gomulka purges" of 1968) which triggered the mass exodus of almost all of Poland's Jewish minority -- including the approximately fourteen thousand Jews who had returned to Poland following the Soviet-Polish Repatriation Agreement of March 25, 1957. The great majority of the Polish Jews eventually went to

Israel. In that context, it is interesting to note that the Soviets apparently, at the time of the signing of the Soviet-Polish Repatriation Agreement, were aware of the distinct possibility that many of the Jewish repatriates eventually would find their way to Israel. This is reflected in a 1957 statement attributed to the then Soviet leader Nikita S. Khrushchev, who reportedly commented that "we knew that many of them [Jewish repatriates] would go to Israel from there [Poland]."[9]

Jewish departures comparable to the Polish exodus also occurred in the immediate postwar period in Romania, Bulgaria, and in most of the other Eastern European countries -- with most of the emigres going to Israel.[10] Therefore, we can see that there was considerable precedence for the Soviet Jewish emigration initiative and that contrary to common belief, the emigration "privilege" is not confined to the Jews alone, although it is highly restricted.

THE MOTIVATIONAL ASPECT

The question of why an individual leaves a country in which he or she was born, grew up, and lived in for a good part of their adult lives is a most difficult question to answer, and in most cases cannot be resolved by a single, simplified explanation. This is especially true of the Soviet Jewish emigration and its related motivational factors.

It should be recognized that the Soviet Jewish propensity to emigrate is greatly increased by the fact that the Soviet Jews are a highly mobile group in terms of residence and life styles. As an ethnic community, they had already experienced two major changes in residence: from their small ethnic communities (shetl) of the Pale in pre-World War I days to urban concentration in the Ukraine and Byelorussia during the Civil War, and from the western border areas to major interior metropolitan areas during World War II. In the process, their attachment to the Yiddish language and centuries-old Jewish cultural tradition was broken. Also, nearly all Soviet Jews have relatives or friends abroad -- hence, they have available international ties which provide both moral and financial support for their emigration aspirations.

A major emigration motivational factor, of course, is the existence of the symbolic homeland, Israel, even though the individual emigrant may ultimately go elsewhere. As Ross points out in his 1973 study on "The Development of Emigration Nationalism Among Soviet Jews," "...if the symbolic homeland and/or center of strength of a group is located beyond the geographic borders of the state of residence, its self-assertion will tend to

184

take the form of an emigration-nationalist movement."[11]

In his study, Ross notes that Soviet Jewish emigration patterns show that entire families, rather than individuals, are the modal departing unit. The decision to emigrate is consensually based within the family unit; and even in those rare cases where there are dissenters, they almost invariably leave also. In addition, Ross discovered that once several members of a Jewish community decide to emigrate, others in the community are also emboldened to leave.[12] Ross also states that Jewish communities in the Soviet Union are tightly although informally knit and provide a firm basis of support and mutual aid for their members.

Another, and equally important factor prompting Jewish emigration is that of traditional "Russian" antisemitism. Reportedly, this phenomenon reasserted itself in considerable magnitude following the 1967 Arab-Israeli war. Furthermore, as we saw earlier, discrimination against the Jews still remains extensive today -- particularly with regard to discrimination in higher education and in employment.

While it may be true that the great majority of the unassimilated, religious Jews of the Soviet "peripheries" who, thus far, constitute the bulk of the emigration, may be motivated primarily by cultural and religious factors, this is not true of the majority of Jews who emigrate from the Soviet heartland. These heartland emigrants, who, in great numbers, are choosing Western destinations other than Israel, appear to be motivated primarily by such secular motives as higher educational opportunities for their children and extended career opportunities for themselves. In other words, these latter emigrants appear to be motivated basically by the desire to get out of the Soviet Union and away from its antisemitic prejudices rather than by a desire to go to any particular "national" destination, such as Israel.

FACTORS INFLUENCING EMIGRATION POLICIES AND PRACTICES

The Leadership Debate

According to Mikhail Zand, the decision reached by the Soviet leadership in early 1971 to allow unprecedented numbers of Jews to emigrate was a victory won by the "liberals" among the leadership over the so-called "neo-Stalinist" leadership faction. According to that same source, the "Jewish policy" advocated by the "neo-Stalinists" had prevailed earlier, but was discredited when the Leningrad trial of the would-be (Jewish) hijackers in December 1970 failed to produce the desired result, i.e., intimidation of Soviet "Zionists." In addition, the Soviet leaders reportedly had not anticipated the magnitude of the adverse international reaction to the trial and to the internal Soviet policies in general. As a consequence, the "liberals" were able to press for a more flexible "Jewish policy", including enlarged Jewish emigration quotas.[13] Moreover, as a result of ensuing events (most notably the blossoming of the U.S.-Soviet détente and its related "obligations" on the Soviet government) the "liberal" elements within the leadership became increasingly wedded to a more relaxed policy position with regard to the Jewish emigration issue -- their prestige and future political fortunes rested not only on the success of détente, but also on the success of the new emigration policies.

Alleged members of the so-called "liberal" wing of the Soviet leadership include Soviet Premier Aleksei N. Kosygin,[14] U.S.S.R. Academy of Sciences Vice-President Aleksei M. Rumyantsev, K.G.B. Chairman Yuri V. Andropov, former trade Union Chief Aleksandr A. Shelepin, and the late Marshal of the Soviet Army and former Warsaw Pact Chief Ivan I. Yakubovsky. Party General Secretary Leonid I. Brezhnev's ideological position has been described as "middle-of-the-road" -- he is for détente and Jewish emigration, but reportedly is not as liberal as Kosygin and Andropov with regard to the possible relaxation of internal policies and practices. Identified as "conservative" and particularly antisemitic are the former Deputy Premier Dmitri Polyansky, former Ukrainian Party Chief P. Shelest, and Party theoretician Mikhail Suslov.[15]

Domestic and Foreign Policy Concerns

In studying the Jewish emigration issue, it soon becomes readily apparent that it is extremely complicated and intricately interwoven into a host of vital Soviet foreign and domestic policy concerns.

Pursuant to domestic policy, the Soviet authorities in confronting the internal dissident challenge[16] were faced with a potentially volatile situation -- one which had to be defused quickly or else it could have spread, with disastrous results, throughout the Soviet Union and perhaps Eastern Europe as well. Emigration (and in extreme cases, outright exile) represented a convenient and logical way to accomplish that end. Consequently, over the years, the authorities have utilized the Jewish emigration conduit as a prime means to dispatch so-called "undesirable" elements (i.e., dissident activists, social malingerers, and in some cases, even hardened criminals) out of the country. As one result,

internal opposition to the regime has been seriously stifled
through the depletion of its most effective leadership.[17]

Conversely, the opening of the emigration gates to the
Jews could set a most dangerous precedent which could prompt
the demand of not only other minority groups to emigrate, but
segments of the Russian group as well. In addition, such a
victory won by the Jewish "nationalists" could be interpreted
by the other national groups that the time was ripe to press the
central authorities for greater autonomy in their own homelands.
Also, the winning of the individual right to emigrate could
oblige the authorities to allow other personal freedoms heretofore largely curtailed, e.g., more unrestricted freedom of
speech, the press, travel, and perhaps even some form of
limited political opposition.

Then, too, there is the interesting observation made by
the prominent Marxist dissident, Roy Medvedev, that if Soviet
citizens gain a choice of whether to emigrate or stay, then the
Soviet government has an obligation to satisfy their needs and
wants. Consequently, Medvedev continues, economic priorities
would have to be shifted from defense and heavy industry to
consumer goods[18] -- a most interesting conjecture!

With regard to foreign policy, the Jewish emigration issue
continues to represent a factor of some importance in ongoing
Soviet foreign relations. This is especially true in the economic
sphere where the Soviets (and the Eastern Europeans as well)
desperately need Western technology and trade if they are to
stay abreast of advancing technology and thus, remain econom-
ically and perhaps even politically viable. As a consequence,
the passage by the United States Congress of the Jackson-Vanik
Amendment to the Trade Act of 1974 which prohibits "the extension of most-favored-nation tariff status, U.S. government credits, credit guarantees, or investment guarantees" to the Soviet
Union and the Eastern European nations (except Poland and Yugoslavia) was a considerable blow to Soviet détente expectations.
However, this is not to say that the Soviets are totally dependent
on trade with the U.S. in their quest for needed Western products
and technological expertise. In fact, the Soviet Union's two
leading Western trade partners in 1977 were West Germany and
Japan -- each of whom did about two and one-half times as much
trade with the Soviet Union as the U.S. did. (According to the
U.S. Commercial Office in Moscow, the total volume of U.S.-
Soviet trade in 1977 fell 26.5 percent to $1.86 billion from
$2.5 billion in 1976. Most of the decline represented a drop
in U.S. exports to the Soviet Union, which fell to $1.6 billion
from $2.3 billion in 1976.) The bulk of the U.S.-Soviet trade

consists of U.S. exports of wheat, corn, and feed grains. Exports of sophisticated U.S. technology amounted to only about $500 million in 1977.[19] Of importance is the fact that the Jackson-Vanik Amendment was specifically tied to the Soviet Jewish emigration issue in that the stipulated congressional prohibitions were prompted by the Soviet denial of Jewish emigration rights and the related levying of assorted exit fee requirements. Another harmful and perhaps even more serious blow to the Soviets was the Stevenson Amendment to the Export-Import Bank Act of 1974, by which the U.S. Congress imposed a limit of $300 million on the amount of Export-Import Bank credits and guarantees that could be provided for U.S. exports to the Soviet Union, unless Congress, by concurrent resolution, approved a higher amount. That Amendment also was influenced by restricted Soviet Jewish emigration practices. In response to these congressional actions, the Soviet Union informed the United States on January 14, 1975, that it would not put the 1972 U.S.-Soviet Trade Agreement into effect.[20]

As pointed out, a prime Soviet motivation for allowing more Jews to emigrate stems from a keen desire to obtain "most-favored-nation" treatment and extensive trade credits from the United States. This perhaps is reflected in the dramatic increase in the total Jewish emigration as evidenced in the 1972 and 1973 emigration figures (31,500 and 33,500 respectively), which occurred at the height of the U.S.-Soviet détente relationship. Correspondingly, there was a dramatic decline of 42 percent in Jewish emigration (to 20,000) in 1974 from that of 1973, following the passage of the mentioned U.S. legislation. Jewish emigration figures for 1975 took a further drop -- to approximately 13,000. However, 1975 was also the year in which the Helsinki Final Act was signed and Soviet hopes were on the rise again that the sought-after most-favored-nation treatment and extended trade credits would be obtained. Relatedly, we see a corresponding liberalization of the Jewish emigration policy in that the urban, well-educated Jews began to replace the "peripheral" Jews as the backbone of the Jewish emigration flow. In addition, there is a corresponding rise in the total Jewish emigration figures for 1976 -- to 14,000.

The Soviet emigration issue also constitutes an important element in Soviet diplomatic maneuverings in the Middle East. For example, it is conceivable that the Soviets might use the "carrot" of increased Jewish emigration as a means to entice the Israelis to reduce their possible intransigence over certain issues in a future Middle East settlement and to allow a Soviet role in the settlement effort. (It may be recalled that renewed Jewish

188

emigration from the Soviet Union coincided with Soviet diplomatic efforts to achieve an Arab-Israeli accommodation following the June 1967 Arab-Israeli conflict.) In addition, some observers speculate that Soviet motives in allowing more Jewish emigration during the early 1970s were partially due to a desire to overload the Israeli domestic budget,[21] and to distort Israel's domestic political balance by feeding into it rightist, anti-communist Soviet Jews who all could be expected to support Israeli rightist political factions. Others have said that the then "liberal" Soviet emigration practices were prompted by a desire to bring complete chaos to an already critical Israeli housing shortage.[22] Also, it must be remembered that even though formal diplomatic relations currently do not exist between the two governments, the Soviets have remained in diplomatic contact with Israel over the years through their diplomatic representatives in the United Nations -- since as one of the two great superpowers the Soviet Union retains important power stakes in the Middle East area. In view of that continuing relationship, it is reasonable to assume that the emigration issue, at one time or another, has, or will, surface as an important item of discussion in the ongoing Soviet-Israeli contacts.[23]

THE SOVIET LEGAL PERSPECTIVE

Regulations Governing Entry and Exit

As Professor George Ginsburgs, the noted Western authority on Soviet law succinctly points out, in Soviet law a citizen does not possess a right to emigrate at will; however, the concept of emigration is not unfamiliar to the Soviet authorities. Consequently, the Regulations on Entry into the U.S.S.R. and Exit from the U.S.S.R. ratified by Resolution of the U.S.S.R. Council of Ministers of June 19, 1959, no. 660, specify that exit from the U.S.S.R. of Soviet citizens is permitted on strength of passports for travel abroad or substitute documents accompanied by an exit visa furnished by the union or republican ministries of foreign affairs, diplomatic missions of the U.S.S.R. Ministry of Foreign Affairs, the ministries of internal affairs of the U.S. S.R., the union and autonomous republics, and their organs, depending on the official position of the interested citizen, his passport category, and location at the time of issuance of the visa. In cases not involving diplomatic or service passports, Soviet citizens going abroad temporarily or for permanent residence receive a _permis de sejour_. Foreign documents and exit visas are issued in accordance with the established procedure on the basis

189

of a written petition from the individual citizen desiring to go
abroad on private business.

Special instructions for the application of these regulations,
with respect to the issuance of documents and visas, were to be
issued by the U.S.S.R. Ministry of Foreign Affairs in consultation
with the U.S.S.R. Ministry of Internal Affairs and the Committee
on State Security (K.G.B.). The method of issuance of documents
and visas was to depend on rules laid down by the Ministry of
Internal Affairs in conjunction with the Ministry of Foreign Affairs,
the Committee on State Security, and the Ministry of Defense.

As Ginsburgs comments, the obvious implication of this
directive is that exit from the Soviet Union, even for permanent
residence, is both possible and legitimate; i.e., whenever the
competent institutions approve a personal request to that effect.
The final word, however, rests with the administrative authorities
and, without their consent, the application will be refused. Moreover, the regulations do not indicate what criteria govern the entire process, presumably allowing these to be defined by the previously referred-to "special" instructions. Consequently, as
Ginsburgs notes, when official emigration permission is granted,
it has been recognized as a unique circumstance and not symp-
tomatic of any public recognition of the inherent freedom of the
individual citizen to emigrate. In that regard, Ginsburgs states
that inasmuch as Soviet law has sanctioned the emigration of
various people over the years, the phenomenon represents, and
locally has always been perceived as, an incidence of political
dispensation constituting a special privilege conferred on the
interested party by the organs of the State and not something that
a person can claim unilaterally, independently of, or in opposition to the regime's expressed wishes.[24]

New regulations concerning entry into and exit from the
U.S.S.R. were ratified by Resolution of the U.S.S.R. Council
of Ministers of September 22, 1970, no. 801. These new regulations essentially reflect the same entry and exit requirements
constituted in the June 19, 1959, regulations. What is interesting is the Council of Ministers' concurrent supplementation and
modification of the schedule of State tariffs pertaining to travel
documents as originally set forth in the Council of People's Commissars Decree 598 of April 29, 1942.[25] Under the new regulations the fees charged for documents connected with travel to
and from the West are discriminatory, doubtless reflecting not
only a desire to make those seeking emigration to the West pay
for that privilege, but also to discourage the emigration practice.
These new tariffs, which apparently were prompted by the Jewish
emigration threat, include a fifteen ruble charge for the official

190

form certifying that the individual has been invited by foreign relatives or acquaintances, a four hundred ruble fee for travel documents, and a five hundred ruble fee for renunciation of Soviet citizenship (in spite of the fact that no known Soviet law exists which compels renunciation of citizenship prior to emigration).[26]

In actual application, the citizenship renunciation and accompanying five hundred ruble fee payment requirement apparently only applies to certain "fascist" country destinations, i.e., Israel, Spain, and South Africa -- in spite of the fact that the actual wording of the decree stipulates fulfillment of both requirements prior to departure for "capitalist countries." With one known exception, both Jewish and non-Jewish families immigrating to the United States, Great Britain, and other such Western countries are excused from both paying the fee and of the need to renounce their Soviet citizenship.[27] Ironically, the stipulated requirements for emigration to "socialist countries" include both the need to relinquish Soviet citizenship and to pay an accompanying fee of fifty rubles. Other documentational fees for these "socialist" emigrants include five rubles for the noted certification form and thirty rubles for travel documents. It is not known if these requirements are actually levied.

In addition, whereas immigrants to Israel are required to relinquish their Soviet passports and travel on laissez-passer documentation; both Jewish and non-Jewish immigrants to the United States and to a wide variety of other Western countries receive regular passports for travel purposes. In that connection, individual Jewish immigrants to the United States have been advised prior to their departure from the U.S.S.R. of the "necessity" later to contact the Soviet Embassy in Washington, D.C., in order to retain their Soviet citizenship status.[28]

A particularly interesting legal question evolves from the renunciation of citizenship requirement and its accompanying mandatory five hundred ruble fee payment. As Ginsburgs notes, there is nothing in the relevant Soviet statutes or ministerial directives which specifies such citizenship renunciation or accompanying payment. On the other hand, most indicative that this innovation is motivated by purely political considerations is supported by the observation that the fee for relinquishing citizenship is not always separately itemized in the receipt issued to the applicant. Apparently, the authorities have decided to allow the matter to be handled at the administrative level and thus, cloud its legal status. In all probability, the citizenship renunciation procedure is prompted by a desire to alert the prospective emigrant of the full gravity of the proposed

191

step and emphasize the finality of the break between the individual and his homeland.[29]

Grounds for Emigration

To date, the Soviet authorities have only sanctioned emigration on grounds of family reunification, i.e., the desire to facilitate the reunification of families separated by war and geopolitical changes in Europe. That exclusive policy was most recently reiterated by Colonel Vladimir Obidin, Head of O.V.I.R., who stated that there is no "social basis" for emigration from the U.S.S.R. and that "family reunion is the only basis for issuing exit permission."[30] In that context, Ginsburgs makes the interesting observation that although the family reunification scheme ostensibly eschews nationality as a criterion for emigration candidacy; emigration, in fact, has been virtually restricted to certain national groups.[31] This reality is most certainly reflected in the current mass exodus of Jews who, no doubt, have been singled out by the leadership for special "consideration" in that regard.

Grounds for Refusal

There are various Soviet grounds for refusal of exit permission. These include the concerns for "the State interest, public morals, and possible harm done to the rights of citizens remaining behind." In addition, the authorities have denied emigration to persons living in the so-called "closed areas," i.e., geographical locations where alleged secret military-related activities are carried out -- such areas as Angarsk, Perm', Krasnoyarsk, and so forth.

Also, individuals serving in the military are denied emigration and in that regard, officials have stated that there is no set policy regarding the required time lapse between active military service and the granting of permission to emigrate -- "These cases are periodically reviewed and denials may be revoked after one, two, or more years, depending on the circumstances."[32]

Another ground for refusal is the possession of "State secrets." This is a particularly amorphous category since the Soviet system perpetuates a continuous over-classification of what constitutes "State secrets"; even access to Western literature in a Soviet public library requires a special "clearance." Consequently, the categories of State secrets are broadly defined, involving an array of both military and economic related

192

matters. Moreover, the authorities, over the years, have been
inconsistent and arbitrary in restricting emigration of citizens
on grounds of possession of State secrets.[33] Closely related
to the question of who has had access to State secrets is the
issue of the declassification of such information. A case in
point is the long-term denial of emigration to the prominent
Jewish scientist, Dr. Veniamin Levich, on the grounds that he
possessed "State secrets" even though his access to such information reportedly was outdated.[34]

With regard to the required "cooling-off" period for emigration applicants who have been engaged in "secret" work,
Mstislav Keldysh, President of the U.S.S.R. Academy of Sciences, remarked in 1972 that any scientist who has been engaged
in "secret" work would be refused permission to emigrate "for
a period of five years after termination of his classified [i.e.,
"secret"] activities." The experiences of individual Jewish
emigrants, however, indicate considerable fluctuation in the
required time interval -- some who had possessed a "first degree" dopusk (security clearance) had been allowed to emigrate
after two years and in some cases after less than two years;
others were obliged to wait the full five years.

The Right of Appeal

With regard to the question of the right of appeal of emigration application rejections, Ginsburgs points out that there
is nothing in Soviet law which prevents the government from
adding emigration matters to the list of items over which the
courts may exercise appropriate supervision. As of this time,
it has not done so; consequently, the emigration issue still remains outside the jurisdiction of the courts. As a result, those
whose efforts to emigrate have been vetoed by the administrative organs have no alternative but "to resort to extrajudicial
methods of advertising their plight and assume all the serious
risks that such a contravention of the written rules entails."[35]

The Soviet View of Compliance

Various authoritative Soviet sources steadfastly maintain
that Soviet emigration procedures operate "in strict accordance"
with Soviet laws and pertinent international agreements. They
specifically point to the provisions of the International Covenant
on Civil and Political Rights, adopted by the United Nations General Assembly on December 16, 1966, and the Final Act of the
Conference on Security and Cooperation in Europe, dated August

1, 1975, as the particular international agreements covering
Soviet emigration commitments. The Soviets maintain that the
appropriate provisions of these particular international agreements specifically support Soviet delay or rejection of emigration applications from persons who "possess State secrets, are
members of the military, or in those cases where emigration in-
fringes on vitally important rights and interests of other citizens,
e.g., minor children or aged parents."[36] In that context, Boris
T. Shumilin, Deputy Minister of Internal Affairs of the Soviet
Union, remarked in an interview in February 1976, that as of
January 1, 1976, the Soviets had "postponed decisions for only
1.6 percent of the overall number of Jewish emigration applicants."[37] In an earlier interview conducted in December 1972,
Shumilin had claimed that "permission to go was given to 95.5
percent of people of Jewish nationality who applied to go to
Israel" during 1972.[38] In the February 1976 interview, Shumilin
also maintained that "in 1975 alone more than 300 people" who
had previously been refused permission to emigrate received exit
permission.[39] He, moreover, claimed in July 1977 that 737
Soviets, whose applications had been previously rejected, received permission in 1976 to leave. He also stated that during
the first five months of 1977, a "further 615 persons in this
situation" received exit permission.[40]

The So-Called "Diploma Tax" and Its Ramifications

Another highly controversial Soviet legal imposition on
emigration (primarily Jewish emigration) was the August 3, 1972,
Presidium of the U.S.S.R. Supreme Soviet Decree ("Decree of
the Presidium of the Supreme Soviet of the U.S.S.R. Concerning
Reimbursement of State Expenditures on Education by Citizens
of the U.S.S.R. Departing for Permanent Residence Abroad")
that citizens of the U.S.S.R. departing for permanent residence
abroad (except those going to socialist countries) were obliged
to reimburse State expenses for higher education and advanced
academic degrees.[41] Oddly enough, although the decree was
confirmed by the Supreme Soviet at its September session, it
was not published until December 27, 1972.[42] The Soviet authorities, at the time, justified their reluctance to publish the
decree by claiming that it was strictly an internal affair of the
U.S.S.R. In support of that position, a law adopted by the
U.S.S.R. Supreme Soviet in 1958 provides for the nonpublica-
tion of decrees (ukazi) and laws (postanovlenie) "not having
general significance or bearing a normative character." The
law also provides that the appropriate organs will make known

194

such laws and decrees to persons affected by them.[43] Publication of the Supreme Soviet decree was followed promptly by the release of the specified educational reimbursement costs in a directive signed by Premier Kosygin and also dated August 3, 1972.[44]

As illustration of the exhorbitance of the stipulated educational reimbursement costs, graduates of universities and institutes above the high school level were obliged to pay anywhere from 4,500 rubles to slightly over 12,000 rubles, depending on the type of training received and the place of study. For example, graduates of the prestigious Moscow State University were charged 12,200 rubles; graduates of "other" universities, 6,000 rubles; graduates of engineering-technical and engineering-economics institutes and higher military academies were charged 7,700 rubles; graduates of agricultural and forestry institutes, 5,600 rubles; etc. Students who did not complete their undergraduate training were required to pay lesser amounts depending on their accumulated years of study. Graduate students who had not defended their dissertations were assessed 1,700 rubles for each year of postgraduate study in addition to the fee for their undergraduate degree. Emigrants who had received the Candidate of Sciences degree were assessed a fee of 5,400 rubles in addition to their fees for undergraduate study, and those possessing the Doctor of Sciences degree were required to remit an additional 7,200 rubles. Consequently, a graduate of Moscow State University, possessing both the Candidate of Sciences and Doctor of Sciences degrees would be liable for fees totaling 24,800 rubles -- i.e., 12,200 rubles for undergraduate work, 5,400 rubles for the Candidate of Sciences degree, and 7,200 for the Doctor of Sciences degree.[45]

As a result of immediate widespread Western criticism of the August 3 decree and the accompanying reimbursement charges, the Soviet authorities were obliged to retreat somewhat from the initial, all-encompassing coverage of the then, as-yet-unpublished State dictum. In mid-October 1972, arbitrary and selective exemptions to the decree were allowed. Later, in an interview with the Novosti Press Agency (distributed to Western newsmen on December 29, 1972), Deputy Minister of Internal Affairs Shumilin announced additional concessions which were subsequently spelled-out in the January 1973 published directive specifying reimbursement fees and other stipulations of the new emigration requirement.

According to the final version of the decree as published in January 1973, invalids of the "first and second group" and men and women who had reached statutory pensionable age

195

(sixty and fifty-five years, respectively) would be totally exempt from having to reimburse the State, invalids of the "third group" might be excused to the extent of 50 percent of the designated sum, and a graduated discount was also allowed to those who had worked a specified number of years, who had earned their diploma without interruption from work or without having been formally enrolled in a graduate program. Also, persons who married citizens of foreign countries were likewise entitled to a 25 to 50 percent rebate, depending on their financial situation, while those who married prior to August 3, 1972, were totally exempt. In addition, citizens who wished to emigrate in order to establish permanent residence in the developing countries could be granted an exemption "in excess of the one foreseen by these instructions to the amount of 70 percent," and persons married to citizens of developing countries could receive an exemption "up to 80 percent, and in individual cases, in full." The directive also authorized the Ministry of Finance together with the Ministry of Internal Affairs, "when there are other justifiable reasons," to excuse Soviet citizens going abroad from repaying the tax in whole or in part. The formalization and issuance of exit visas to persons emigrating abroad for permanent residence was entrusted by the directive to the agencies of the U.S.S.R. Ministry of Internal Affairs after the persons concerned presented receipts from the U.S.S.R. State Bank confirming that the monies due in reimbursement for State expenses for education had been paid. The final statement of the directive stipulated that these regulations did not apply to U.S.S.R. citizens emigrating for permanent residence in socialist countries.[46]

The Soviet authorities attempt to justify the enactment of this measure by maintaining that conditions of emigration from a country lie exclusively within that country's sphere of domestic jurisdiction and, therefore, every state has the sovereign right to adopt whatever laws in this realm deemed appropriate or necessary. In addition, the Soviets argue that when a country spends impressive sums of money on free educational benefits for its peoples, it should have the inherent right to protect itself from the consequences of a prospective major "brain drain." In that regard, the Soviet spokesmen mistakenly claim that the educational tax is in accord with the UNESCO General Council Resolution 1,243 of 1970, which, on the contrary, was designed to counter the "brain drain" from the developing countries. (The 1970 UNESCO Resolution urged members to "take appropriate measures to restrict encouragement of foreign scientists to leave or not return to their [native] countries" (Italics added), and did not, as the Soviets allege, call on them to restrict emigration

196

of their own scientists.) The Soviets also maintain that the controversial tax was not directed to the Jewish emigrants per se, but affected "all emigrants" regardless of specific ethnic affiliation.[47]

In the face of mounting worldwide criticism and more importantly, the prospective loss of desired trade concessions from the United States in the form of "most-favored-nation" treatment and favorable trade credits, the highly controversial education tax was finally "suspended" by the Soviet authorities on March 19, 1973. While in effect (from August 3, 1972, to March 19, 1973), Soviet official sources maintain that only some nine hundred out of a total twenty thousand Jewish emigrants (or 4.5 percent) actually paid the required tax.[48] However, one high-ranking Soviet official, Vladimir S. Alkhimov, Vice-Minister of Foreign Trade, has stated that "10 percent" of the total Jewish emigration during that period was obliged to pay the tax. This corresponds with most Western estimates that between 10 and 15 percent paid.[49]

Official Israeli sources view the education tax as designed specifically to deter the more educated and "valuable" Jews of the R.S.F.S.R. from seeking emigration. According to these same Israeli sources, another and possibly equally important Soviet aim was to discourage young Jews from attempting to enroll in universities and institutes of higher education.[50] Georgy A. Arbatov, Director of the U.S.A. and Canada Institute, Moscow, however, commented immediately prior to the suspension that suspension of the tax could instead result in increased discrimination against Jews in their quest for higher education. He inferred that the official attitude, in such cases, might very well be "why waste the people's money on individuals who eventually will desert the Soviet Union and its people."[51] A prime Soviet motivation for imposing the controversial tax was reportedly also its revenue-raising potential -- the tax was said to earn the equivalent of $2 to $3 million each month during its period of application.[52]

THE PROCEDURAL REQUIREMENTS

Soviet citizens desiring to leave the Soviet Union for either temporary or permanent residence abroad must obtain the permission of the appropriate State authorities. In that context, in order to obtain permission to go to Israel the following documents, properly executed, must be presented to the local office of Visas and Registration (Otdel Vizy I Registratsii - O.V.I.R.) of the Ministry of Internal Affairs.

197

1) An affadavit or vyzov from a relative in Israel which states the relationship of the relative to the Soviet citizen, invites the Soviet citizen to Israel, and promises to support the Soviet citizen after arrival. The vyzov next has to be notarized by the relative in Israel and taken to the Finnish Embassy, which represents the Soviet interests in that country. There the document is certified and the relative mails it to the prospective emigrant in the Soviet Union. The mailed vyzov is valid for one year.[53]

2) An application and questionnaire, executed in duplicate, for each person departing, sixteen years of age and older. The questionnaire forms are issued by O.V.I.R. upon presentation of the vyzov and must be typed.

3) An autobiography, at the end of which must be indicated the identification of the foreign relative the applicant intends to join.

4) A "reference" from the place of residence (the Housing Office, the Apartment House Office, the Housing Management Office) indicating the number and relationship of members of the family, at the end of which it must be stated that it was issued for presentation to O.V.I.R.

5) A statement to O.V.I.R. from each of the applicant's remaining parents, consenting to the applicant's departure for permanent residence in Israel. The signatures of the parents must be certified by the Housing Office at their place of residence. If the parents are deceased, their death certificates must be submitted to the O.V.I.R.

6) A statement to O.V.I.R. from the other parent of a minor child, if that parent remains in the U.S.S.R., consenting to the applicant's departure. That parent's signature must be certified by the Housing Office at his or her place of residence.

7) Eight photographs, 4 x 8 cm. of the applicant are to be provided to O.V.I.R. for documentational purposes.

8) A receipt from the U.S.S.R. State Bank certifying the payment of a fee of forty rubles for "exit visa processing.

9) A postcard with the applicant's current address for subsequent notification purposes.

Up to January 1976, Jewish emigration applicants were also required to obtain a "reference" or so-called kharakteristika from his or her place of employment. The "reference" had to be signed by the director of the plant or office, the local Party official, and the trade union representative. Those who were not employed or on pension had to obtain a reference from their Housing Office, indicating their social status. Should the applicant have children in school or university, a kharakteristika had to be obtained for them as well.

Of all the formal emigration requirements thrust on the individual applicant, the kharakteristika requirement was the most traumatic. As Ginsburgs points out, when the authorities first demanded that such a document be produced for emigration purposes, the result was utter confusion, for the management of the factory or institution where the applicant was employed had no experience in such matters and in the standard bureaucratic practice refused to do what was not stated in the existing regulations. Aside from the uncertainty as to what precisely was expected of them, the managerial staff was faced with a serious dilemma -- a negative response might lead to embarrassing inquiries as to why a person without proper qualifications features on the payroll to begin with; a positive reply might call for explanations as to why the directors were willing to assist so valuable an individual to leave the Soviet Union. Under such circumstances, the safest solution was to ignore the request, and this is exactly what many employers did when first confronted with what must have appeared to them as an unsolvable situation. In addition, through the kharakteristika exercise, the applicant's desire to emigrate became known, and, given the climate of opinion in Soviet society, seldom missed exposing the applicant to such unpleasant personal experiences as ostracism and public condemnation, dismissal from the job, harassment, intimidation, and on occasion, even pressure tactics to make him change his mind.

In lieu of the kharakteristika, subsequent applicants (commencing in January 1976) were required to submit a so-called spravka (or informational sheet) signed only by the applicant's employer and merely attesting to the applicant's length of service at that particular employment.[54] Also, the validity of the spravka was extended to one full year from the previous (kharakteristika) period of six months.[55]

Other revisions to the formalized Jewish emigration procedure include both positive and negative remedial actions, depending on the prevailing political climate and related Soviet policy objectives. For example, beginning in December 1975, the Soviets adopted several remedial procedures of a positive nature in an attempt to project an image of compliance with the 1975 "Helsinki Accords." First of all, the Soviets reduced the required exit fees payment by one hundred rubles; the new total payment now includes 260 rubles for an external passport or laissez-passer documentation and a forty ruble application fee.

199

These new fees were instituted in January 1976 and reportedly
have been uniformly applied. Remaining unchanged, however,
is the required five hundred ruble "renunication of citizenship"
fee charged Jewish emigrants bound for Israel. Also, under a
new regulation enacted on December 23, 1975, any applicant
refused permission to emigrate is eligible for a full refund of
the forty ruble application fee.[56] Moreover, unsuccessful can-
didates, as of January 1976, are entitled to a review by "higher
visa offices" of their case every six months instead of the former
once a year review procedure. In addition, applicants for emigration are to be processed on a local basis rather than
being referred to "higher authority" in most cases. (However,
the local O.V.I.R.s had always played a crucial if ambiguously
defined role in the emigration process, and it is not clear that
this action represents, in fact, a "change.") Furthermore, the
following three grounds for emigration refusal are specified
by the authorities -- if approval is against "the State interest,
if it adversely affects public morals, or if it harms the rights of
citizens remaining in the U.S.S.R."[57]

On the negative side, intermittent emigration procedural
alterations have included, inter alia, the refusal by individual
local O.V.I.R. offices to accept extended vyzovs; the refusal
of exit permission because the sponsoring relative had relocated
to the United States, whereas, that same sponsoring relative
had left the U.S.S.R. with an exit visa for Israel; the restriction
of exit permission to applicants receiving vyzovs from close relatives only, such as a "parent, child, or sibling"; the necessity
for applicants to have their emigration applications inspected
initially by local police officials; the requirement that all emigration applications must be typed; the interception and distribution of mailed vyzovs from Israel by local police organs; and
the placing of more stringent restrictions on apartment transfers
by departing emigrants.[58]

In addition to these procedural requirements, the aspiring
emigrant, upon notification of exit permission, must turn over
to the authorities his internal passport, birth certificate, diplomas from educational installations, labor record book, military
service records, retirement certificate, diplomas and certificates
for learned degrees and titles, membership certificates of creative
artists' unions, and a statement from the "Housing Operations
Office" that the applicant's living space had been vacated and
no claims were registered against the applicant in that regard.
(The applicant can, however, have these documents authenticated
for the purpose of giving them legal validity abroad.) In addition,
the departing emigrant and family are subject to stringent export

200

restrictions of personal possessions.[59] Also, all emigrants
with exit visas for Israel must obtain Israeli entry visas from
The Netherlands Embassy in Moscow (which represents the Israelis in the Soviet Union) regardless of their individual exit
and transit routes.

THE EXTERNAL "STAGING" AREAS

The only current external "staging" area for Jews emigrating from the Soviet Union is Vienna, Austria. They travel to
Vienna either by Austrian State Railways from Budapest, Hungary,
or by Aeroflot directly from Moscow. Most emigrants, more than
60 percent, reportedly prefer to travel by train because they can
carry more baggage.
From July 1971 through January 1977, there were approximately 109,000 Soviet Jewish emigrants who processed through
the Vienna transit facility.[60] This figure represents the overwhelming percentage of the Soviet Jewish emigration total since
those Jews who proceed directly from the Soviet Union to the
United States and to other Western countries (as well as those
relatively few Jews who, up to October 1973, traveled via
Bucharest) represent a small fraction of the total emigration flow.
Between 1971 and the 1973 Middle East War, when the emigration rate was at its highest, emigrating Soviet Jews were processed through an Israeli-run facility at Schoenau Castle, located
outside Vienna. However, after a Palestinian terrorist attack on
an emigre train bound for Vienna a few days before the war broke
out, the Austrian government closed the Schoenau facility. It
later opened new transit facilities which, unlike Schoenau, are
under Austrian auspices. The Schoenau facility was controlled
by the "Jewish Agency" (Sokhnut) -- the semiofficial institution
responsible for the immigration of Jews to Israel.
Those Jewish emigrants who seek resettlement in Western
countries other than Israel upon arrival in Vienna are placed
under the care of the "Hebrew Immigrant Aid Society" (otherwise
known as HIAS), a private American-based organization which
sends them on to a HIAS center in Rome, Italy, for further processing. The average stay in Vienna is several days at most, whereas in Rome, the stay can last anywhere from three weeks to six
months, depending primarily on the bureaucratic machinations of
the preferred country of resettlement.[61]
Until October 1973, another external transit processing
point for Jews emigrating from the Soviet Union was that of
Bucharest, Romania.[62] This transit route which began in October 1972 catered almost exclusively to Jews emigrating from

201

Soviet Moldavia and the Southern Ukraine areas. These emigrants arrived in Bucharest on trains from either Chernovtsy or Kishinev were processed exclusively by the Israeli Embassy in Bucharest, and departed on the first available El Al flight to Israel -- sometimes within two hours after arrival. As a matter of deliberate policy, the Government of Romania had no contact with the emigrants.

THE EMIGRATION FLOW

The Alleged "Quota System"

Allegations have been made over the years by various sources that the Soviets impose specific Jewish emigration quotas for the individual Soviet geographical areas. For example, Leonard Schroeter in his book, The Last Exodus, states that:

> ...The [emigration] pattern established in November-December 1971, of approximately 2,500 Jews per month, continued through 1972-73. The number was not constant; there were slow periods in the midsummer (presumably attributable to the fact that OVIR workers were on summer vacation) and high points at the end of the year (which some have attributed to OVIR's need to meet a quota and stay on the Soviet "plan").[63] (Italics added.)

This allegedly geographically based quota "plan" is perhaps given credence by the decided imbalance between emigration from the Soviet heartland and that from the peripheral areas. (The "peripheral" Jews comprise the great bulk of the emigration statistics thus far.) Such a quota system also would be consonant with inherent Soviet centralist concepts and known quota allocation proclivities. In addition, the occupational make-up of the Jewish emigration flow thus far reflects strong centralized control over the emigration selection process; i.e., the relative numbers of educated emigrants still constitute a decided minority of the total emigration flow.

Statistical Data

"Hard" statistical data pertinent to the Soviet Jewish emigration flow are difficult to specify -- it depends upon the source[64] and as we shall see later in this chapter, specificity is also hindered by the recent phenomenon known as the "dropout" syndrome, i.e., those Jewish emigrants who "drop out" at the transit stop-over in Vienna, Austria, and opt for immigration elsewhere than Israel. Another statistical complication is the fact that some Jews remain in the Soviet Union even after completing all the exit procedural requirements. For example, an official Soviet source notes that there were "more than 2,000" Jews in that category in 1972.[65] Consequently, statistical data presented in this chapter although reflecting both Western and Soviet-sourced materials should not be construed as definitive statistical accountings. Hopefully, they are accurate approximations, but approximations nonetheless.

Emigration prior to 1971 (1948-70). Official Soviet sources state that between 1948 and 1971 approximately 21,000 Jews left the Soviet Union for Israel.[66] This overall figure contrasts with the Western figure of approximately 24,000 for that same period.[67]

Emigration in 1971. Approximately 14,000 Jews were permitted to emigrate from the U.S.S.R. in 1971. This represented a significant increase from the approximately 1,000 Jews who were allowed to leave in all of 1970.[68] It should be noted that the Western-sourced figure of 14,000 compares favorably with the official Soviet figure of 13,700 given by Party General Secretary Brezhnev in a Western press interview.[69]

Emigration in 1972. According to Western-sourced data, there were approximately 31,500 Jews who emigrated from the Soviet Union in 1972. This compares with the official Soviet figure of 29,800 offered by Party Secretary General Brezhnev in a Western press release of June 14, 1973. The 1972 emigration flow was comprised primarily (approximately 90 percent) of low-skilled Georgian and unassimilated "Western" Jews.[70]

Of interest is the fact that the number of Jews applying for exit permits increased considerably during 1972. Relatedly, the backlog of individuals (some of whom may have represented entire family groups) who had received invitations (vyzovs) to emigrate, but who had not yet departed, reportedly reached more than 35,000 at the end of 1971.[71]

Emigration in 1973. Jewish emigration in 1973 reached a record high of approximately 33,500 emigrants,[72] an approximate 11 percent increase over the 1972 total.[73] As in 1972, nearly 90 percent of the emigrants originated from the peripheral areas. The R.S.F.S.R., which alone accounts for approximately 38 percent of the total Jewish population as recorded in the 1970 All-Union Census, apparently contributed less than 10 percent of the total Jewish emigration for 1973.[74]

Of particular significance about the 1973 emigration figures is the continuing low emigration flow from Moscow and Leningrad. Moscow, which contained nearly 40 percent of the total Jewish scientific community in 1971, apparently accounted for only approximately 5 percent of the Jewish emigration in 1973. Also, emigration from the Chernovtsy region and from the other border areas of the former Czechoslovak-Transcarpathian Oblast' and the former Polish area of L'vov undoubtedly continued to constitute a significant majority of the Jewish exodus from the Ukrainian S.S.R. and is possibly designed to clear sensitive border areas of what Soviet authorities may consider residents of questionable loyalty. It is reported that well over half of the postwar Chernovtsy Jewish community of 70,000 by 1974 had emigrated and that the flow was still continuing at a high level. The Georgian emigration dropped to second place (behind the Ukrainian flow) in the overall 1973 emigration totals. Another factor worth mentioning is the Brezhnev statement to a visiting group of U.S. Senators in 1974 that of the 61,000 Jews who had applied for emigration in 1973, 60,200 applications had been granted by the authorities.[75]

Emigration in 1974. There was a total of approximately 20,000 Jewish emigrants who left the Soviet Union in 1974.[76] This total represents a drop of 42 percent from 1973. Also, by the end of 1974 more than a third of the Jewish imigrants with visas for Israel were going elsewhere, mainly to the United States.[77]

Western sources attribute the 1974 decline to the lapse in the U.S.-Soviet détente relationship, increased harassment of would-be emigrants by the Soviet authorities, and to the growing indecision of potential applicants. (The Soviets, during 1974, reportedly increased the bureaucratic red tape involved in exit application, e.g., police clearances, typewritten applications, dismissal from work, etc.). The Soviets, on the other hand, argue that Soviet Jews had become disillusioned about life in Israel; e.g., alleged unemployment, an "increasingly acute" housing shortage, inflation, etc.

Official Soviet sources claim that as of January 1, 1975, only 1,420 Jewish emigration requests were outstanding and that 1,500 Soviet Jews who had received exit permission for Israel in 1973-74 did not leave.[78]

Emigration in 1975. The total Jewish emigration from the Soviet Union in 1975 was approximately 13,000, with a monthly average of approximately 1,000.[79] This total is approximately 35 percent below the 1974 total and 62 percent down from 1973.

Jews who received exit permission in 1975 tended to come from Odessa, the Baltic States, and the Western Ukraine as well as from the Caucasus and Central Asia.

The most significant factor of the 1975 Jewish emigration flow was the increased concentration of emigrants from a few large cities, particularly Moscow, Leningrad, Kiev, and Odessa. Odessa was the single largest source of Jewish emigrants in 1975, having approximately 15 percent of the total Jewish emigration. Whereas, Moscow was the second largest with approximately 9 percent of the emigration total. Also in 1975, Jewish emigration from Leningrad constituted approximately 7 percent of the total Jewish emigration (emigrants from Leningrad only comprised approximately 3 percent of the total in 1973).

Among the Soviet Republics, Georgian Jewish emigration in 1975 was approximately 11 percent of the total; and emigration from the R.S.F.S.R., Eastern Ukraine, and Byelorussia comprised about 43 percent of the total (whereas, in previous years, emigration from these three areas averaged about 15 percent of the total). Ukrainian Jewish emigration in 1975 was approximately 40 percent of the total.[80]

Reportedly, fully 37 percent of the Soviet immigration to Israel during the period 1971-75 came from the Georgian, Bukharan (Central Asia), and Mountain (Dagestan and Azerbaidzhan) Jewish communities. Nearly half of the Israeli immigrants were from the so-called Western borderlands -- the Baltic Republics, West Ukraine, Byelorussia, Moldavia, and Transcarpathian Ukraine. Only 14 percent reportedly came from the Soviet heartland during that same period.[81]

Emigration in 1976. Jewish emigration in 1976 was approximately 14,000[82] and approximated the 1975 monthly emigration average of 1,000. As in 1975, there was a concentration of emigrants from a few large cities, i.e., Odessa, Moscow, Leningrad, and Kiev. Also, as in 1975, Odessa was the single largest source of emigrants and in fact, also experienced the largest emigration increase over 1975 -- approximately 1,100. As a result, Odessa's share of the total emigration climbed from approximately 15 percent in 1975 to about 21 percent in 1976. Whereas Moscow's emigration position remained virtually unchanged -- approximately 9 percent in 1975 versus about 9 percent in 1976. Leningrad, however, raised its emigration share from approximately 7 percent in 1975 to about 8 percent in 1976.

Among the Soviet republics, the Ukrainian emigration share increased from about 40 percent in 1975 to approximately 46 percent in 1976 -- largely as a result of the increased emigration flow from Odessa. Conversely, there was an emigration

decrease of approximately 2 percent each for the R.S.F.S.R.,
Georgia, and Azerbaidzhan. Correspondingly, less than half
as many emigrants departed Dagestan in 1976 than in 1975, a
decrease of from about 7 percent to approximately 3 percent.

Of particular significance is that approximately 45 percent
of the total Jewish emigration in 1976 came from the four cities
of Odessa, Moscow, Leningrad, and Kiev.[83] This meant that
the orthodox, unassimilated Jews from the rural and non-Russian
areas of the Soviet Union, i.e., the "Oriental" and "Western"
Jews, who comprised the bulk of the emigration flow in previous
years, were being replaced by the urban, well-educated, assimilated "Core" Jews from the Soviet heartland. In addition, the
Soviet authorities in 1976 allowed several long-term Jewish
"refuseniks"[84] (otkazniki) to leave the Soviet Union -- the most
prominent of whom was Aleksandr Lunts.

Soviet motivation for allowing larger numbers of urban,
well-educated Jews to depart in 1976 and finally also allowing
several long-term "refuseniks" to leave, probably stems from
several factors. First of all, the Soviets have been sensitive
to international criticism of their performance in the human rights
area, especially since the signing of the Helsinki Final Act in
August 1975. In that regard, despite the fact that Israel is not
a signatory, emigration from the Soviet Union to that country
has become an important Soviet defense against Western criti-
cisms of Moscow's compliance with the Final Act's provisions.
A second motivational factor probably concerns continuing Soviet
desires to obtain "most-favored-nation" treatment and extensive
trade credits from the United States. With regard to the Soviet
concession in allowing certain "refuseniks" to emigrate, this
probably is motivated by a desire to appear to comply with the
spirit of the "Helsinki Accords" and also, to get rid of several
prominent dissident activists who were creating internal problems.

Concerning Soviet emigration policies and practices in
1976, a charge is levied by Joseph Almogi, Chairman of the
Jewish Agency, and Eugene Gold, Chairman of the American Committee for Soviet Jewry, that "55,000 Soviet Jews had applied
to emigrate in 1976 and only 14,000 were permitted to leave."
They also claim that there still remained in the Soviet Union
180,000 Jews who had applied to emigrate.[85] Conversely,
Soviet Deputy Interior Minister Shumilin claimed in a July 1977
Soviet press article that 737 Jewish emigration applicants whose
applications had been previously denied received exit permission
in 1976. That same official also denied the Israeli claim that
over one million Jews wish to emigrate and that 180,000 emigration applications had been submitted to the Soviet authorities.[86]

Emigration in 1977. Jewish emigration in 1977 rose to
approximately 17,000, an approximate increase of 16 percent
over 1976. Less than 15 percent of those who left during the
first six months of 1977 were over sixty-two years of age, and
more than one-half of all emigrants were either professionals
or skilled workers, with only 2 percent listed as unskilled.
Again, the urban, well-educated Jews mainly from the major
cities of Odessa, Moscow, Leningrad, and Kiev constituted
the bulk of the emigration flow.[87]

Also, according to Shumilin, during the first five months
of 1977, a "further 615" previously rejected applicants were
allowed to leave the Soviet Union. He also claimed that as of
June 1, 1977, only about 2,600 Jewish emigration applications
were then currently under review by the authorities. In addition,
that same official stated that whereas before 1974 an average
of 2,200 emigration applications were submitted on a monthly
basis by Jews, during the "past three or four years that number
has halved and is now 900 to 1,000 per month."[88]

Emigration in 1978 (First Five Months). Approximately
9,507 Jews were permitted to leave the Soviet Union for Israel
during the first five months of 1978, an approximate increase of
66 percent over the some 5,735 who left in the first five months
of 1977. If the current trend continues, Jewish emigration from
the Soviet Union for 1978 could reach as high as 22,000, the
highest total since 1973. However, in decided contrast to
recent years, the current Jewish emigration reportedly is predominantly blue-collar and nonurban. Relatedly, there is very
little Jewish emigration from either Moscow or Leningrad.

Soviet motivation for allowing more Jews to emigrate in
1978 is linked both to the influence of the Belgrade meeting of
the signatories of the Helsinki Final Act and to continuing Soviet
desires for U.S. tariff and trade credit concessions.[89]

The Vienna "Dropout" (noshrim) Syndrome

In recent years, commencing with the sudden rise in the
number of urban, well-educated Jews emigrating from the Soviet
Union, a new phenomenon appeared on the Jewish emigration
scene -- that of ever-increasing percentages of Jewish emigrants
changing direction at the Vienna, Austria, transit point and pro-
ceeding to Western countries other than Israel for resettlement.
This trend represents a most serious problem for the Israelis,
both in terms of international prestige and in the more substantive areas of Israeli Jewish population growth and internal Israeli
politics.

TABLE 13
Jewish Emigration from the Soviet Union -- 1971-77

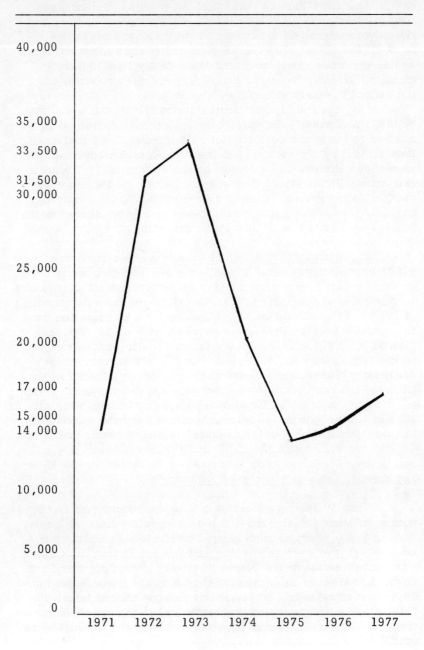

As can be seen by the figures provided in the following tables, the "dropout" reality became increasingly significant beginning in 1974. (From 1968 until June 1976, about 131,000 Jews left the U.S.S.R., of whom 111,000 settled in Israel and 20,000 elsewhere.)[90]

The reasons for the rather high Vienna dropout rates in the past several years are varied; however, it appears, as noted, that a primary factor involves the change in the composition of the emigration flow from a decidedly rural prominence to one in which the urban, well-educated, and mostly nonreligious "Core" Jews constitute a majority.[91] These "Core" Jews apparently have little if any cultural affinity with the State of Israel, having been cut off from Jewish traditions for most of their lives. As previously mentioned, their motivation for leaving the Soviet Union basically appears to be that of wanting to get away from the Soviet system and its built-in antisemitic prejudices rather than any desire to go to the Jewish "national homeland." Also, since many of the new Jewish emigrants are professional persons, there is a greater ambition and need to pursue individual careers in the most advantageous environment -- for many that means going to the United States, the "center of world capitalism." In addition, a sizable number of emigrants are accustomed to the cold Russian climate and consequently are apparently hesitant to resettle in the temperate Israeli zone. Also, there are those who are opposed to the "socialist" system of government in Israel and prefer to resettle in a strictly capitalist environment like the United States or Canada. Others are worried, inter alia, about the volatile Middle East situation, Israel's inflation, reported serious housing shortage, alleged unemployment situation (particularly for skilled and professional labor), necessity to learn Hebrew, currency devaluation, and general economic difficulties. In that regard, it is known that detailed descriptions of the Israeli realities, both good and bad, are transmitted regularly to would-be emigrants from relatives and friends who have already resettled in Israel. In addition, as noted previously in this study, the Soviet authorities, for years, have conducted an intensive anti-Israeli propaganda campaign, one designed to thwart Jewish emigration to Israel. Evidently, all of these factors play a role in producing the referred-to "dropout" syndrome.

In an effort to combat the increasing "dropout" rate, the Israeli government in July 1976 established the so-called Prime Minister's "Committee of Eight,"[92] made up of four Israeli officials and four representatives of the American Jewish charitable organizations to study the "dropout" problem. At that time, the

TABLE 14
The Vienna "Dropout" Rate*

	Proportion not Going to Israel	
Year	Number	Percentage
1971	59	0.4
1972	219	0.7
1973	1,451	4.5
1974	3,879	18.7
1975	4,926	37.0
1976	6,089	48.9
1977 (First three months only)[93]	1,716	52.5

*Emanuel Litvinoff, ed., "Emigrants Who Turn Away From Israel,"
Insight 1 (April 1975): 2; "Israel, U.S. Jews Split Over Soviet
Emigrants," Washington Post, 10 November 1976; Kurier (Vienna,
Austria), 22 October 1976; Division of Research and Statistics,
HIAS, Statistical Abstract 15 (Fourth Quarter, 1974): 1; Zvi
Gitelman, "Research on the U.S.S.R. Based on Interviews with
Soviet Emigres: A Conference Report and Research Proposal," p.2.

TABLE 15
Percentages of "Dropouts" by City of Origin*

City	1973	1974	1975
Moscow	25	55	72
Leningrad	27	54	73
Odessa	19	72	90
Kiev	10	49	70
Vilna	2	7	16
Riga	7	29	51
Kishinev	0.6	3.13	9

*Zvi Gitelman, "Research on the U.S.S.R. Based on Interviews
with Soviet Emigres: A Conference Report and Research Proposal",
p. 13; Kurier (Vienna, Austria), 22 October 1976.

Israeli authorities reportedly were considering several possible courses of action designed to overcome the "dropout" threat. Those contemplated action alternatives included, inter alia, the possible curtailment of all administrative and financial aid to Jews who decide to resettle in Western countries other than Israel. However, in the face of reported opposition from the American Jewish community, and the Austrian government as well, the Israeli officials decided not to alter the existing procedures. Consequently, American Jewish assistance to those Jews who seek resettlement in the United States and elsewhere would continue as before;[94] also, the Vienna transit processing procedure would remain unchanged. It should be noted that in addition to their own nationalist concerns, the Israeli officials were afraid that the Soviet Union possibly would use the question of the ultimate destination of the emigrants as a pretense for further curtailment of the emigration flow.[95]

The flow of "dropouts" to non-Israel destinations. A statistical account. According to a HIAS statistical report of 1974, of the 3,067 Soviet Jews assisted by that organization from 1967 through 1973, 2,560 (83 percent) went to the United States, 233 (11 percent) went to Canada, and the remaining 6 percent were resettled in Western Europe, Australia, and Latin America.

The absolute number of Soviet Jews arriving in the United States in 1974 with HIAS assistance was 3,490 compared with 1,449 in 1973, an increase of 141 percent.

Of the total 4,110 Soviet Jews assisted by HIAS in 1974, resettlement destinations were as follows: United States, 84.9 percent; Canada, 9.6 percent; Australia/New Zealand, 2.9 percent; Western Europe, 2.2 percent; and, Latin America, 0.3 percent. In absolute numbers, Canada accepted 398 Soviet Jews in 1974 (an increase of 103 percent over 1973) and Australia and New Zealand accepted 82 and 37, respectively. Of the 3,490 Soviet Jews going to the U.S. in 1974, 45 percent resettled in the New York metropolitan area and the remainder in some thirty-three states and the District of Columbia.[96]

The number of HIAS-assisted Soviet Jews arriving in the United States in 1975 was 5,250. Whereas, for the first nine months of 1976, of a total of 5,502 HIAS-assisted Soviet Jews, 4,681 (85 percent) went to the United States; 472 (9 percent) went to Canada; 241 (4 percent) went to Australia and New Zealand; 107 (2 percent) went to West European countries; and 1 went to Latin America.[97]

211

TABLE 16
Soviet Jewish Arrivals in the United States*[98]

1972	1973	1974	1975	1976 (January to September 30)
453	1,449	3,490	5,250	4,681

Total to United States
1972 - September 30, 1976

15,323

*Figures were obtained from the Soviet Jewry Research Bureau, National Conference on Soviet Jewry (New York, NY).

During the first nine months of 1977, HIAS assisted 6,358 Soviet Jews, an increase of 16 percent over the corresponding period for 1976. In addition, Soviet Jews accounted for 92 percent of the HIAS overall caseload. Of the Soviet Jews assisted by HIAS, 5,615 (88 percent) went to the United States; 315 (5 percent) went to Australia and New Zealand; 270 (4 percent) went to Canada; 143 went to Western Europe; and 15 to Latin America. The preponderant number -- 3,893 or 69 percent -- continued to come from the Ukraine, S.S.R., followed by 21 percent from the R.S.F.S.R.[99]

The U.S. prerogative. Recognizing the need for substantial funds to help the increased number of Soviet Jewish emigrants in the early 1970s, President Nixon issued a Presidential Determination accompanying the foreign assistance act in May 1972 for $2 million to "aid Soviet refugees" during the fiscal year of 1972. Of that total, $1.85 million went to the 32-nation Intergovernmental Committee for European Migration (I.C.E.M.) for travel costs and $150,000 went to the American-operated U.S. Refuge Program (U.S.R.P.) to assist refugee resettlement in Israel.[100]

In fiscal year 1973, with the number of Jewish emigrants increasing, the U.S. Congress took the initiative and appropriated $50 million for "assistance to Israel or another suitable country, including assistance for resettlement...of Jewish or other similar refugees from the Union of Soviet Socialist Republics."[101]

TABLE 17

Republic of Origin of HIAS-Assisted Soviet Jewish Immigrants
to the U.S. in 1976 (January to September 30)*

| Republic | Number of Arrivals | | |
	Male	Female	Total
Armenia, S.S.R.	1	1	2
Azerbaidzhan, S.S.R.	14	10	24
Byelorussia, S.S.R.	48	52	100
Estonia, S.S.R.	3	2	5
Georgia, S.S.R.	42	43	85
Kazakhstan, S.S.R.	12	7	19
Latvia, S.S.R.	60	59	119
Lithuania, S.S.R.	22	20	42
Moldavia, S.S.R.	116	126	242
R.S.F.S.R.	516	530	1,046
Tadzhikistan, S.S.R.	1	5	6
Ukraine, S.S.R.	1,454	1,514	2,968
Uzbek, S.S.R.	8	6	14
Not Listed	7	2	9
Total	2,304	2,377	4,681

*Division of Research and Statistics, HIAS, Statistical Abstract
17 (Third Quarter, 1976): 15.

The HIAS-assisted arrivals came from 13 of the 15 Soviet
republics. The preponderant number of HIAS-assisted U.S.S.R.
arrivals -- 2,698 persons (63 percent of the total) -- continues
to come from the Ukrainian, S.S.R., followed by the Russian
Soviet Federated Socialist Republic (22 percent). The 667 from
the other 11 republics constituted 14 percent of the total.

The Congress subsequently provided $36.5 million in fiscal year 1974. Of this $86.5 million total, $75.5 million was given to the Israeli "Jewish Agency" to assist the costs of resettling emigrants in Israel. These U.S. government funds are administered by the U.S. Department of State, Office of Coordinator of Human Rights and Humanitarian Affairs, and go to the Jewish Agency through the United Israel Appeal, Inc. (U.I.A.), a voluntary agency accredited to the U.S. government. Aid is furnished under the 1972 Foreign Relations Authorization Act, which authorizes the Secretary of State to assist Israel or suitable countries in the resettlement of "Jewish or other similar refugees" from the U.S.S.R.[102]

In fiscal year 1975, $40 million was authorized and of that amount, approximately $5 million was allocated for purposes of transportation and maintenance for Soviet (Jewish) emigrants en route to countries other than Israel, mainly the United States, and an additional $900,000 was allocated for direct assistance to American (Jewish) resettlement agencies -- $300 per immigrant. Although there are precedents for official American government assistance to political refugees from communist countries (both from Hungary in 1956 and from Cuba since the 1960s), subsidization of American Jewish resettlement agencies is a new phenomenon.[103]

In fiscal year 1976, $20 million was authorized and in fiscal year 1977 an authorization of $25 million was granted for Soviet (Jewish) resettlement.

In January 1977, a U.S. Department of State allocation of $2 million was made to assist Soviet (Jewish) refugees not resettling in Israel. In March 1977, the U.S. House of Representatives International Relations Subcommittee on International Operations voted $20 million in assistance to Israel "for resettling refugees from the Soviet Union and Romania" for fiscal year 1978.[104]

In order to assist these Soviet emigrants further, the U.S. government since August 1973, has utilized the "parole" authority under Section 212 (D) (5) of the U.S. Immigration and Nationality Act as a primary means to expedite the entry into the United States of Soviet Jews who drop out of the Israeli pipeline upon reaching the Vienna, Austria, staging point.[105] This action was necessitated by the dramatic increase in the numbers of these Jews applying for U.S. immigration upon reaching Rome, Italy. As of January 1, 1977, there was an accumulation of 4,000 such individuals in Rome seeking U.S. entry.[106]

214

The Jewish "Overflow" problem in Western Europe. As a result of the increased number of Soviet Jews "dropping out" of the Israel immigration pipeline in Vienna, Austria and the accelerated arrival in Western Europe of Soviet Jewish "departees" from Israel (i.e., those Jews who first had resettled in Israel and then had left), an "overflow" of Jewish emigrants developed in several Western European areas beginning in 1973.[107] For example, in Rome, Italy, in September 1973 there were a reported 800 Soviet Jews seeking help to immigrate to the United States, approximately 380 of whom had first resettled in Israel. Subsequently, in Rome in January 1975, there was a reported backlog of over 2,000 Soviet Jews seeking resettlement in countries other than Israel; and as noted earlier, as of January 1, 1977, there was an accumulation of 4,000 Soviet Jews in Rome seeking U.S. immigration. In addition to Rome, similar Soviet Jewish "overflows" were occurring in West Berlin and in Brussels, Belgium.

In Brussels, in September 1974, there were more than 900 Soviet Jews, the great majority of whom were Israeli "departees," desiring resettlement in Western countries other than Israel. A comparable situation developed in West Berlin where beginning in August 1973, an influx of 546 Soviet Jewish emigrants appeared on the scene. Of these, only 15 had come directly to West Berlin from Vienna, Austria; the others had first resettled in Israel.[108] This sudden influx created official concern in both Brussels and West Berlin because of possible Arab terrorist activity, the possible effect on relations with the Soviets, and also, the added burden placed on the local economies. Consequently, Soviet Jewish immigration to other Western areas was expedited -- particularly to the U.S. where the "parole" system was activated as an expeditious means.

The "Direct" Channel Alternative

In addition to those Jews who immigrate to non-Israeli destinations after "dropping out" of the Israeli immigration channel in Vienna, Austria, there are those Jews who immigrate to these destinations directly from the Soviet Union. Such Jews comprised 71 percent of the total "direct" Soviet immigration to the U.S. in 1972 (or 358 in absolute numbers); 66.2 percent (or 502) in 1973; 61 percent (or 622) in 1974; 50.3 percent (or 585) in 1975; and 35.1 percent (or 239) for the period January to April 1976.[109] There were 223 "direct" Jewish U.S. immigrants from January through July 1977 -- a 41 percent drop from the comparable 1976 period.[110]

TABLE 18
Soviet Jewish "Direct" Immigrants to the U.S. -- For Selected
Years Between 1959 and 1969*

Year	Total "Direct" Immigrants	Estimated Jews
1959	40	0 (Percent of total)
1960	342	25 (7 ")
1961	114	8 (7 ")
1965	287	35 (12 ")
1966	298	16 (5 ")
1967	266	51 (19 ")
1968	238	52 (22 ")
1969	288	128 (44 ")

*Based on statistical data provided by the U.S. Immigration
and Naturalization Service.

THE EFFECT OF JEWISH EMIGRATION ON THE SOVIET DOMESTIC
SCENE

On the Other "Nationalities"

There appears to be ample evidence that the Soviet authorities are indeed vitally concerned that the emigration of Jews
might strengthen national feelings among the other "nationalities."
This fear is based on the very real threat which nationalism represents to the very foundations of the centralized Party-controlled
system. Various individual American official visitors to the Soviet
Union in recent years have come away with the distinct impression
that the Soviet leaders are very concerned about the Jewish "situation" and the possibility that the discontent so prevalent among
the Jews might spread to other minority groups.

It, for instance, is known that non-Jewish groups have been
impressed by the Jewish success and some, like the Volga Germans,
have copied the Jewish emigration activist program in seeking their
own emigration objectives. However, as noted earlier in this study,
most non-Jewish "nationalities" differ fundamentally from the Jews
in that the other "nationalities" seek to perpetuate their national
communities in the historic homelands currently located within the
Soviet Union.[111] Consequently, these groups reject large-scale
emigration as a desirable national objective and in fact view
mass departures as a threat to the preservation of their national
homelands and their eventual liberation from Russian domination.
At the same time, these non-Jewish groups welcome the international

216

attention which the Jews have drawn to their cause and the accompanying international interest in what is going on inside the Soviet Union. They hope that through this international awareness and related leadership concessions to the Jews that some long-term beneficial effect will come to their own nationalist aspirations.

On Dissidence

As noted previously, there is substantial factual evidence available to suggest that the Soviet authorities are using the Jewish emigration channel as a means to rid the Soviet society of harmful dissident activists -- Jew and non-Jew alike. In fact, through the selective use of the emigration availability, the authorities have, to a large extent, controlled the activist dissident movement inside the Soviet Union.[112] However, there is the converse reality that the availability of an emigration "escape hatch" might possibly embolden dissident activism, encourage new generations of dissident activists, and also, foster future across-the-board opposition to the regime.

On the Jews Who Remain

The specter of renewed anti-semitism and a deteriorating Jewish situation in the Soviet Union was raised in 1973 by both Soviet and Western observers. For example, the previously mentioned Georgy A. Arbatov commented on the possibility of antisemitic consequences resulting from the passage of the Jackson-Vanik Amendment. He noted that should the Jackson-Vanik Amendment be enacted, it "would revive antisemitism in the Soviet Union, because it would give Soviet Jews a special status and treatment."[113] Also, former U.S. Deputy Secretary of State Kenneth Rush speculated that the passage of the Jackson-Vanik legislation would represent a "grave danger" for Soviet Jews by "bringing about a counterproductive reaction in Russia, producing antisemitism."[114] Another Western observer, Leonard Schapiro, put it in an even more drastic perspective when he commented that:

> Both Israel and to some extent the [American] Jewish communities behave as if the only problem were to help those Soviet Jews who wish to do so to emigrate, and ignore the much greater problem of what will happen to those who stay, to those who either wish to become or remain assimilated Soviet citizens, or to live as Jews in their [Soviet] homeland. No one has ever suggested that this category of Jews is anything other than the great majority, numbered in millions. What is going to happen to these people when the Soviet Union decides that it has let out

a sufficient number of Jews to satisfy American critics, or
to get rid of the troublemakers, or to appease foreign left-
wing opinion, or whatever motive it may be acting on?
Millions of Soviet Jews will then be at the mercy of a police
regime, infuriated by the fact that it has had to release its
hold over the lucky ones who escaped, and ready to exact
vengeance on those who are left behind.[115]

As spelled out in previous portions of this study, officially
sanctioned anti-Jewish discriminatory policies and practices
largely have been a part of the Soviet system since the late 1930s
and have continued, with brief respites since. It is also apparent
that the recent mass exodus of Jews, commencing in the early
1970s, has added to the fervor of this antisemitic feeling. This
is reflected in the consensus reportedly prevalent in the Soviet
leadership circles and other segments of the population that the
Jews who emigrate are "traitors", comparable only in notoriety
to the earlier mass migrations following the Revolution and after
the two World Wars.[116] As noted previously, this feeling of
distrust, undoubtedly, has "spilled over" onto those loyal Jewish
citizens who thus far have decided to remain in the Soviet
Union. It is perhaps safe to assume, therefore, that as time
goes on and more and more Jews depart, those Jews remaining
will be subject to increasing discrimination. It would also appear feasible that as a result of increased discrimination, many
Jews will feel less secure and even though "assimilated" will
eventually seek to emigrate. This insecurity on the part of
"assimilated" Jews is perhaps captured best in the following
Hannah Arendt observation:

> The behavior patterns of assimilated Jews...created
> a Jewish type that is recognizable everywhere....Jews
> were transformed into a social group whose members shared
> certain psychological attributes and reactions, the sum
> total of which was supposed to constitute "Jewishness."
> In other words, Judaism became an involved personal prob-
> lem for every individual Jew. (Italics added.)[117]

It is believed that this depiction most vividly illustrates the current dilemma of "assimilated" Jews in the Soviet Union -- out-
wardly, the appearance of social acceptance and conformity,
but inwardly, mounting fears of inferiority and deepening personal despair.

218

On Science and Technology

Over the years, Soviet authorities have defended their largely
restrictive Jewish emigration policies and practices under the all-
pervasive need to "protect State secrets" and to prevent a resultant
"brain-drainage."

In support of the Soviet "brain-drainage" contention is the
reported Israeli information that nearly 40 percent of the Soviet
Jewish immigration to that country, in recent years, has consisted
of persons with some post-secondary education. Also, of the total
HIAS-assisted Soviet Jewish immigration to the United States in the
first nine months of 1976, 48 percent (or 1,422 persons) were "highly-
trained and/or university educated." Also, as noted in detail earlier,
starting in 1975, more and more urban, well-educated Jews were
leaving the Soviet Union. This trend continued through 1977.[118]
(See Table 19 which follows for occupational details of Soviet
Jewish emigrants settling in the U.S. during the first nine months
of 1976.)

However, in spite of these undeniable realities, the view expressed earlier that the alleged "brain-drain" contention has little
validity at least in the long-term perspective is repeated here.
(A view which, on occasion, has been supported even by official
Soviet spokesmen.)[119] To recapitulate briefly, the Moscow-Lenin-
grad scientific-technological community where reportedly the great
bulk of the Jewish scientists are located (perhaps as high as 40 percent) has yet to be demonstrably affected by the recent Jewish exodus. Moreover, Jewish representation in the Soviet scientific-
technological community has undergone a continual and drastic
reduction in force over the past twenty-five years or so -- from a
Jewish representation of 15.46 percent of the total scientific community in 1950 to a mere 6.17 percent in 1975. In addition, as
previously noted, the Soviet leadership apparently made a fateful
decision, initially in the late 1930s and most recently reiterated
in the early 1970s, to purge Jews from "all responsible positions"
and to replace them with appropriate "Soviet" replacements. It
appears that this policy largely has been carried out.[120] Also, as
previously noted, Jewish emigration during the first five months of
1978 once again was composed predominantly of blue-collar and
nonurban Jews.[121] The educated, urban Jews apparently were stay-
ing put.

A perhaps conclusive indication that the alleged "brain-
drain" concern is not actually all that crucial to continuing
Soviet scientific-technological development is evidenced by
the continuing restrictions directed against Jews, ranging from
the denial of higher educational opportunities to discriminatory
job and career-development policies. Finally, as mentioned

219

TABLE 19
The Occupational Categories of HIAS-Assisted Soviet Jewish Immigrants to the U.S. for the First Nine Months of 1976*

Occupation	Male	Female	Total	Percent of Total Arrivals	Percent of Labor Force
Professionals	300	493	793	17	27
Engineers	322	85	407	9	14
Technicians	107	115	222	5	8
White Collar (Managerial, Clerical, Sales)	119	370	489	10	17
Blue Collar (Machine Trades, Bench-work, Structural)	482	82	564	12	19
Service	140	226	355	8	12
Transportation	64	1	65	1	2
Unskilled	12	7	19	–	–
Not Listed	4	4	8	–	–
Not in Labor Force	754	994	1,748	37	
(Children)	(160)	(154)	(314)		
(Housewives)	(–)	(152)	(152)		
(Students)	(481)	(412)	(893)		
(Retired)	(113)	(276)	(389)		
Total	2,304	2,377	4,681		

*Division of Research and Statistics, HIAS, Statistical Abstract 17 (Third Quarter, 1976): 14

previously, there is the feeling of distrust of all Jews, regardless of their individual emigration desires, which apparently has pervaded the Soviet society -- and which not only places the individual Jew in a state of continuous limbo, but also denies his services to the State.

NOTES

1. The dates and information relating to the Israeli immigration "waves" are from Leonard J. Fein, Israel: Politics and People (Boston: Little, Brown & Co., 1968).
2. J.B. Schectman, "The U.S.S.R., Zionism, and Israel," in The Jews in Soviet Russia since 1917, ed. Lionel Kochan (London, New York, Toronto: Oxford University Press, 1970), p. 116
3. The great majority of these individuals were living in the former Polish territories annexed by the Soviets in 1939.
4. Korey, Soviet Cage, p. 191.
5. Ibid.
6. West German sources estimated in 1973 that 180,000 ethnic Germans (about one-tenth of the estimated Soviet German population) were actively seeking emigration.
7. U.S., Foreign Broadcast Information Service (F.B.I.S.) vol. 3, Moscow and the Departure of Soviet Citizens from the U.S.S.R., 14 July 1977, R-1 [Hereafter cited as F.B.I.S., Soviet Departures]; Radio Liberty, Research Report no. RL 26/77, February 1, 1977, More Ethnic Germans Seek to Emigrate from the U.S.S.R.
8. According to statistical data provided by the U.S. Immigration and Naturalization service.
This dramatic increase in the number of direct Armenian immigrants to the United States is due, in part, to the fact that Lebanon, Cyprus, Greece, and France had stopped issuing entry visas to them.
9. As quoted in Korey, Soviet Cage, p. 193.
10. Royal M. Wharton, "Soviet Exit Policies Affect East-West Trade," Human Events (25 November 1972), p. 13. [Hereafter cited as Wharton, Human Events].
11. Ross, "Alienation and Self-Image," p. 3.
12. Ibid., pp. 9, 11.
13. Zand, Jewish Question.
14. Who in a speech in Riga, Latvia, in July 1965 reportedly had denounced "the manifestation of...antisemitism" as "absolutely alien to and in contravention to the [Soviet] world view." See Pravda (Moscow), 19 July 1965.

15. See "The Insider Who Came Out," Washington Post, 10 July 1977; Radio Liberty, Target Area Listener Report, no. 200-70, June 22, 1970, Soviet Leadership Divided on Anti-Semitism?"; Pravda (Moscow), 19 July 1965; Linden, Revival of Russian Patriotism, pp. 26-27; Associated Press (Moscow), 29 November 1976; and Reuters (Moscow), 25 September 1975.

16. As represented by the entire spectrum of internal dissident groups and personalities; e.g., Andrei Sakharov, individual nationalist groups like the Ukrainian Nationalist Movement, the assorted religious-oriented dissident elements, the human rights groups, etc.

17. "Soviet Dissident Allowed to Leave," New York Times, 4 June 1976.

18. "Soviet [sic] Stiffen Jews' Penalties," Baltimore Sun, 1 September 1976.

19. See "Trade With Soviet [sic] Fell 26.5% in 1977; U.S. Exports Down," New York Times, 29 March 1978; and "Soviet Trade Disappoints American Firms," New York Times, 29 January 1978.

20. U.S., Congress, Senate, Senator Henry M. Jackson of Washington Speaking for the Amendment of the Trade Reform Act of 1974, Amendment No. 2000, 93d Cong. 2d Sess., December 13, 1974, Congressional Record 120:174; U.S., Congress, Senate, Committee on Foreign Relations, Report of a Conference Between Members of the U.S. Senate and Delegates to the Supreme Soviet of the Soviet Union, Moscow and Leningrad, June 29-July 5, 1975 (Washington, D.C.: Government Printing Office, 1975), pp. 5-6; U.S., Department of State, Bureau of Public Affairs, Office of Media Services, Press Conference, Soviets Reject Trade Agreement, January 14, 1975.

21. "Why is Russia Letting Jews Go To Israel?" Washington Evening Star, 23 February 1972. The cost of absorbing Soviet Jews in Israel in 1974 was over $500 million a year. Institute for Jewish Policy Planning and Research of the Synagogue Council of America, Analysis, no 47, Special Issue, November 1, 1974, "Which Promised Land? The Realities of American Absorption of Soviet Jews," p. 1 [Hereafter cited as Synagogue Council, "American Absorption"].

22. There may be some validity in these charges since Israeli officials have freely admitted problems related to the recent Soviet immigration flow, e.g., housing shortage, the lack of professional employment opportunities, need for extensive retraining programs, etc. The Israelis characterize new Soviet immigrants as a "most difficult group to absorb."

222

23. Synagogue Council, "American Absorption"; Evans and Novak article, Washington Post, 24 January 1972; "Why Russia Lets More Jews Go," London Observer, 9 January 1972.

24. George Ginsburgs, "Soviet Law and the Emigration of Soviet Jews," Soviet Jewish Affairs, 3 (1973): 3-4 [Hereafter cited as Ginsburgs, "Soviet Law"].

25. English language translations of the new entry and exit regulation and travel tariff changes are provided as Appendices to this study.

26. New emigration measures promulgated in January 1976 reduced the four hundred ruble travel documents fee to three hundred rubles; however, the five hundred ruble fee for renunciation of Soviet citizenship, obligatory for those going to Israel, remains in effect. Dependents sixteen years of age and under are not required to renounce their Soviet citizenship and to pay the accompanying five hundred ruble fee -- such dependents automatically lose citizenship through the parents' citizenship renunciation action.

27. The one exception was a Jewish family which emigrated from Chernovtsy in 1972.

28. Polozhenie o v'yezde v S.S.S.R. i o vyezde iz S.S.S.R., utverzhdennoe postanovleniem, No. 801 Soveta Ministrov S.S.S.R., 22 Sentyabrya 1970 g. [Concerning confirmation of the statute on entry into and departure from The Union of Soviet Socialist Republics] No. 801, Council of Ministers of the U.S.S.R., 22 September 1970 g.

29. Ginsburgs, "Soviet Law," pp. 14-15. Of related interest is the amendment to Israel's 1952 Nationality Law, entitled "Nationality (Amendment No. 3) Law, 5731, 1971" which passed on May 17, 1971. It adds a new paragraph to Section 2 of the Nationality Law which grants Israeli nationality even before the immigrant arrives in Israel. The New Jerusalem Post, 18 May 1971.

30. "Soviet Defends Its [sic] Record on Allowing Emigration," New York Times, 21 January 1977 [Hereafter cited as New York Times, "Soviet Defends"].

31. Ginsburgs, "Soviet Law," pp. 8-9.

32. Emigration from the U.S.S.R.-Situation in 1974 (Moscow: A samizdat [self-published] document "published" by unknown authors on November 18, 1974), p. 4.

33. "Soviets deny hundreds of Jews visas over 'state secrets'," Chicago Sun-Times, 25 November 1976; Radio Liberty, Research Report no. RL 82/77, April 13, 1977, State Secrets and the Right to Emigrate.

223

34. Dr. Levich first applied for emigration in 1972. He reportedly finally received exit permission in October 1978. See "Soviet Physicist, Aided by Kennedy, Is Granted Permission to Emigrate," Washington Post, 24 October 1978.

35. Ginsburgs, "Soviet Law," pp. 7-8.

36. V.M. Chkhikvadze,"Human Rights and the Ideological Struggle," Sovetskoye gosudarstvo i pravo [The Soviet state and law] (April 1977), pp. 100-108 [Hereafter cited as Chkhikvadze, "Human Rights"]; U.S., Foreign Broadcast Information Service (F.B.I.S.) vol. 3, no. 244, Novoye Vremya Scores Reports on Emigration from U.S.S.R., 18 November 1976, R-9.

37. Other official Soviet sources claim that for the period 1970 through 1975, 98.4 percent of all exit visas applied for were granted. U.S., Foreign Broadcast Information Service (F.B.I.S.), vol. 3, Kudryavtsev Interviewed on Human Rights Issue, 23 March 1977, R-1; New York Times, "Soviet Defends"; American Association for Slavic Studies, "Soviet Freedoms," p. 5. Also, according a TASS article of September 4, 1975, "...since World War Two only 1,973 persons had their applications to Israel denied -- 1.6 percent of applicants." Reuters (Moscow), 4 September 1975.

38. In June 1974, a "highly placed" Soviet official commented that 13,704 Jewish applicants (or 83 percent) were allowed to leave the U.S.S.R. in 1971 and 29,821 Jewish applicants (or 95 percent) were let go in 1972. "Brezhnev Jews," United Press (Moscow), 19 June 1974.

39. "The Soviet View of Emigration," New York Times, 3 February 1976; "On the Departure of Soviet Citizens for Other Countries," Novosti (Moscow), 26 December 1972 [Hereafter cited as Novosti, "Departure of Soviet Citizens"].

40. F.B.I.S., "Soviet Departures."

41. It is of interest that the Communist regimes in both Poland and Czechoslovakia preceded the Soviet initiative in implementing emigration educational tax fees. Polish emigres, during the "great Jewish exodus" after the war, were compelled to reimburse the State approximately nine thousand U.S. dollars (equivalency) for their studies completed in Poland. Czech fees range from one to ten thousand Czech crowns -- equivalent to one-half to five months average salary in 1972. Wharton, Human Events, p. 14.

42. Vedomosti Verkhovnogo Soveta S.S.S.R. [Herald of the Supreme Soviet of the U.S.S.R.], no. 52 (Moscow: Izdanie Verkhovnogo Soveta S.S.S.R., 1972), item 519.

43. See Article 3 of the Presidium of the U.S.S.R. Supreme Soviet Decree of June 19, 1958, concerning "The Procedure for Publishing and Putting Into Force Legislative Acts of the U.S.S.R.," as contained in Vedomosti Verkhovnogo Soveta S.S.S.R. [Herald of the Supreme Soviet of the U.S.S.R.], no.

14 (Moscow: Izdanie Verkhovnogo Soveta S.S.S.R., 1958), item 275.

44. See Sobranie postanovlenii pravitel'stva S.S.S.R. [Collected resolutions of the U.S.S.R. Council of Ministers], no. 1, 1973, item 4. English language translations of both the "Educational Tax" decree and the accompanying specified educational reimbursement costs are provided as Appendices to this study. See also "Soviet [sic] Publishes Fee for Emigration," New York Times, 24 January 1973.

45. As cited in Sobranie postanovlenii pravitel'stva S.S.S.R. [Collected resolutions of the U.S.S.R. Council of Ministers], no. 1, 1973, item 4. According to a statement attributed to Mr. David Korn, Chairman of the "Washington, D.C. Soviet Jewish Committee," on August 22, 1972, Soviet officials in Moscow expected Jews in the United States to pay the required educational tax fees for the penalized Jewish emigrants. Reuters (Washington, D.C.), 23 August 1972.

46. Sobranie postanovlenii pravitel'stva S.S.S.R. [Collected resolutions of the U.S.S.R. Council of Ministers] no. 1, 1973, item 4; Novosti, "Departure of Soviet Citizens."

47. U.S., Foreign Broadcast Information Service (F.B.I.S.), vol. 3, Text of Abrasimov Letter to Mitterand on Soviet Jews, 8 September 1972, F-1; Novosti, "Departure of Soviet Citizens"; U.S., Foreign Broadcast Information Service (F.B.I.S.), vol. 3 Soviet Official in C.S.S.R. Paper on Emigration Practice, 27 January 1973, J-1; U.S., Foreign Broadcast Information Service (F.B.I.S.), vol. 3, Repayment for Education Before Emigration Defended, 28 September 1972, A-11; "Just Measure and Zionist Insinuations," New Times (Moscow) 38 (September 1972):10-11; U.S., Foreign Broadcast Information Service (F.B.I.S.), vol. 3, International Law Upholds State's Restrictions on Emigres, 12 September 1972, J-14. Few ethnic German emigrants (not more than twenty to thirty) were required to pay the educational tax. Most other national emigrants likewise escaped the brunt of the tax burden.

48. "Soviets Halt Tax on Exit, Inform U.S.," Washington Post, 19 April 1973; United Press (Washington, D.C.), 18 April 1973. One Soviet source, Victor Louis, said it was the "most controversial Soviet law of all time." "Soviet Education Tax," Yedi ot Aharonot (Tel Aviv), 21 March 1973.

49. See "Exit Fee Dropped for Many, Soviet Aide Says," Washington Evening Star, 3 May 1973.

50. "Israelis Assess Soviet Exit Fees," New York Times, 17 August 1972 [Hereafter cited as New York Times, "Israelis Assess"].

225

51. Washington Post, 28 February 1973.

52. New York Times, "Israelis Assess."

53. For "socialist" countries (except Yugoslavia) anyone can extend the vyzov. For the rest of the world, however, a mother, father, sister, brother, wife, husband, or child must extend the vyzov. However, the Soviet authorities have been somewhat lenient with regard to Jewish emigration practices -- vyzovs from distant relatives, friends, and even complete strangers, for the most part, have been readily accepted. Ginsburgs, "Soviet Law," p. 9.

54. There have been isolated reports that individual local O.V.I.R. offices have, on occasion, demanded that the new spravka document also be signed by the local Party official and trade union representative "just like the kharakteristika."

55. Pamyatka ot'ezzhayushchemu [Advice to those leaving] (Moscow: A samizdat [self-published] document "published" by unknown authors in November 1974) [Hereafter cited as Samizdat, Departure Advice]; see also Consular Section, American Embassy, Moscow, Procedure for Obtaining Exit Documentation From the Union of Soviet Socialist Republics (April 1970).

56. See Vedomosti Verkhovnogo Soveta S.S.S.R. [Herald of the Supreme Soviet of the U.S.S.R.] no. 1 (Moscow: Izdanie Verkhovnogo Soveta S.S.S.R., January 7, 1976), item 2.

57. "Soviet [sic] Ease Emigration," Washington Post, 18 January 1976; Chkhikvadze, "Human Rights"; Reuters (Moscow), 21 January 1976.

58. "New Exit Rules Curb Soviet Jews," Washington Post, 21 March 1974; "Emigration of Soviet Jews Declines, But Reasons are Disputed," New York Times, 26 May 1974.

59. Samizdat, Departure Advice.

60. Official Soviet sources claim that a total of 141,600 Jews (including dependents) left the Soviet Union for Israel between 1945 and 1977. U.S., Foreign Broadcast Information Service (F.B.I.S.), vol. 3, Emigration Data Cited: Refutes 'Zionist' Exaggeration, 14 July 1977, R-1.

61. "Israel, U.S. Jews Split Over Soviet Emigrants," Washington Post, 10 November 1976 [Hereafter cited as Washington Post, "Israel, U.S. Jews Split"]. Rome is the primary processing point for those Vienna "dropouts" who desire U.S. immigration -- a U.S. Immigration and Naturalization Service Office is situated at the American Embassy in Rome.

62. The Bucharest transit facility was in operation only from October 1972 until October 1973, when it was unilaterally closed by the Romanian authorities.

226

63. Leonard Schroeter, The Last Exodus (New York: Universe Books, 1974), p. 352.

64. Soviet-sourced data usually differ from Western-sourced data, and in some instances, there are internal discrepancies in both.

65. U.S., Foreign Broadcast Information Service (F.B.I.S.), vol. 3, Soviet Official Explains Emigration Policy to Novosti, 4 January 1973, J-6.

66. U.S., Foreign Broadcast Information Service (F.B.I.S.), vol. 3, 'Exodus' of Jews a Trickle, Many Wish to Return, 16 March 1973, J-1.

67. U.S., Department of State, Bureau of Public Affairs, GIST -- Soviet Jewish Emigration (July 1977) [Hereafter cited as U.S., Department of State, GIST]; National Conference on Soviet Jewry, Information Sheet, Emigration Statistics -- Soviet Jews [Hereafter cited as National Conference on Soviet Jewry, Emigration Statistics].

68. U.S.,Department of State, GIST. According to press reports at the time, Party General Secretary Brezhnev stated in Moscow in 1971 that 992 Jews had emigrated in 1970. Reuters (Moscow), 2 January 1974.

69. Reuters (Moscow), 2 January 1972.

70. U.S., Department of State, GIST; "Soviet Emigration to Israel Hits Record," Washington Evening Star, 4 January 1973; National Conference on Soviet Jewry, Emigration Statistics.

71. See "Jewish Emigration Vexes Kremlin," Christian Science Monitor, 14 March 1972.

72. Official Soviet sources state that 35,000 Jews emigrated from the U.S.S.R. to Israel in 1973. Reuters (Moscow), 4 September 1975.

73. U.S., Department of State, GIST; "Vance: Soviet-Bloc Rights Gains Scant," Washington Post, 7 June 1977.

74. Based on estimates by author; see also Katz, The Jews, "Nationalism," p. 5.

75. U.S., Department of State, GIST; estimates by author; Katz, The Jews, "Nationalism," p. 5; United Press International (Camp David, Maryland), 20 June 1973.

76. Official Soviet sources claim that 21,000 Soviet Jews emigrated in 1974. Reuters (Moscow), 4 September 1975.

77. U.S., Department of State, GIST.

78. Novoye Vremya (Moscow), 31 January 1975.

79. U.S., Department of State, GIST.

80. Author's estimates based on statistical data accrued at the Vienna, Austria, transit facility.

227

81. Zvi Gitelman, "Research on the U.S.S.R. Based on Interviews with Soviet Emigres: A Conference Report and Research Proposal" (Based on a conference sponsored by the Research and Development Committee of the American Association for the Advancement of Slavic Studies, December 19-20, 1976, University of Michigan, Ann Arbor), p. 3 [Hereafter cited as Gitelman, "Research on the U.S.S.R."].

82. 1976 was the first year since 1973 in which the Jewish emigration rate exceeded that of the immediately preceding year.

83. Author's estimates based on statistical data accrued at the Vienna, Austria, transit facility.

84. Also known as "refusedniks" -- those emigration applicants who are not allowed to leave the Soviet Union because of alleged possession of State secrets or who otherwise in some manner do not measure up to the imposed Soviet exit requirements.

85. Davar (Tel Aviv), 15 March 1977.

86. F.B.I.S., "Soviet Departures." The Soviets claim that from 1945 until December 31, 1975, approximately 122,000 Jews or "5 percent of the total Soviet Jewish population," emigrated. See Literaturnaya Gazeta (Moscow), 11 February 1976; Associated Press (Moscow), 22 January 1976.

87. At the time of the writing of this study, statistics were not available on the regional origins of the emigrants. See National Conference on Soviet Jewry, News Bulletin, no. 119, January 16, 1978, p. 2.

88. F.B.I.S., "Soviet Departures."

89. "Soviet [sic] Letting More Jews Leave; U.S. Group Backing Trade Credits," New York Times, 11 June 1978 [Hereafter cited as New York Times, "Soviet Letting More Jews Leave"].

90. Kurier (Vienna, Austria), 22 October 1976 (The Kurier article concerns "possible Austro-Israeli confrontation" over Soviet Jewish emigration, commenting specifically on the "dropout" problem. It also provides specific "dropout" figures.); Washington Post, "Israel, U.S. Jews Split"; Division of Research and Statistics, HIAS, Statistical Abstract 15 (Fourth Quarter, 1974): 1 [Hereafter cited as HIAS, Statistical Abstract (vol., quarter, year)]; Gitelman, "Research on the U.S.S.R.," p. 2. To these "dropout" figures must be added the number of Soviet Jews who initially went to Israel and subsequently left -- for example, including these Israeli "departees" in the 1975 figures would raise the 1975 "dropout" rate to 46 percent instead of the listed 37 percent.

91. Reportedly, "more than" 80 percent of the Jews who left Moscow in the first five months of 1978 did not go to Israel.

228

"Dropout" figures for other major Soviet cities are equally strik-
ing. See "Coping in Israel. Many Soviet Jews Find Transition
Is Difficult," Washington Post, 22 May 1978 [Hereafter cited as
Washington Post, "Coping in Israel"].

92. Later expanded to a "Committee of Ten."

93. At the time of the writing of this study these were the
only figures available. (Subsequent data suggest that the "dropout"
rate averaged "well over" 50 percent for the remainder of 1977 and
the first five months of 1978. See Washington Post, "Coping in
Israel"; Soviet Jewry Research Bureau, National Conference on Soviet Jewry, News Bulletin, no. 125, May 15, 1978 , "Emigration
Statistics.")

94. However, HIAS, as of September 1973, did cut off assistance to those Jews who first had immigrated to Israel and then
had sought resettlement elsewhere. "Refugee Soviet Jews 'denied
aid to settle'," Daily Telegram (London), 4 June 1976 [Hereafter
cited as Daily Telegram, "denied aid to settle"]; Synagogue Council, "American Absorption," p. 12; Kurier, (Vienna, Austria), 22
October 1976.

95. Daily Telegram, "denied aid to settle"; "Israel Acts to
Keep Soviet Jews Coming," New York Daily News, 18 July 1976;
Washington Post, "Israel, U.S. Jews Split"; Kurier (Vienna, Austria),
22 October 1976.

96. HIAS, Statistical Abstract 15 (Fourth Quarter, 1974): 1,
22, 24-25, 27; Emanuel Litvinoff, ed., "Emigrants Who Turn Away
From Israel," Insight 1 (April 1975):3 [Hereafter cited as Litvinoff,
"Emigrants Who Turn Away"].

97. HIAS, Statistical Abstract 17 (Third Quarter, 1976):1,14.

98. In 1975, three-quarters of the Jewish imigrants to the
U.S. came from the Soviet heartland, and in 1976, 85.5 percent
came from there. Gitelman, "Research on the U.S.S.R.," p. 3;
HIAS, Statistical Abstract 17 (Third Quarter, 1976): 15.

99. National Conference on Soviet Jewry, News Bulletin,
no. 119, January 16, 1978, p. 3.

100. Both of these refugee organizations were created in
the early 1950s to help refugees from Eastern Europe and the Middle
East. U.S., Department of State, Bureau of Public Affairs, Office
of Media Services, Special Report No. 15, U.S. Assistance to
Soviet Jews in Israel (April 1975) [Hereafter cited as U.S., Department of State, U.S. Assistance].

101. Ibid.

102. Synagogue Council, "American Absorption."

103. Ibid.

104. Soviet Jewry Research Bureau, National Conference on
Soviet Jewry, News Bulletin, no. 108, May 2, 1977, "Soviet Refugee Assistance to Israel," p. 4.

105. The parole authority also has been used for the Hungarian refugees in 1956, the Cuban refugees in the 1960s, and the Indochina refugees in the mid-1970s.

106. "U.S. Will Admit 4,000 Refugees," Baltimore Sun, 14 January 1977.

107. Also, as of June 1976, there were a reported approximately 300 Soviet Jews who had returned to Vienna, Austria, from Israel seeking repatriation to the U.S.S.R. As of August 22, 1977, this "returnee" figure reportedly had risen to 500 to 700 individuals. Reuters (Vienna), 3 December 1976; "Emigre Jews, Wanted by No One, Stagnate in Austria," Washington Post, 22 August 1977.

108. "West Berlin Destination For Some Soviet Jews," New York Times, 4 November 1973; "West Berlin Restricting Entry of Jews From the Soviet Union," New York Times, 4 December 1974; "West Berlin is Curbing Immigration by Jews," New York Times, 27 January 1975.

109. As noted earlier, the Soviet Armenian "direct" U.S. immigration figures rose dramatically in 1976.

110. Based on statistical data provided by the U.S. Immigration and Naturalization Service.

During the period 1973-77 there were very few "direct" Jewish immigrants to the U.S. from the larger Soviet Jewish communities of Moscow, Leningrad, Kiev, and Odessa.

111. However, individual non-Jews have gotten out of the Soviet Union via the Jewish emigration channel either by claiming nonexistent Jewish forebears or through "marriages of convenience" with Jewish spouses, which are dissolved immediately upon exiting -- the so-called "Emigration Jews" mentioned earlier. See Litvinoff, "Emigrants Who Turn Away," p. 9.

112. "Soviet Dissident Allowed to Leave," New York Times, 4 June 1976.

113. Washington Post, 28 February 1973; Jewish Telegraph Agency, 28 February 1973.

114. New York Times, 30 March 1973.

115. Leonard Schapiro, review of The Soviet Cage: Antisemitism in Russia, by William Korey, and Jewish Nationality and Soviet Politics: The Jewish Sections of the C.P.S.U., 1917-1930 by Zvi Y. Gitelman, in The New York Review of Books, 19 July 1973, p. 4.

116. "Moscow vs. Zionism," New York Post, 11 November 1976; "Soviet Jews in 9 Cities Claim Official Drive is Fostering 'Pogrom Atmosphere'," Los Angeles Times, 3 February 1977.

117. Arendt, Totalitarianism, p. 66.

118. Gitelman, "Research on the U.S.S.R.," p. 5; HIAS, Statistical Abstract 17 (Third Quarter, 1976): 14.

119. See U.S., Foreign Broadcast Information Service (F.B.I.S.), vol. 3, Tass [sic] Commentator Yuriy Kornilov Writes, 19 September 1972, A-12. According to Kornilov there "has never been a brain-drain" situation in the Soviet Union.

120. As mentioned earlier, current Jewish representation in the Soviet scientific community, higher educational institutions, diplomatic corps, military, etc., is drastically down from earlier years.

121. New York Times, "Soviet Letting More Jews Leave."

7
Conclusion

A basic conclusion of this study is that the official Soviet policy position toward the Jews is fundamentally an ambivalent one. Soviet theory professes one viewpoint, while actual Soviet practice often enacts another. In that context, the Soviet "Jewish" theoretical position has not changed at all since the inception of the regime in 1917. It still denies "nationhood" status to the Jews, believes that the only real solution to the Jewish "problem" lies in total assimilation and that attempts to preserve or revive Jewish "nationalism" are not only "socially retrogressive," but counter to the basic teachings of both Marx and Lenin. As the results of this study amply illustrate, the persistent Soviet theoretical viewpoint is classical antisemitism in its purest form.

On the other hand, Soviet practice continues to treat the Jews as a distinct "nationality," often equal in national stature to the officially recognized nationalities. (Of course, this officially expressed equality most often coincides with negative or regulatory governmental policy actions.) This dichotomy is depicted most clearly in such governmental actions as the listing of Yevrei (Jewish) in the "nationality" section of the obligatory internal passport document; the official establishment of a "Jewish Autonomous Oblast'" which, in itself, denotes distinct "national" status (and its endorsement by leading Party officials of the day as the new "Jewish national homeland"); and the creation of a "Jewish Commissariat" within the 1918 Commissariat for Nationality Affairs. Even today, the Jewish minority regularly is afforded the descriptive term of "nation." This is reiterated everywhere. In a recent description of the "nations" (narody) of European Russia, Jews are even listed as one of the osnovnie narody ("basic nations") and their "national" language (narodnyi yazik) as "Yiddish," and their own autonomous region is emphasized.[1] A most recent exemplar of this official "national"

232

designation is even found in the May 1976 Party publication, Partiinaya Zhizn' (Party Life), where the Jews are prominently displayed as a distinct "nationality" (natsional'nyi).[2] Countless other official writings commit the same identificational "error," a practice which, as noted previously, has drawn the ire of the Party ideologues.[3]

One entirely unexpected research revelation, however, is the steadfast refusal of the succeeding Soviet regimes, from Lenin to Brezhnev, to acknowledge the Jewish problem as part of the overall nationalities issue, at least in official pronouncements. In that respect, the successive leaderships have adhered to a singular tragic policy objective -- the complete destruction of Judaism, both ethnically and culturally.

Ironically, one is also struck by the awareness that the same typically "Russian" nature which characterized the Tsarist approach to "solving" the Jewish question has been retained by succeeding Bolshevik-Soviet regimes. For example, Tsars Aleksandr I (1801-25) and Nicholas I (1825-55) both faced Jewish problems similar to those of the Bolsheviks and later, the Soviets. In seeking to resolve their Jewish situations, both Tsars attempted the total assimilation of the Jews, as did subsequent Bolshevik and Soviet regimes. In that effort, Nicholas I opened special Yiddish language schools like the Bolsheviks and for the same purpose -- to undermine Judaism and to promote "statist" loyalties among the Jewish citizenry. In addition, both Tsar Aleksandr I and Tsar Nicholas I sought to institute large-scale Jewish resettlements for which they, too, sought foreign financing and other material support. Furthermore, restrictive minority (Jewish) educational quotas were as much a fact of life under the Tsars as they are in the contemporary Soviet Union. Also, Jewish emigration and all of its ramifications was as prevalent in Tsarist times as it is today.[4] But unlike Tsarist rule, the Jews in contemporary Soviet society are not allowed the "freedom" voluntarily to cast off their "Jewishness" by merely claiming that they are no longer "Jews"; their "Jewishness" is decided for them by the State, regardless of their own stated preferences.

With regard to the current situation, we have seen in this study the detrimental effect which the Jewish issue has had on certain Soviet foreign policy expectations, i.e., the denial of "most-favored-nation status" and extended trade credits from the United States. In addition, there are even indications that the continuation of the current Jewish difficulties (and the possible ripening of other Soviet "nationalities" issues as well) may adversely affect Soviet Party relations with other communist parties. This possibility is especially pertinent with regard to Soviet Party relations with members of the Eurocommunist bloc.[5]

In addition, the longevity of the Jewish problem may be considerably extended if it does prove true that the majority of Jews will not emigrate and perhaps never will. That circumstance could not help but have a continuing effect on the other "national" and dissident groups. In that respect, it should be reiterated that individual Jewish activist leaders recently have stated their intention not only to focus on Jewish emigration rights, but also, on religious and political rights, and for a better life in general for Jews in the Soviet Union.[6] In other words, to attempt to regain Jewish "national" rights -- a most pertinent objective, particularly, when one recalls Hannah Arendt's observation that the "loss of national rights also entails the loss of political and human rights."[7] That redirection of effort, interestingly, coincides not only with the stated aims of other "national" and dissident groups, but, also with the reported view of President Carter's National Security Adviser Zbigniew Brzezinski. According to a press article, Brzezinski reportedly stated that "it would certainly be within the rules of peaceful coexistence, as the Soviet leaders have defined it," if the West were to give "some realistic encouragement of pluralism via nationalism and separatism" in the Soviet Union.[8] A most interesting projection, particularly in view of the continuing Jewish troubles.

At this juncture, mention should be made of the author's predetermined disposition to render as objective and factual account of the status of Soviet Jewry as possible, without biased or moralistic inclusions. The premise being to let the facts more or less speak for themselves (which it is believed they have with devastating reality). However, it is exceedingly difficult to ignore the human tragedy which has exemplified Jewish life in the Soviet Union and before its inception, Tsarist Russia. Traditionally, the Jews have constituted an alien "they" in a society to which they individually have made significant contributions. As noted previously in this study, Jews in the Soviet Union are the tragic victims of the continuing dichotomy in official "Jewish" policy practices, i.e., the contradiction between "total assimilation" and extensive exclusion. This is particularly ironic when one considers the leading role played in the establishment and early years of the communist regime by such leading "Jewish" revolutionary figures as Trotsky, Kamenev, Zinoviev, Kaganovich, Litvinov, and others. Moreover, the Jewish "stigma" remains in spite of the important revolutionary roles played by these communist zealots and their counterparts today. The Jews are damned if they do and damned if they don't. Those Jews who

234

seek to retain their "Jewishness" and practice traditional cultural observances are singled out for exceptional coercive measures by the authorities. The Jews who, on the other hand, desire complete assimilation into the general population are not allowed to do so; they are continually reminded of their "Jewishness" through official policy exclusion and popular antisemitic mentality. Previously in this study, a comparison was made of the Jewish plight in the Soviet Union with that of Jews under Nazi rule. The comparative note was offered that the Soviet Jewish situation was not as totally destructive as that of the German Jewish example; i.e., the German Jews were physically annihilated, whereas, the Soviet situation was "restrained primarily to ethnocultural deprivation." However, perhaps this comparison fails to depict accurately the actual reality of the Soviet Jewish predicament. Perhaps, the psychological scars which are borne by most Jews in the Soviet Union today are, in a sense, as totally destructive as the physical annihilation experienced by the Jews in Nazi Germany. When one considers the overwhelming pervasiveness of the stigma of Jewish identity in Soviet society today, one cannot help but believe that the Soviet Jewish experience is a most devastating one. As one survivor of Nazi totalitarian antisemitism remarked, "I experienced a definite Jewish identity which affected the entire spectrum of my existence and colored all my thoughts and actions." A depiction which undoubtedly characterizes the Soviet Jewish experience today. Here is a people who have been singled out, more than any other ethnic group, for exceptional governmental pressures to deny their cultural heritage and to embrace, with all haste, the sanctioned culture of the new Soviet State. Yet, in spite of this "pioneering" role, Jews in the Soviet Union continue to be treated as second class citizens. Therefore, as substantiated by the extensive factual evidence presented in this study, the final judgment must be made that the Soviet Jewish experience constitutes a human tragedy of considerable magnitude. One which requires an urgent resolution, both in the interest of the Soviet Jews themselves and also perhaps in the interest of the continued viability of the Soviet State.

Consequently, as can be seen from these brief concluding remarks, the Soviet Jewish problem is complex, potentially eruptive, and full of possible pitfalls for the ongoing Soviet leadership. This is especially pertinent in view of the relative influence which the Jewish situation has on both national and dissident groups, and the fact that there does not appear to be any imminent or easy solution to the Jewish predicament on the horizon.

Finally, in view of the severity of current Soviet "Jewish" policies and practices, it appears evident that any Soviet Jew who desires to maintain his "Jewishness" has only one alternative -- to leave the Soviet Union. Many will choose to do so; others, perhaps the great majority, will attempt an accommodation, if indeed they can, with the realities of the Soviet social system. Their lot will not be an easy one.

NOTES

1. See Narody Evropeiskoi Chasti S.S.S.R. [Nations of the European U.S.S.R.] (Moscow: Gosudarstvennoe Izdatel' stvo, 1964), 1:23, 2:832-33.
2. Party Life, p. 16.
3. F.B.I.S., "Pravda Official Rebukes."
4. Judd L. Teller, The Kremlin, The Jews, and the Middle East (New York and London: Thomas Youseloff, 1957), pp. 20-23; Greenberg, Jews in Russia, II:59-62, 73.
5. See Radio Free Europe Research, Non-Ruling CPs: Italy, November 21, 1972, "Soviet Anti-Semitism Poses Problem for PCI."
6. The Economist, "We'll Stay."
7. Arendt, Totalitarianism, pp. 299-300.
8. "101 problems for Mr [sic] Brezhnev," The Economist, 19 March 1977.

Appendices

TABLE 20
The Jewish Population of the U.S.S.R. in 1970 as Compared to
the General Population -- According to Republic, Region, and
Oblast'*

| Autonomous Republic, Region, and Oblast' | Absolute Numbers | | Percentage of Jews in General Population |
	General Population	Jews	
(1)	(2)	(3)	(4)
U.S.S.R.	241,720,134	2,150,707	0.88
R.S.F.S.R.	130,079,210	807,915	0.62
Northwest Region (Rayon)	12,156,960	176,904	1.45
Arkhangel'sk Oblast'	1,401,289	–	–
Vologda Oblast'	1,295,897	–	–
Leningrad City	3,949,501	162,587	4.11
Leningrad Oblast'	1,435,729	5,879	0.41
Murmansk Oblast'	799,527	2,684	0.33
Novgorod Oblast'	721,471	–	–
Pskov Oblast'	875,293	2,335	0.27
Karel' A.S.S.R.	713,451	1,580	0.22
Komi A.S.S.R.	964,802	1,839	0.19
Central Region (Rayon)	27,651,573	319,956	1.16
Briansk Oblast'	1,581,950	11,476	0.73
Vladimir Oblast'	1,510,913	–	–
Ivanovo Oblast'	1,339,110	1,764	0.13
Kalinin Oblast'	1,717,237	3,456	0.20
Kaluga Oblast'	994,876	2,278	0.23
Kostroma Oblast'	870,575	–	–
City of Moscow	7,061,008	251,523	3.56
Moscow Oblast'	5,774,529	36,316	0.63
Orel Oblast'	931,028	–	–
Riazin Oblast'	1,411,590	–	–

TABLE 20

(1)	(2)	(3)	(4)
Smolensk Oblast'	1,106,066	5,316	0.48
Tula Oblast'	1,952,467	4,857	0.25
Yaroslav Oblast'	1,400,224	2,970	0.21
Volga-Viat Region (Rayon)	8,347,817	16,845	0.20
Gorkiy Oblast'	3,682,484	16,845	0.46
Kirov Oblast'	1,727,348	-	-
Mariy A.S.S.R.	684,748	-	-
Mordvin A.S.S.R.	1,029,562	-	-
Chuvash A.S.S.R.	1,233,675	-	-
Central Black Earth Region (Rayon)	7,998,214	11,085	0.13
Belgorod Oblast'	1,261,140	-	-
Voronezh Oblast'	2,526,928	6,434	0.25
Kursk Oblast'	1,473,864	4,651	0.31
Lipetsk Oblast'	1,224,344	-	-
Tambov Oblast'	1,511,938	-	-
Povolzh Region (Rayon)	18,575,426	55,376	0.30
Astrakhan Oblast'	867,483	3,462	0.40
Volgograd Oblast'	2,322,910	5,042	0.22
Kuybyshev Oblast'	2,750,926	18,678	0.68
Penzen Oblast'	1,555,970	-	-
Saratov Oblast'	2,454,083	11,992	0.49
Ul'ianov Oblast'	1,224,748	-	-
Bashkir A.S.S.R.	3,818,075	6,681	0.17
Kalmyk A.S.S.R.	267,993	-	-
Tatar A.S.S.R.	3,131,238	9,521	0.30
North Caucasus Region (Rayon)	14,280,644	66,872	0.46
Krasnodar Region (Kray)	4,509,807	7,726	0.17
Stavropol Region (Kray)	2,305,780	6,140	0.27
Rostov Oblast'	3,831,262	18,190	0.47
Dagestan A.S.S.R.	1,428,540	22,149	1.55
Kabardino-Balkar A.S.S.R.	588,203	5,578	0.95

TABLE 20

(1)	(2)	(3)	(4)
North Osetin A.S.S.R.	552,581	2,044	0.37
Checheno-Ingush A.S.S.R.	1,064,471	5,045	0.47
Ural Region (Rayon)	15,185,916	51,927	0.34
Kurgan Oblast'	1,085,560	–	–
Orenburg Oblast'	2,049,976	6,885	0.33
Perm Oblast'	3,023,443	8,096	0.27
Sverdlovsk Oblast'	4,319,741	21,269	0.49
Udmurt A.S.S.R.	1,417,675	–	–
Cheliabinsk Oblast'	3,228,801	15,677	0.48
Western Siberia Region (Rayon)	12,109,501	27,338	0.22
Altay Region (Kray)	2,670,261	–	–
Kemerov Oblast'	2,918,353	5,012	0.17
Novosibirsk Oblast'	2,505,249	11,864	0.47
Omsk Oblast'	1,823,831	8,081	0.44
Tomsk Oblast'	785,706	2,381	0.30
Tyumen Oblast'	1,406,101	–	–
Eastern Siberia Region (Rayon)	7,463,434	17,202	0.23
Krasnoiarsk Region (Kray)	2,961,991	5,349	0.18
Irkutsk Oblast'	2,313,410	8,029	0.35
Chitin Oblast'	1,144,918	1,714	0.15
Buriat A.S.S.R.	812,251	2,090	0.26
Tuva A.S.S.R.	230,864	–	–
Far East Region (Rayon)	5,780,509	24,391	0.42
Primorsk Region (Kray)	1,721,285	3,832	0.22
Khabarovsk Region (Kray)	1,345,907	18,913	1.40
The Jewish Autonomous Oblast' of Birobidzhan (which is part of the Khabarovsk Region)	172,449	11,452	6.64
Amur Oblast'	793,449	–	–
Kamchatka Oblast'	287,612	–	–

TABLE 20

(1)	(2)	(3)	(4)
Magadan Oblast'	352,481	1,646	0.47
Sakhalin Oblast'	615,652	-	-
Yakut A.S.S.R.	664,123	-	-
Kaliningrad Oblast'[1]	731,936	4,525	0.61
Total number of Jews spread among autonomous republics, regions, and oblasts where their number is not given in the census. (This figure is obtained by subtracting the number of Jews in oblasts, where their number is not given, from the number of Jews in the republic.)		35,494	
Ukraine, S.S.R.	47,126,517	777,126	1.65
Dneper and Donetsk Region (Rayon)	20,056,672	241,765	1.20
Voroshilovgrad Oblast'	2,750,566	12,539	0.46
Dnepropetrovsk Oblast'	3,342,962	62,287	2.07
Donetsk Oblast'	4,891,979	39,988	0.82
Zaporozh Oblast'	1,774,749	20,242	1.14
Kirovograd Oblast'	1,259,398	7,729	0.61
Poltava Oblast'	1,706,217	10,768	0.63
Sumi Oblast'	1,504,679	4,725	0.31
Kharkov Oblast'	2,826,122	76,487	2.71
Southwest Region (Rayon)	20,689,231	361,811	1.77
Vinnitsa Oblast'	2,131,902	42,251	1.98
Volyn Oblast'[2]	974,454	-	-

[1]Kaliningrad Oblast' is the northern part of eastern Prussia, which was annexed by the U.S.S.R. after World War II (the southern part was annexed by Poland).

[2]The total number of Jews in the oblasts of Volyn and Ternopol which is not given is 3,294. (This figure is arrived at by subtractin the number of Jews in all oblasts of the Ukraine, where their number is given, from the number of Jews in the whole republic.)

240

TABLE 20

(1)	(2)	(3)	(4)
Zhitomir Oblast'	1,626,608	35,706	2.19
Transcarpathia Oblast'	1,056,799	10,862	1.03
Ivano-Frankovsk Oblast'	1,249,271	3,584	0.28
Kiev City	1,631,908	152,006	9.31
Kiev Oblast'	1,834,021	12,628	0.69
L'vov Oblast'	2,428,868	27,721	1.14
Rovno Oblast'	1,047,605	2,527	0.24
Ternopol' Oblast'[1]	1,152,668	–	–
Khmelnits Oblast'	1,615,373	16,089	1.00
Cherkass Oblast'	1,534,993	10,643	0.69
Cherigov Oblast'	1,559,874	10,335	0.66
Chernovots Oblast'	844,877	37,459	4.43
South Region (Rayon)	6,380,614	170,886	2.68
Krym Oblast'	1,813,502	25,614	1.41
Nikolayev Oblast'	1,148,118	17,978	1.56
Odessa Oblast'	2,389,006	117,233	4.91
Kherson Oblast'	1,029,988	10,061	0.98
Byelorussia S.S.R.	9,002,338	148,011	1.64
Brest Oblast'	1,294,550	5,015	0.39
Vitebsk Oblast'	1,370,006	17,343	1.27
Gomel' Oblast'	1,533,304	42,312	2.76
Grodno Oblast'	1,120,395	3,199	0.28
Minsk City	916,949	47,057	5.13
Minsk Oblast'	1,540,130	7,278	0.47
Mogilev Oblast'	1,227,004	25,807	2.10
Uzbek S.S.R.	11,799,429	102,855	0.87
Andizhan Oblast'	1,059,174	4,404	0.41
Bukhara Oblast'	933,656	8,421	0.90
Kashkadar Oblast'	801,480	2,452	0.30
Namangan Oblast'	847,510	–	–
Samarkand Oblast'	1,468,884	15,964	1.09
Surkhandar' Oblast'	662,027	–	–

[1] The total number of Jews in the oblasts of Volyn and Ternopol' which is not given is 3,294. (This figure is arrived at by subtracting the number of Jews in all oblasts of the Ukraine, where their number is given, from the number of Jews in the whole republic.

241

TABLE 20

(1)	(2)	(3)	(4)
Syrdar' Oblast'	575,461	–	–
Tashkent City	1,384,509	55,758	4.03
Tashkent Oblast'	1,478,785	3,611	0.24
Fergansk Oblast'	1,331,972	9,200	0.69
Khorezm Oblast'	553,707		
Kara-Kalpak, A.S.S.R.	702,264		
Total number of Jews in oblasts where their number was not given		3,045	–
Moldavia S.S.R.	3,568,873	98,072	2.75
Georgia S.S.R.	4,686,358	55,382	1.18
Tbilisi City	891,928	19,579	2.20
Regions subject to republic administration	2,898,282	28,400	0.98
Abkhaz A.S.S.R.	486,959	4,372	0.90
Adzhar, A.S.S.R.	309,768	1,546	0.50
South Osetin Autonomous Oblast'	99,421	1,485	1.49
Azerbaidzhan S.S.R.	5,117,081	41,288	0.81
Baku City	1,265,515	29,760	2.35
Regions subject to republic administration	3,499,066	11,521	0.35
Nakhichevan A.S.S.R.	202,187	–	–
Nagorno-Karabakh Autonomous Oblast'	150,313	–	–
Jews in oblasts where their number is not given		7	
Latvia S.S.R.	1,364,127	36,680	1.55
Riga City	731,831	30,581	4.18
Kazakh S.S.R.	12,008,726	27,689	0.21
Alma-Ata City	729,633	9,180	1.26
Aktyubinsk Oblast'	550,582	–	–
Alma-Ata Oblast'	712,148	–	–

TABLE 20

(1)	(2)	(3)	(4)
Eastern Kazakhstan Oblast'	845,251	–	–
Gur'yev Oblast'	499,577	–	–
Dzhambul Oblast'	794,320	–	–
Karaganda Oblast'	1,552,056	5,040	0.32
Kzyl-Orda Oblast'	491,780	1,090	0.22
Kokchetav Oblast'	589,204	–	–
Kustanay Oblast'	889,621	–	–
Pavlodar Oblast'	697,947	–	–
North Kazakhstan Oblast'	555,830	–	–
Semipalatinsk Oblast'	713,827	–	–
Taldi-Kurgan Oblast'	610,046	–	–
Turgay Oblast'	221,441	–	–
Uralsk Oblast'	531,077	–	–
Tselinograd Oblast'	754,955	–	–
Chimkent Oblast'	1,287,431	3,310	0.26
Jews in oblasts where their number was not given		9,069	
Lithuania S.S.R.	3,128,236	23,564	0.75
Vilnius City	372,100	16,491	4.43
Takzhik S.S.R.	2,899,602	14,615	0.50
Dushanbe City	375,744	11,424	3.04
Regions subject to republic administration	1,488,341	–	–
Leninabad Oblast'	937,721	2,251	0.24
Autonomous Oblast' of Gorno-Badakhshan	97,796	–	–
Jews in districts where their number was not given		940	
Kirghiz S.S.R.	2,932,805	7,680	0.26
Frunze City	430,618	5,962	1.38
Regions subject to republic administration	770,956	–	–
Issyk-Kul Oblast'	311,922	–	–

TABLE 20

(1)	(2)	(3)	(4)
Naryn Oblast'	186,358	–	–
Osh Oblast'	1,232,881	–	–
Jews in oblasts where their number was not given		1,718	
Estonia S.S.R.	1,356,079	5,288	0.39
Tallinn City	362,706	3,754	1.03
Turkmen S.S.R.	2,158,880	3,494	0.16
Ashkhabad City	256,224	1,246	0.49
Regions subject to republic administration	412,438	–	–
Mary Oblast'	622,343	–	–
Tashauz Oblast	410,920	–	–
Chardzhoy Oblast'	456,955	799	0.17
Jews in oblasts where their number was not given		1,499	
Armenia S.S.R.	2,491,873	1,048	0.04

*Council of Ministers, Soviet Census of 1970 4.

TABLE 21
Jewish Population in U.S.S.R. Compared to the General Population in the 1959 and 1970 Censuses*

	1959 Census			1970 Census			Changes			
	General Population Number	Jews Number	%	General Population Number	Jews Number	%	General Population Number	% 1959	Jews Number	% 1970
U.S.S.R.	208,826,650	2,267,814	1.1	241,720,134	2,150,707	0.9	+32,893,484	115.7	-117,107	94.84
R.S.F.S.R.	111,534,306	875,307	0.7	130,079,210	807,915	0.6	+18,544,904	116.6	-67,392	92.34
Ukraine	41,869,046	840,314	2.0	47,126,517	777,126	1.6	+5,257,471	112.6	-63,188	92.52
Byelorussia	8,055,714	150,084	1.9	9,002,338	148,011	1.6	+946,624	111.8	-2,073	98.67
Moldavia	2,884,477	95,107	3.3	3,568,873	98,072	2.7	+684,396	123.7	+2,965	103.15
Uzbek	8,119,103	94,344	1.2	11,799,429	102,855	0.9	+3,680,326	145.3	+8,511	108.42
Georgia	4,044,045	51,582	1.3	4,686,358	55,382	1.2	+642,313	115.9	+3,800	105.76
Azerbaidzhan	3,697,717	40,204	1.1	5,117,081	41,382	0.8	+1,419,364	138.4	+1,084	102.73
Latvia	2,093,458	36,592	1.7	2,364,127	36,680	1.6	+270,669	112.9	+88	100.00
Kazakh	9,294,741	28,048	0.3	13,008,726	27,689	0.2	+3,713,985	140.0	-359	98.57
Lithuania	2,711,445	24,672	0.9	3,128,236	23,564	0.8	+416,791	115.4	-1,180	96.00
Tadzhik	1,980,547	12,414	0.6	2,899,602	14,615	0.5	+919,055	146.4	+2,201	117.74
Kirghiz	2,065,837	8,610	0.4	2,932,805	7,680	0.3	+866,968	142.0	-903	89.19
Estonia	1,196,791	5,436	0.5	1,356,079	5,288	0.4	+159,288	113.3	-148	98.14
Turkmen	1,516,375	4,078	0.3	2,158,880	3,494	0.2	+642,505	142.4	-584	85.67
Armenia	1,763,048	1,024	0.05	2,491,873	1,048	0.04	+728,825	141.3	+24	102.34

*Council of Ministers, Soviet Census of 1959; Council of Ministers, Soviet Census of 1970 4.

TABLE 22
Jewish Rural Population -- According to the Censuses of 1959
and 1970*

Republic	1959	1970	Changes Number	Changes Percent of 1959
U.S.S.R.	106,112	45,056	-60,056	-56.5
R.S.F.S.R.	45,079	21,401	-23,678	-52.5
Ukraine	30,280	12,888	-17,392	-57.4
Uzbek	4,421	3,076	-1,345	-30.4
Byelorussia	5,593	2,546	-3,047	-54.5
Moldavia	6,791	2,182	-4,609	-67.9
Kazakh	2,748	1,307	-1,441	-52.4
Georgia	7,752	914	-6,838	-88.2
Azerbaidzhan	1,287	476	-811	-63.0
Kirghiz	669	339	-330	-49.3
Latvia	464	316	-148	-31.9
Lithuania	261	213	-48	-18.4
Tadzhik	448	192	-256	-57.1
Estonia	136	124	-12	-8.8
Turkmen	133	52	-81	-60.9
Armenia	50	30	-20	-40.0

*Ibid.

TABLE 23
Jewish Population in the Primary Cities in the Republics (1970)*

| Republic and City | Absolute Numbers | Percentage of Total Jewish Population | |
		In given republic	In U.S.S.R.
U.S.S.R.	2,150,707		100.0
R.S.F.S.R.	807,915	100.0	37.6
Moscow	251,523	31.1	11.7
Leningrad	162,587	20.1	7.6
Ukraine,S.S.R.	777,126	100.0	36.1
Kiev	152,006	19.6	7.1
Byelorussia,S.S.R.	148,011	100.0	6.9
Minsk	47,057	31.8	2.2
Uzbek, S.S.R.	102,855	100.0	4.8
Tashkent	55,758	54.2	2.6
Moldavia, S.S.R.	98,072	100.0	4.6
Kishinev	49,905	50.9	2.3
Georgia, S.S.R.	55,382	100.0	2.6
Tbilisi	19,579	35.3	0.9
Azerbaidzhan, S.S.R.	41,288	100.0	1.9
Baku	29,716	72.0	1.4
Latvia, S.S.R.	36,680	100.0	1.7
Riga	30,581	83.4	1.4
Kazakh, S.S.R.	27,689	100.0	1.3
Alma-Ata	9,180	33.1	0.4
Lithuania, S.S.R.	23,564	100.0	1.1
Vilnius	16,491	70.0	0.8
Tadzhik, S.S.R.	14,615	100.0	0.7
Dushanbe	11,424	78.2	0.5
Kirghiz, S.S.R.	7,680	100.0	0.4
Frunze	5,962	77.6	0.3
Estonia, S.S.R.	5,288	100.0	0.2
Tallinn	3,754	71.0	0.2
Turkmen, S.S.R.	3,494	100.0	0.2
Ashkabad	1,246	35.7	0.1
Armenia, S.S.R.	1,179	100.0	0.1
Yerevan	----(No figures given)----		

*Council of Ministers, Soviet Census of 1970 4.

TABLE 24

The Jewish Urban and Rural Population of the U.S.S.R. According to the Censuses of 1959 and 1970 -- By Republic and Oblast'*

Republic	Urban Population			Rural Population			Urban & Rural Population		
	1959	1970	%	1959	1970	%	1959	1970	%
(1)	(2)	(3)	(4)	(5)	(6)	(7)	(8)	(9)	(10)
U.S.S.R.	2,161,702	2,104,651	97.3	106,112	45,056	43.4	2,267,814	2,150,707	94.8
R.S.F.S.R.	830,228	786,514	94.7	45,079	21,401	47.5	875,307	807,915	92.3
Leningrad City	168,641	162,587	96.4	-	-	-	168,641	162,578	96.4
Leningrad Oblast'	4,618	4,831	104.6	1,453	1,048	72.1	6,053	5,879	97.1
Murmansk Oblast'	2,884	2,318	80.4	156	366	234.6	3,040	2,684	88.3
Pskov Oblast'	2,750	2,223	80.8	275	112	40.7	3,025	2,335	77.2
Karel' A.S.S.R.	-	1,470	-	-	110	-	-	1,580	-
Komi A.S.S.R.	-	1,594	-	-	245	-	-	1,839	-
Kaliningrad Oblast'	4,268	4,386	102.8	252	139	55.2	4,520	4,525	100.0
Briansk Oblast'	13,326	11,348	85.2	381	128	33.6	13,707	11,476	83.7
Ivanovo Oblast'	-	1,730	-	-	34	-	-	1,764	-
Kalinin Oblast'	-	3,317	-	-	139	-	-	3,456	-
Kaluga Oblast'	-	2,278	-	-	149	-	-	2,278	-
Moscow City	239,246	251,523	105.1	-	-	-	239,246	251,523	105.1
Moscow Oblast'	43,355	28,259	65.2	19,682	8,057	40.9	63,037	36,316	57.6
Smolensk Oblast'	-	5,122	-	-	194	-	-	5,316	-
Tula Oblast'	-	4,660	-	-	197	-	-	4,857	-
Yaroslav Oblast'	-	2,931	-	-	39	-	-	2,970	-
Gorkly Oblast'	17,827	16,695	93.7	447	150	33.6	18,274	16,845	92.2
Voronezh Oblast'	5,610	5,824	103.8	587	610	103.9	6,197	6,434	103.8
Kursk Oblast'	-	4,581	-	-	70	-	-	4,651	-
Astrakhan Oblast'	-	3,369	-	-	93	-	-	3,462	-
Volgograd Oblast'	-	4,903	-	-	139	-	-	5,042	-
Kuybyshev Oblast'	19,690	18,468	93.8	495	210	42.4	20,185	18,678	92.5
Saratov Oblast'	13,004	11,651	89.6	815	341	41.8	13,819	11,992	86.8
Bashkir A.S.S.R.	7,167	6,589	91.9	300	92	30.7	7,467	6,681	89.5
Tatar A.S.S.R.	10,112	9,434	93.3	248	87	35.1	10,360	9,521	91.9
Krasnodar Region (Kray)	-	7,173	-	-	533	-	-	7,726	-
Stavropol Region (Kray)	-	5,789	-	-	351	-	-	6,140	-
Rostov Oblast'	20,516	17,944	87.5	348	246	70.7	20,864	18,190	87.2

TABLE 24

	(1)	(2)	(3)	(4)	(5)	(6)	(7)	(8)	(9)	(10)
Orenburg Oblast'		8,248	6,681	81.0	468	204	43.6	8,716	6,885	79.0
Perm Oblast'		-	7,852	-	-	244	-	-	8,096	-
Sverdlovsk Oblast'		25,291	20,942	82.0	725	327	45.1	26,016	21,296	81.8
Chellabinsk Oblast'		18,611	15,485	83.2	337	192	57.0	18,948	15,677	82.3
Kemerovo Oblast'		-	4,938	-	-	74	-	-	5,012	-
Novosibirsk Oblast'		12,184	11,752	96.5	245	112	45.7	12,429	11,864	95.5
Omsk Oblast'		9,175	7,970	86.9	283	111	39.2	9,458	8,081	83.4
Tomsk Oblast'		-	2,303	-	-	78	-	-	2,381	-
Krasnolarsk Region (Kray)		-	5,112	-	-	237	-	-	5,349	-
Irkutsk Oblast'		9,727	7,823	80.4	586	206	35.2	10,313	8,029	77.9
Chitin Oblast'		-	1,477	-	-	264	-	-	1,471	-
Buriat A.S.S.R.		2,224	1,807	85.0	447	283	63.3	2,691	2,090	77.7
Primorsk Region (Kray)		-	3,264	-	-	568	-	-	2,832	-
Khabarovsk Region (Kray)[1]		7,959	7,048	88.6	535	494	92.3	8,494	7,542	88.8
Birobidzhan Oblast'		11,977	10,275	85.8	2,292	1,177	51.4	14,269	11,452	80.8
Magadan Oblast'		-	1,466	-	-	180	-	-	1,646	-
Dagestan A.S.S.R.		20,501	21,652	105.6	926	497	53.7	21,427	22,149	103.4
Kabardino-Balkar A.S.S.R.		3,365	5,458	162.2	196	120	73.2	3,529	5,578	158.1
Checheno-Ingush A.S.S.R.		4,981	4,855	97.5	242	190	78.5	5,233	5,045	96.6
North Osetin A.S.S.R.		2,012	2,015	100.0	70	29	41.4	2,082	2,044	98.2
Republic of the Ukraine		810,031	764,238	94.3	30,280	12,888	42.6	840,311	777,126	92.5
Donetsk & Dnepr Region									241,765	
Voroshilovgrad Oblast'		13,795	12,460	90.3	144	79	54.9	13,939	12,539	90.0
Dnepropetrovsk Oblast'		72,430	68,776	95.0	826	511	61.9	73,256	69,287	94.6
Donetsk Oblast'		42,256	39,834	94.3	245	154	62.9	42,501	39,988	94.1
Zaporozh Oblast'		20,113	19,843	98.7	698	399	57.2	20,811	20,232	97.3
Kirovograd Oblast'		8,640	7,358	85.2	865	371	42.9	9,505	7,729	81.3
Poltava Oblast'		12,007	10,600	88.2	280	168	60.0	12,287	10,768	87.7
Sumi Oblast'		6,025	4,624	76.7	234	101	43.2	6,259	4,725	75.5
Kharkov Oblast'		83,740	76,211	91.0	452	276	61.1	84,192	76,487	90.8

[1]Without the Autonomous Jewish District of Birobidzhan, which is included in the Khabarovsk Region. The data for the former is given separately.

249

TABLE 24

	(1)	(2)	(3)	(4)	(5)	(6)	(7)	(8)	(9)	(10)
Southwest Region (Rayon)									361,811	
Vinnitsa Oblast'		41,648	38,787	93.1	8,509	3,464	40.7	50,157	42,241	84.2
Volyn Oblast'		-	-	-	-	-	-	-	-	-
Zhitomir Oblast'		39,805	35,131	88.3	2,243	575	25.6	42,048	35,706	84.9
Transcarpathia Oblast'		9,226	9,042	98.0	2,943	1,820	61.8	12,169	10,862	89.3
Ivano-Frankovsk Oblast'		-	3,529	-	-	55	-	-	3,548	-
Kiev City		153,466	152,006	99.0	-	-	-	153,466	152,006	99.0
Kiev Oblast'		13,886	12,251	88.2	897	377	42.0	14,768	12,628	85.5
L'vov Oblast'		29,701	27,584	93.9	329	137	41.6	30,030	27,721	92.3
Rovno Oblast'		-	2,459	-	-	68	-	-	2,527	-
Ternopol' Oblast'		-	-	-	-	-	-	-	-	-
Khmelnits Oblast'		17,733	15,685	88.5	1,317	404	30.7	19,050	16,089	84.5
Cherkass Oblast'		12,281	10,463	85.2	829	180	21.7	13,110	10,643	81.2
Chernigov Oblast'		12,220	10,229	83.7	342	106	31.0	12,562	10,335	82.3
Chernovots Oblast'		40,717	37,221	91.4	1,423	238	16.7	42,140	37,459	88.9
South Region (Rayon)									170,886	
Krym Oblast'		26,815	24,089	89.8	2,675	1,525	57.0	26,374	25,614	97.1
Nikolayev Oblast'		19,028	17,417	91.5	1,249	561	44.9	20,277	17,978	88.7
Odessa Oblast'		118,962	116,280	97.7	2,415	953	39.5	121,377	117,233	96.6
Kherson Oblast'		9,556	9,768	102.2	881	293	33.1	10,437	10,061	96.4
Byelorussian Republic		144,491	145,465	100.7	5,593	2,546	45.5	150,084	148,011	98.6
Brest Oblast'		5,715	4,879	85.4	297	136	45.8	6,012	5,015	83.4
Vitebsk Oblast'		18,092	16,926	93.4	894	417	46.6	18,986	17,343	91.4
Gomel Oblast'		42,913	41,619	97.0	2,094	693	33.1	45,007	42,312	94.0
Grodno Oblast'		3,513	3,068	87.3	232	131	56.5	3,745	3,199	85.4
Minsk City		38,842	47,057	121.1	-	-	-	38,842	47,057	121.1
Minsk Oblast'		7,638	6,452	84.5	1,416	826	58.3	9,054	7,278	80.4
Mogilev Oblast'		27,778	25,464	91.7	660	343	52.0	28,438	25,807	90.7

250

TABLE 24

(1)	(2)	(3)	(4)	(5)	(6)	(7)	(8)	(9)	(10)
Uzbek Republic	89,823	99,799	111.0	4,421	3,076	69.6	94,344	102,855	109.0
Andizhan Oblast'	5,011	4,472	89.2	588	130	22.1	5,599	4,404	78.7
Bukhara Oblast'	6,122	8,244	134.7	302	177	58.6	6,242	8,121	126.4
Kashkadar Oblast'	–	2,184	–	–	268	–	–	2,452	–
Samarkand Oblast'	12,855	14,360	111.7	1,661	1,604	96.6	14,496	15,964	110.1
Surkandar' Oblast'	2,583	–	–	493	–	–	3,076	–	–
Tashkent City	50,455	55,785	110.6	–	–	–	50,445	55,758	110.5
Tashkent Oblast'	4,264	3,146	73.8	948	465	49.1	5,212	3,611	69.3
Fergansk Oblast'	8,301	9,149	110.2	387	51	13.2	8,688	9,200	105.9
Moldavian Republic	88,316	95,890	108.6	6,791	2,182	32.1	95,107	98,072	103.1
Georgian Republic	43,830	54,468	124.3	7,752	914	11.8	51,285	55,382	108.0
Tiblisi City	17,333	19,579	113.0	97	–	–	–	19,579	–
Regions subject to administration of republic	20,106	27,645	137.5	7,374	755	10.2	27,580	28,400	103.0
Abkhaz A.S.S.R.	3,124	4,253	136.1	208	119	57.2	3,332	4,372	131.2
Adzhar A.S.S.R.	1,585	1,511	95.3	32	35	109.4	1,617	1,546	95.6
Autonomous Region of South Osetin	1,682	1,480	88.0	41	5	12.2	1,723	1,485	86.2
Azerbaidzhan Republic	38,917	40,812	104.9	1,287	476	37.0	40,204	41,288	102.7
Baku City	29,197	29,716	101.8	–	–	–	29,197	29,716	101.8
Regions subject to administration of republic	9,634	11,052	114.7	1,270	469	36.9	10,904	11,521	105.7
Latvian Republic	36,128	36,364	100.7	464	316	68.1	36,592	36,680	100.2
Riga City	30,267	30,581	101.0	–	–	–	30,267	30,581	101.0

251

TABLE 24

(1)	(2)	(3)	(4)	(5)	(6)	(7)	(8)	(9)	(10)
Kazakh Republic	25,300	26,382	104.3	2,748	1,307	47.6	28,048	27,689	98.7
Alma-Ata City	8,462	9,180	109.0	-	-	-	8,425	9,180	109.0
Karagandin Oblast'	4,792	4,336	103.0	207	104	50.2	4,999	5,040	100.8
Kyzl-Orda Oblast'	1,045	1,070	102.4	56	20	35.7	1,101	1,090	99.0
Chimkent Oblast'	2,965	3,143	106.0	308	167	54.2	3,273	3,310	101.1
Lithuanian Republic	24,411	23,351	95.7	261	213	81.6	24,672	23,564	95.5
Vilnius City	16,354	16,491	100.8	-	-	-	16,354	16,491	100.8
Tadzhik Republic	11,967	14,423	120.5	488	192	42.9	12,415	14,615	117.7
Dushanbe City	8,720	11,424	131.0	-	-	-	8,720	11,424	131.0
Regions subject to administration of republic	3,239	-	-	434	-	-	3,673	-	-
Leninabad Oblast'	-	2,215	-	-	36	-	-	2,251	-
Kirghiz Republic	7,941	7,341	92.4	669	339	50.7	8,610	7,680	89.2
Frunze City	5,840	5,962	102.1	-	-	-	5,840	5,962	102.1
Regions subject to administration of republic	610	-	-	472	-	-	1,082	-	-
Estonian Republic	5,300	5,164	97.4	136	124	91.2	5,436	5,288	97.3
Tallinn City	3,714	3,754	101.1	-	-	-	3,714	3,754	101.1
Turkmen Republic	3,954	3,442	87.2	133	52	39.1	4,078	3,494	85.7
Ashkhabad City	1,276	1,246	97.6	-	-	-	1,276	1,246	97.6
Charshan Oblast'	-	788	-	-	11	-	-	799	-
Armenian Republic	974	1,018	104.5	50	19	38.0	1,024	1,048	102.3

*Council of Ministers, Soviet Census of 1959; Council of Ministers, Soviet Census of 1970 4.

252

TABLE 25
Jewish Population in Six Primary Cities of the U.S.S.R. According
to the Censuses of 1959 and 1970*

City	1959 (in 000's)	1970 (in 000's)	Growth Number (in 000's)	Growth Percentage of 1959
Moscow	239.2	251.5	12.3	5.1
Minsk	38.8	47.1	8.3	21.4
Kishinev	42.9	50.0	7.1	16.6
Tashkent	50.4	55.8	5.4	10.7
Tbilisi	17.3	19.6	2.3	13.3
Dushanbe	8.7	11.4	2.7	31.0

*Ibid.

TABLE 26
Jewish Population in Primary Cities of Eight Republics as Compared to the Total Jewish Population of the Same Republics (1970)*

Republic	Number of Jews (in 000's)	Capital City	Number of Jews (in 000's)	Percentage of total Jews in Republic
Uzbek	102.8	Tashkent	55.8	54.3
Moldavia	98.1	Kishinev	50.0	51.0
Azerbaidzhan	41.3	Baku	29.7	71.9
Latvia	36.7	Riga	30.6	83.4
Lithuania	23.6	Vilnius	16.5	69.9
Tadzhik	14.6	Dushanbe	11.4	78.1
Kirghiz	7.7	Frunze	6.0	77.9
Estonia	5.3	Tallinn	3.8	71.7

*Council of Ministers, Soviet Census of 1970 4.

TABLE 27
Jews and Other "Minorities" Whose Numbers Declined in Comparison to Russians, Ukrainians, and the
General Population (1970 Compared to 1959)*

Nationality	1959 Census	1970 Census	Change Numbers	Change Percentage	Those who declared their national language to be their mother language (in percentage) 1959	Those who declared their national language to be their mother language (in percentage) 1970
Total population of U.S.S.R.	208,826,650	241,720,134	+32,893,484	+15.8	94.3	93.9
Russians	114,113,579	129,015,140	+14,901,561	+13.1	99.8	99.8
Ukrainians	37,252,930	40,753,246	+3,500,316	+9.3	87.7	85.7
Jews	2,267,814	2,150,707	-117,107	-5.2	21.5	17.7
Mordavians	1,285,116	1,262,670	-22,554	-1.6	78.1	77.8
Poles	1,380,232	1,167,523	-212,759	-15.2	45.2	32.5
Karals	167,278	146,081	-12,197	-12.5	71.3	63.0
Finns	92,717	84,750	-7,967	-8.6	59.5	51.0
Czechs	24,557	20,981	-3,567	-14.5	49.0	42.9
Slovaks	14,641	11,658	-2,983	-20.4	61.2	52.0
Wopses	16,374	8,281	-8,093	-49.4	46.1	34.3
Karaites	5,727	4,571	-1,156	-20.2	13.9	12.8
Albanians	5,258	4,402	-856	-16.3	79.0	50.7

*Council of Ministers, Soviet Census of 1959; Council of Ministers, Soviet Census of 1970 4.

TABLE 28
Married Jews in the U.S.S.R. According to Age and Sex in Four Republics (1970)*

Republic	Total over 16 M	Total over 16 F	16 – 19 M	16 – 19 F	20 – 29 M	20 – 29 F	30 – 39 M	30 – 39 F	40 – 49 M	40 – 49 F	50 – 59 M	50 – 59 F	60 and older M	60 and older F
Ukraine	78.8	57.1	1.4	5.7	40.9	56.9	88.2	82.5	94.6	79.1	94.9	60.4	86.5	36.9
Byelorussia	76.7	57.5	1.0	3.4	39.4	51.0	89.8	81.9	96.0	78.5	95.9	60.2	87.3	38.4
Moldavia	78.4	63.2	2.1	6.3	44.8	60.6	92.2	87.3	96.5	85.3	96.2	69.7	87.6	41.7
Latvia	74.2	58.7	1.3	3.7	39.4	53.8	86.2	82.0	92.4	80.6	92.0	66.6	83.4	36.0

Percent of Those Married at Age:

*Council of Ministers, Soviet Census of 1970 4.

255

TABLE 29
Comparison by Age of Jews and Russians in the R.S.F.S.R.
(1970)*

Age Group	Jews		Russians	
	Number	Percent	Number	Percent
Total	807,915	100.0	107,747,630	100.0
0 - 10	56,002	7.0	19,269,970	18.0
11 - 15	34,335	4.2	10,872,898	10.1
16 - 19	31,375	3.9	8,049,168	7.5
20 - 29	88,006	10.9	14,006,485	13.0
30 - 39	121,675	15.0	17,365,923	16.1
40 - 49	129,563	16.0	14,864,679	13.8
50 - 59	131,592	16.2	10,237,941	9.5
60 and older	213,379	26.4	12,985,378	12.0

*Ibid.

256

TABLE 30
Comparison of Men and Women in the Jewish Population of the U.S.S.R. According to the 1970 Census*

	Total Number of Jews	Men	Women					
			Number	Percentage of women in general Jewish population	Number of Women for Every 100 Men	Surplus of Women	
						Number	Percentage
U.S.S.R.	2,150,707	988,009	1,162,698	54.1	117.0	174,689	100.0
R.S.F.S.R.	807,915	378,902	492,013	53.1	113.2	50,111	28.7
Ukraine	777,126	345,038	432,078	55.6	125.2	87,030	49.8
Byelorussia	148,011	57,483	80,528	54.4	119.3	13,045	7.5
Uzbek	102,855	48,417	54,483	52.9	112.4	6,021	3.4
Georgia	55,382	26,094	29,288	52.9	112.2	3,194	1.8
Azerbaidzhan	41,288	18,761	22,527	54.6	120.1	3,766	2.2
Lithuania	23,564	11,389	12,175	51.7	106.9	786	0.4
Moldavia	98,072	45,110	52,962	54.0	117.4	7,852	4.5
Latvia	86,680	17,659	19,021	51.9	107.7	1,362	0.8
Estonia	5,288	2,657	2,631	49.8	99.0	-26	–
Kirghiz	7,680	3,605	4,075	53.1	113.0	470	0.3
Tadzhik	14,615	7,016	7,569	51.8	107.4	523	0.3
Armenia	1,048	478	570	54.4	119.2	92	–
Turkmen	3,494	1,711	1,783	51.0	104.2	72	–
Kazakh	27,689	13,649	14,040	50.7	102.9	391	0.2

*Ibid.

257

TABLE 31
The Working Jewish Population in the U.S.S.R. According to
Sex, Type of Community, and Education (1970)*

				Per 1000 people in working population having education			
(1)	Higher	Higher, Incomplete	High School, Vocational	High School, General	High School, Incomplete	Total Higher and High School	Primary
	(2)	(3)	(4)	(5)	(6)	(7)	(8)
R.S.F.S.R.							
Rural and urban population							
Both sexes	468	41	173	139	113	934	50
Men	486	45	163	123	110	927	57
Women	447	37	185	159	115	943	40
Urban population							
Both sexes	471	41	173	140	111	936	48
Men	490	45	162	123	109	929	56
Women	449	37	185	160	114	945	39
Rural population							
Both sexes	362	32	185	119	156	854	105
Men	367	33	179	115	155	849	113
Women	352	31	195	127	157	862	92
Ukraine							
Rural and urban population							
Both sexes	283	39	214	236	143	915	64
Men	286	42	200	218	148	894	81
Women	279	36	230	255	137	937	45
Urban population							
Both sexes	284	39	215	236	142	916	62
Men	287	43	200	218	148	896	79
Women	280	36	230	256	137	939	44

258

TABLE 31

(1)	(2)	(3)	(4)	(5)	(6)	(7)	(8)
Rural population							
Both sexes	190	23	197	199	178	787	155
Men	189	20	162	200	179	750	181
Women	192	27	246	199	178	842	117
Byelorussia							
Rural and urban population							
Both sexes	248	35	210	208	197	898	84
Men	256	37	186	186	200	868	110
Women	240	34	231	230	193	928	57
Urban population							
Both sexes	247	35	209	209	198	898	85
Men	254	37	188	187	202	868	110
Women	239	22	230	232	194	928	57
Rural population							
Both sexes	340	54	235	146	112	857	80
Men	358	39	194	147	122	860	104
Women	315	75	290	146	98	924	48
Moldavia							
Rural and urban population							
Both sexes	184	38	161	233	197	813	145
Men	181	38	138	217	208	782	167
Women	186	39	188	252	185	850	114
Urban population							
Both sexes	183	38	161	235	198	815	142
Men	181	38	138	219	208	784	167
Women	186	38	187	254	186	851	114
Rural population							
Both sexes	198	42	180	145	192	757	165
Men	201	35	134	157	206	733	185
Women	193	52	247	127	171	790	135

TABLE 31

(1)	(2)	(3)	(4)	(5)	(6)	(7)	(8)
Latvia							
Rural and urban population							
Both sexes	285	66	159	211	160	881	96
Men	295	68	148	190	164	865	109
Women	273	63	172	235	155	898	82
Urban population							
Both sexes	284	66	159	211	160	880	96
Men	294	68	148	190	164	864	109
Women	273	63	172	235	156	890	82
Rural population							
Both sexes	373	45	179	174	129	900	70
Men	407	33	154	163	138	895	81
Women	321	64	218	192	115	910	51

*Ibid., Vols. 3 and 4.

TABLE 32
The Jewish Population in Five Republics -- According to Sex,
Type of Community, and Education (In 1959 and 1970)*

	Per 1000 people having education aged 10 years and up						
	Higher	Higher, Incomplete	High School, Vocational	High School, General	High School, Incomplete	Total Higher and High School	Primary
(1)	(2)	(3)	(4)	(5)	(6)	(7)	(8)
R.S.F.S.R.							
Urban and rural population							
Both sexes -- 1959	267	57	120	173	147	764	152
Both sexes -- 1970	344	55	135	172	118	824	116
Men -- 1959	300	63	121	147	146	777	158
Men -- 1970	391	62	132	143	114	842	113
Women -- 1959	240	52	119	195	148	754	147
Women -- 1970	304	49	137	197	122	809	118
Urban population							
Both sexes -- 1959	270	58	119	175	146	768	150
Both sexes -- 1970	346	55	134	173	117	825	114
Men -- 1959	305	65	119	149	144	782	155
Men -- 1970	393	62	132	143	113	843	111
Women -- 1959	242	52	118	198	147	757	146
Women -- 1970	305	50	137	198	121	811	117
Rural population							
Both sexes -- 1959	204	40	137	136	174	691	193
Both sexes -- 1970	274	34	146	125	151	730	165
Men -- 1959	214	41	139	123	177	694	211
Men -- 1970	301	36	147	117	150	751	165
Women -- 1959	194	39	135	151	170	689	174
Women -- 1970	242	31	145	135	152	705	166

261

TABLE 32

(1)	(2)	(3)	(4)	(5)	(6)	(7)	(8)
Birobidzhan							
Urban and rural population							
Both sexes - 1959	29	9	76	54	236	404	338
Both sexes - 1970	45	9	108	95	290	547	292
Men - 1959	30	9	60	58	225	382	389
Men - 1970	56	11	80	104	296	547	321
Women - 1959	28	9	89	50	244	420	300
Women - 1970	36	8	129	88	289	517	270
Urban population							
Both sexes - 1959	29	9	77	57	239	411	333
Both sexes - 1970	26	10	109	98	295	558	284
Men - 1959	31	9	63	62	226	391	382
Men - 1970	57	12	83	107	301	560	311
Women - 1959	28	9	88	53	249	427	297
Women - 1970	38	8	128	92	291	557	262
Rural population							
Both sexes - 1959	27	7	72	36	222	362	397
Both sexes - 1970	31	3	100	69	251	454	362
Men - 1959	23	5	47	40	224	339	427
Men - 1970	51	4	55	81	255	446	402
Women - 1959	28	9	92	32	220	381	320
Women - 1970	16	2	134	60	247	459	331
Ukraine							
Urban and rural population							
Both sexes - 1959	141	33	115	167	196	652	206
Both sexes - 1970	195	37	150	214	151	747	160
Men - 1959	156	35	120	156	195	662	222
Men - 1970	221	43	152	198	151	765	100
Women - 1959	131	31	111	176	197	646	194
Women - 1970	175	32	148	226	152	733	160
Urban population							
Both sexes - 1959	143	33	114	170	197	657	205
Both sexes - 1970	197	37	150	215	151	750	158
Men - 1959	157	36	119	158	197	667	221
Men - 1970	223	43	153	199	150	768	159
Women - 1959	132	30	110	180	197	649	194
Women - 1970	176	32	148	227	152	735	158

TABLE 32

(1)	(2)	(3)	(4)	(5)	(6)	(7)	(8)
Rural population							
Both sexes - 1959	108	30	130	90	170	528	225
Both sexes - 1970	120	19	128	149	159	575	246
Men - 1959	116	27	131	100	167	541	243
Men - 1970	134	18	115	160	163	590	253
Women - 1959	100	33	129	81	174	517	207
Women - 1970	105	20	140	137	155	557	239
Byelorussia							
Urban and rural population							
Both sexes - 1959	109	32	110	135	220	606	235
Both sexes - 1970	164	37	142	179	188	710	190
Men - 1959	113	32	109	125	218	597	265
Men - 1970	183	40	136	166	190	715	201
Women - 1959	105	31	111	143	222	612	211
Women - 1970	148	34	147	189	187	705	181
Urban population							
Both sexes - 1959	106	30	108	136	223	603	237
Both sexes - 1970	163	37	142	180	189	711	190
Men - 1959	110	31	108	126	220	595	267
Men - 1970	181	40	136	167	191	715	201
Women - 1959	102	29	108	145	225	609	213
Women - 1970	148	34	147	190	188	707	180
Rural population							
Both sexes - 1959	183	70	171	98	151	673	186
Both sexes - 1970	223	43	167	125	127	683	191
Men - 1959	170	57	151	101	163	651	209
Men - 1970	253	34	146	121	130	684	183
Women - 1959	188	83	189	96	139	695	164
Women - 1970	192	51	184	129	123	679	198
Latvia							
Urban and rural population							
Both sexes - 1959	142	46	84	201	214	687	214
Both sexes - 1970	209	72	119	214	159	773	163
Men - 1959	151	50	83	171	216	671	238
Men - 1970	236	77	117	185	162	777	165
Women - 1959	134	43	84	226	213	700	194
Women - 1970	185	67	121	241	157	771	162

TABLE 32

(1)	(2)	(3)	(4)	(5)	(6)	(7)	(8)
Urban population							
Both sexes - 1959	141	46	83	202	215	687	214
Both sexes - 1970	209	72	119	215	160	775	164
Men - 1959	150	50	83	172	216	671	239
Men - 1970	236	78	117	185	162	778	165
Women - 1959	134	43	83	227	213	700	194
Women - 1970	185	67	121	241	157	771	162
Rural population							
Both sexes - 1959	199	25	128	247	211	170	179
Both sexes - 1970	262	37	133	180	129	741	129
Men - 1959	214	24	95	147	234	714	191
Men - 1970	295	35	110	168	133	741	121
Women - 1959	174	26	181	148	174	703	161
Women - 1970	215	41	165	198	124	743	141
Moldavia							
Urban and rural population							
Both sexes - 1959	83	23	71	129	214	520	293
Both sexes - 1970	126	34	112	198	190	660	227
Men - 1959	93	23	64	115	221	516	322
Men - 1970	142	37	107	189	200	675	234
Women - 1959	76	23	77	141	208	525	270
Women - 1970	112	32	116	206	181	647	222
Urban population							
Both sexes - 1959	81	22	69	132	216	520	295
Both sexes - 1970	126	34	111	200	190	661	227
Men - 1959	90	22	62	116	223	513	326
Men - 1970	141	37	107	191	200	676	233
Women - 1959	74	22	74	144	210	524	271
Women - 1970	112	32	115	207	182	648	222
Rural population							
Both sexes - 1959	114	39	104	99	190	546	261
Both sexes - 1970	134	33	127	123	172	589	245
Men - 1959	131	39	90	98	202	560	272
Men - 1970	153	33	104	132	184	606	257
Women - 1959	97	39	118	99	177	530	250
Women - 1970	115	35	151	113	159	571	233

*Council of Ministers, Soviet Census of 1959; Council of Ministers, Soviet Census of 1970, Vols. 3,4.

264

TABLE 33

The Educational Levels of Three Ethnic Groups: Jews, Russians, and the Local National Majority in the Working Population in Five Republics (1970)*

| | Every 1000 employed persons having education | | | | | | |
	Higher	Higher, Incomplete	High School, Vocational	High School, General	High School, Incomplete	Total Higher and High School	Primary
(1)	(2)	(3)	(4)	(5)	(6)	(7)	(8)
R.S.F.S.R.							
Russians							
Both sexes	65	12	115	143	328	663	255
Men	65	12	94	133	342	646	294
Women	65	12	136	153	313	679	219
Jews							
Both sexes	468	41	173	139	113	934	50
Men	486	45	162	123	110	927	57
Women	447	37	185	159	115	943	40
Ukraine							
Ukrainians							
Both sexes	47	10	90	182	308	637	253
Men	51	10	79	188	331	659	255
Women	43	9	100	176	286	614	252
Jews							
Both sexes	283	39	214	236	143	915	64
Men	286	42	200	218	148	894	81
Women	279	36	230	255	137	937	45
Russians							
Both sexes	98	17	143	224	294	776	169
Men	100	18	128	211	312	769	188
Women	96	16	158	238	275	783	149

TABLE 33

(1)	(2)	(3)	(4)	(5)	(6)	(7)	(8)
Byelorussia							
Byelorussians							
Both sexes	40	10	83	143	279	555	326
Men	43	10	66	139	315	573	339
Women	36	10	98	148	245	537	314
Jews							
Both sexes	248	35	210	208	197	898	84
Men	256	37	189	186	200	868	110
Women	240	33	231	230	193	928	57
Russians							
Both sexes	141	22	187	227	258	835	131
Men	137	21	174	219	282	833	144
Women	145	23	201	237	231	837	116
Moldavia							
Moldavians							
Both sexes	23	7	39	76	290	435	315
Men	28	7	35	81	318	469	336
Women	19	7	44	70	264	404	295
Jews							
Both sexes	184	38	161	233	197	813	143
Men	181	38	138	217	208	782	167
Women	186	39	188	252	185	850	114
Russians							
Both sexes	111	22	160	203	281	777	159
Men	106	21	132	197	312	168	182
Women	115	22	185	208	254	784	139
Latvia							
Latvians							
Both sexes	59	21	123	135	320	658	261
Men	53	21	108	103	345	630	289
Women	64	21	138	166	295	684	235
Jews							
Both sexes	285	66	159	211	160	881	96
Men	295	68	148	190	164	865	109
Women	273	63	172	235	155	898	82

TABLE 33

(1)	(2)	(3)	(4)	(5)	(6)	(7)	(8)
Russians							
Both sexes	77	21	128	165	290	681	230
Men	81	22	123	149	313	688	244
Women	73	21	134	181	268	677	216

*Council of Ministers, Soviet Census of 1970, Vols. 3,4.

TABLE 34
The Working Jewish Population Having High School (Complete and Incomplete) and Higher Education (Complete and Incomplete) in Four Soviet Republics -- According to Sex (1959 and 1970)*

	Per 1000 People		Rate of Increase	
	1959	1970	Number	Percent
Ukraine				
Both sexes	814	915	101	11.2
Men	770	894	124	11.6
Women	871	937	66	10.8
Byelorussia				
Both sexes	783	898	115	11.5
Men	726	868	142	11.9
Women	852	928	76	10.9
Latvia				
Both sexes	823	881	58	10.7
Men	779	865	86	11.1
Women	884	898	14	10.2
Moldavia				
Both sexes	673	813	140	12.1
Men	604	782	178	12.9
Women	787	850	63	10.8

*Council of Ministers, Soviet Census of 1959; Council of Ministers, Soviet Census of 1970, Vols. 3,4.

TABLE 35
Percentage of Speakers of Jewish Dialects of the Total Jewish
Population in Several Selected Regions (1970)*

Republics or Districts	Percentage of Speakers of Jewish Dialects	
U.S.S.R.	25 percent	
R.S.F.S.R.	19	"
Moscow City	17	"
Moscow Oblast'	21	"
Leningrad City	15	"
Leningrad Oblast'	19	"
Dagestan, A.S.S.R.	88	"
Kabardino-Balkar, A.S.S.R.	81	"
North Osetin, A.S.S.R.	36	"
Checheno-Ingush, A.S.S.R.	57	"
Ukraine, S.S.R.	18	"
Kiev City	16	"
Kiev Oblast'	28	"
Khmel'nitsk Oblast'	31	"
Transcarpathia Oblast'	54	"
Chernovots Oblast'	54	"
Byelorussia, S.S.R.	28	"
Minsk Oblast'	36	"
Mogilev Oblast'	36	"
Tadzhik, S.S.R.	64	"
Moldavia, S.S.R.	52	"
Uzbek, S.S.R.[1]	42	"
Georgia, S.S.R.	82	"
Those who speak Georgian	59	"
Those who speak other dialects	23	"
Azerbaidzhan, S.S.R.[2]	47	"
Lithuania, S.S.R.	63	"
Latvia, S.S.R.	49	"

[1] The Uzbek Republic is the place of principal concentration of
Bukharan Jews.
[2] Concentration of Mountain Jews who speak Tati.
*Council of Ministers, Soviet Census of 1970 4: 9, 20-321,
331-83.

TABLE 36
Languages Spoken by Jews According to Republic, Community, and Sex (1970)*

(1)	Number of Jews	Who declare that the Jewish dialect is			Percent of all Jews	Who declare that their mother tongue is	
		their mother tongue	a second well-known language	Total (3+4)		Russian	Other Languages
	(2)	(3)	(4)	(5)	(6)	(7)	(8)
U.S.S.R.	2,150,707	381,078	166,566	547,644	25.46	1,682,798	86,381
Men	988,009	167,295	70,376	237,671	24.05	779,038	41,676
Women	1,162,698	213,783	96,190	309,973	26.66	903,760	45,155
Urban population	2,104,651	367,447	163,953	531,400	25.25	1,665,295	81,909
Rural population	46,056	13,631	2,613	16,244	35.27	27,503	4,922
R.S.F.S.R.	807,915	94,971	76,866	171,837	21.26	709,502	3,442
Men	378,902	42,372	33,336	75,708	19.98	334,593	1,937
Women	429,013	52,599	43,530	96,129	22.41	374,909	1,505
Urban Population	768,514	90,900	75,085	166,075	21.11	692,313	3,211
Rural Population	21,401	3,921	1,781	5,762	26.92	17,189	231
Ukraine	777,126	102,190	55,277	157,467	20.26	654,620	17,936 (Ukrainian)
Men	345,048	42,252	22,232	64,484	18.69	293,509	8,046
Women	432,078	59,938	33,045	92,983	21.52	361,111	9,890
Urban Population	764,238	97,514	54,742	152,256	19.92	649,206	15,343
Rural Population	12,888	4,676	535	5,211	40.43	5,414	2,593
Byelorussia	148,011	26,391	15,517	41,908	28.31	118,608	2,911 (Byelorussian)
Men	67,483	10,649	5,484	17,133	25.39	55,378	1,406
Women	80,528	15,742	9,033	24,755	30.77	63,230	1,505
Urban Population	145,465	25,860	15,395	41,255	28.36	116,912	2,600
Rural Population	2,546	531	122	653	25.65	1,696	311

TABLE 36

(1)	(2)	(3)	(4)	(5)	(6)	(7)	(8)	
Uzbek, S.S.R.	102,855	38,621	4,896	43,517	42.31	47,308	322	(Uzbeki)
Men	48,417	17,946	2,150	20,096	41.51	22,337	152	
Women	54,343	20,675	2,746	23,421	43.02	24,971	180	
Urban Population	99,779	36,745	4,870	41,615	41.71	46,758	223	
Rural Population	3,076	1,876	26	1,902	61.83	550	109	
Georgia	55,382	12,809	548	13,357	24.12	10,359	32,032	(Georgian)
Men	26,094	6,054	228	6,282	24.07	4,556	15,407	
Women	29,228	6,755	320	7,075	24.15	5,803	16,625	
Urban Population	54,468	12,730	541	13,271	24.36	10,142	31,418	
Rural Population	914	79	7	86	9.41	217	614	
Azbaidzhan, S.S.R.	41,288	17,067	2,134	19,201	46.50	23,187	936	(Azerbaidzhani)
Men	18,761	7,746	907	8,653	46.12	10,524	446	
Women	22,527	9,321	1,227	10,548	46.82	12,663	490	
Urban Population	40,812	16,678	2,125	18,803	46.07	23,107	932	
Rural Population	476	389	9	398	83.61	80	4	
Lithuania	23,564	14,587	265	14,852	63.03	8,237	667	(Lithuanian)
Men	11,389	6,839	133	6,972	61.22	4,165	342	
Women	12,175	7,748	132	7,880	65.72	4,072	325	
Urban Population	23,351	14,449	264	14,713	63.01	8,178	655	
Rural Population	213	138	1	139	65.26	56	12	
Estonia	5,288	1,139	173	1,312	24.81	3,699	408	(Estonian)
Men	2,657	523	87	610	22.96	1,897	214	
Women	2,631	616	86	702	26.68	1,805	191	
Urban Population	5,164	1,130	169	1,299	25.15	3,598	395	
Rural Population	124	9	84	93	75.00	101	13	

270

TABLE 36

(1)	(2)	(3)	(4)	(5)	(6)	(7)	(8)	
Kirghiz, S.S.R.	7,680	2,048	526	2,574	33.51	5,332	–	(Kirghiz)
Men	3,605	927	213	1,140	31.62	2,515	–	
Women	4,075	1,121	308	1,429	35.07	2,817	–	
Urban Population	7,341	1,935	517	2,452	33.40	5,113	–	
Rural Population	339	113	9	122	35.99	219	–	
Kazakh, S.S.R.	27,689	6,322	1,310	7,632	27.54	20,744	1	(Kazakh)
Men	13,649	2,976	596	3,572	26.17	10,352	1	
Women	14,040	3,346	714	4,060	28.92	10,392	–	
Urban Population	26,382	5,964	1,284	7,248	27.47	19,827	1	
Rural Population	1,307	358	26	384	29.38	917	–	
Moldavia	98,072	43,795	7,345	51,140	52.14	53,476	578	(Moldavian)
Men	45,110	19,186	3,210	22,396	49.65	25,527	298	
Women	52,962	24,609	4,135	28,744	54.27	27,949	280	
Urban Population	95,890	42,527	7,261	49,788	51.92	52,735	434	
Rural Population	2,182	1,268	84	1,352	61.96	744	144	
Latvia	36,680	16,946	1,174	18,120	49.40	19,166	435	(Latvian)
Men	17,659	7,862	539	8,401	47.57	9,494	243	
Women	19,021	9,084	635	9,719	51.10	9,672	192	
Urban Population	36,364	16,863	1,169	18,032	49.59	18,972	399	
Rural Population	316	83	5	88	27.85	194	36	
Tadzhik, S.S.R.	14,615	2,914	282	3,196	21.87	5,457	6,184	(Takzhik)
Men	7,046	1,396	123	1,492	21.17	2,683	2,966	
Women	7,569	1,545	159	1,704	22.51	2,774	3,218	
Urban Population	14,423	2,813	280	3,093	21.44	5,379	6,172	
Rural Population	192	101	2	103	53.65	78	12	

TABLE 36

(1)	(2)	(3)	(4)	(5)	(6)	(7)	(8)	
Armenia	1,048	222	29	251	23.95	801	13	(Armenian)
Men	478	97	17	114	23.85	368	6	
Women	570	125	12	137	24.03	433	7	
Urban Population	1,018	208	29	237	23.28	786	13	
Rural Population	30	14	–	14	46.67	15	–	
Turkmen, S.S.R.	3,494	1,056	224	1,280	36.63	2,302	3	(Turki)
Men	1,711	497	116	613	35.83	1,143	1	
Women	1,783	559	108	667	37.41	1,159	2	
Urban Population	3,442	1,041	222	1,263	36.69	2,272	2	
Rural Population	52	15	2	17	32.69	30	1	

*Ibid.

272

TABLE 37
Urban/Rural Speakers of Jewish Dialects According to Sex (1970)*

	Males		Females		Total	
	Number	Percent	Number	Percent	Number	Percent
Total Jewish Population						
Urban and Rural	988,009	100.0	1,162,698	100.0	2,150,707	100.0
Speakers of a Jewish dialect as mother language	167,295	16.9	213,783	18.4	381,078	17.7
Speakers of a Jewish dialect as a second, well-known language	70,376	7.1	96,190	8.3	166,566	7.7
Total speakers of a Jewish dialect	273,671	24.0	309,973	26.7	547,644	25.5
Total Urban Population	963,652	100.0	1,140,990	100.0	2,104,651	100.0
Speakers of a Jewish dialect as mother language	160,498	16.7	260,949	18.1	367,447	17.5
Speakers of a Jewish dialect as a second, well-known language	69,070	7.2	94,883	8.3	163,953	7.8
Total speakers of a Jewish dialect	229,568	23.8	301,832	26.4	531,400	25.3
Total Rural Population	24,357	100.0	21,699	100.0	46,056	100.0
Speakers of a Jewish dialect as mother language	6,797	27.9	6,834	31.5	13,631	29.6
Speakers of a Jewish dialect as a second, well-known language	1,306	5.4	1,307	6.0	2,613	5.8
Total speakers of a Jewish dialect	8,103	33.3	8,141	37.5	16,244	35.3

*Ibid.

TABLE 38

Use of Jewish Dialects According to Republic and Administrative Region (1970)*

Republic and Geographic Administrative Region	Number of Jews	Who speak a Jewish dialect as their		Total (3+4)	Percentage of all Jews who speak a Jewish dialect (5:2)
		Mother tongue	Second well-known language		
(1)	(2)	(3)	(4)	(5)	(6)
Culture Area A[1]	1,613,384	170,233	142,036	312,269	19.35
R.S.F.S.R.	753,589	66,905	74,924	141,829	18.82
Leningrad City	162,587	8,454	16,409	24,863	15.29
Leningrad Oblast'	5,879	520	589	1,109	18.96
Murmansk Oblast'	2,684	134	141	275	10.25
Pskov Oblast'	2,335	363	330	693	29.68
Karel', A.S.S.R.	1,580	111	63	174	11.01
Komi, A.S.S.R.	1,839	186	126	312	16.96
Kaliningrad Oblast'	4,525	354	343	697	15.40
Briansk Oblast'	11,476	1,477	1,520	2,997	26.11
Ivanovo Oblast'	1,764	201	131	332	18.82
Kalinin Oblast'	3,456	317	360	677	19.59
Kaluga Oblast'	2,278	201	215	416	18.26

[1]Areas in which live principally Ashkenazic ("Core") Jews, Soviet citizens since 1917.

274

TABLE 38

(1)	(2)	(3)	(4)	(5)	(6)
Moscow City	251,523	19,071	23,657	42,728	16.99
Moscow Oblast'	36,316	3,869	3,912	7,781	21.42
Smolensk Oblast'	5,316	601	688	1,289	24.25
Tula Oblast'	4,857	453	325	778	16.02
Yaroslav Oblast'	2,970	195	286	481	16.19
Gorki Oblast'	16,845	2,325	2,273	4,598	17.30
Voronezh Oblast'	6,434	455	505	960	14.92
Korsk Oblast'	4,651	734	505	1,319	28.40
Astrakhan Oblast'	3,462	562	390	952	27.50
Volgograd Oblast'	5,042	500	426	926	–
Kuybyshev Oblast'	18,678	2,472	2,418	4,890	26.20
Saratov Oblast'	11,992	1,565	1,318	2,946	24.57
Bashkir, A.S.S.R.	6,681	1,055	680	1,735	25.97
Tatar, A.S.S.R.	9,521	2,043	1,130	3,173	33.33
Krasnodar Region (Kray)	7,726	1,019	599	1,618	20.90
Stavropol Region (Kray)	6,140	946	618	1,564	25.50
Rostov Oblast'	18,190	1,045	1,513	2,558	14.06
Orenburg Oblast'	6,885	1,204	827	2,031	29.50
Perm Oblast'	8,096	1,102	842	1,944	24.01
Sverdlovsk Oblast'	21,269	2,107	2,202	4,309	20.30
Cheliabinsk Oblast'	15,677	2,181	1,664	3,845	24.50
Kemerov Oblast'	5,012	531	353	884	17.64
Novosibirsk Oblast'	11,864	829	658	1,487	12.53
Omsk Oblast'	8,081	731	529	1,260	15.59
Tomsk Oblast'	2,381	260	186	446	18.73

TABLE 38

(1)	(2)	(3)	(4)	(5)	(6)
Krasnoiarsk Oblast'	5,349	500	314	814	15.22
Irkutsk Oblast'	8,029	570	577	1,147	14.28
Chitin Oblast'	1,741	96	102	198	11.37
Buriat, A.S.S.R.	2,090	140	119	259	12.39
Primorsk Region (Kray)	3,832	204	197	401	10.46
Khabarovsk Region (Kray)	18,913	2,805	2,591	5,396	28.53
Birobidzhan Oblast'	11,452	1,970	1,699	3,669	32.04
Magadan Oblast'	1,646	93	108	201	12.21
Kaliningrad Oblast'	4,525	354	343	697	15.40
Kazakh Republic	27,689	6,322	622	6,944	25.08
Ukrainian Republic	692,309	71,902	51,537	123,439	17.83
Voroshilovgrad Oblast'	12,539	894	1,011	1,905	15.19
Dnepropetrovsk Oblast'	69,287	3,631	4,635	8,266	11.93
Donetsk Oblast'	39,988	1,997	2,869	4,866	12.17
Zaparodzh Oblast'	20,242	1,162	1,123	2,285	11.29
Kirovograd Oblast'	7,729	903	586	1,482	19.30
Poltava Oblast'	10,768	1,120	819	1,939	18.00
Sumi Oblast'	4,725	444	412	856	18.10
Kharkov Oblast'	76,487	3,686	5,389	9,075	11.90
Vinnitsa Oblast'	42,251	11,347	2,536	13,883	32.90
Zhitomir Oblast'	35,706	8,772	2,295	11,067	30.10
Kiev City	152,006	12,216	11,648	23,864	15.70
Kiev Oblast'	12,628	2,907	632	3,539	28.00
Khmel'nitsk Oblast'	16,089	4,060	843	4,903	30.50
Cherkass Oblast'	10,643	2,143	796	2,939	27.60
Chernigov Oblast'	10,335	1,362	662	2,024	19.60

TABLE 38

(7)	(2)	(3)	(4)	(5)	(6)
Krym Oblast'	25,614	2,324	2,189	4,513	17.60
Nikolayev Oblast'	17,978	1,426	1,223	2,649	14.73
Odessa Oblast'	117,233	10,763	11,034	21,797	18.60
Kherson Oblast'	10,061	745	835	1,580	15.70
Byelorussian Republic	139,797	25,104	14,953	40,057	28.65
Mogilev Oblast'	25,807	5,148	4,166	9,264	35.90
Vitebsk Oblast'	17,343	3,066	1,909	4,915	28.30
Gomel' Oblast'	42,312	9,595	3,439	13,034	30.80
Minsk City	7,278	2,069	534	2,603	35.90
Minsk Oblast'	47,057	5,286	4,955	10,241	21.76
Culture Area B[1]	256,635	107,677	13,181	120,858	47.09
Lithuania	23,564	14,587	265	14,852	63.00
Latvia	36,680	16,946	1,174	18,120	49.40
Estonia	5,288	1,139	173	1,312	24.80
West Byelorussia	8,214	1,287	564	1,851	22.50
Grodno Oblast'	8,199	481	161	642	20.10
Brest Oblast'	5,015	806	403	1,209	24.10
West Ukraine	84,817	29,923	3,660	33,583	39.60
Rovno Oblast'	2,527	444	114	558	22.10
Volyn and Ternopol' Oblasts[2]	2,664				
L'vov Oblast'	27,721	4,287	1,597	5,884	21.20

[1]Regions annexed by the U.S.S.R. during World War II.
[2]There is no breakdown of linguistic data for Jews of the districts of Volyn and Ternopol'.

TABLE 38

(1)	(2)	(3)	(4)	(5)	(6)
Ivano-Frankovsk Oblast'	3,584	957	132	1,089	30.40
Transcarpathia Oblast'	10,862	5,866	42	5,908	54.40
Chernovots Oblast'	37,459	18,369	1,775	20,144	53.80
Moldavia, S.S.R.	98,072	43,795	7,345	51,140	52.10
Culture Area C[1]	261,178	133,524	9,471	142,995	54.75
R.S.F.S.R.	34,816	26,755	832	27,587	79.23
Dagestan, A.S.S.R.	22,149	19,212	219	19,431	87.70
Kabardino-Balkar, A.S.S.R.	5,578	4,400	132	4,532	81.25
North Osetin, A.S.S.R.	2,044	959	134	729	35.66
Checheno-Ingush, A.S.S.R.	5,045	2,548	347	2,895	57.49
Azerbaidzhan, S.S.R.	41,288	17,067	2,134	19,201	46.50
Georgia, S.S.R.[2]	55,382	12,809	548	45,389	81.95
		32,032			
Armenia, S.S.R.	1,048	222	29	251	23.95
Uzbek, S.S.R.	102,855	38,621	4,896	43,517	42.31
Takzhik, S.S.R.[3]	14,615	2,914	282	3,196	21.87
Kirghiz, S.S.R.	7,680	2,048	526	2,574	33.51
Turkmen, S.S.R.	3,494	1,056	224	1,280	36.63

[1]Regions in which Oriental Jews live (Georgians, Bukharans, and Mountain Jews).
[2]Georgian is spoken by Georgian Jews, and it is considered their national language. 32,032 Jews in Georgia declared Georgian as their mother tongue. 12,809 additional Jews declared other Jewish dialects (apparently Yiddish and Tati) as their mother tongue. In sum, 45,389 Jews declared a Jewish dialect to be their everyday language. 10,359 Jews declared Russian to be their mother tongue.

³The Bukharan Jews who live in the Tadzhik Republic are speakers of Tadzhik. In the report of the census, it was not specified what are the national languages which 2,914 Jews in the Tadzhik Republic declared as their mother tongue. It is reasonable to assume that the intention was principally for Ashkenazik Jews who are speakers of Yiddish. 6,814 Jews declared Takzhik as their mother tongue. In this instance, Tadzhik is the official state language, their national language, and also the mother tongue of the Bukharan Jews. Another 282 Jews declared their national language to be a second and well-known language. In sum, in the Tadzhik Republic, 9,380 Jews -- 64.18 percent -- declared their use of Jewish dialects.

*Ibid.

TABLE 39
Languages Spoken by Jews of the R.S.F.S.R. According to Age Group (1970)*

	Total	Mother Tongue			Second Well-Known Language		
		Jewish Dialect	Russian	Other Languages	Jewish Dialect	Russian	Other Languages
Total	807,915	94,971	709,502	3,442	76,866	86,749	48,454
At ages of							
0 – 10	56,002	8,148	47,568	286	209	5,840	58
11 – 15	34,355	4,274	29,909	152	262	4,076	117
16 – 19	31,375	3,096	28,017	262	611	3,061	1,794
20 – 29	88,006	7,115	80,284	607	2,903	6,837	6,018
30 – 39	121,563	8,993	112,259	423	5,283	8,307	7,539
40 – 49	129,563	10,785	118,322	456	10,148	9,887	8,582
50 – 59	131,592	13,965	117,114	513	17,974	13,001	11,430
60 and older	213,379	37,710	175,094	575	39,345	34,825	11,783

*Ibid., p. 373

PERTINENT CIVIL AND NATIONAL RIGHTS GUARANTEES
PROVIDED IN THE U.S.S.R. ALL-UNION CONSTITUTION
OF 1936*

Article 110

Judicial proceedings are conducted in the language of the
Union Republic, Autonomous Republic or Autonomous Region,
persons not knowing this language being guaranteed the opportunity of fully acquainting themselves with the material of the
case through an interpreter and likewise the right to use their
own language in court.

Article 121

Citizens of the U.S.S.R. have the right to education...
instruction in schools being conducted in the native language.

Article 123

Equality of rights of citizens of the U.S.S.R., irrespective
of their nationality or race, in all spheres of economic, government, cultural, political, and other public activity, is an unde-
feasible law. Any direct or indirect restriction of the rights of,
or, conversely, the establishment of any direct or indirect privileges for, citizens on account of their race or nationality, as
well as any advocacy of racial or national exclusiveness or
hatred and contempt, is punishable by law.

Article 124

In order to ensure to citizens freedom of conscience, the
church in the U.S.S.R. is separated from the state, and the
school from the church. Freedom of religious worship and freedom of anti-religious propaganda is recognized for all citizens.

Article 126

In conformity with the interests of the working people,
and in order to develop the organizational initiative and political

*Konstitutsiya (osnovnoi zakon) Soyuza Sovetskikh Sotsial-
isticheskikh Respublik [The Constitution (basic law) of the Union
of Soviet Socialist Republics] (Moscow: Izdatel'stvo Izvestiya
Sovetov Deputatov Trudyashchikhsya S.S.S.R., 1960), pp. 23-29.

281

activity of the masses of the people, citizens of the U.S.S.R.
are guaranteed the right to unite in public organizations:...
co-operative societies, youth organizations...cultural, technical and scientific societies;...

Article 135

　　All citizens of the U.S.S.R., who have reached the age
of eighteen, irrespective of race or nationality, sex, religion,
education, domicile, social origin, property status, or past
activities, have the right to vote in the election of deputies.
　　Every citizen of the U.S.S.R. who has reached the age of
twenty-three is eligible for election to the Supreme Soviet of the
U.S.S.R., irrespective of race or nationality, sex, religion, education, domicile, social origin, property status, or past activities.

PERTINENT CIVIL AND NATIONAL MINORITY RIGHTS GUARANTEES PROVIDED IN THE U.S.S.R. ALL-UNION CONSTITUTION OF 1977*

This is a society of mature socialist social relations, in which a new historical community of people, the Soviet people, has emerged through the drawing together of all social strata and on the basis of the juridical and actual equality of all nations and nationalities.

II. The State and the Individual

Chapter 6. Citizenship of the U.S.S.R.: Equality of Citizens

Article 34

Citizens of the U.S.S.R. shall be equal before the law, irrespective of origin, social and property status, nationality or race, sex, education, language, attitude toward religion, type or character of occupation, domicile or other particulars.

Equality of rights of citizens of the U.S.S.R. shall be insured in all fields of economic, political, social, and cultural life.

Article 36

Soviet citizens of different nationalities [natsional'nosti] and races shall have equal rights.

The exercise of these rights shall be insured by the policy of all-round development and drawing together of all nations and nationalities of the U.S.S.R., education of citizens in the spirit of Soviet patriotism and socialist internationalism, and the opportunity for using the mother tongue and the languages of the other peoples of the U.S.S.R.

Any and all direct or indirect restriction of the rights of, or the establishment of direct or indirect privileges for citizens on grounds of race or nationality, and likewise any advocacy of racial or national exclusiveness, hostility or contempt, shall be punishable by law.

---

*F.B.I.S., Constitution Text.

Chapter 7. The Basic Rights, Freedoms, and Duties of
Citizens of the U.S.S.R.

Article 45: Citizens of the U.S.S.R. shall have the right to
education

The opportunity for instruction in schools in the mother
tongue [shall be guaranteed].

Article 51

In conformity with the aims of building communism citizens
of the U.S.S.R. shall have the right to join public organizations
facilitating development of their political activity and initiative,
and satisfying their diverse interests.

Article 52

Freedom of conscience, that is, the right to profess any
religion and perform religious rites or not profess any religion,
and to conduct atheistic propaganda, shall be recognized for all
citizens of the U.S.S.R. Incitement of hostility and hatred on
religious grounds shall be prohibited.
The church in the U.S.S.R. shall be separated from the
state, and the school from the church.

Article 54

Citizens of the U.S.S.R. shall be guaranteed inviolability
of the person. No person shall be subjected to arrest other than
by decision of a court of law, or with the sanction of a prosecutor.

Article 55

Citizens of the U.S.S.R. shall be guaranteed inviolability
of the home. No person shall without lawful grounds enter a
home against the will of the persons residing in it.

Article 56

The privacy of citizens, of secrecy of correspondence,
telephone conversations, and telegraphic messages shall be protected by law.

284

Article 57

Respect for the individual, protection of the rights and freedoms of Soviet man shall be the duty of all state organs, public organizations, and officials.

Chapter 11. Autonomous Oblast' and Autonomous Okrug

Article 86

The Russian Soviet Federated Socialist Republic shall include the following autonomous oblasts:* Adygeskaya, Gorno-Altaiskaya, Yevreiskaya [Jewish], Karacheyevo-Cherkesskaya, Khakasskaya. (Italics added.)

Chapter 20. Courts of Law and Arbitration

Article 158

Judicial proceedings shall be conducted in the language of the union or autonomous republic, autonomous oblast' or autonomous okrug, or in the language spoken by the majority of the population in the given locality. Persons participating in the case not conversant with the language in which the judicial proceedings are conducted shall have the right to fully [sic] acquaint themselves with the materials of the case, to participate in court proceedings through an interpreter, and to address the court of law in their own language.

---

*Denotes a smaller "national" entity.

RELEVANT HUMAN AND NATIONAL MINORITY RIGHTS PROVISIONS IN THE BASIC UNITED NATIONS CHARTER*

WE THE PEOPLES OF THE UNITED NATIONS DETERMINED

...to reaffirm faith in fundamental human rights, in the dignity and worth of the human person, in the equal rights of men and women, and of nations large and small,...

Chapter I. Purposes and Principles

Article 1

The purposes of the United Nations are:...
2. To develop friendly relations among nations based on respect for the principle of equal rights and self-determination of peoples,...
3. To achieve international co-operation in solving international problems of an economic, social, cultural, or humanitarian character, and in promoting and encouraging respect for human rights and for fundamental freedoms for all without distinction as to race, sex, language, or religion;...

Article 13

1. The General Assembly shall initiate studies of and make recommendations for the purpose of:...
(b) promoting international co-operation in the economic, social, cultural, educational, and health fields, and assisting in the realization of human rights and fundamental freedoms for all without distinction as to race, sex, language, or religion.

Chapter IX. International and Economic and Social Co-operation

Article 55

The United Nations shall promote:...
(c) universal respect for, and observance of, human rights and fundamental freedoms for all without distinction as to race, sex, language, or religion.

---

*United Nations, Yearbook of Human Rights for 1947, Part 3; Brownlie, Basic Documents, pp. 93-96, 101.

Article 56

All Members pledge themselves to take joint and separate action in co-operation with the Organization for the achievement of the purposes set forth in Article 55.

Chapter XII. International Trusteeship System

Article 76

The basic objectives of the trusteeship system, in accordance with the Purposes of the United Nations laid down in Article 1 of the present Charter, shall be:...
(c) to encourage respect for human rights and for fundamental freedoms for all without distinction as to race, sex, language, or religion, and to encourage recognition of the interdependence of the peoples of the world;...

PERTINENT HUMAN AND NATIONAL MINORITY RIGHTS
PROVISIONS OF THE UNITED NATIONS "UNIVERSAL
DECLARATION OF HUMAN RIGHTS" (December 10, 1948)*

Article 1

All human beings are born free and equal in dignity and
rights. They are endowed with reason and conscience and
should act towards one another in a spirit of brotherhood.

Article 2

Everyone is entitled to all the rights and freedoms set forth
in this Declaration, without distinction of any kind, such as race,
color, sex, language, religion, political or other opinion, national or social origin, property, birth or other status.

Article 6

Everyone has the right to recognition everywhere as a person before the law.

Article 7

All are equal before the law and are entitled, without any
discrimination to equal protection of the law. All are entitled to
equal protection against any discrimination in violation of this
Declaration and against any incitement to such discrimination.

Article 13

1. Everyone has the right to freedom of movement and
residence within the borders of each state.
2. Everyone has the right to leave any country, including
his own, and to return to his country.

Article 15

1. Everyone has the right to a nationality.
2. No one shall be arbitrarily deprived of his nationality
nor denied the right to change his nationality.

*U.N. Doc. A/811; United Nations, Official Records, p.
71; United Nations, Yearbook on Human Rights for 1948, pp. 457-
68.

Article 18

   Everyone has the right to freedom of thought, conscience, and religion; this right includes freedom to change his religion or belief, and freedom, either alone or in community with others and in public or private, to manifest his religion or belief in teaching, practice, worship, and observance.

Article 19

   Everyone has the right to freedom of opinion and expression; this right includes freedom to hold opinions without interference and to seek, receive, and impart information and ideas through any media and regardless of frontiers.

Article 21

   1. Everyone has the right to take part in the government of his country, directly or through freely chosen representatives.
   2. Everyone has the right of equal access to public service in his country.

Article 22

   Everyone, as a member of society, has a right to...social and cultural rights indispensable for his dignity and the free development of his personality.

Article 23

   1. Everyone has the right to work, to free choice of employment, to just and favorable conditions of work, and to protection against unemployment.

Article 26

   1. Everyone has the right to education...higher education shall be equally accessible to all on the basis of merit.
   3. Parents have a prior right to choose the kind of education that shall be given to their children.

PERTINENT HUMAN AND NATIONAL MINORITY RIGHTS
PROVISIONS OF THE "INTERNATIONAL AGREEMENT
ON THE ELIMINATION OF ALL FORMS OF RACIAL
DISCRIMINATION" (December 21, 1965)*

Part I

Article 1

1. In this Convention, the term "racial discrimination"
shall mean any distinction, exclusion, restriction or preference
based on race, colour, descent, or national or ethnic origin
which has the purpose or effect of nullifying or impairing the
recognition, enjoyment or exercise, on an equal footing, of
human rights and fundamental freedoms in the political, economic,
social, cultural or any other field of public life.

Article 2

(a)   Each State Party undertakes to engage in no act or
practice of racial discrimination against persons, groups of persons or institutions and to ensure that all public authorities and
public institutions, national and local, shall act in conformity
with this obligation;...
(c)   Each State Party shall take effective measures to review
governmental, national, and local policies, and to amend, rescind
or nullify any laws and regulations which have the effect of creating or perpetuating racial discrimination wherever it exists;...

2. State Parties shall, when the circumstances so warrant,
take, in the social, economic, cultural, and other fields, special
and concrete measures to ensure the adequate development and
protection of certain racial groups or individuals belonging to
them, for the purpose of guaranteeing them the full and equal enjoyment of human rights and fundamental freedoms. These measures shall in no case entail as a consequence the maintenance
of unequal or separate rights for different racial groups after the
objectives for which they were taken have been achieved.

Article 4

State Parties condemn all propaganda and all organizations
which are based on ideas or theories of superiority of one race
or group of persons of one colour or ethnic origin, or which attempt

*Brownlie, Basic Documents, pp. 237-42.

290

to justify or promote racial hatred and discrimination in any form, and undertake to adopt immediate and positive measures designed to eradicate all incitement to, or acts of, such discrimination and, to this end, with due regard to the principles embodied in the Universal Declaration of Human Rights and the rights expressly set forth in Article 5 of this Convention, inter alia:

(a) Shall declare an offence punishable by law all dissemination of ideas based on racial superiority or hatred, incitement to racial discrimination, as well as all acts of violence or incitement to such acts against any race or group of persons of another colour or ethnic origin, and also the provision of any assistance to racist activities, including the financing thereof;

(b) Shall declare illegal and prohibit organizations, and also organized and all other propaganda activities, which promote and incite racial discrimination, and shall recognize participation in such organizations or activities as an offense punishable by law;

(c) Shall not permit public authorities or public institutions, national or local, to promote or incite racial discrimination.

Article 5

In compliance with the fundamental obligations laid down in Article 2 of this Convention, State Parties undertake to prohibit and to eliminate racial discrimination in all its forms and to guarantee the right of everyone, without distinction as to race, colour, or national or ethnic origin, to equality before the law, notably in the enjoyment of the following rights:

(a) The right to equal treatment before the tribunals and all other organs at administering justice;...

(c) Political rights, in particular the rights to participate in elections-to vote and to stand for election-on the basis of universal and equal suffrage, to take part in the Government as well as in the conduct of public affairs at any level and to have equal access to public service;

(d) Other civil rights, in particular;

(i) The right to freedom of movement and residence within the border of the state;

(ii) The right to leave any country, including one's own, and to return to one's country;

(iii) The right to nationality;...

(vii) The right to freedom of thought, conscience, and religion;

(viii) The right to freedom of opinion and expression;

(ix) The right to freedom of peaceful assembly and association;

(e) Economic, social, and cultural rights, in particular:
    (i) The rights to work, to free choice of employment,
...

PERTINENT HUMAN AND NATIONAL MINORITY RIGHTS
PROVISIONS OF THE "INTERNATIONAL COVENANT ON
ECONOMIC, SOCIAL, AND CULTURAL RIGHTS"
(December 16, 1966)*

PREAMBLE

The State Parties to the present Covenant,
*****
Recognizing that, in accordance with the Universal Declaration of Human Rights...agree upon the following articles:

Part I

Article 1

1. All peoples have the right of self-determination. By virtue of that right they freely determine their political status and freely pursue their economic, social, and cultural development.

Part II

Article 2

2. The State Parties to the present Covenant undertake to guarantee that the rights enunciated in the present Covenant will be exercised without discrimination of any kind as to race, color, sex, language, religion, political or other opinion, national or social origin, property, birth or other status.

Part III

Article 7

The State Parties to the present Covenant recognize the right of everyone to the enjoyment of just and favourable conditions of work, which ensure, in particular:...
(c) Equal opportunity for everyone to be promoted in his employment to an appropriate higher level, subject to no considerations other than those of seniority and competence;...

---

*United Nations, Yearbook on Human Rights for 1966, pp. 437-41.

Article 13

1. The State Parties to the present Covenant recognize the right of everyone to education.

2. The State Parties to the present Covenant recognize that, with a view to achieving the full realization of this right;
...

(c) Higher education shall be made equally accessible to all, on the basis of capacity, by every appropriate means,...

3. The State Parties to the present Covenant undertake to have respect for the liberty of parents and, when applicable, legal guardians, to choose for their children schools, other than those established by the public authorities, which conform to such minimum educational standards as may be laid down or approved by the State and to ensure the religious and moral education of their children in conformity with their own convictions.

PERTINENT HUMAN AND NATIONAL MINORITY RIGHTS
PROVISIONS OF THE "INTERNATIONAL COVENANT ON CIVIL
AND POLITICAL RIGHTS" (December 16, 1966)*

PREAMBLE

The State Parties to the present Covenant,
****
Recognizing that in accordance with the Universal Declaration of Human Rights,...agree upon the following articles:

Part I

Article 1

All peoples have the right of self-determination. By virtue
of that right they freely determine their political status and freely
pursue their economic, social, and cultural development.

Part II

Article 2

1. Each State Party to the present Covenant undertakes to
respect and to ensure to all individuals within its territory and
subject to its jurisdiction the rights recognized in the present
Covenant, without distinction of any kind, such as race, color,
sex, language, religion, political or other opinion, national or
social origin, property, birth or other status.

Part III

Article 12

1. Everyone lawfully within the territory of a State shall,
within that territory, have the right to liberty of movement and
freedom to choose his residence.
2. Everyone shall be free to leave any country, including
his own.
3. The above-mentioned rights shall not be subject to any
restrictions except those which are provided by law, are necessary
to protect national security, public order (ordre public),...public

*United Nations, Yearbook on Human Rights for 1966, pp.
442-50.

health or morals or the rights and freedoms of others, and are consistent with the other rights recognized in the present Covenant.

4. No one shall be arbitrarily deprived of the right to enter his own country.

Article 14

1. All persons shall be equal before the courts and tribunals.

3. In the determination of any criminal charge against him, everyone shall be entitled to the following minimum guarantees, in full equality:

(a) To be informed promptly and in detail in a language which he understands of the nature and cause of the charge against him;...

Article 18

1. Everyone shall have the right to freedom of thought, conscience, and religion. This right shall include freedom to have or to adopt a religion or belief of his choice, and freedom, either individually or in community with others and in public or private, to manifest his religion or belief in worship, observance, practice, and teaching.

2. No one shall be subject to coercion which would impair his freedom to have or to adopt a religion or belief of his choice.

3. Freedom to manifest one's religion or beliefs may be subject to such limitations as are prescribed by law and are necessary to protect the public safety, order, health, or morals or the fundamental rights and freedoms of others.

4. The States Parties to the present Covenant undertake to have respect for the liberty of parents and, when applicable, legal guardians to ensure the religious and moral education of their children in conformity with their own convictions.

Article 19

1. Everyone shall have the right to hold opinions without interference.

2. Everyone shall have the right to freedom of expression; this right shall include freedom to seek, receive, and impart information and ideas of all kinds, regardless of frontiers, either orally, in writing or in print, in the form of art, or through any media of his choice.

Article 20

2. Any advocacy of national, racial, or religious hatred that constitutes incitement to discrimination, hostility or violence shall be prohibited by law.

Article 24

1. Every child shall have, without any discrimination as to race, colour, sex, language, religion, national or social origin, property or birth, the right to such measures of protection as are required by his status as a minor, on the part of his family, society, and the State.
3. Every child has a right to acquire a nationality.

Article 25

Every citizen shall have the right and the opportunity, without any of the distinctions mentioned in Article 2 and without unreasonable restrictions:
(a) To take part in the conduct of public affairs, directly or through freely chosen representatives;
(b) To vote and to be elected at genuine periodic elections which shall be by universal and equal suffrage and shall be held by secret ballot, guaranteeing the free expression of the will of the electors;
(c) To have access, on general terms of equality, to public service in his country.

Article 26

All persons are equal before the law and are entitled without any discrimination to the equal protection of the law. In this respect, the law shall prohibit any discrimination and guarantee to all persons equal and effective protection against discrimination on any ground such as race, colour, sex, language, religion, political or other opinion, national or social origin, property, birth or other status.

Article 27

In those States in which ethnic, religious, or linguistic minorities exist, persons, belonging to such minorities shall not be denied the right, in community with other members of their group, to enjoy their own culture, to profess and practice their own religion, or to use their own language.

PERTINENT HUMAN AND NATIONAL MINORITY RIGHTS
PROVISIONS OF THE "CONFERENCE ON SECURITY AND
COOPERATION IN EUROPE" (August 1, 1975)*

1.

(a) Declaration on Principles Guiding Relations Between
Participating States.

VII. Respect for human rights and fundamental freedoms,
including the freedom of thought, conscience, religion or belief

The participating States will respect human rights and fundamental freedoms, including the freedom of thought, conscience,
religion or belief, for all without distinction as to race, sex, language, or religion.

They will promote and encourage the effective exercise of
civil, political, economic, social, cultural, and other rights and
freedoms all of which derive from the inherent dignity of the human person and are essential for his free and full development.

Within this framework the participating States will recognize and respect the freedom of the individual to profess and practice, alone or in community with others, religion or belief acting
in accordance with the dictates of his own conscience.

The participating States on whose territory national minorities exist will respect the right of persons belonging to such
minorities to equality before the law, will afford them the full
opportunity for the actual enjoyment of human rights and fundamental freedoms and will, in this manner, protect their legitimate
interests in this sphere.

The participating States recognize the universal significance
of human rights and fundamental freedoms, respect for which is an
essential factor for the peace, justice, and well-being necessary
to ensure the development of friendly relations and co-operation
among themselves as among all States.

They will constantly respect these rights and freedoms in
their mutual relations and will endeavour jointly and separately,
including in co-operation with the United Nations, to promote
universal and effective respect for them.

They confirm the right of the individual to know and act
upon his rights and duties in this field.

In the field of human rights and fundamental freedoms, the
participating States will act in conformity with the purposes and

---

*U.S., Conference on Security, pp. 75, 77, 80-81, 113-15,
120, 126-27, 131.

principles of the Charter of the United Nations and with the
Universal Declaration of Human Rights. They will also fulfill
their obligations as set forth in the international declarations
and agreements in this field, including inter alia, the International Covenants on Human Rights, by which they may be bound.

Co-operation in Humanitarian and Other Fields.*

1. Human Contacts

The participating States,...
        Make it their aim to facilitate freer movement and contacts,
individually and collectively, whether privately or officially,
among persons, institutions, and organizations of the participating States, and to contribute to the solution of the humanitarian
problems that arise in that connextion [sic],...
        (a) Contact and Regular Meetings on the Basis of Family
            Ties
        In order to promote further development of contacts on the
basis of family ties the participating States will favorably consider applications for travel with the purpose of allowing persons
to enter or leave their territory temporarily, and on a regular
basis if desired, in order to visit members of their families.
        (b) Reunification of Families
        The participating States will deal in a positive and human-
itarian spirit with the applications of persons who wish to be
reunited with members of their family, with special attention
being given to requests of an urgent character such as requests
submitted by persons who are ill or old.
        They will deal with applications in this field as expedi-
tiously as possible.
        They will lower where necessary the fees charged in con-
nexion [sic] with these applications to ensure that they are at
a moderate level.
        Applications for the purpose of family reunification which
are not granted may be renewed at the appropriate level and will
be reconsidered at reasonably short intervals by the authorities
of the country of residence or destination, whichever is concerned; under such circumstances fees will be charged only when
applications are granted.
        They confirm that the presentation of an application con-
cerning family reunification will not modify the rights and obligations of the applicant or of members of his family.

---

*This section of the Final Act is commonly referred to as
the "Basket III" portion of the Agreement.

(d) Travel for Personal or Professional Reasons.

They confirm that religious faiths, institutions, and organizations, practicing within the constitutional framework of the participating States, and their representatives can, in the field of their activities, have contacts and meetings among themselves and exchange information.

3. Co-operation and Exchanges in the Field of Culture.

National minorities or regional cultures. The participating States, recognizing the contribution that national minorities or regional cultures can make to co-operation among them in various fields of culture, intend, when such minorities or cultures exist within their territory, to facilitate this contribution, taking into account the legitimate interests of their members.

4. Co-operation and Exchanges in the Field of Education.

(a) Teaching Methods....

National minorities or regional cultures. The participating States, recognizing the contribution that national minorities or regional cultures can make to co-operation among them in various fields of education, intend, when such minorities or cultures exist within their territory, to facilitate this contribution, taking into account the legitimate interests of their members.

300

CONCERNING CONFIRMATION OF THE STATUTE ON
ENTRY INTO AND DEPARTURE FROM THE
UNION OF SOVIET SOCIALIST REPUBLICS

The Council of Ministers USSR decrees:

1. Confirm the attached Statute on Entry into and Departure from the Union of Soviet Socialist Republics.

Put the Statute into force beginning January 1, 1971.

2. Instruct the Ministry of Justice USSR in coordination with the ministries and departments concerned to submit to the Council of Ministers USSR, in connection with the issuance of this decree, proposals on recognizing and changing the decisions of the USSR Government, which have lost their validity.

Chairman of the
Council of Ministers USSR   A. Kosygin

Deputy Director of the Administration of
Affairs of the Council of Ministers USSR

K. Selivanov

Moscow, the Kremlin, September 22, 1970   No. 801

Confirmed

by decree of the Council of Ministers
USSR

September 22, 1970   No. 801

STATUTE

On Entry into and Departure from the Union of Soviet
Socialist Republics

CONFIRMED
by decree of the Council of
Ministers USSR
September 22, 1970 No. 801

STATUTE

On Entry into and Departure from the Union of Soviet
Socialist Republics

Entry into the Union of Soviet Socialist Republics.

1. Entry into the Union of Soviet Socialist Republics by
Soviet citizens shall be authorized by valid Soviet diplomatic,
official, regular civilian foreign passports, seamen's passports,
and return certificates.
    Soviet citizens permanently residing abroad, who hold
valid Soviet regular civilian foreign passports shall be authorized
to depart for the Union of Soviet Socialist Republics when their
passports contain a notation regarding removal from the register
in connection with their departure for the Soviet Union, made by
Soviet embassies, missions, and consulates.

2. Entry into the Union of Soviet Socialist Republics by
citizens of foreign countries and by stateless persons shall be
authorized by valid overseas passports, or by substitute documents, bearing Soviet entry visas, unless another entry procedure has been established by agreement between the Union of
Soviet Socialist Republics and the country in question.

3. Visas for entry into the Union of Soviet Socialist Republics for citizens of foreign countries and also for stateless
persons shall be issued abroad by Soviet embassies, missions,
and consulates or, in individual cases, by Soviet representatives especially authorized for that purpose.

    Visas for departure from the USSR may in appropriate
cases also be issued on the territory of the Union of Soviet
Socialist Republics (exit-entry visas), upon the departure of
citizens abroad for a limited period of time. Such visas shall

302

be issued by the Ministry of Foreign Affairs USSR, the Ministry of Internal Affairs USSR, the ministries of internal affairs of union and autonomous republics, the administrations of internal affairs of the executive committees of the krai, oblast', and municipal councils of workers' deputies, in accordance with the established procedure.

4. Permits for crossing the boundary of the USSR by crews of transportation services going abroad shall be subject to special regulation.

Departure from the Union of Soviet Socialist Republics.

5. Departure from the Union of Soviet Socialist Republics by Soviet citizens shall be authorized by the valid documents enumerated under paragraph 8, a-g of this statute.

6. Departure of foreign citizens as well as stateless persons from the Union of Soviet Socialist Republics shall be authorized by valid foreign passports or by substitute documents bearing exit visas, unless another procedure for departure is established by agreement between the Union of Soviet Socialist Republics and the country concerned.

7. Visas for departure from the Union of Soviet Socialist Republics shall be issued by the Ministry of Foreign Affairs USSR, the ministries of foreign affairs of the union republics, diplomatic agencies of the Ministry of Foreign Affairs USSR, the Ministry of Internal Affairs USSR, the ministries of internal affairs of union and autonomous republics, the administrations of internal affairs of the executive committees of krai, oblast', and municipal councils of workers' deputies, in accordance with established procedure.
Visas for departure of foreign citizens and stateless persons from the Union of Soviet Socialist Republics may also be issued abroad (entry-exit visas) when entering the USSR for a limited period of time. Such visas shall be issued by Soviet embassies, missions, and consulates or, in individual cases, by Soviet representatives especially authorized for that purpose.

Documents authorizing the crossing of the state boundary of the USSR.

8. Citizens of the Union of Soviet Socialist Republics may, for the purpose of departure from the USSR, residence

abroad, and return to the USSR, be issued the following:
a) diplomatic passports
b) official passports
c) seamen's passports
d) regular civilian foreign passports
In the absence of the enumerated documents a certificate of return to the USSR may be issued.

9. Diplomatic, official, and regular civilian foreign passports for citizens of the Union of Soviet Socialist Republics going abroad shall be issued by the Ministry of Foreign Affairs USSR and the ministries of foreign affairs of the union republics in accordance with paragraphs 13, 14, and 16-18 of this statute.

For citizens of the Union of Soviet Socialist Republics who are abroad, diplomatic, official, and regular civilian passports and certificates for return to the USSR shall be issued by Soviet embassies, missions, and consulates or, in individual cases, by Soviet representatives especially authorized for that purpose.

10. In lieu of the certificates issued formerly, official passports shall also be issued in accordance with established procedure by the Ministry of Internal Affairs USSR, and the ministries of internal affairs of the union republics, for persons leaving on official assignments for socialist countries; and regular civilian foreign passports -- by the Ministry of Internal Affairs USSR, the ministries of internal affairs of the union and autonomous republics, the administrations of internal affairs of the executive committees of the krai, oblast', and municipal councils of workers' deputies.

11. Seamen's passports shall be issued to citizens of the Union of Soviet Socialist Republics by port captains of the Ministry of the Merchant Marine and fisheries port captains of the Ministry of Fisheries USSR.

12. Stateless persons residing on the territory of the USSR shall be issued the required documents with exit visas for departure from the Soviet Union. Such documents shall be issued in accordance with established procedure by the Ministry of Internal Affairs USSR, the ministries of internal affairs of the union and autonomus republics, the administrations of internal affairs of the executive committees of krai, oblast', and municipal councils of workers' deputies.

304

13. Diplomatic passports shall be issued:

a) To members and candidate members of the Central Committee of the Communist Party of the Soviet Union; to members and candidate members of the Central Committees of the communist parties of the union republics; to members of the Central Auditing Commission CPSU, and to members of the auditing commissions of the communist parties of the union republics; to secretaries of the krai and oblast' committees of the CPSU and the communist parties of union republics; and to responsible officials of the apparatus of the CPSU Central Committee;

b) To the Chairman of the Presidium of the Supreme Soviet of the USSR and his deputies; to the chairmen of the Presidia of the Supreme Soviets of union and autonomous republics and their deputies; to members of the Presidium of the Supreme Soviet USSR and members of the Presidia of the Supreme Soviets of union and autonomous republics; to the Secretary of the Presidium of the Supreme Soviet USSR and the secretaries of the Presidia of the Supreme Soviets of union and autonomous republics; to deputies of the Supreme Soviet USSR and deputies of the Supreme Soviets of union and autonomous republics; to the Chief of the Secretariat and the heads of department of the Presidium of the Supreme Soviet USSR; to the assistants of the Chairman of the Presidium of the Supreme Soviet USSR;

c) To the Chairman of the Council of Ministers and his deputies; to the chairmen of.the councils of ministers of union and autonomous republics and their deputies; to ministers of the USSR and the chairmen of State Committees of the USSR, the leaders of central State establishments of the USSR, the union and autonomous republics, and their deputies; to the chairmen of the executive committees of krai and oblast' councils of workers' deputies; to members of the collegia of the Ministries and State Committees of the USSR; to the Manager of Affairs of the Council of Ministers USSR; to the deputy managers of affairs of the Council of Ministers USSR, the heads of secretariats, and the assistants of the Chairman and the deputy chairmen of the Council of Ministers USSR; the department heads of the Administration of Affairs of the Council of Ministers USSR;

d) To ambassadors and envoys of the USSR, counselors, first, second, and third secretaries, attaches of the Ministry of Foreign Affairs USSR, the ministries of foreign affairs of the union republics, the embassies, and missions of the USSR, and also Soviet consuls generals, consuls, vice-consuls, consular agents, and secretaries of consulates general and consulates; to diplomatic couriers;

e) To military, naval, and air attaches and their assistants;

f) To commercial representatives of the USSR and their deputies, commercial counselors, counselors for economic affairs, and their deputies and to commercial attaches;

g) To heads and members of government delegations of the USSR and the union republics at international conferences, meetings and negotiations; to heads, representatives, and members of delegations of the USSR and the union republics at meetings of the UN and its bodies, specialized agencies of the UN, at inter-governmental conferences of international organizations;

h) To Soviet employees of international organizations performing functions comparable to diplomatic functions;

14. Official passports shall be issued:

a) To employees of ministries, departments, and other State institutions, and enterprises of the USSR, the union and autonomous republics, who go abroad on official business;

b) To correspondents of the Telegraphic Agency of the Soviet Union attached to the Council of Ministers USSR [TASS] and of the newspapers Izvestiya and Pravda.

15. Seamen's passports shall be issued to citizens of the USSR who are crew members of vessels sailing abroad under the Ministry of the Merchant Marine and the Ministry of Fisheries USSR.

16. Regular civilian foreign passports shall be issued to Soviet citizens, besides those enumerated in paragraphs 13-15 of these Regulations, to those going abroad on official, public, and private business, and also to Soviet citizens permanently residing abroad.

17. To wives and children under 18 years of age and to unmarried daughters over 18, accompanying persons enumerated in paragraphs, 13, 14, and 16, or traveling to join them, there shall be issued the appropriate diplomatic, official, and regular civilian foreign passports. Children up to 16 years of age may also be entered in the passport of one of their parents or of persons with whom they are traveling.

18. Documents for departure from the USSR, residence abroad, and return to the USSR shall be issued in accordance with established procedures upon the written application of the

ministries, departments, and organizations of the USSR concerned, and also upon the application of citizens going abroad on private business.

19. Foreign visas for those leaving on official assignments shall be obtained through the Ministry of Foreign Affairs USSR, the representatives of the Soviet Union abroad, the ministries of foreign affairs of the union republics, the embassies and missions of the USSR abroad; for those traveling on private business -- by direct application of the citizens to the foreign missions.

ON AMENDMENTS AND CHANGES OF DECREE NO. 598
OF THE COUNCIL OF PEOPLE'S COMMISSARS,
DATED APRIL 29, 1942,
"SCHEDULES OF GOVERNMENTAL FEES."

The Council of Ministers USSR decrees:

1. Be it established that for the issuance to citizens of
the USSR of certificates of invitation abroad from relatives and
acquaintances, and for statements of invitation from persons
residing in capitalist countries the following governmental fees
shall be charged:
a) for the issuance of certificates of invitation -- 5
rubles.
b) for statements of invitation from persons residing in
capitalist countries -- 15 rubles.

2. Be it established that for regular civilian foreign passports for persons going abroad on private business a fee of 1
ruble shall be charged.

3. Paragraphs 9, 10, 11, 18, and 19 of Decree No. 598
of the Council of People's Commissars dated April 29, 1942,
"Schedules of Governmental Fees," shall read as follows:

"9. For the issuance to citizens of the USSR, foreigners,
and stateless persons permanently residing in the USSR (except
for political emigres) of documents authorizing departure for
abroad (excluding diplomatic passports):
a) to socialist countries for temporary and permanent
residence - - 30 rubles;
b) to other countries for temporary and permanent residence -- 400 rubles.

10. For entering any changes in the documents issued
for the departure from the USSR of Soviet citizens, foreigners,
and stateless persons, permanently residing in the USSR (except
for political emigres) -- 5 rubles.

10a. For the issuance to citizens of the USSR of certificates of invitation abroad -- 5 rubles.

10b. For statements of invitation from persons residing
in capitalist countries for temporary and permanent residence
-- 15 rubles.

308

11. For applications from foreigners and stateless persons (except for political emigres) regarding receipt of USSR citizenship -- 5 rubles.

18. For applications of political emigres regarding receipt of USSR citizenship -- 50 kopeks.

19. For applications regarding relinquishment of USSR citizenship:
a) from persons residing abroad -- 5 rubles.
b) from persons residing in the USSR and intending to leave later for socialist countries -- 50 rubles;
c) from persons residing in the USSR and intending to leave later for capitalist countries -- 500 rubles."

Chairman of the
Council of Ministers USSR   A. Kosygin

Deputy Director of the Administration of Affairs
of the Council of Ministers USSR   K. Selivanov

Moscow, the Kremlin, September 22, 1970 No. 803

DECREE BY THE SUPREME SOVIET OF THE USSR

519   On Reimbursement by USSR Citizens Who Are Departing
       for Permanent Residence Abroad of State Educational
       Expenditures*

The Presidium of the Supreme Soviet of the USSR decrees:

It shall be established that USSR citizens who depart for
permanent residence abroad (except those departing to socialist
countries) shall be obliged to reimburse State expenditures for
education at an institution of higher learning, for graduate study,
for medical internship, for graduate study at a higher military
school, and for receipt of the corresponding academic degree.
       The extent and conditions of reimbursement of the expend-
itures indicated above shall be determined in accordance with a
procedure to be established by the Council of Ministers of the
USSR.

N. Podgorny
Chairman of the Presidium of the Supreme Soviet
of the USSR

M. Georgadze
Secretary of the Presidium of the Supreme Soviet
of the USSR

Moscow, Kremlin. August 3, 1972.
   No. 3198--VIII

---

*In compliance with this Decree, the Council of Ministers
of the USSR has adopted a Resolution which is being published
in the Collected Resolutions of the Government of the USSR, No.
1, 1973.

LISTING OF EDUCATION REIMBURSEMENTS BY
EMIGRATING SOVIET CITIZENS

(Resolution of the Council of Ministers: "On Reimbursement by USSR Citizens Who Are Departing for Permanent Residence Abroad of State Education Expenditures"; Moscow, Sotsialisticheskaya Zakonnost', No. 4, April 1973, signed to press 13 March 1973, pp. 75-76.)

In accordance with the Decree of the Presidium of the Supreme Soviet of the USSR of 3 August 1972, entitled "On reimbursement by USSR citizens who are departing for permanent residence abroad of State educational expenditures,"[1] the Council of Ministers of the USSR resolves:

1. To approve the Directive (appended hereto), prepared by the Ministry of Finance of the USSR, the Ministry of Higher and Secondary Specialized Education of the USSR, and the Ministry of Internal Affairs of the USSR, on the extent and conditions of reimbursement by USSR citizens who are departing for permanent residence abroad of State expenditures for education at an institution of higher learning, for graduate study, for medical internship, for graduate study at a higher military school, and for receipt of the corresponding academic degree.

2. To authorize the Ministry of Finance of the USSR, with the participation of the Ministry of Internal Affairs of the USSR, in extraordinary cases when there exist justifiable reasons, to exempt, partially or in full, USSR citizens who are departing for permanent residence abroad from reimbursement of State expenditures for education at an institution of higher learning, for graduate study, for medical internship, for graduate study at a higher military school, and for receipt of the corresponding academic degree.

A. Kosygin
Chairman,
Council of Ministers of the USSR

M. Smirtyukov
Executive Officer,
Council of Ministers of the USSR

Moscow, Kremlin, 3 August 1972, No. 573.

[1]. See Vedomosti Verkhovnogo Soveta SSSR [Record of the Supreme Soviet of the USSR], 1972, No. 52, p. 519.

Approved
by the Resolution of the Council
of Ministers of the USSR
of 3 August 1972, No. 573

Directive
On Reimbursement by USSR Citizens Who Depart for
Permanent Residence Abroad of State Edpenditures for
Education

1. USSR citizens who depart for permanent residence abroad
shall reimburse State expenditures for education at USSR institutions of higher learning in the following amounts:

(in thousands of rubles)

In event of gradua-tion from institu-tions of higher learning or study during the last year of the acad-emic program	In event of education for				
	one years	two years	three years	four years	five years
Moscow State University. 12.2	2.4	4.9	7.3	9.8	-
Other universities....... 6.0	1.2	2.4	3.6	4.8	-
Engineering-technical, engineering-economics, and higher military insti-tutions of learning....... 7.7	1.5	3.1	4.6	6.1	-
Agricultural and Forestry. 5.6	1.1	2.3	3.4	4.5	-
Medical, pharmaceutical, stomatological, and physical education...... 8.3	1.4	2.8	4.2	5.6	7.0
Economics, law, pedagog-ical, history and library sciences institutes and cultural institutes....... 4.5	0.9	1.8	2.7	3.6	-
Institutes and departments of foreign languages..... 6.8	1.4	2.8	4.1	5.5	-
Institutes of arts (conser-vatories, theater, art, and literature).......... 9.6	1.9	3.8	5.7	7.7	-

312

2. Persons who have done graduate study, medical internship, graduate study at a higher military school or who have an academic degree shall, in addition to reimbursing State expenditures for receiving higher education, as provided in paragraph 1 of this Directive, be liable as follows:

(a) persons who have done graduate study, medical internship, or graduate study at a higher military school, but who have not successfully defended a dissertation -- 1.7 thousand rubles for each year of education;

(b) persons who have been awarded the academic degree of Candidate of Sciences -- 5.4 thousand rubles;

(c) persons who have been awarded the academic degree of Doctor of Sciences (in addition to the amounts stipulated in subparagraph (b) of this paragraph) -- 7.2 thousand rubles.

3. The following USSR citizens who are departing for permanent residence abroad are exempted from reimbursement of State expenditures for education at an institution of higher learning, for graduate study, for medical internship, for graduate study at a higher military school and for receipt of the corresponding academic degree, as provided by paragraphs 1 and 2 of this Directive, as follows:

(a) invalids of groups One and Two -- in full. Group Three invalids may be exempted from the above specified reimbursement in amounts up to 50 percent;

(b) men who have reached age 60 and women who have reached age 55 -- in full;

(c) men with length of service of no less than 25, 15, and 8 years, and women with length of service of no less than 20, 12, and 6 years -- in amounts of 75, 50, and 25 percent respectively;

(d) persons who have studied at an institution of higher learning, have done graduate work or graduate work at a higher military school without interruption of employment -- in an amount of 50 percent;

(e) persons who have married citizens (subjects) of foreign states -- in amounts between 25 and 50 percent with account being taken of their material situation, while persons who were married prior to 3 August 1972 -- in full;

(f) persons who have graduated from institutions of higher learning on the basis of examinations without regular attendance at lectures, as well as those who have been awarded the academic degree of Candidate of Sciences without graduate study, medical internship or graduate study at a higher military school -- in an amount of 75 percent.

USSR citizens who are departing for permanent residence in developing countries may be exempted from reimbursement of expenditures for education and receipt of an academic degree, in addition to the amounts of expenditure reimbursement reduction stipulated in this paragraph of the Directive, in an amount of up to 70 percent, while persons who have married citizens (subjects) of those countries in an amount of up to 80 percent, and in individual cases -- in full.

A partial or full exemption from reimbursement of expenditures for education and receipt of an academic degree shall also be granted by the Ministry of Finance of the USSR, with the participation of the Ministry of Internal Affairs of the USSR, when there are other justifiable reasons.[1]

4. The amounts specified in paragraphs 1 through 3 of the present Directive shall be accepted by branches of the State Bank of the USSR and credited to income in the Union budget.

5. Processing and issuance of exit visas to persons departing for permanent residence abroad shall be performed by agencies of the Ministry of Internal Affairs of the USSR upon presentation by said persons of receipts, issued by branches of the State Bank of the USSR, showing payment of amounts as reimbursement of State expenditures for education.

6. The present Directive does not pertain to USSR citizens who are departing for permanent residence in socialist countries.

| Ministry of Finance of the USSR | Ministry of Higher and Secondary Specialized Education of the USSR | Ministry of Internal Affairs of the USSR |

---

[1]. This paragraph is given in the version adopted by the resolution of the Council of Ministers of the USSR of 26 October 1972, No. 872.

THE PROGRAM OF THE COMMUNIST PARTY OF THE SOVIET
UNION. THE TASKS OF THE PARTY IN THE FIELD
OF NATIONAL RELATIONS*

Under socialism the nations flourish and their sovereignty
grows stronger. The development of nations does not proceed
along lines of strengthening national barriers, national narrow-
mindedness, and egoism, as it does under capitalism, but along
lines of their association, fraternal mutual assistance, and
friendship. The appearance of new industrial centres, the pros-
pecting and development of mineral deposits, the virgin land
development project, and the growth of all modes of transport
increase the mobility of the population and promote greater intercourse between the peoples of the Soviet Union. People of
many nationalities live together and work in harmony in the
Soviet republics. The boundaries between the constituent republics of the USSR are increasingly losing their former significance, since all the nations are equal, their life is based
on a common socialist foundation, the material and spiritual
needs of every people are satisfied to the same extent, and
they are all advancing together to the common goal -- communism. Spiritual features deriving from the new type of social
relations and embodying the finest traditions of the peoples of
the USSR have taken shape and are common to Soviet men and
women of different nationalities.

Full-scale communist construction constitutes a new
stage in the development of national relations in the USSR in
which the nations will draw still closer together until complete
unity is achieved. The building of the material and technical
basis of communism leads to still greater unity of the Soviet
peoples. The exchange of material and cultural values between
nations becomes more and more intensive, and the contribution
of each republic to the common cause of communist construction increases. Obliteration of distinctions between classes
and the development of communist social relations make for a
greater social homogeneity of nations and contribute to the
development of common communist traits in their culture, morals, and way of living, to a further strengthening of their
mutual trust and friendship.

With the victory of communism in the USSR, the nations
will draw still closer together, their economic and ideological
unity will increase, and the communist traits common to their
spiritual makeup will develop. However, the obliteration of
national distinctions, and especially of language distinctions,

315

is a considerably longer process than the obliteration of class distinctions.

The Party approaches all questions of national relationships arising in the course of communist construction from the standpoint of proletarian internationalism and firm pursuance of the Leninist nationalities policy. The Party neither ignores nor over-accentuates national characteristics.

The Party sets the following tasks in the sphere of national relations:

(a) to continue the all-round economic and cultural development of all the Soviet nations and nationalities, ensuring their increasingly fraternal co-operation, mutual aid, unity, and affinity in all spheres of life, thus achieving the utmost strengthening of the Union of Soviet Socialist Republics; to make full use of, and advance the forms of, national statehood of the peoples of the USSR;

(b) in the economic sphere, to continue to pursue the line of comprehensive development of the economies of the Soviet republics; effect a rational geographic location of production and a planned working of natural wealth, and promote socialist division of labour among the republics, unifying and combining their economic efforts, and properly balancing the interests of the state as a whole and those of each Soviet republic. The extension of the rights of the Union Republics in economic management having produced substantial positive results, such measures may also be carried out in the future with due regard to the fact that the creation of the material and technical basis of communism will call for still greater inter-connection and mutual assistance between the Soviet republics. The closer the intercourse between the nations and the greater the awareness of the countrywide tasks, the more successfully can manifestations of parochialism and national egos, be overcome.

In order to ensure the successful accomplishment of the tasks of communist construction and the co-ordination of economic activities, inter-republican economic organs may be set up in some zones (notably for such matters as irrigation, power grids, transport, etc.).

The Party will continue its policy ensuring the actual equality of all nations and nationalities with full consideration for their interests and devoting special attention to those areas of the country which are in need of more rapid development. Benefits accumulating in the course of communist construction must be fairly distributed among all nations and nationalities;

(c) to work for further all-round development of the socialist cultures of the peoples of the USSR. The wide scale of communist construction and the new victories of communist ideology are enriching the cultures of the peoples of the USSR, which are socialist in content and national in form. The ideological unity of the nations and nationalities is growing, and there is a rapproachement of their cultures. The historical experience of socialist nations shows that national forms do not ossify; they change, advance, and draw closer together, shedding all outdated traits that contradict the new living conditions. An international culture common to all the Soviet nations is developing. The cultural treasures of each nation are increasingly augmented by works acquiring an international character.

Attaching decisive importance to the development of the socialist content of the cultures of the peoples of the USSR, the Party will promote their further mutual enrichment and rapprochement, the consolidation of their international basis, and thereby the formation of the future single world-wide culture of communist society. While supporting the progressive traditions of each people, and making them the property of all Soviet people, the Party will in all ways further new revolutionary traditions of the builders of communism common to all nations;

(d) to continue promoting the free development of the languages of the peoples of the USSR and the complete freedom for every citizen of the USSR to speak, and to bring up and educate his children, in any language, ruling out all privileges, restrictions or compulsions in the use of this or that language. By virtue of the fraternal friendship and mutual trust of peoples, national languages are developing on a basis of equality and mutual enrichment.

The existing process of the voluntary study of Russian in addition to the native language is of positive significance, since it facilitates reciprocal exchanges of experience and access of every nation and nationality to the cultural gains of all the other peoples of the USSR, and to world culture. The Russian language has, in effect, become the common medium of intercourse and co-operation between all the peoples of the USSR;

(e) to pursue consistently as heretofore the principles of internationalism in the field of national relations; to strengthen the friendship of peoples as one of the most important gains of socialism; to conduct a relentless struggle against manifestations and survivals of nationalism and chauvinism of all types, against trends of national narrow-mindedness and exclusiveness, idealisation of the past and the veiling of social contradictions in the history of peoples, and against obsolete customs and habits which hinder communist construction. The growing scale of communist construction calls for the continuous exchange of trained personnel among nations. Manifestations of national aloofness in the indoctrination and employment of workers of different nationalities in the Soviet republics are impermissible. The liquidation of manifestations of nationalism is in the interests of all nations and nationalities of the USSR. Every Soviet republic can continue to flourish and strengthen only in the great family of fraternal socialist nations of the USSR.

---

*Programma: Ustav KPSS [The Program and Statutes of the CPSU] (Moscow: State Publishing House of Political Literature, 1962).

318

Sources Consulted

PRIMARY SOURCES

A most important primary data source used in this study
is comprised of over two hundred individual U.S. Department
of State cables, dispatches, and memoranda. In addition,
countless other governmental data were perused for background
and general informational purposes. Unfortunately, existing
U.S. government regulations preclude the actual listing of
these materials in this study.

Soviet Publications

Byuleten N.K.V.D., R.S.F.S.R., no. 37, 1929.
Central Statistical Administration of the Council of Ministers,
    U.S.S.R. Itogi vsesoyuznoi perepisi naseleniya 1959
    goda [Results of the all-union population census of 1959].
    16 vols. Moscow: "Statistika," 1962.
Central Statistical Administration of the Council of Ministers,
    U.S.S.R. Itogi vsesoyuznoi perepisi naseleniya 1970
    goda [Results of the all-union population census of 1970].
    7 vols. Moscow: "Statistika," 1973. Vol. 3: Uroven'
    obrazovaniya naseleniya S.S.S.R. [The educational level
    of the population of the U.S.S.R.]; vol. 4: Natsional'nyi
    sostav naseleniya S.S.S.R. [The national makeup of the
    population of the U.S.S.R.].
Central Statistical Administration of the U.S.S.R., Census
    Division. Vsesoyuznaya perepis' naseleniya 1926 goda
    [The all-union population census of 1926]. Moscow:
    Gosudarstvennoe Izdatel'stvo, 1929.
Istoriya Sovetskoi Konstitutsiya (v dokumentakh) 1917-1956
    [The History of the Soviet Constitution (in documents)
    1917-1956]. Moscow: Gosudarstvennoe Izdatel'stvo Yuri-
    dicheskoi Literatury, 1957.

319

Kommunisticheskaya akademiya komissiya po izucheniyu natsional'nogo voprosa [The Communist academy commission
for the study of the nationality question]. Natsional'naya
politika VKP (b) v tsifrakh [The nationality policy of the
VKP (b) (Communist Party) in figures]. Moscow: Izdatel'-
stvo Kommunisticheskoi Akademii, 1940.
Konstitutsiya (osnovnoi zakon) Soyuza Sovetskikh Sotsialisticheskikh Respublik [The Constitution (the basic law) of
the Union of Soviet Socialist Republics]. Moscow:
Izdatel'stvo "Izvestiya Sovetov Deputatov Trudyashchikhsya S.S.S.R.," 1960.
Lenin, Vladimir Il'ich. Natsional'nii vopros [The National
question]. Moscow: Gosudarstvennoe Izdatel'stvo, 1936.
_____. Polnoe sobranie sochinenii [Full collection of works].
5th ed., 55 vols. Vol. 12: "Sotsialism i religiya"
["Socialism and Religion"]; vol. 17: "Ob otnoshenii
rabochii partii k religii" ["Concerning the attitude of the
workers' party toward religion"]. Moscow: Gosudarst-
vennoe Izdatel'stvo, 1960.
_____. Selected Works. 12 vols. Vol. 4. New York: Inter-
national Publishers, 1943.
_____. Sochineniya [Collected Works]. 2d ed. 45 vols.
Moscow: Gosudarstvennoe Izdatel'stvo, 1961.
_____. Sochineniya [Collected Works]. 3d ed. 30 vols.
Moscow: Gosudarstvennoe Izdatel'stvo, 1926-32.
_____. Sochineniya [Collected Works]. 3d ed. 30 vols.
Vol. 17: Kriticheskie zametki po natsional'nomu voprosu
[Critical notes on the national question]. Moscow:
Gosudarstvennoe Izdatel'stvo, 1926-32.
_____. The Right of Nations to Self-Determination. New York:
International Publishers, 1951.
Marx, Karl. A World Without Jews. Translated and introduction
by Dagobert D. Runes. New York: Philosophical Library,
1959.
_____. Karl Marx, Selected Works. Edited by V. Adoratsky.
2 vols. Moscow: Marx-Engels Institute, 1933; New
York: International Publishers, 1933.
_____. The Civil War in France. Introduction by Frederick
[sic] Engels. New York: International Publishers, 1933.
Marx, Karl and Engels, Frederick [sic]. Karl Marx and Fred-
erick Engels: Collected Works. 45 vols. Vol. 4: The
Holy Family or Critique of Critical Criticism: Against
Bruno Bauer and Company. New York: International Pub-
lishers, 1975.

_____. Manifesto of the Communist Party. New York: International Publishers, 1932.

_____(Friedrich) . Selected Correspondence, 1846-1895. London: Martin Lawrence, Ltd., 1934.

_____. The German Ideology. Moscow: Marx Engels Institute, 1964.

Narodnoe Khozyaistvo S.S.S.R., 1922-1972, Yubileniyi Yezhegodnik [National Economy of the U.S.S.R., 1922-1972, Jubilee Yearbook]. Baku: Azerbaidzhan Gosudarstvennoe Izdatel'stvo, 1972.

Narodnoe Khozyaistvo S.S.S.R. v 1960 [The National Economy of the U.S.S.R. in 1960]. Moscow: Izdatel'stvo "Statistika," 1961.

Narodnoe Khozyaistvo S.S.S.R. v 1962 [The National Economy of the U.S.S.R. in 1962]. Moscow: Izdatel'stvo "Statistika," 1963.

Narodnoe Khozyaistvo S.S.S.R. v 1964 [The National Economy of the U.S.S.R. in 1964]. Moscow: Izdatel'stvo "Statistika," 1965.

Narodnoe Khozyaistvo S.S.S.R. v 1965 [The National Economy of the U.S.S.R. in 1965]. Moscow: Izdatel'stvo "Statistika," 1966.

Narodnoe Khozyaistvo S.S.S.R. v 1967 [The National Economy of the U.S.S.R. in 1967]. Moscow: Izdatel'stvo "Statistika," 1968.

Narodnoe Khozyaistvo S.S.S.R. v 1968 [The National Economy of the U.S.S.R. in 1968]. Moscow: Izdatel'stvo "Statistika," 1969.

Narodnoe Khozyaistvo S.S.S.R. v 1969 [The National Economy of the U.S.S.R. in 1969]. Moscow: Izdatel'stvo "Statistika," 1970.

Narodnoe Khozyaistvo S.S.S.R. v 1970 [The National Economy of the U.S.S.R. in 1970]. Moscow: Izdatel'stvo "Statistika," 1971.

Narodnoe Khozyaistvo S.S.S.R. v 1972 [The National Economy of the U.S.S.R. in 1972]. Moscow: Izdatel'stvo "Statistika," 1973.

Narodnoe Khozyaistvo S.S.S.R. v 1973 [The National Economy of the U.S.S.R. in 1973]. Moscow: Izdatel'stvo "Statistika," 1974.

Narodnoe obrazovanie, nauka i kul'tura v S.S.S.R.: statisticheskii sbornik [National education, science and culture in the U.S.S.R.: statistical material]. Moscow: "Statistika," 1971.

Narodnoe obrazovanie, nauka i kul'tura v S.S.S.R.: statisticheskii sbornik [National education, science and culture
in the U.S.S.R.: statistical material]. Moscow: "Statistika," 1977.

Narody Evropeiskoi Chasti S.S.S.R. [Nations of the European
U.S.S.R.]. Moscow: Gosudarstvennoe Izdatel'stvo,
1964.

Novaya sistema narodnogo obrazovaniya v S.S.S.R. [The new
system of popular education in the U.S.S.R.]. Moscow:
1960.

Pechat' S.S.S.R. v 1968 godu [Publications of the U.S.S.R. in
the year 1968]. Moscow: Izdatel'stvo "Kniga," 1969.

Pechat' S.S.S.R. v 1969 godu [Publications of the U.S.S.R. in
the year 1969]. Moscow: Izdatel'stvo "Kniga," 1970.

Pechat' S.S.S.R. v 1970 godu [Publications of the U.S.S.R. in
the year 1970]. Moscow: Izdatel'stvo "Kniga," 1971.

Polozhenie o v'yezde v S.S.S.R. i o vyezde iz S.S.S.R., utverzhdennoe postanovleniem, No. 801 Soveta Ministrov
S.S.S.R., 22 Sentyabrya 1970 g. [Concerning confirmation of the statute on entry into and departure from the
Union of Soviet Socialist Republics]. No. 801, Council
of Ministers of the U.S.S.R., 22 September 1970.

Prakticheskoe reshenie natsional'novo voprosa v Belorusskoi
S.S.R. [The practical resolution of the national question
in Byelorussia, S.S.R.]. Part I. Minsk: 1927.

Sbornik zakonov i ukazov prezidiuma verkhovnogo soveta
S.S.S.R., 1938-1967 [A collection of the laws and de-
crees of the presidium of the supreme soviet of the
U.S.S.R., 1938-1967]. 3 vols. Moscow: Izdatel'stvo
"Izvestiya Sovetov Deputatov Trudyashchikhsya S.S.S.R.,"
1971.

Sobranie postanovlenii pravitel'stva S.S.S.R. [Collected resolutions of the U.S.S.R. Council of Ministers], no. 1,
1973.

Sobranie uzakonenii i rasporyazhenii rabochekrest'yanskovo
pravitel'stva R.S.F.S.R. [Collected laws and directives
of the workers-peasants council of the R.S.F.S.R.],
no. 35, 1929.

Sovetskie Konstitutsii: Spravochik [Soviet Constitutions: A
Reference Book]. Moscow: Gosudarstvennoe Izdatel'-
stvo Politicheskoi Literatury, 1975.

S.S.S.R. v Tsifrakh v 1974 godu: Kratkii Statisticheskii
Sbornik [The U.S.S.R. in Figúres in 1974: A Brief
Statistical Account]. Moscow: Izdatel'stvo "Statistika,"
1975.

Stalin, Joseph. Leninism. 2 vols., Eng. ed. Moscow and
Leningrad: State Publishing House, 1934.
_____. Marxism and Linguistics. New York: International
Publishers, 1951.
_____. Marxism and the National and Colonial Question.
Moscow: Foreign Languages Publishing House, 1940.
_____. Sochineniya [Collected Works]. 13 vols. Moscow:
Gosudarstvennoe Izdatel'stvo, 1946-
Statisticheskoe Upravlenie Goroda Moskvy [Statistical Direc-
torate of the City of Moscow]. Moskva v Tsifrakh,
1966-1970: Kratkii Statisticheskii Sbornik [Moscow in
Figures, 1966-1970: A Brief Statistical Account]. Moscow:
Izdatel'stvo "Statistika," 1972.
Statisticheskoe Upravlenie Goroda Moskvy [Statistical Direc-
torate of the City of Moscow]. Moskva v Trifrakh,
1971-1975: Kratkii Statisticheskii Sbornik [Moscow in
Figures, 1971-1975: A Brief Statistical Account]. Moscow:
Izdatel'stvo "Statistika," 1976.
Tretii vserossiiskii s'yezd sovetov rabochikh, soldatskikh
i krest'yanskikh deputatov [The third all-Russian con-
gress of the soviets of workers, soldiers and peasants
deputies]. St. Petersburg, 1918.
Ugolovnyi Kodeks R.S.F.S.R. [Criminal Codes of the R.S.F.
S.R.]. Moscow: Gosudarstvennoe Izdatel'stvo Yuridi-
cheskoi Literatury, 1922.
Ugolovnyi Kodeks R.S.F.S.R. Moscow: Gosudarstvennoe Izda-
tel'stvo Yuridischeskoi Literatury, 1953.
Ugolovnyi Kodeks R.S.F.S.R. Moscow: Gosudarstvennoe Izda-
tel'stvo Yuridicheskoi Literatury, 1964.
Ugolovnyi Kodeks R.S.F.S.R. Moscow: Gosudarstvennoe Izda-
tel'stvo Yuridischeskoi Literatury, 1967.
Unidentified public (Znanie) lecturer, Moscow, March 21, 1973.
Vedomosti R.S.F.S.R., 33 (869) [Herald of the R.S.F.S.R.].
August 14, 1975.
Vedomosti Verkhovnogo Soveta S.S.S.R. [Herald of the Supreme
Soviet of the U.S.S.R.], no. 11. Moscow: Izdanie Verk-
hovnogo Soveta S.S.S.R., 1938.
Vedomosti Verkhovnogo Soveta S.S.S.R. [Herald of the Supreme
Soviet of the U.S.S.R.], no. 14. Moscow: Izdanie Verk-
hovnogo Soveta S.S.S.R., 1958.
Vedomosti Verkhovnogo Soveta S.S.S.R. [Herald of the Supreme
Soviet of the U.S.S.R.], no. 52. Moscow: Izdanie Verk-
hovnogo Soveta S.S.S.R., 1972.
Vedomosti Verkhovnogo Soveta S.S.S.R. [Herald of the Supreme
Soviet of the U.S.S.R.], no. 1. Moscow: Izdanie Verk-
hovnogo Soveta S.S.S.R., 1976.

Vestnik Statistiki [Statistical Material] 11. Moscow: Main
    Statistical Administration, 1965.
Vestnik Statistiki [Statistical Material] 4. Moscow: Main
Statistical Administration, 1974.

U.S. Publications

American Association for the Advancement of Slavic Studies.
    The Current Digest of the Soviet Press. Columbus,
    Ohio: American Association for the Advancement of
    Slavic Studies, March 7, 1976. Vol. 28, no. 7,
    "Soviet Freedoms Defined and Defended."
_____. The Current Digest of the Soviet Press. Columbus,
    Ohio: American Association for the Advancement of
    Slavic Studies, January 19, 1977. Vol. 28, no. 51,
    "Jewish Culture Seen Thriving in the U.S.S.R."
_____. The Current Digest of the Soviet Press. Columbus,
    Ohio: American Association for the Advancement of
    Slavic Studies, August 10, 1977. Vol. 29, no. 28,
    "Soviet Ethnic Integration: What Is It?"
Consular Section, American Embassy, Moscow. Procedure
    for Obtaining Exit Documentation From the Union of
    Soviet Socialist Republics (April 1970).
DeWitt, N. Education and Professional Employment in the
    U.S.S.R. Prepared for the National Science Foundation
    by the Office of Scientific Personnel, Washington, D.C.,
    U.S. Government Printing Office, 1961.
Joint Publications Research Service. General Secretary
    Brezhnev's Report at the 24th C.P.S.U. Congress.
    Arlington, Va.: Joint Publications Research Service,
    December 20, 1971. Special Report No. 54742-1.
Law Library of Congress. Church and State Under Communism.
    Washington, D.C.: Law Library of Congress, 1964.
U.S. Congress. Senate. Committee on Finance. Exchange of
    Letters Between Secretary of State Henry A. Kissinger
    and Senator Henry M. Jackson of Washington. Wash-
    ington, D.C., October 18, 1974.
U.S. Congress. Senate. Senator Henry M. Jackson of Wash-
    ington Speaking for the Amendment of the Trade Reform
    Act of 1974. Amendment No. 2000. 93d Cong., 2d sess.,
    December 13, 1974. Congressional Record, vol. 120.
U.S. Congress. Senate. Senator Henry M. Jackson of Wash-
    ington Speaking about East-West Trade and Freedom of
    Emigration. 94th Cong., 1st sess., January 30, 1975.
    Congressional Record, vol. 121.

324

U.S. Congress. Senate. Senator Henry M. Jackson Newsletter. Washington, D.C., October 11, 1973. Text of Senator Jackson's speech at the Pacem in Terris Conference, Washington, D.C., on that same date.

U.S. Congress. Senate Committee on Foreign Relations. Report of a Conference Between Members of the U.S. Senate and Delegates to the Supreme Soviet of the Soviet Union, Moscow and Leningrad, June 29-July 5, 1975. Washington, D.C.: U.S. Government Printing Office, 1975.

U.S. Department of State. Bureau of Public Affairs. GIST -- Soviet Jewish Emigration (July 1977).

U.S. Department of State, Bureau of Public Affairs. Office of Media Services. U.S. Trade Policy and Detente. Testimony of Secretary of State Henry A. Kissinger before the Senate Committee on Finance. Washington, D.C., March 7, 1974.

U.S. Department of State. Bureau of Public Affairs. Office of Media Services. U.S.-Soviet Relations. Special Report No. 6. Statement of Secretary of State Henry A. Kissinger before the Senate Foreign Relations Committee. Washington, D.C., September 19, 1974.

U.S. Department of State. Bureau of Public Affairs. Office of Media Services. The Trade Reform Act. Testimony of Secretary of State Henry A. Kissinger before the Senate Committee on Finance. Washington, D.C., December 3, 1974.

U.S. Department of State. Bureau of Public Affairs. Office of Media Services. Soviets Reject Trade Agreement. Press Conference. Washington, D.C., January 14, 1975.

U.S. Department of State. Bureau of Public Affairs. Office of Media Services. Conference on Security and Cooperation in Europe, Final Act. Washington, D.C.: U.S. Government Printing Office, 1975.

U.S. Department of State. Bureau of Public Affairs. Office of Media Services. Special Report No. 15. U.S. Assistance to Soviet Jews in Israel (April 1975).

U.S. Department of State. Bureau of Public Affairs. Office of Media Services. State of the World. Speech by President Gerald R. Ford before a joint session of Congress. Washington, D.C., April 10, 1975.

U.S. Department of State. Bureau of Public Affairs. Office of Media Services. The American Role in East-West Trade. Statement of Robert S. Ingersoll, Deputy Secretary of State, before the Senate Commerce Committee. Washington, D.C., December 12, 1975.

U.S. Foreign Broadcast Information Service (F.B.I.S.). Vol.
7, Special Report, <u>Text of Khrushchev Draft Program at
the 22nd C.P.S.U. Congress</u>, October 1961.

U.S. Foreign Broadcast Information Service (F.B.I.S.). Vol.
3, <u>U.S.S.R. Domestic Affairs--Briefs</u>, 24 July 1970.

U.S. Foreign Broadcast Information Service (F.B.I.S.). Vol.
3, <u>Text of Abrasimov Letter to Mitterand on Soviet Jews</u>,
8 September 1972.

U.S. Foreign Broadcast Information Service (F.B.I.S.). Vol.
3, <u>International Law Upholds State's Restrictions on
Emigres</u>, 12 September 1972.

U.S. Foreign Broadcast Information Service (F.B.I.S.). Vol.
3, <u>Moscow Refutes Western Propaganda on Jewish Emi-
gration</u>, 12 September 1972.

U.S. Foreign Broadcast Information Service (F.B.I.S.). Vol.
3, <u>Tass [sic] Commentator Yuriy Kornilov Writes</u>, 19
September 1972.

U.S. Foreign Broadcast Information Service (F.B.I.S.). Vol.
3, <u>Repayment for Education Before Emigration Defended</u>,
28 September 1972.

U.S. Foreign Broadcast Information Service (F.B.I.S.). Vol.
3, <u>Soviet Official Explains Emigration Policy to Novosti</u>,
4 January 1973.

U.S. Foreign Broadcast Information Service (F.B.I.S.). Vol.
3, <u>Soviet Official in C.S.S.R. Paper on Emigration Prac-
tice</u>, 27 January 1973.

U.S. Foreign Broadcast Information Service (F.B.I.S.). Vol.
3, <u>'Exodus' of Jews a Trickle, Many Wish to Return</u>, 16
March 1973.

U.S. Foreign Broadcast Information Service (F.B.I.S.). Vol.
3, <u>Soviet Newspapers Report Ratification of Rights Pacts,</u>
28 September 1973.

U.S. Foreign Broadcast Information Service (F.B.I.S.).
<u>Trends in Communist Propaganda</u>, 31 October 1973.
"Pravda Official Rebukes Soviet Press for Softness on
Zionism."

U.S. Foreign Broadcast Information Service (F.B.I.S.). Vol.
3, <u>Soviet Decrees on Passport System, Registration;
Decrees 109 and 110 of the U.S.S.R. Government</u>, 5 November 1974.

U.S. Foreign Broadcast Information Service (F.B.I.S.).
<u>Trends in Communist Propaganda,</u> 18 December 1974.
"Podgorny, Red Star Register Dissent from Detente
Mood."

U.S. Foreign Broadcast Information Service (F.B.I.S.). Vol.
3, Moscow Claims Drop in Number of Jewish Emigrants
to Israel, 5 November 1975.
U.S. Foreign Broadcast Information Service (F.B.I.S.). Vol.
3, Emigration Procedures Simplified 'Quite Recently',
22 January 1976.
U.S. Foreign Broadcast Information Service (F.B.I.S.). Vol.
3, no. 222, Preparations for Census, 16 November 1976.
U.S. Foreign Broadcast Information Service (F.B.I.S.). Vol.
3, no. 244, Novoye Vremya Scores Reports on Emigration from U.S.S.R., 18 November 1976.
U.S. Foreign Broadcast Information Service (F.B.I.S.). Vol.
3, Concerning an Anti-Soviet Campaign, 13 December
1976.
U.S. Foreign Broadcast Information Service (F.B.I.S.). Vol.
3, Izvestiya Rebuts Zionist Claims About Soviet Jews,
12 January 1977.
U.S. Foreign Broadcast Information Service (F.B.I.S.). Vol.
3, Izvestiya Denies Existence of 'Jewish' Question,
14 January 1977.
U.S. Foreign Broadcast Information Service (F.B.I.S.). Vol.
3, Kudryavtsev Interviewed on Human Rights Issue,
23 March 1977.
U.S. Foreign Broadcast Information Service (F.B.I.S.). Vol.
3, Special Report, Text of U.S.S.R. Constitution,
7 June 1977.
U.S. Foreign Broadcast Information Service (F.B.I.S.). Vol.
3, Emigration Data Cited: Refutes 'Zionist' Exaggeration, 14 July 1977.
U.S. Foreign Broadcast Information Service (F.B.I.S.). Vol.
3, Moscow and the Departure of Soviet Citizens from
the U.S.S.R., 14 July 1977.

United Nations Publications

United Nations. Commission on Human Rights, 5 January 1961.
Study of Discrimination in Education (Doc. E/CN.4/Sub.
2/210).
United Nations. Commission on Human Rights, 20 December
1963. Periodic Reports on Human Rights Covering the
Period 1960-1962 (Doc. C/CN.4/Add.2).
United Nations. General Assembly, 10 December 1948. Univer-
sal Declaration of Human Rights (A/811).

United Nations. General Assembly, 25 September 1963. <u>Mani-</u>
<u>festations of Racial Prejudice and Religious Intolerance</u>
(A/5473).
United Nations. <u>Official Records of the Third Session of the</u>
<u>General Assembly</u>. Lake Success, N.Y.: United Nations,
1948.
United Nations. <u>Yearbook for 1948-49</u>. Lake Success, N.Y.:
United Nations, 1950.
United Nations. <u>Yearbook on Human Rights for 1947</u>. Lake
Success, N.Y.: United Nations, 1947.
United Nations. <u>Yearbook on Human Rights for 1948</u>. Lake
Success, N.Y.: United Nations, 1948.
United Nations. <u>Yearbook on Human Rights for 1966</u>. Lake
Success, N.Y.: United Nations, 1966.

UNPUBLISHED SECONDARY SOURCES

Baron, Salo. "Cultural Reconstruction of Russian Jewry." Prepared for delivery at the Congregation Shaar Hashomayim,
Westmount, Quebec, Canada, November 18, 1971.
Gitelman, Zvi Y. "Assimilation, Acculturation, and National
Consciousness Among Soviet Jews." Prepared for delivery
at the annual meeting of the American Historical Association, New Orleans, December 1972.
_____. "Research on the U.S.S.R. Based on Interviews with
Soviet Emigres: A Conference Report and Research Proposal." Based on a conference sponsored by the Research
and Development Committee of the American Association
for the Advancement of Slavic Studies, December 19-20,
1976, University of Michigan, Ann Arbor.
Linden, Carl A. <u>Soviet Politics and the Revival of Russian</u>
<u>Patriotism</u>. Washington, D.C.: The Institute of Sino-
Soviet Studies, the George Washington University, n.d.
Ross, Jeffrey A. "Alienation and Self-Image: The Development
of Emigration-Nationalism Among Soviet Jews." Prepared
for delivery at the annual meeting of the International
Studies Association, New York, March 14-17, 1973.

PUBLISHED SECONDARY SOURCES

Books

Akhapkin, Yuri. <u>First Decrees of Soviet Power</u>. London: Lawrence & Wishart, 1970.

328

Alliluyeva, Svetlana. Twenty Letters to a Friend. New York: Harper & Row, 1967.

Armstrong, John A. Ideology, Politics, and Government in the Soviet Union. rev. ed. New York: Praeger Publishers, 1967.

Arendt, Hannah, The Origins of Totalitariantsm. New York and London: Harcourt, Brace, Jovanovich, 1951.

Aronson, Gregor, et al. Russian Jewry, 1917-1967. Translated by Joel Carmichal. New York and London: Thomas Yoseloff, 1969.

A Study Group of Members of the Royal Institute of International Affairs. Nationalism. London: Oxford University Press, 1939.

Avineri, Shlomo. The Social and Political Thought of Karl Marx. London and New York: Cambridge University Press, 1968.

Baron, Salo. The Russian Jew Under Tsars and Soviets. New York and London: The Macmillan Co., and Collier Macmillan Publishers, 1964.

Bauer, Bruno. The Capacity of Today's Jews and Christians to Become Free. Zurich and Winterthur: Georg Herwegh, 1843.

Bauer, Raymond A., Inkeles, Alex, and Kluckhohn, Clyde. How The Soviet System Works: Cultural, Psychological, and Social Themes. Cambridge, Mass.: Harvard University Press, 1956.

Begun, Vladimir. Polzuchaya kontrrevolyutsia [Creeping Counterrevolution]. Minsk: Izdatel'stvo "Belarus," 1974.

Belenki, M.S. Judaism. Moscow: The Political Literature Publishing House, 1974-75.

Belloc, Hilaire. The Jews. Boston, New York: Houghton Mifflin Co., 1922.

Bloom, Solomon F. The World of Nations: A Study of the National Implications in the Work of Karl Marx. New York: Columbia University Press, 1941.

Bohlen, Charles Eustis. Witness to History, 1929-1969. New York: W.W. Norton, 1973.

Brodsky, R. The Truth About Zionism. Moscow: Novosti, 1974-75.

Brownlie, Ian. Basic Documents on Human Rights. Oxford: Clarendon Press, 1971.

Bruk, S.I. and Apenchenko, V.S., eds. Atlas Narodov Mira [Atlas of the Peoples of the World]. Moscow: Glavnoe

Upravlenie Geodeziii i Kartografii Gosudarstvennogo
Geologicheskogo Komiteta S.S.S.R., 1964.
Bunyan, James, and Fisher, H.H. The Bolshevik Revolution,
1917-1918. Stanford, Calif.: Stanford University Press,
1934.
Burmistrova, T. Yu. Teoriya sotsialisticheskoi natsii [Theory
of socialist nations]. Leningrad: Izdatel'stvo Leningrad-
skogo Universiteta [Leningrad University Press], 1970.
Cang, Joel. The Silent Millions - A History of the Jews in
the Soviet Union. London: Rapp and Whiting, Ltd.,
1969.
Chkhikvadze, V.M., ed. The Soviet State and Law. Moscow:
Progress Publishers, 1969.
Cohen, Richard, ed. Let My People Go. New York: Popular
Library, 1971.
Conquest, Robert, ed. Soviet Nationalities Policy in Practice.
London, Sidney, Toronto: The Bodley Head, 1967.
Denisov, Andrei, and Kirichenko, M. Soviet State Law. Mos-
cow: Foreign Languages Publishing House, 1960.
Deutsch, Karl W. National and Social Communication: An In-
quiry in the Foundations of Nationality. 2d ed. Cam-
bridge, Mass.: M.I.T. Press, 1966.
Deutscher, Isaac. Stalin, A Political Biography. New York:
Oxford University Press, 1949.
Dimanshtein, S., ed. Yidn in F.S.S.R. [Jews in the U.S.S.R.].
Moscow: Zamlbuch, Der Emes, 1935.
Division of Research and Statistics, HIAS. Statistical Abstract
15 (Fourth Quarter, 1974): 1-15.
Division of Research and Statistics, HIAS. Statistical Abstract
17 (Third Quarter, 1976): 1-15.
Djilas, Milovan. Conversations With Stalin. New York: Har-
court, Brace & World, 1962.
Dubnow, Simon M. History of the Jews in Russia and Poland:
From the Earliest Times Until the Present Day. 3 vols.
Translated by I. Friedlander. Philadelphia: The Jewish
Publication Society of America, 1916-20.
Dupre, Louis K. The Philosophical Foundations of Marxism.
New York and Chicago: Harcourt, Brace & World, 1966.
Dymtryshyn, Basil. U.S.S.R.: A Concise History. New York:
Charles Scribner's Sons, 1965.
Eliav, Arie L. (Ben-Ami). Between Hammer and Sickle. New
York: Signet Books, 1969.
Emerson, Rupert. From Emigre to Nations: The Rise of Self-
Assertion of Asian and African Peoples. Cambridge,
Mass.: Harvard University Press, 1960.

330

Encyclopedia Judaica. Vol. 10. Jerusalem, Israel: Keter Publishing House, Ltd., 1971.

Fedoseyev, P.N., et al. Leninizm i natsional'nyi vopros v sovremennykh usloviyakh [Leninism and the national question under contemporary conditions]. 2d ed. Moscow: Politizdat, 1974.

Fein, Leonard J. Israel: Politics and People. Boston: Little, Brown & Co., 1968.

Fischer, George. The Soviet System and Modern Society. New York: Atherton Press, 1969.

Gilboa, Yeloshua A. The Black Years of Soviet Jewry. Translated by Yosef Schacter. Boston: Little, Brown & Co., 1971.

Gitelman, Zvi Y. Jewish Nationality and Soviet Politics. The Jewish Sections of the C.P.S.U., 1917-1930. Princeton, N.J.: Princeton University Press, 1972.

_____. Soviet Immigrants in Israel. New York: Institute for Jewish Policy Planning and Research of the Synagogue Council of America, 1972.

Goldberg, B.Z. The Jewish Problem in the Soviet Union: Analysis and Solution. Foreword by Daniel Mayer. New York: Crown Publishing Co., 1961.

Goldhagen, Erich, ed. Ethnic Minorities in the Soviet Union. New York: Praeger Publishers, 1968.

Goldman, Guild G. Zionism Under Soviet Rule (1917-1928) New York: Herzl Press, 1960.

Gouzenko, Igor. The Iron Curtain. New York: Dutton Publishers, 1948.

Greenberg, Louis. The Jews in Russia: The Struggle for Emancipation. 2 vols. New York: Schocken Books, 1976.

Halevy, Jacob. Genocide of a Culture: The Execution of the 24. London: World Jewish Congress, 1972.

Harper, Samuel N., and Thompson, Ronald. The Government of the Soviet Union. 2d ed. Toronto, New York, London: D. Van Nostrand Co., Inc., 1949.

Ingles, Jose D. Study of Discrimination in Respect of the Right of Everyone to Leave Any Country, Including His Own, and to Return to His Country. Lake Success, N.Y.: United Nations, 1963.

Kann, Robert A. The Multinational Empire: Nationalism and National Reform in the Habsburg Monarchy. 2 vols. New York: Columbia University Press, 1950.

Karchev, A.G. Brak i sem'ya v S.S.S.R. [Marriage and Family in the U.S.S.R.]. Moscow: Izdatel'stvo "Statistika," 1964.

Karol, Alexander G. Soviet Research and Development. Cambridge, Mass.: The M.I.T. Press, 1966.

Katz, Zev, ed. Attitudes of Major Soviet Nationalities. 5 vols. Cambridge, Mass.: M.I.T. Center of International Studies, 1973. Vol. 5: The Jews in the Soviet Union, by Zev Katz.

Kohn, Hans. The Idea of Nationalism, A Study in Its Origins and Background. New York: Macmillan Co., 1944.

Kolarz, Walter. Religion in the Soviet Union. New York: Frederick A. Praeger, 1961.

Korey, William. The Soviet Cage, Anti-Semitism in Russia. New York: The Viking Press, 1973.

Kozlov, V.I. Dinamika chislennosti narodov: metologiya issledovannia i osnovne faktory [The dynamics of population statistics: research methodology and basic facts]. Moscow: "Nauka," 1969.

Kurman, M.V. and Lebedinskii, I.V. Naselenie bol'shogo sotsialisticheskogo goroda [The population of a large socialist city]. Moscow: Izdatel'stvo "Statistika," 1968.

Levin, Alfred. Foreword to The Jews in Russia: The Struggle for Emancipation, by Louis Greenberg. New York: Schocken Books, 1976.

Lorimer, Frank. The Population of the Soviet Union: History and Prospects. Geneva: League of Nations, 1946.

Macartney, Carlile Aylmer. National States and National Minorities. London: Oxford University Press, 1934.

Masaryk, Thomas Garrigue. The Spirit of Russia: Studies in History, Literature, and Philosophy. 2d ed. 3 vols. London: Allen & Unwin; New York: Macmillan Publishers, 1955-67.

Mishin, V. Obshchestvennii progress [Social progress]. Gorkii: Volgo-Vyatsko Knizhnoe Izdatel'stvo, 1970.

Mitin, N., ed. The Ideology of International Zionism. Moscow: The Political Literature Publishing House, 1974-75.

Morris, William, ed. The American Heritage Dictionary of the English Language. New College ed. Boston, New York, Atlanta, Dallas, Palo Alto: Heritage Publishing Co., Inc. and Houghton Mifflin Co., 1975.

Pipes, Richard E. The Formation of the Soviet Union: Communism and Nationalism, 1917-1923. Cambridge, Mass.: Harvard University Press, 1954.

Rabinovich, Solomon. Jews in the Soviet Union. Moscow: Novosti Agency Publishing House, 1967.

Rigby, T.H. Communist Party Membership in the U.S.S.R., 1917-67. Princeton, N.J.: Princeton University Press, 1968.

Rothenberg, Joshua. The Jewish Religion in the Soviet Union.
New York: K.T.A.V. Publishing House, Inc., 1971.
Sabine, George H. A History of Political Theory. New York:
Henry Holt & Co., 1937.
Sachar, Abram Leon. A History of the Jews. New York: Alfred
A. Knopf Publishers, 1972.
Safarov, G. Marks o natsional 'no-kolonial'nom voprose [Marx
on the national-colonial question]. Moscow: Gosudar-
stvennoe Izdatel'stvo, 1928.
Sakharov, Andrei. Progress, Coexistence, and Intellectual
Freedom. New York: W.W. Norton, 1970.
Savtsov, V.Y., and Rozenblum, N.Y. The Black Webs of
Zionism. Kiev: Literature of the Ukraine, 1974-75.
Schapiro, Leonard. The Communist Party of the Soviet Union.
rev. & enl. ed. New York: Vintage Books, 1971.
Schectman, Joseph. Star in Eclipse: Russian Jewry Revisited.
New York: Thomas Yoseloff Publishers, 1961.
Schlesinger, Rudolf. Federalism in Central and Eastern Europe.
London: K. Paul, Trench, Trubner & Co., 1945.
_____, ed. The Nationalities Problem and Soviet Administra-
tion. Translated by W.W. Gottlieb. London: Routledge
& Kegan Paul, 1956.
Schroeter, Leonard. The Last Exodus. New York: Universe
Books, 1974.
Schulman, Elias. A History of Jewish Education in the Soviet
Union. New York: K.T.A.V. and Brandeis University
Press, 1971.
Schwarz, Solomon M. The Jews in the Soviet Union. Syracuse,
N.Y.: Syracuse University Press, 1951.
_____. Yevrei v Sovetskom Soyuze (1939-1965) [Jews in the
Soviet Union: 1939-1965]. New York: The American Jew-
ish Committee, 1966.
Shaeen, Samad. The Communist (Bolshevik) Theory of National
Self-Determination. The Hague and Bandung: W. Van
Hoeve Ltd., 1956.
Shaffer, Harry G. The Soviet Treatment of Jews. New York,
London, Washington: Praeger Publishers, 1974.
Sitnikov, G.O. and Verest, G.B. Together They Do Black
Business. Kiev: Novye Knigi Ukrainy, 1974-75.
Smal-Stocki, Roman. The Captive Nations: Nationalism of the
Non-Russian Nations in the Soviet Union. New York:
Bookman Associates, 1960.
Smolar, Boris. Soviet Jewry Today and Tomorrow. New York:
Macmillan Co.; London: Collier-Macmillan Ltd., 1971.

Solzhenitsyn, Aleksandr. The Gulag Archipelago, 1918-1956. Translated by Thomas P. Whitney. New York: Harper & Row, 1973.

Souvarine, Boris. Stalin, A Critical Survey of Bolshevism. New York: Longmans, Green & Co., 1939.

Soviet Jews: Facts and Fiction. Moscow: Novosti Press Agency Publishing House, 1972.

Studenikina, S.S., gen. ed. Istoriya sovetskoi konstitutsii v dokumentakh 1917-1956 [The History of the soviet constitution in documents 1917-1956]. Moscow: Gosudarstvennoe Izdatel'stvo, 1957.

Talbot, S., ed. Khrushchev Remembers. Introduction by E. Crankshaw. Boston: Little, Brown & Co., 1970.

Teller, Judd L. The Kremlin, the Jews, and the Middle East. New York and London: Thomas Youseloff, 1957.

_____. Scapegoat of the Revolution. New York: Charles Scribner's Sons, 1954.

The American Jewish Committee. American Jewish Yearbook 1976. New York: The American Jewish Committee, 1976.

Tobia, Henry. The Jewish Bund in Russia from its Origins to 1905. Stanford, Calif.: Stanford University Press, 1972.

Vernadsky, George. A History of Russia. 6th rev. ed. New Haven: Yale University Press, 1961.

Vishinskii, Andrei Y., ed. The Law of the Soviet State. Translated by H.W. Babb. New York: Macmillan Publishers, 1948.

Voronel, Aleksandr and Yakhot, Viktor, eds. Jewishness Rediscovered: Jewish Identity in the Soviet Union. New York: Academic Committee on Soviet Jewry and the Anti-Defamation League of B'nai B'rith, 1974.

Vozniak, N.V. Their True Face. Kiev: Novye Knigi Ukrainy, 1974-75.

Werth, Alexander. Russia: Hopes and Fears. New York: Simon and Schuster, 1969.

Wesson, Robert G. The Russian Dilemma. New Brunswick, N.J.: Rutgers University Press, 1974.

West, Benjamin. Struggles of a Generation: The Jews Under Soviet Rule. Tel Aviv: Massadah Publishing Co., Ltd., 1959.

Wolf, Lucien, ed. The Legal Sufferings of the Jews in Russia. Introduction by Professor A.V. Dicey. London: T. Fisher Unwin, 1912.

Wolfe, Bertram D. Three Who Made a Revolution. New York: Dial Press, 1948.

334

Yarmolinsky, Avrahm. The Jews and Other Nationalities Under the Soviets. New York: Vanguard Press, 1948.
Zhukov, Dmitri. Against Zionism and Israeli Aggression. Moscow: Nauka Publishing House, 1974.

ARTICLES AND PERIODICALS

"A Union of Equals." Literaturnaya Gazeta [Literary Gazette] (Moscow), 1 December 1976, p. 10.
Abramsky, C. "The Biro-Bidzhan Project." In The Jews in Soviet Russia since 1917, pp. 62-75. Edited by Lionel Kochan. London, New York, Toronto: Oxford University Press, 1970.
Aleksandrov, V. "The Latest Anti-Soviet Fulminations." International Affairs 11 (1972): 79-81.
Altshuler, Mordekhai. "Mixed Marriages Amongst Soviet Jews." Soviet Jewish Affairs 6 (December 1970): 30-33.
Arbatov, G.A. "U.S. Foreign Policy and the Scientific and Technical Revolution." SShA: Ekonomika, Politika, Ideologiya 11 (November 1973): 3-16.
Armstrong, John A. "Soviet Foreign Policy and Anti-Semitism." Perspectives on Soviet Jewry (1971), pp. 62-75.
Aspaturian, Vernon L. "The Non-Russian Nationalities." In Prospects for Soviet Society, pp. 143-98. Edited by Allen Kassof. New York: Praeger Publishers, 1968.
Baron, John. "The Control Mechanism." In Understanding the Solzhenitsyn Affair: Dissent and Its Control in the U.S.S.R., pp. 8-13. Edited by Ray S. Cline. Washington, D.C.: The Center for Strategic and International Studies, Georgetown University, 1974.
Begun, Vladimir. "An Unwanted Invasion." Neman, no. 1 (1972).
Bromlei, Yurii V. "Ethnic Aspects of Contemporary National Processes." Istoriya S.S.S.R. 3 (May-June 1977): 19-28.
Bruk, S.I., and Kozlov, V.I. "Etnograficheskaya nauka i perepis' naseleniya 1970 goda" [The Ethnographical science and the population census for 1970]. Sovetskaya Etnografiya 6 (Moscow: 1967): 3-20.
_____. "Voprosy o natsional'nosti i yazkike v predstoyashchei perepisi naseleniya" [Questions about nationality and language in the forthcoming population census]. Vestnik Statistiki [Statistical Material] 3 (Moscow: 1968): 32-37.
Brumberg, Joseph and Brumberg, Abraham. "Sovyetish Heymland." In The Unredeemed, Anti-Semitism in the Soviet Union, pp. 83-96. Edited by R.I. Rubin. Chicago: Quadrangle,

335

1968. This article also appears in Goldhagen, Erich, ed. Ethnic Minorities in the Soviet Union. New York: Praeger Publishing Co., 1968, pp. 274-312.

Checinski, Michael. "Soviet Jews and Higher Education." Soviet Jewish Affairs 2 (1973): 1-16.

Chkhikvadze, V.M. "Human Rights and the Ideological Struggle." Sovetskoye gosudarstvo i pravo [The Soviet state and law] (April 1977), pp. 100-08.

Conference on "Interaction of Cultures of Peoples of U.S.S.R." Sovetskaya Estonia 30 (November 1976).

Decter, Moshe. "Jewish National Consciousness in the Soviet Union" and "Epilogue." Perspectives on Soviet Jewry (1971), pp. 1-41, 17-104.

Deutsch, Karl W. "Social Mobilization and Political Development." American Political Science Review 60 (September 1961): 493-514.

Division of Research and Statistics, HIAS. Statistical Abstract 15 (Fourth Quarter, 1974): 1-27.

_____. Statistical Abstract 17 (Third Quarter, 1976): 1-15.

"Economic Crimes in the Soviet Union." Journal of the International Commission of Jurists (Summer Issue 1964), pp. 3-47.

Emigration from the U.S.S.R. - Situation in 1974. Moscow: A samizdat [self-published] document "published" by unknown authors on November 18, 1974.

Ettinger, S. "The Jews in Russia at the Outbreak of the Revolution." In The Jews in Soviet Russia since 1917, pp. 14-28. Edited by Lionel Kochan. London, New York, Toronto: Oxford University Press, 1970.

Friedberg, Maurice. "The Plight of Soviet Jews." Problems of Communism (November 1970), pp. 17-26.

Gantskaya, O.A., and Debets, G.F. "O graficheskom izobrazhenii rezul'tatov statisticheskogo obsledovaniya mezhnatsional'nykh brakov" [Concerning the graphical representation of the statistical results of the investigation of intermarriages]. Sovetskaya Etnografia 3 (Moscow: 1966): 109-18.

Ginsburgs, George. "Soviet Law and the Emigration of Soviet Jews." Soviet Jewish Affairs 3 (1973): 3-19.

Grishin, V.M. "Problemy natsional'no-gosudarstvennogo stroitelstva v pervoi sovetskoi konstitutsii," [The problems of nation-state building in the first Soviet Constitution]. Voprosy Istorii K.P.S.S. [Questions on the History of the C.P.S.U.] 7 (1968): 21-34.

"How Many Jews Are There in the Soviet Union?" Soviet Life (July 1972), p. 53.

Inkeles, Alex. "Anti-Semitism as an Instrument of Soviet Policy." Perspectives on Soviet Jewry (1971), pp. 76-85.

Institute for Jewish Policy Planning and Research of the Synagogue Council of America. Analysis, no. 47, Special Issue, November 1, 1974. "Which Promised Land? The Realities of American Absorption of Soviet Jews."

"Just Measure and Zionist Insinuations." New Times (Moscow) 38 (September 1972): 10-11.

Kapeluish, Yakov. "Yidn in Sovetnfarband" (Jews in the Soviet Union). Sovetish Heimland 9 (1974): 173-82.

Katlin, V. "Putting the Record Straight." New Times 2 (January 1973): 17.

Khanazarov, K. Kh. "Mezhnatsional'nye braki--odna iz progressivnykh sblizheniya sotsialisticheskikh natsii" [Intermarriages--one of the progressive drawing-togethers of socialist nations]. Obschestvennye Nauki v Uzbekistane [The Social Sciences in Uzbekistan] 10 (1964): 29-30.

Khronika Tekushchikh Sobytii [Chronicle of Current Events] , no. 41 (August 3, 1976).

Kohn, Hans. "Soviet Communism and Nationalism: Three Stages of a Historical Development." In Soviet Nationality Problems, pp. 43-71. Edited by Edward Allworth. New York and London: Columbia University Press, 1971.

Kon, I. "Dialektika razvitiya natsii" [Dialectic of the development of nations]. Novyi mir 3 (Moscow: 1970): 133-49.

Lendvai, Paul. "Jews Under Communism." Commentary (December 1971), pp. 67-74.

Linevski, A. "The Role of the Ethnographer in Soviet Construction in the North." In The Nationalities Problem and Soviet Administration, pp. 109-22. Edited by Rudolf Schlesinger. Translated by W.W. Gottlieb. London: Routledge & Kegan Paul, 1956.

Literaturnaya Gazeta [Literary Gazette] (Moscow), 24 January 1973, p. 13.

Literaturnaya Gazeta (Moscow), 11 February 1976.

Litvinoff, Emanuel, ed. "Captive Scientists: Their Central Role in the Struggle for Freedom." Insight 1 (May 1975): 1-2.

_____. "Emigrants Who Turn Away From Israel." Insight 1 (April 1975): 1-3.

_____. "Jews as a Soviet Nationality, A Statistical Analysis."
Insight 1 (October 1975): 1-7.
_____. "Open Assault on Jews and Judaism." Insight 1
(July 1975): 1-8.
Medvedev, Roy A. Blishnevostochnii konflikt i yevreiskii
vopros v S.S.S.R. [The near-eastern conflict and the
Jewish question in the U.S.S.R.]. Moscow: A samiz-
dat [self-published] document authored in May 1970.
Miller, Jacob. "Soviet Theory on the Jews." In The Jews in
Soviet Russia since 1917, pp. 44-61. Edited by Lionel
Kochan. London, New York, Toronto: Oxford University
Press, 1970.
Morgenthau, Hans J. "The Jews and Soviet Foreign Policy."
Perspectives on Soviet Jewry (1971), pp. 86-91.
National Conference on Soviet Jewry. Information Sheet.
Emigration Statistics -- Soviet Jews.
_____. News Bulletin, no. 119, January 16, 1978.
Newth, J.A. "A Statistical Study of Intermarriage Among Jews
in Part of Vilnius (Vilno--U.S.S.R.)." Bulletin on Sov-
iet Jewish Affairs 1 (1968): 64-69.
Newth, J.A., and Katz, Zev. "Proportions of Jews in the Com-
munist Party of the Soviet Union." Bulletin on Soviet
and East European Affairs 4 (1969): 37-38.
Nove, Alec, and Newth, J.A. "The Jewish Population: Demo-
graphic Trends and Occupational Patterns." In The
Jews in Soviet Russia since 1917, pp. 125-58. Edited
by Lionel Kochan. London, New York, Toronto: Oxford
University Press, 1970.
Novoye Vremya [New Time] 31 (January 1975).
Novoye Vremya [New Time] 16 (April 1976):30.
Pamyatka ot'ezzhayushchemu [Advice to those leaving]. Mos-
cow: A samizdat [self-published] document "published"
by unknown authors in November 1974.
Partiinaya Zhizhn' [Party Life] 10 (May 1976): 13-24.
"Preparations for the 50th Anniversary of the Formation of the
Union of Soviet Socialist Republics." Partiinaya Zhizn'
[Party Life] 5 (March 1972): 3-13.
Radio Free Europe Research. Non-Ruling CPs: Italy (21 Nov-
ember 1972). "Soviet Anti-Semitism Poses Problems
for PCI."
Radio Liberty. Background Information Report, no. AR-8-73,
June 8, 1973.
Radio Liberty. Listener Report no. 13-73. March 6, 1973.
Pyatigorsk Listener to RL Speaks of Jewish Communities
Springing Up in Siberia.

Radio Liberty. Radio Liberty Bulletin, no. 16. April 22, 1977.
Radio Liberty. Research Report no. RL-235/73. July 26, 1973.
An Intensification of the Antisemitic Campaign in the
Soviet Press.
Radio Liberty. Research Report no. 2-77. January 1, 1977.
Emigration from the U.S.S.R. in the Post-Helsinki
Period.
Radio Liberty. Research Report no. RL 26/77. February 1,
1977. More Ethnic Germans Seek to Emigrate from the
U.S.S.R.
Radio Liberty. Research Report no. RL 82/77. April 13, 1977.
State Secrets and the Right to Emigrate.
Radio Liberty. Target Area Listener Report, no. 200-70. June
22, 1970. Soviet Leadership Divided on Anti-Semitism?
Redlich, Shimon. "The Jewish Antifascist Committee in the
Soviet Union." Jewish Social Studies 31 (January 1969):
25-36.
Rigby, T.H. "Addendum to Dr. Rigby's Article on C.P.S.U.
Membership." Soviet Studies 28 (October 1976): 615
Rothenberg, Joshua. "Jewish Religion in the Soviet Union."
In The Jews in Soviet Russia since 1917, pp. 159-87.
Edited by Lionel Kochan. London, New York, Toronto:
Oxford University Press, 1970.
_____. "The Fate of Judaism in the Communist World." In
Religion and Atheism in the U.S.S.R. and Eastern
Europe, pp. 223-39. Edited by Bohdan R. Bociurkiw
and John W. Strong. Toronto: University of Toronto
Press, 1973.
Salsberg (Saltzberg), J.B. "Anti-Semitism in the U.S.S.R.?"
Jewish Life (February 1957), p. 38. Cited by William
Korey, The Soviet Cage, Anti-Semitism in Russia, p.
53. New York: Viking Press, 1973.
Samoilenko, V.F. "V.I. Lenin's Works 'Critical Notes on the
Nationalities Question' and 'On the Right of Nations to
Self-Determination'." Voprosy Istorii K.P.S.S. [Ques-
tions on the History of the C.P.S.U.] 11 (November
1976): 92-102.
Sautin, I. "Naselenie strany i sotsializma" [The population
of the country and of socialism]. Bolshevik 10 (May
1940): 10-25.
Schapiro, Leonard. Introduction to The Jews in Soviet Russia
since 1917, pp. 1-13. Edited by Lionel Kochan. London, New York, Toronto: Oxford University Press, 1970.

_____. Review of The Soviet Cage, Anti-Semitism in Russia, by William Korey, and Jewish Nationality and Soviet Politics: The Jewish Sections of the C.P.S.U., 1917-1930, by Zvi Y. Gitelman. The New York Review of Books, 19 July 1973, pp. 3-5.

Schechtman, J.B. "The U.S.S.R., Zionism, and Israel." In The Jews in Soviet Russia since 1917, pp. 99-124. Edited by Lionel Kochan. London, New York, Toronto: Oxford University Press, 1970.

Silver, Brian. "Social Mobilization and the Russification of Soviet Nationalities." American Political Science Review 68 (March 1974): 45-66.

Soviet Analyst (2 March 1972).

Soviet Jewry Research Bureau. National Conference on Soviet Jewry. News Bulletin, no. 108, May 2, 1977. "Soviet Refugee Assistance to Israel."

Soviet Jewry Research Bureau. National Conference on Soviet Jewry. News Bulletin, no. 125, May 15, 1978. "Emigration Statistics."

Soviet Life, May 1972, p. 17.

Soviet Life, October 1972, pp. 17, 48.

Tartakower, Arieh. "The Jewish Problem in the Soviet Union." Jewish Social Studies 31 (January 1969): 285-306.

Tarent'eva, L.N. "Opredelenie svoie natsional'noi prinadlezhnosti podrostkami v natsional'no-smeshannykh semyakh" [The Determination of the national affiliation of children of nationally-mixed families]. Sovetskaya Etnografiya 3 (Moscow: 1969): 20-30.

Trofimenko, G.A. "The U.S.S.R. and the United States: Peaceful Coexistence as the Norm of Mutual Relations." SShA: Ekonomika, Politika, Ideologiya 2 (February 1974): 3-17.

Watson, Hugh Seton. "Nationalism and Imperialism." In The Impact of the Russian Revolution, 1917-1967. The Influence of Bolshevism on the World Outside Russia. London: Oxford University Press for the Royal Institute for International Affairs, 1967. Cited by Hans Kohn, "Soviet Communism and Nationalism: Three Stages of a Historical Development." In Soviet Nationality Problems, pp. 223-39. Edited by Edward Allworth. New York and London: Columbia University Press, 1971.

Weinryb, B.D. "Antisemitism in Soviet Russia." In The Jews in Soviet Russia since 1917, pp. 288-320. Edited by Lionel Kochan. London, New York, Toronto: Oxford University Press, 1970.

Wharton, Royal M. "Soviet Exit Policies Affect East-West Trade." Human Events (25 November 1972), pp. 11-14.
Zand, Mikhail. Yevreiskii vopros v S.S.S.R. (Tezisy) [The Jewish Question in the U.S.S.R.: Theses]. Moscow: a samizdat [self-published] document authored in May 1970.
Zinich, V.T., and Naulko, V.I. "Kul'turno-bytovoe sblizhenie narodov Ukrainskogo S.S.R." [The cultural-social drawing together of the peoples of the Ukrainian S.S.R.]. Sovetskaya Etnografiya 6 (November-December 1972): 28-37.

Press Items

Associated Press (Moscow), 29 November 1974.
Associated Press (Moscow), 1 July 1975.
Associated Press (Moscow), 22 January 1976.
"Brezhnev-Jews." United Press (Moscow), 19 June 1974.
"Coping in Israel, Many Soviet Jews Finding Transition Is Difficult." Washington Post, 22 May 1978.
Davar (Tel Aviv), 15 March 1977.
"December 10 Is Human Rights Day: In the Struggle for Genuine Humanism." Izvestiya (Moscow), 10 December 1976.
"Drive on Dissidents Creates 'Ominous Atmosphere.'" Washington Post, 5 June 1977.
"Emigration of Soviet Jews Declines, But Reasons are Disputed." New York Times, 26 May 1974.
"Emigre Jews, Wanted by No One, Stagnate in Austria." Washington Post, 22 August 1977.
Evans and Novak. Washington Post, 24 January 1972.
"Exit Fee Dropped for Many, Soviet Aide Says." Washington Evening Star, 3 May 1973.
"Facts Refute Slander of Zionists." Tribuna (Prague), 17 October 1973.
"Invitations to Nowhere." Vechernaya Moskva (Moscow), 1 February 1975.
"Israel Acts to Keep Soviet Jews Coming." New York Daily News, 18 July 1976.
"Israel, U.S. Jews Split Over Soviet Emigrants." Washington Post, 10 November 1976.
"Israelis Assess Soviet Exit Fees." New York Times, 17 August 1972.
Izvestiya (Moscow), 27 July 1918.
Izvestiya (Moscow), 25 May 1945.

"Jewish Emigration Vexes Kremlin." Christian Science Monitor, 14 March 1972.

Jewish Telegraph Agency, 28 February 1973.

Kurier (Vienna, Austria), 22 October 1976.

London Observer, 13 January 1963.

Los Angeles Times, 12 June 1977.

"Moscow Ratifies 2 U.N. Covenants on Human Rights." New York Times, 28 September 1973.

"Moscow vs. Zionism." Washington Post, 11 November 1976.

Nasha strana [Our country] (Israel), 17 May 1976.

National Guardian, 25 June 1956.

"New Exit Rules Curb Soviet Jews." Washington Post, 21 March 1974.

New York Times, 15 January 1931.

New York Times, 30 March 1973.

New York Times, 16 June 1977.

"Official Jewish Leaders in Soviet Union Seek Link to International Groups." New York Times, 27 November 1976.

"101 Problems for Mr [sic] Brezhnev." The Economist, 19 March 1977.

"On the Departure of Soviet Citizens for Other Countries." Novosti (Moscow), 26 December 1972.

Pravda (Moscow), 28 December 1932.

Pravda (Moscow), 30 November 1936.

Pravda (Moscow), 2 November 1961.

Pravda (Moscow), 28 February 1963.

Pravda (Moscow), 8 March 1963.

Pravda (Moscow), 19 July 1965.

Radio Australia, 15 January 1975.

Realites (Paris), May 1957.

"Refugee Soviet Jews 'denied aid to settle'." Daily Telegram (London), 4 June 1976.

Reuters (Moscow), 2 January 1972.

Reuters (Moscow), 2 January 1974.

Reuters (Moscow), 4 September 1975.

Reuters (Moscow), 25 September 1975

Reuters (Moscow), 21 January 1976.

Reuters (Vienna), 3 December 1976.

Reuters (Washington, D.C.), 23 August 1972.

Sovetskaya Rossiya [Soviet Russia] (Moscow), 27 September 1973.

"Soviet Charges [sic] a Key Jewish Human-Rights Activist With Treason." New York Times, 2 June 1977.

"Soviet Defends Its [sic] Record on Allowing Emigration." New York Times, 21 January 1977.

"Soviet Delegates Warmly Greeted by Mennonites." Washington Post, 28 July 1978.
"Soviet Dissident Allowed to Leave." New York Times, 4 June 1976.
"Soviet Dissidents Feel Pinch of Customs, Currency Rules." Washington Post, 15 June 1976.
"Soviet [sic] Ease Emigration." Washington Post, 18 January 1976.
"Soviet Education Tax." Yedi ot Aharanot (Tel Aviv), 21 March 1973.
"Soviet Emigration to Israel Hits Record." Washington Evening Star, 4 January 1973.
"Soviet Halt Tax on Exit, Inform U.S." Washington Post, 19 April 1973.
"Soviet Jews in 9 Cities Claim Official Drive is Fostering 'Pogrom Atmosphere'." Los Angeles Times, 3 February 1977.
"Soviet [sic] Letting More Jews Leave; U.S. Group Backing Trade Credits." New York Times, 11 June 1978.
"Soviet Physicist, Aided by Kennedy, Is Granted Permission to Emigrate." Washington Post, 24 October 1978.
"Soviet Publishes [sic] Fee for Emigration." New York Times, 24 January 1973.
"Soviets Deny hundreds of Jews visas over 'state secrets'." Chicago Sun-Times, 25 November 1976.
"Soviet Stiffen [sic] Jews' Penalties." Baltimore Sun, 1 September 1975.
"Soviet Trade Disappoints American Firms." New York Times, 29 January 1978.
TASS (Moscow), 24 July 1918.
TASS (Moscow), 5 June 1977.
"The Fate of a Russian Pariah." Washington Post, 3 April 1976.
"The Insider Who Came Out." Washington Post, 10 July 1977.
The New Jerusalem Post, 18 May 1971.
"The Soviet View of Emigration." New York Times, 3 February 1976.
"The Truth About Jews in the U.S.S.R." Moscow News, 21 February 1976.
"Trade With Soviet [sic] Fell 26.5% in 1977; U.S. Exports Down." New York Times, 29 March 1978.
"Two Moscow Jews Face Charge of 'Hooliganism' After Protest." Christian Science Monitor, 3 November 1976.
United Press (Washington, D.C.), 18 April 1973.
United Press International (Camp David, Maryland), 20 June 1973.

"U.S., Fulfilling Promise, Signs 11-Year-Old Rights Pact at
    U.N." New York Times, 6 October 1977.
"U.S. Will Admit 4,000 Refugees," Baltimore Sun, 14 January
    1977.
"Vance: Soviet-Bloc Rights Gains Scant." Washington Post
    7 June 1977.
Vechernaya Moskva [Evening Moscow] , 7 December 1976.
Washington Post, 28 February 1973.
"We'll Stay, But Not Quietly." The Economist, 6 August 1977.
"West Berlin Destination For Some Soviet Jews." New York
    Times, 4 November 1973.
"West Berlin is Curbing Immigration by Jews." New York Times,
    27 January 1975.
"West Berlin Restricting Entry of Jews From the Soviet Union."
    New York Times, 4 December 1974.
"Why Russia Lets More Jews Go?" London Observer, 9 January
    1972.

Index

346

349

351

Shtern, Mikhail, 169
Shumilin, Boris T., 194-95, 206
Shvartser, Veniamin W., 84
Shvartsman, Osher, 82
Sik, Ota, 156
Silver, Brian, 56-57, 59, 62-63
Sitnikov, G.O., 171
"Sliyanie" (fusion of nationalities), 129, 151
Smidovich, Peter, 86
Social and Political Thought of Karl Marx, 3
"Social mobilization," 56, 59, 86, 155, 184
Social Revolutionary Party, 114
Sokolnikov, Grigory, 112, 115
Sources of Soviet law, 121
South Africa, 131, 191
"Sovetish Heimland," 82
Soviet administrative law, 122
Soviet All-Union constitution of 1936, 74, 79, 128
Soviet All-Union constitution of 1977, 128-30, 133, 135, 140, 172
Soviet civil law, 122
Soviet collective-farm law, 122
Soviet concept of "Socialist Legality," 123
Soviet constitution of 1918, 126
Soviet corrective-labor law, 123
Soviet criminal law, 123
Soviet entry-exit regulations, 189-201
Soviet family law, 123
Soviet financial law, 122

Soviet international private law, 122
Soviet international public law, 123
"Sovietization," 58, 62
Soviet Jewry Research Bureau, National Conference on Soviet Jewry, 212
Soviet labor law, 122
Soviet land law, 122
Soviet-Nazi "Nonaggression Pact" (August 22, 1939), 74, 157
Soviet-Polish Repatriation Agreement (1957), 181-84
Soviet repatriation program, 183
Soviet state or constitutional law, 121
Spain, 191
Spanish repatriates, 182
Stalin, Joseph, 5, 14-24, 61-62, 76, 87-89, 125, 152-53, 155-61
"Statute Concerning the Organization of the Jews" (1804), 105
"Statute of Conscription and Military Service" (1827), 105
Stevenson Amendment (Export-Import Bank Act of 1974), 188
"Study of Discrimination in Respect to the Right of Everyone to Leave Any Country, Including His Own, and to Return to His Country" (1963), 134
Suslov, Mikhail S., 150, 153, 186
Sverdlov, Yakov, 112
Tadzhik, 30, 37-38
"Theses on the Immediate Tasks of the Party in Connection with the National Program" (1921), 124

352

To the Jewish Workers, 12
Toth, Robert C., 168
Transcarpathia, 29
Trotsky, Leon, 112, 114
Tsilionok, Boris, 169
Types of Soviet law, 121
Ukraine, 18, 29, 35-39, 41,
    44, 46, 64-65, 68, 104,
    114-15, 119, 131, 160,
    202, 204-06, 212-13
Ukrainian Rada, 17
"UNESCO Convention Against
    Discrimination in Educa-
    tion," 79
Union supreme soviets, 117,
    119, 121
United Israel Appeal (U.I.A.),
    214
United Jewish Socialist Work-
    ers' Party (Farainigte),
    111, 115
United Nations, 131- 35,
    142
United States, 4, 108, 140,
    167, 183-88, 191, 197,
    200-01, 204, 209, 211-
    16, 219-20, 233
"Universal Declaration of
    Human Rights" (1948),
    131-34, 138-39
University of the Toilers of
    the East, 20-21
Uritskii, M., 112
U.S. Foreign Relations Auth-
    orization Act (1972), 214
U.S. Refugee Program (U.S.
    R.P.), 212
U.S.-Soviet détente, 186-
    88, 204, 234
U.S.-Soviet trade (1976-77),
    187-88
U.S. Trade Act of 1974, 187
Utin, Nicholas, 109
Uzbek S.S.R., 35, 37-38

"Vechernaya Moskva," 83
Verest, G.V., 171
Vergelis, Aron, 82
Vernadsky, George, 110
Vienna, Austria, 201, 203, 207,
    214-15
Volga Germans, 63, 182-83,
    216
Voronel, Aleksandr, 165-66
Vozniak, N.V., 171
West Berlin, 215
"Western" ("Zapadniki") Jews,
    29, 89, 206
Whitlam, John, 164
Witte, Count, 110
Workers, 2-3, 16, 18, 20, 24,
    128, 133, 202
World War I, 6, 184
World Without Jews, 4-5
Yakubovsky, Ivan I., 186
"Yeshiva," 73, 77
Yevrei" (Jewish), 34, 126, 232
Yiddish, 10, 11, 13, 29, 56,
    61, 63, 64, 78, 80-82, 108,
    111, 113, 125, 184, 232-
    33
Yugoslavia, 131, 137, 187
Zand, Mikhail, 163-64, 166,
    185
"Zemlya i Volya" (Land and Free-
    dom), 109
Zhemchuzhina (Madame Molotov),
    157
Zhukov, Dmitri, 171
Zinoviev, Georgy, 112
Zionism, 10-11, 23, 76, 88-
    90, 114-15, 154-55, 159,
    162, 170-72, 183, 186
Zionist Party, 111, 115
Zionist Workers' Party, 111
Zundelevich, Aaron, 109

DATE DUE

Jun13 80FAC			
MAR 17 84 C			
Mar. 26			
APR 6 '84			
MAR 22 '85 X			
MAY 31 '88 S			
JUN 01 PAID			
JUN 15 '88 S			
MAY 15 95 S			
MAY 2 1995			
GAYLORD			PRINTED IN U S A.